From
MORNING
to
EVENING

From MORNING to EVENING
Every Day With Jesus

MIKE W. IRELAND

XULON PRESS

Xulon Press
2301 Lucien Way #415
Maitland, FL 32751
407.339.4217
www.xulonpress.com

© 2019 by Mike W. Ireland

All rights reserved solely by the author. The author guarantees all contents are original and do not infringe upon the legal rights of any other person or work. No part of this book may be reproduced in any form without the permission of the author. The views expressed in this book are not necessarily those of the publisher.

Unless otherwise indicated, Scripture quotations taken from the English Standard Version (ESV). Copyright © 2001 by Crossway, a publishing ministry of Good News Publishers. Used by permission. All rights reserved. Scripture quotations taken from the Holy Bible, New International Version (NIV). Copyright © 1973, 1978, 1984, 2011 by Biblica, Inc.™. Used by permission. All rights reserved.

Printed in the United States of America.

ISBN-13: 978-1-5456-7978-4

Dedication

To my grandchildren:
AIDAN
BRENDEN
CARTER
CHASE
ETHAN
HANNAH
JACY
JOSHUA
LANDON
TRISTEN
and
BRYAN, more than a grandchild, also a son

Preface

Jesus is the most incredible person of human history. The division of the centuries is determined by his arrival in long-ago Israel. Sunday gatherings of worshipers across the globe testify to his continuing influence. He is the subject of many thousands and thousands of songs and books. When decisions are being weighed, people ask, "What would Jesus do?" Millions of prayers to God are closed by an appeal to the name of Jesus. Every year the world pauses to remember his birth and his resurrection. And the quest to discover the real Jesus continues to this day.

Never was there a more beautiful life. Yet if a committee of the wisest and best people had been formed to develop a portrait of the perfect person, we would never have thought of the person of Jesus. If the most powerful and most resourceful among us had been chosen to develop a plan for how one person could teach us and show us the best way to live, we still would never have thought of Jesus. If the most spiritual and religious among us had convened to develop a plan for how one person could show us the Father, we still would never have thought of someone like Jesus. If the best and brightest minds among us had come together to develop a plan for saving the world from sin, we still would never have thought of Jesus. It is no wonder that we did not recognize him. We were looking for someone entirely different.

His claim to be the Son of God is found in all four Gospels. Matthew, Mark, Luke and John present Jesus as the long-awaited Jewish Messiah and the Savior of the world. The Gospel writers never hesitate in declaring that Jesus is the fulfillment of prophecies, the healer of all diseases, the worker of miracles, the teacher of God's word, and the only way to the Father. While each one writes from his own perspective, with his own target audience and his own agenda, these four early disciples are united in their view of Jesus.

Although the Gospels share some things in common with the "biographies" or "lives" written in the Graeco-Roman world, they are not biographies as we are accustomed. No effort is made to present Jesus' life in its entirety. Beyond the birth stories, only one childhood story (Luke 2:42) is told. No details are shared about his home life, his education, his interaction with siblings or playmates, his changing appearance into a man, or his views about himself and his world. It is his ministry, begun when he was about thirty years old (Luke 3:23), that receives the greatest attention by the writers. It is at this point that his long-awaited mission begins in earnest and it is in this mission that we discover what God has done for us.

Yet many modern Biblical scholars reject the idea that Jesus was anything more than a man. Their arguments seem to run along two lines: the unreliability of the Gospels and the Christian community controlling the information. These critics consider the Gospels the result of a process of storytelling and mythmaking by the early Christians. The church, it is argued, had its own propaganda machine at work in order to maintain control of the general populace. Most critics seem willing to grant that Jesus was an exceptional teacher with a kind and compassionate nature. However, there is great reluctance to say that Jesus was divine.

This cynical view of the Gospels and disparaging opinion of the church has resulted in numerous provocative portraits of Jesus in recent years. From magician to political radical, from social justice advocate to eschatological prophet, from con man to delusional rabbi, Jesus has been portrayed by well-known Bible scholars endeavoring to provide clarity to the mystery surrounding the real identity of Jesus. While the portraits vary in numerous details, they share one very important conclusion: Jesus was only a mere man.

The search for the real Jesus won't be satisfied by questioning the reliability of first century writers or reading between the lines or accusing the church of spinning propaganda. To know Jesus, one must read the Gospels. Those who saw him and heard him and those whose lives were forever changed by him have something to say about him. Also, Jesus must be allowed to speak for himself.

This is not an appeal to ignore the Synoptic problem or difficult passages. This is not an effort to dissuade us from asking tough questions of the text, considering Jesus in his cultural context, or examining what the early church fathers said about him. Also, there is no effort made in this volume to determine which Gospel was written first, how the writers might have shared information, to whom the letters were written, or why there appear to be occasional differences as well as remarkable similarities in their respective records. Rather, this is a plea that we simply listen to Matthew, Mark, Luke, and John, to hear what they say about Jesus, and to hear what Jesus says about himself.

In an effort to encourage the reading of the four Gospels over the course of a year and to give the reader a sense of direction and a coherent way of looking at Jesus, the devotional readings in this book are taken from harmonizing the four Gospels. Establishing historical sequence in the life of Jesus is not without its challenges. Also, reading the Gospels

Preface

"horizontally" – comparing accounts – may mislead us into thinking that we have one portrait of Jesus instead of four unique ones. It is assumed that the Gospels are historical narratives reflecting each writer's individual purpose, perspective and style. However, a harmony is a wonderful tool for studying the Gospels and the life of Christ. By inviting all the writers' participation where relevant, the reader sees the fullest picture possible.

But the primary goal of this reading is not to critically evaluate how the accounts relate to each other but to see the man. We want to see Jesus by watching him and listening to him. A harmony simply provides us a structure for doing so.

Two particular harmonies have been helpful in determining the sequence of textual readings. An older volume (1904), **A Harmony of the Gospels for Historical Study** by William Stevens and Ernest Burton makes use of the Revised Version of 1881. More recently (1988), Robert Thomas and Stanley Gundry developed **The NIV Harmony of the Gospels**.

A verse or two (**English Standard Version**) from the primary text appears at the top of each page. After the passage, there will be a primary text designation followed by parentheses containing any parallels in the other Gospels. This allows the reader to consider what the other writers recorded about a particular event or saying in the life of Jesus. In this way, every verse in all four Gospels is included in this yearlong reading.

The reader is encouraged to read the primary text before reading the devotional page. While the comments are intended to prompt contemplation of the text, they are not intended to replace it. The most important words are those found in the Gospels.

One of the benefits of a devotional book is that it helps the reader to focus. By the use of a selected text the reader's attention is directed toward certain ideas or concepts. The contemplation of these ideas or concepts is intended to help one focus on the things that matter most.

The focus of this volume is Jesus. Every page is intended to draw the reader's attention to the most extraordinary person who ever lived. Even more, the texts and accompanying thoughts are designed to impress upon the reader that this extraordinary person is today's most important person. As the ancient writer said, "Jesus Christ is the same yesterday and today and forever" (Hebrews 13:8).

This volume is my effort to encourage and assist you in your desire to know Jesus and in your efforts to walk with him each day. From morning to evening, whatever each day brings, be sure that it brings Jesus and you together.

But he was wounded for our transgressions; he was crushed for our iniquities; upon him was the chastisement that brought us peace, and with his stripes we are healed.

Isaiah 53

JANUARY 1

Jesus was on the lips of the prophet seven hundred years before the infant was born in Bethlehem. How amazing is that?

God was coming! But this wasn't God coming in a whirlwind or showing Himself in a burning bush. God wasn't simply trying to show His power in a pillar of fire or manifesting His presence in a cloud. God was actually and really coming – in person!

The plan was simple: He would come among us and live as we live. He would be born as we are and grow up as we do. He would play as a child and work as a man. He would be just another fellow in Galilee.

In this way, He would know us and we could know Him. In sharing our experiences, feeling our pains, knowing our fears, and understanding our hearts, He could give us what we needed most and we could trust Him. Could there ever be better news? God was coming to us!

So, God came just as He planned, but we didn't recognize Him. He spoke the very words we needed to hear, but we didn't believe Him. He showed us how to live, what He actually had in mind when He made us, but we rejected His ways, choosing instead to keep living as we had always lived. When we had had enough of His words and His ways, we punished Him for both. Even so, He never argued for His rights or freedoms. He never raised a hand to fight back. He never called for the angels who did His bidding. In unimaginable humility and surrender, He just accepted what we gave Him.

Having abused Him without mercy, we did the unthinkable: we killed Him. Actually, what was unthinkable was that He accepted it. With that, we thought the matter was over.

Seven hundred years in advance God knew what He was going to do for us and He knew what we were going to do to Him. Still, here came **Jesus**.

> **... it seemed good to me also, having followed all things closely for some time past, to write an orderly account for you, most excellent Theophilus, that you may have certainty concerning the things you have been taught.**
>
> **Luke 1:1-4**

JANUARY 2

Jesus is the story. But who experienced the greater anticipation? Luke who began writing about Jesus? Or, Theophilus who picked up the finished product and began to read? Perhaps, the heart of each was beating fast. Maybe they both realized that this was no ordinary story.

Imagine Theophilus' excitement as he opened the manuscript and began to pour over the words. It was more than a journey of knowledge. It was an adventure in living! No one ever lived like Jesus!

Or, put yourself in Luke's place: sitting down to write about Jesus. How would you decide what to write? Which stories would you include? What words of Jesus would you report? How would you begin? How would you conclude?

Luke wanted to take Theophilus on a journey through the life of Jesus. Luke's idea was not to recount every event or detail every experience. This was not to be a fact-finding trip. It was, instead, a daily walk through the villages of Jesus' days and into the lives of those who saw him and talked to him. It was to be like one of those field trips where no one comes back unchanged.

But make no mistake: spending everyday with Jesus can bring some discomfort. Seeing his life makes us more sensitive to our own. Time with Jesus exposes our weaknesses, unmasks our pretensions, uncovers our fears, and reveals our sins. Necessary, but not very pleasant.

But here is the best part. On this walk you can see yourself as God sees you, you can see life as it is meant to be lived, you can observe the very best in the human spirit, and you can find answers to life's most difficult questions. Theophilus may be the name on the page, but it might just as well be your name because Luke is writing to you, too!

Luke knew that no one ever walked with Jesus and stayed the same. No one! So, let the journey begin! Just you and **Jesus**.

> In the beginning was the Word, and the Word was with God, and the Word was God. He was in the beginning with God. All things were made through him, and without him was not anything made that was made.
>
> John 1:1-3

JANUARY 3

Jesus is the "Logos," the Word. Only John calls him that. Perhaps, John was trying to connect with his culture.

Imagine writing to someone from a different culture, to someone whose religious beliefs are very different than your own. You want to introduce them to Jesus. What would you say? How would you begin?

Would you start with a story from Jesus' life? Would you begin with an Old Testament prophecy? Would you focus first on some particular teaching?

"Logos" (Word) was a term widely recognized and used by the Greeks. It was not personal, but it was a supreme idea or principle over all things. Just as the Jews had their own ideas about God's relationship to humans, so the Greek culture used certain ideas to describe the link between God and humanity.

"Logos" is more than just the word spoken; it is the meaning of the word, too. As the Word, Jesus is the living portrait of God, an expression of God's mind to us. His words and ways are what God wants to reveal about Himself. "The Son is the radiance of God's glory and the exact representation of his being..." (Hebrews 1:3). Everything you want to know about God can be found in Jesus.

Okay. When it comes to the subject of God, we are in over our heads. The questions are many and the answers are beyond us. But while there is mystery, there is also revelation: the Word was the very essence, the very character, the very nature of God. "For in Christ all the fullness of Deity lives in bodily form...." (Colossians 2:9). Whatever may be said about God is actually seen in the person of Jesus.

John says, "I want to tell you about the most extraordinary person. He was in the beginning with God. He is Deity! And nothing was made without him!"

Today may offer you the opportunity to present him. How would you introduce **Jesus?**

He came as a witness, to bear witness about the light, that all might believe through him.
The true light, which enlightens everyone, was coming into the world.
John 1:4-9

JANUARY 4

Jesus is the light in an otherwise dark, dark world. Perhaps, that is why John writes like a man offering hope to the hopeless or like a fellow pointing the dying toward a cure.

Proud of our achievements, our social, technological and scientific progress, we find it difficult to admit that we live in a world of darkness. "The Dark Ages" are history. The light of learning shines brighter than ever! Yet, for all of our claims, we have made no real progress in conquering the basic ills of humanity: fear, hate, injustice. Our planet seems as plagued by war, crime, and racism as ever.

We have made enormous improvements in making our own lives more comfortable but we still struggle with lust, greed and hate in our hearts. We have made wonderful changes in matters of health, but our society is still plagued by drug and alcohol addiction. We publish more books each year on self-improvement than were written in all of history, yet we seem to find ourselves always searching for that one right idea or view that will bring us happiness and fulfillment.

We cannot solve our darkness problem. No matter how we try, we cannot find our own way. We need help. We need Light.

There is nothing like a working flashlight when you have to crawl under a car at night to do a bit of automotive repair or when you're tromping through the forest after sundown. The light gives guidance to your hands and certainty to your steps. It reveals those things that are truly valuable and beneficial while exposing what is worthless, even dangerous, to you.

Jesus, of course, is more than your flashlight! But when you are trying to steady yourself on a dark, uneven path or trying to determine what truly matters in the midst of dark days, there is nothing like the Light that comes from heaven.

Today, you can see the valuable and recognize the dangerous because the blessing of light comes to you in the person of **Jesus**.

He came to his own, and his own people did not receive him. But to all who did receive him, who believed in his name, he gave the right to become children of God, who were born, not of blood nor of the will of the flesh nor of the will of man, but of God.

John 1:10-13

JANUARY 5

Jesus was not what they expected. But really, who did expect a poor, ordinary-looking guy to be the Messiah? Who really thought the Savior of the world would start as a carpenter before turning to preaching? And who really could see that, beneath the poverty of his surroundings and the character of his companions, there was really a king? It was too much to swallow then and it does not go down any easier now.

Although these were Jesus' people, they rejected him. Well, most did. Not everyone was offended. There were a few who could see beneath the surface, who could recognize God among them. "To those who believed in his name, he gave the right to become children of God." He gave them the right to become something they could never be without him!

Now, see if these two ideas don't put a smile on your face all day: God wants you in His family and He is the very person to make it happen!

Every person who would enter God's family must come in by being born again. This is not by inheritance, not by human ancestry. You cannot get into the family of God by being raised in a religious home.

This new birth is not by human decision. You cannot make yourself a member of God's family by positive thinking or by making a resolution or by deciding to live a good life.

God does it! This new birth is accomplished by God in the hearts of those who accept Jesus. Without that trust, nothing will happen.

The most incredible thing has happened in your life! You are a child of God! But it is no accident. God planned for you from the beginning. Everything He has done was with you in mind. All His work was His expression of love for you. And He said it all and He said it best in **Jesus**.

> **And the Word became flesh and dwelt among us, and we have seen his glory, glory as of the only Son from the Father, full of grace and truth.**
>
> **John 1:14**

JANUARY 6

Jesus was (is) the unique God-man in human history. He "pitched his tent" among us. He lived within the limitations of space and time, and he endured with us the experiences of hunger and thirst, fatigue and suffering.

So, why did we reject him? The simplest explanation would be that we did not know that he was God. But that would be the wrong answer. We did not crucify Jesus because he was God — we did not believe he was God! We were both astounded and offended because we did not know that he was human. Not human as you and I are, but human as God created us to be!

For the first time we were in the presence of someone who was living the very life God intended us to live. This was a man who always spoke the truth, whose every action was based on love, whose thoughts, words and actions were pure, and who lived every moment of every day doing only the will of the Father.

Jesus was exactly the person we were created to be. But we were offended because we did not like the kind of person he was! Imagine that! We were looking at our best selves and we hated what we saw!

What is God saying to us by this action of becoming flesh? God believes in us! He came and made himself a member of a family of criminals to show us how to live. In spite of our sordid history of cruelty and injustice to one another and our rejection of Him, God resolutely maintained that we could, by trusting Him, make good and wise choices, that we could live as He created us to live.

Can you believe that? God believes in you! It is no wonder that you believe in Him; the wonder is that He believes in you! But He does! And everything God has ever done has been done because of His faith in you.

Whenever you doubt, you need only look at **Jesus**.

No one has ever seen God; the only God, who is at the Father's side, he has made him known.

John 1:15-18

JANUARY 7

Jesus was (is) our very best look at God. God was among us in a way unlike He had ever been before. We had seen the burning bush and we had spoken with His messengers. We had witnessed His glory on Mt. Sinai, but we had never seen God like this.

In Jesus we are privileged to know the heart of God. But how can it be that Jesus alone can show us God unlike anyone ever has? Because, of all the people who have walked on this planet, not one person has ever come from the presence of God. Except Jesus. Now God was walking around on the earth like us.

God now had ears. He heard our fussing and grumbling, and our pleading. And with those ears he heard us cry, "Crucify him!" But no matter what he heard us say, he never closed his ears to us and he never quit loving us.

God now had eyes. He watched the way we treated one another. He looked into our searching eyes and our longing hearts. But even when he saw us turn away from him, he never quit loving us.

God now had arms and hands. Those arms and hands welcomed, caressed and loved people. Before he left us, he stretched out his arms so we could hammer nails into his hands. But he never quit loving us.

God now had legs and feet. They took him all over the countryside to towns and villages, into the houses, the synagogues and the temple. He walked around until we nailed his feet to the wood, but he never quit loving us.

Jesus, as man, was the truth about God. Do you want to know how God feels about you? Do you want to know what God thinks about your sins? Do you want to know what God wants for your life? Do you want to know how much God loves you? Look at **Jesus**.

> A book of the genealogy of Jesus Christ the son of David, the son of Abraham. Abraham was the father of Isaac....and Jacob the father of Joseph, the husband of Mary, of whom was born Jesus, who is called Christ.
>
> Matthew 1:1-17 (Luke 3:23b-38)

JANUARY 8

Jesus' family tree certainly had it all. Abraham, Isaac and Jacob made their mark in Old Testament history. Boaz and Ruth helped bring along a future king named David. David, the giant slayer, was the father of the wisest of men, Solomon. Kings like Jehoshaphat, Hezekiah and Josiah were some of the bright spots among Judah's leaders.

But shake any family tree and a few nuts will fall. Fellows like Rehoboam, Abijah and Joram were all wicked kings. And even among the more notables there were some pretty serious moral failures. Jacob was a liar and a deceiver. Judah was a fornicator. And then there is David: an adulterer and a murderer.

So, why did Matthew and Luke provide lists of hard-to-pronounce names that make for boring reading? Doesn't Matthew understand the importance of grabbing the reader's attention from the opening line? Why begin the most important story in the history of the world with stuff that reads like a phone book? And why should Luke even care about Jewish genealogy? He is a Gentile.

Surely the answers rest in the purposes of the respective writers. Matthew wrote to convince his Jewish readers that Jesus of Nazareth is, indeed, the Messiah foretold in the Old Testament. Luke, on the other hand, wrote to highlight the humanity of Jesus and to emphasize that Jesus was the Savior of the whole world.

Turning the pages of the family album, while rehearsing the stories of those long since gone, reminds us of two of life's most important lessons: life is brief and everyone leaves a story. The names once belonged to living people. Each one left behind their story. We are writing ours even now.

But genealogy, especially that of Jesus, is primarily about God: God at work in the lives of men and women to accomplish His purpose. And even now, today, God is working in your life to accomplish His purpose: your salvation through His Son, **Jesus**.

> "...and he will go before him in the spirit and power of Elijah, to turn the hearts of the fathers to the children, and the disobedient to the wisdom of the just, to make ready for the Lord a people prepared."
> Luke 1:5-17

JANUARY 9

Jesus' arrival did not create any great expectations among the locals. In fact, other than a few shepherds, no one really paid much attention. The same, however, could not be said for the arrival of John. People expected this child to be something special!

Descendants of Aaron, Zechariah ("Yahweh remembers") and his wife Elizabeth ("the oath of God") were both of priestly families. They were a lovely couple whose primary concern was pleasing their God.

It is easy to imagine the great joy that accompanied their wedding. Two families united in happiness by the marriage of their children. But time brought heartache: Elizabeth was barren. Naturally, Zechariah had prayed about this many, many times.

Many years are behind them now. A long-ago hope dismissed. Their disappointment replaced by a reluctant acceptance. But their faithfulness to God was unchanged.

Zechariah had lived for this experience: to be the priest who officiated at the altar. This really was a once-in-a-lifetime kind of thing. Finally, the lot had fallen on him!

And then the unthinkable! After four hundred years without a prophetic word or a divine utterance, an angel appeared to this elderly gentleman who was already living out a dream.

Zechariah was both surprised and afraid! Who could blame him? Angel sightings were rare!

Good news: a baby is coming! The angel named the baby, foretold his success, described his character, and identified the purpose of his life. Like Elijah of old, this John was to be a mighty instrument for God.

God broke in on Zechariah's day to give him the best news: the time was right for God to come! John would be the man who would prepare us for His arrival. John would announce God. He would introduce us to **Jesus**.

And the angel answered him, "I am Gabriel. I stand in the presence of God, and I was sent to speak to you and to bring you this good news.
Luke 1:18-25

JANUARY 10

Jesus was no accident. In fact, Jesus was God's plan from the beginning. Through Abraham, Isaac, and Jacob, through Boaz and David, God was working out His plan for your redemption.

John was part of that plan. So, he, too, was no accident. But that should have been obvious when an angel appeared to announce his coming.

Gabriel. What did he look like? Wings? Halo? Glowing? And did Zechariah realize he was talking to an angel? If he did, why was he so reluctant to accept Gabriel's message?

"I am Gabriel. I stand in the presence of God, and I have been sent to speak to you and to tell you this good news." Wow! Good news straight from God Himself!

But we want assurance. We want some guarantee. We want God to tell us when and how so we can feel certain about what is happening. Like Zechariah, we are amazingly slow to believe even when the message is from God Himself!

Rarely do we get a visit from an angel. But what we do get are the daily blessings of reading and seeing the unfolding plan of God in His Word and experiencing the reality of that plan in our own lives. Every sunrise and sunset is a guarantee of Who is running the universe. Every genuine believer is evidence of 'good news' coming to reality. Every returning prodigal is a sign of the Spirit's work in the heart. 'Good news' is all around us!

"Alright," said Gabriel. "You want a sign, you've got a sign: silence."

Zechariah went home to the privacy and obscurity of his village where he would have several months to ponder his doubt and the sign. Before long, Elizabeth, a senior citizen, became pregnant. That must have stirred the gossip birds down at the market. But old Zechariah knew that John was coming.

John. "God is gracious." He was 'good news' to an old couple. But he would announce the best 'good news' of all. John was going to announce **Jesus**.

And Mary said to the angel, "How will this be, since I am a virgin?" And the angel answered her, "The Holy Spirit will come upon you, and the power of the Most High will overshadow you; therefore the child to be born will be called holy—the Son of God."

Luke 1:26-38

JANUARY 11

Jesus was born of a virgin. God said so. But how can we believe it? Maybe the answer lies in the heart of Mary.

A pregnant virgin is an oxymoron. The very idea has been hotly debated for centuries. Questions swirl around the meaning of ancient words, the interpretation of prophetic passages, and the reality of miracles. Critics have accused Christians of concocting this tale to cover up the adulterous behavior of Mary or claimed that this was an attempt to elevate Jesus to a status equal to the Greek gods.

Obviously, Luke believed Mary was a virgin. But more important, there seems to be no confusion in Mary's mind. Gabriel said, "Mary, you are going to have a son." Her reply: "Hold it one moment, Mr. Gabriel, there is a small problem. I have never been with a man." Mary was old enough to know that it 'takes two to tango' and she knew she hadn't even been to the dance!

She also knew that she was placing herself and her marriage in danger. What would Joseph say? What would people think? Nine months of awkward explanations and the lingering gossip. What about the law? The law regarded a betrothed woman who became pregnant as an adulteress and subject to stoning.

Mary might have said, "I am not old enough to do this," or "This is not the way I dreamed it would be." But instead she said, "Okay. I'll do it!"

Mary's story is lovely and inspirational because she had a lovely heart. She surrendered to God's plan for her life. Today will be an opportunity for you to do the same. "Okay, I'll do it!" With that you sound just like Mary.

What a special person to have been chosen to give birth to **Jesus**.

> And Mary said, "My soul magnifies the Lord, and my spirit rejoices in God my Savior, for he has looked on the humble estate of his servant.
>
> **Luke 1:39-56**

JANUARY 12

Jesus and John were connected even before they saw one another at the Jordan River, even before they knew about the work of the other. With her own exciting news to share, Mary hurried off to congratulate Elizabeth. It is a scene not too difficult to imagine: a couple of women talking about their pregnancies! All the details about morning sickness, doctor's visits and special cravings. Of course, neither of these women should have been pregnant right now! What laughter and tears they must have shared as they told their own stories.

Perhaps, they imagined together what their sons would become. Maybe they dreamed of the grandchildren that would certainly follow. Mostly, each praised God for His goodness to them and each expressed faith in His plan.

After the first century, various stories spread about Mary. Most of them would die over time, but several survived. The "Assumption," the "Immaculate Conception," and her "perpetual virginity" are among the better-known ideas circling around Mary even to this day.

These, and other stories about Mary, are best explained by the human tendency to make saints and heroes of the dead. Those we admire often become even greater with time. Legends grow up around them.

Also, early Christians went to an extreme in their efforts to defend the reputation of Mary against vulgar attacks by the pagans regarding the virgin birth, as well as addressing controversies that questioned the humanity of Jesus and his relationship to Mary and Joseph. Perhaps, it was inevitable that such beliefs about her would come from all this attention.

But in contrast to these views that exalt her, Mary's words provide us with nothing more than the picture of a humble and grateful woman. She knew she was blessed, but she also knew that she was undeserving and that God had been gracious to her. He was holy and mighty and merciful.

And Mary recognized something else as well. Like you, she, too, needed a Savior. That Savior would be the child she carried. **Jesus.**

> ...and all who heard them laid them up in their hearts, saying, "What then will this child be?" For the hand of the Lord was with him.
>
> **Luke 1:57-80**

JANUARY 13

Jesus and his kingdom did not arrive without announcement. God sent an announcer. The announcer's name was John.

After nine months of hand signals and writing notes, the day had finally come. Zechariah must have been about to split to tell someone what happened to him when he served at the altar in the temple. The birth of John was viewed by friends and relatives as an act of God's mercy on this elderly couple. So, there was much joy to be shared.

The eighth day of the child's life was special. This was the day of circumcision and the day the child was officially named. The expectation was that he would be named Zach Jr. after his father. But Elizabeth said that this baby would be called John. Surprised, the folks appealed to Zechariah for resolution to this. Still mute, he wrote on a tablet that the boy's name was John. Zechariah had learned through his experience in silence that God should be believed and obeyed. Immediately, he was set free to speak again. No surprise: he first praised God. Now this family was the talk of the region. The events surrounding the birth of John got people asking, "What will this child be?"

Zechariah had had nine months to think about that. His answer is found in the lines of his hymn. First, he praises God for His faithfulness. Then, he writes about the role his son will play in God's unfolding plan.

"What will this child be?" Zechariah could answer that question, "My son will be a prophet who prepares the way for God!" What an honor! What a task!

But isn't that the privilege and task you have been given? Isn't it also your mission to tell everyone about Jesus and the wonderful truth about his coming?

The prophets had been silent for 400 years. There was no vision in the land. There was little hope and the light of God in Israel had all but gone out. Now, there was someone to tell of what God was doing.

And there still is. You. You can use today to tell others about **Jesus**.

> Now the birth of Jesus Christ took place in this way. When his mother Mary had been betrothed to Joseph, before they came together she was found to be with child from the Holy Spirit.
>
> Matthew 1:18-25

JANUARY 14

Jesus was born to Joseph and Mary. There was not any question about his mother. The identity of his father was an issue from the moment of conception.

He struggled with her story but he cared too much to expose her to public shame. If Joseph said the baby was his, it would be a lie. If he accused Mary of unfaithfulness, she would certainly be harmed. Joseph decided that he would put her away as the law demanded, but do it privately to spare her the public humiliation. He would do his best to exit this matter quickly and quietly and then try and get on with his life.

Then, there was angelic intervention. The couple would live under a cloud, as though guilty of immorality. Joseph accepted the responsibility of caring for a woman thought to have been a fornicator, and rearing a child thought to be illegitimate.

Joseph was the quiet one in all that happened. Four Gospels but not one quote from Joseph. Most folks involved in the unfolding drama talked. Some even sang. Everyone seemed to say something: kings, priests, scribes, relatives, neighbors. Even shepherds. But not Joseph. He said nothing. Whatever he thought, whatever his viewpoint on it all, he said nothing. He just obeyed.

Joseph was a righteous man. He obeyed the word of God, whether written in the laws of Moses or uttered in dreams by angels. He obeyed, and his obedience made a marriage where there might have been divorce. Obedience saved Mary from those who would have shamed her. Obedience saved his son from Herod's hatred.

Joseph was the silent, but obedient man of the story. His obedience was not decided by his understanding of what God was doing and neither was it determined by his personal convenience. Joseph was asked to adjust his entire life to God's plan. And Joseph did.

Joseph may not have been his "real" father, but what an example for **Jesus**.

> For to us a child is born, to us a son is given; and the government shall be upon his shoulder, and his name shall be called Wonderful Counselor, Mighty God, Everlasting Father, Prince of Peace.
> Isaiah 9:6-7; Isaiah 7:14; Colossians 2:9-10

JANUARY 15

Jesus came as a baby. Only God could plan that.

There is nothing more basic to human life than childbirth, and there is nothing more incredible than the arrival of this small life into the world.

Imagine how Mary felt! She really was holding a miracle! And more than that, the destiny of humanity was bound up in this child!

The child would arrive in the most usual way and he would be one of us. But he would also be the Son of God. Humanity and deity in one person. Incarnation.

But why a baby? Why not a strapping man whose size immediately commanded attention? Why not as a scholar/philosopher with a high IQ and lots of degrees behind his name? Why not as a warrior king capable of inspiring men by his mere presence? Why a baby?

If God intended to be one of us, why make it so difficult to recognize Him? Why such humble beginnings and such ordinary looks? If He was coming to establish a kingdom that would never be destroyed, why did it have to be only in hearts? Why couldn't there be a palace and a throne?

The story of Jesus is not just the story of some child destined for greatness or even the story of how one life can make a difference in many lives. This is the story of God coming to be in our skin so that God and we could eat and fish together, so we could laugh and sing together, so we could cry and mourn together, so we could believe and hope together, and so we could die and live always together.

Jesus came as a baby because God wanted you to know how far He would go in order to bring you home to be with Him. Jesus came as a baby because God wanted you to know how small He would become in order to give you more than you could ever imagine for yourself. Because God was always planning for you, He planned for baby **Jesus**.

> And she gave birth to her firstborn son and wrapped him in swaddling cloths and laid him in a manger, because there was no place for them in the inn.
>
> **Luke 2:1-7**

JANUARY 16

Jesus was coming! Mary grew larger, more uncomfortable....then Joseph said, "We have to go register in Bethlehem." What a journey that was! There were so many people and no place to stay.

Finally, they were allowed to stay in a stable. And that's when the baby came! As a mother, she wished for a better beginning for her child, but the baby comes when the baby comes. So, she did what a mother does. She concerned herself with the needs of the baby. Mary wrapped him in strips of cloth and laid him in a manger. For now, it was all she could do.

His birth was a well-kept secret of God. Only a handful of people even noticed. It was just another day in Bethlehem. Shopkeepers were busy minding their stores. Women were picking over produce. Priests were attending to the daily rituals of religion.

We occasionally catch glimpses of the rich and famous striding through the world with their entourage. Surrounded by bodyguards and with much fanfare, they soak up the attention of everyone around them.

In contrast, God's arrival went practically unnoticed but for some nearby shepherds. God's entry point was an animal shelter. The only piece of furniture was a feeding trough. There were more animals than humans to greet him.

But that humble beginning was God's way of getting close to you so that you could be close to Him. God wanted to close the gap between Himself and you. Only this kind of beginning could accomplish that. If God had arrived in glory and splendor, you would have been overwhelmed, intimidated, even fearful. If God had come in the power and might that are His, you might never have drawn near to Him. Remember: even the shepherds were terrified when angels appeared to announce his arrival! But God doesn't want you to be afraid.

This humble beginning was God's way of helping you to understand that God was approachable. And that message was loud and clear in baby **Jesus**.

"For unto you is born this day in the city of David a Savior, who is Christ the Lord.
And this will be a sign for you: you will find a baby wrapped in swaddling cloths and lying in a manger."

Luke 2:8-20

JANUARY 17

Jesus is here! The hope of the world is now entrusted to an infant. And we have never been so near God.

One of life's most exciting and delightful experiences is calling people to tell them about the arrival of your new baby. Of course, the ladies always want to know those details — how long was she in labor, how much does the baby weigh, how long is the little one, etc. Most men are content to know its here, has a name, and everyone is okay. But for all concerned the arrival of a baby is the best news!

The shepherds were doing what shepherds always do: taking care of sheep. Suddenly, one of those messenger angels appeared to them. Now, in their entire lives never had an evening under the stars been interrupted by an angel. Not surprisingly, they were terrified.

There is certainly nothing surprising about the angels making the announcement. But who would have planned to start with shepherds? After all, these guys ranked pretty low on the social scale. The business of tending sheep did not attract a lot of upwardly mobile people. In fact, these fellows were probably pretty hard characters: rough, tough, dirty and ceremonially unclean. In other words, they did not get a lot of baby announcements.

But here they were: listening to angels singing to them! And here they were: kneeling and looking into the face of God before anyone (except Mary and Joseph)! Here they were: being the first to tell others of their amazing experience!

Why did God choose these shepherds to be the first to hear the best news? Was God showing that the good news was for everyone? Was God demonstrating that He was approachable to all?

Answers may be hard to find. But this we know: these shepherds would never look at the nighttime sky quite the same again. After all, they had heard the angels singing and they had looked into the face of God. His name was **Jesus**.

> ... Simeon took him up in his arms and blessed God and said, "Lord, now you are letting your servant depart in peace, according to your word; for my eyes have seen your salvation..."
>
> Luke 2:21-38

JANUARY 18

Jesus was the firstborn of Joseph and Mary. Faithful to God, these parents presented their firstborn before the Lord. But Joseph and Mary didn't come into the temple carrying a sign. Still, there were two aged folks, Simeon and Anna, who recognized the Messiah in the child.

What do you want to do before you die? Parachute out of a plane? Bungee jump off a bridge? Run a marathon? What do you have to do before you can say life is full and complete? "Lord, you can take me now!"

Simeon, "righteous and devout," lived to see the Messiah. He has ordered his days, adjusted his lifestyle in anticipation of this moment. "Now," he says, "God, you can take me."

But is our situation any different than his? Don't we, too, live with a promise of the Lord's return? Shouldn't we order our days, adjust our lifestyle in anticipation of his coming?

In the birth stories of Matthew and Luke, only one person seems to have grasped the real nature of what God had set in motion. Simeon recognized that this child was going to bring change, even to the heart of Mary. In fact, the birth of Jesus would change everything!

The world might appear unchanged. After all, the Herod family still ruled, Roman troops still occupied the land, and Jews still resented both. But around this infant, people were changing. Some were excited and worshiped; others were afraid. No one stayed the same.

Luke's other witness was Anna, a widow for more than six decades. We don't know very much about her. People probably thought she was strange. After all, a woman so consumed by her religion that she lived in the temple was not usual. Also, she was a prophetess. Everyone knew how eccentric prophet-types were.

But, like Simeon, she knew what mattered. She knew that this child was cause for excitement. Then, she did the most natural thing when one discovers really, really good news. She told people about **Jesus**.

And behold, the star that they had seen when it rose went before them until it came to rest over the place where the child was. When they saw the star, they rejoiced exceedingly with great joy.
Matthew 2:1-11

JANUARY 19

Jesus was born in the time of King Herod. Now, for most folks, who is king or president when one is born is not usually a matter of any special note. But then, most leaders would not see the birth of a baby as a threat to their rule.

Herod was plagued by insecurity. Perhaps, he had good reason. The Jews did not think much of him because he was just partly Jewish. The Romans were suspicious of him because he was partly Jewish. So, he often saw conspiracy in those around him. The news of a child "who has been born king of the Jews" was just one more conspiracy theory.

Questions abound regarding the Magi. Were there three men? What made them think that this star would lead them to the king of the Jews? Did their gifts have special meaning? What happened to these gifts? What exactly did they do when they worshiped the baby?

And who were these guys? We don't know their names, although there are some traditions about their names. One of those comes from an early sixth century Greek manuscript in Alexandria. It gives these names: Melchior, Caspar, and Balthsar.

Tradition has also given them faces. In the painting, "Adoration of the Magi," we discover that Melchior was the oldest and his gift was the gold. Caspar is the youngest and he gave the frankincense. Balthsar was the African who brought the gift of myrrh. But the painting is not Scripture.

Of course, some have suggested that things might have been different, at least more practical, if the wise men had been wise women. They would have arrived on time, helped deliver the baby, cleaned the stable, made a casserole, and brought practical gifts, like diapers and baby powder.

What we do know is that these wise men found the child by following the star. The star was God's work and God's work is all about people coming to **Jesus**.

> But when Herod died, behold, an angel of the Lord appeared in a dream to Joseph in Egypt, saying, "Rise, take the child and his mother and go to the land of Israel, for those who sought the child's life are dead."
>
> Matthew 2:12-23 (Luke 2:39)

JANUARY 20

Jesus was only a child but already he was threatened by the world he came to save. We don't want a king over our lives, even if he comes as a baby.

The wise men probably had a strong feeling about Herod. After all, these *are* wise men. But the dream settled the matter.

It was also a dream that sent Joseph and family packing. Joseph again responds to a message from an angel of the Lord by being obedient. Under the cover of darkness, the little family departed for Egypt.

Eventually, Herod realized that the Magi were not going to report back. So, he came up with an alternate plan. If he could not locate the specific child, he would simply eliminate all of the possibilities.

Matthew's record tells us that Herod had thought to inquire of the wise men as to "the exact time the star had appeared" (2:7). Thus, the slaughter of the babies of Bethlehem involved all "who were two years old and under, in accordance with the time he had learned from the Magi" (Matthew 2:16). By this Matthew indicates that Jesus could have been up to two years old at the time of the Magi's visit.

Sometimes we will do anything we can to keep Christ out of our lives, because we, too, feel threatened. We may not be a king and have power over armies. We may not be into killing babies, but we are still adamant that we are not going to let Jesus take control.

Think about it: folks are happy to let Jesus be a baby in a manger, but not so willing to let him be the sovereign King and Lord that he is. What about you?

Perhaps, this explains how we can tolerate the trappings of Christmas, but we find it difficult to really give ourselves to Christ. We enjoy singing the songs of the infant, but we struggle to accept the authority of the man, **Jesus**.

> And he said to them, "Why were you looking for me? Did you not know that I must be in my Father's house?"
>
> Luke 2:40-52

JANUARY 21

Jesus was concerned for the things of his Father, even at the age of 12. What was Jesus like as a twelve-year-old? How did he get along with other kids? What were his favorite games? Was he competitive? What did his brothers and sisters think of him? And that really big question: What did Jesus know about himself and when did he know it? Evidently, those are things we don't need to know.

When they departed Jerusalem, Jesus was not with his parents, but they did not know it. They probably traveled in a caravan and the men and women were not always together. Each probably supposed that Jesus was with the other.

If you have ever become separated from your child at a mall or ballpark, you can understand their feelings when they discovered he was missing. Panic, fear, dread, desperation. As parents, they probably felt guilty for not doing a better job of keeping their eyes on him.

The temple rabbis were the most learned, the most spiritual of Israel's teachers. But we can be sure that they never expected to meet a twelve-year-old like Jesus! Where did this young fellow get such a grasp of Scripture?

Jesus was missing for three days. Did you ever wonder where Jesus slept during this time? And where did he get food? Did anyone stop to ask where this boy's parents might be?

The reaction of Joseph and Mary when they found him was typical of parents. Surprise, relief, and anger. At the same time we are hugging our child we are telling him/her, "If you ever do that again, I'll.... !"

The exchange is an eye-opener! Mary spoke of "your father," but Jesus emphasized God as "my Father." Jesus recognized his unique relationship to God and that he had a mission, and all of this at the age of twelve!

There is nothing more important than knowing who you are and why you are here. Such knowledge seems to take care of most things. Above all, it helps you determine your priorities. "I must be about the things of my Father," said **Jesus**.

As it is written in Isaiah the prophet, "Behold, I send my messenger before your face, who will prepare your way, the voice of one crying in the wilderness: 'Prepare the way of the Lord, make his paths straight,'"

Mark 1:1-6 (Matthew 3:1-6; Luke 3:1-6)

JANUARY 22

Jesus could hardly have found an announcer who was more peculiar than John the Baptizer. John may have come from what appeared to be a traditional Jewish family but he was anything but traditional.

Given his experiences and our impressions of him, he probably would have done well on the television series "Survivor." Then again, he might have been the first one voted off the island because of the things he said.

John the Baptist was not particularly diplomatic. Calling people poisonous snakes on their way to hell is hardly the way to win friends. No one would accuse John of trying to sugar coat anything.

Remember that the events surrounding his birth were so unusual that the people asked, "What then is this child going to be?" Cut from a special piece of cloth, possessing great conviction and determination, believing passionately in the cause, and willing to make the ultimate sacrifice to reach the goal, John was clearing a path for God!

The "voice" could be heard and the people came from Jerusalem and the surrounding region to hear John preach. He must have been very good. He touched their hearts. "They confessed their sins and were baptized by him in the Jordan River."

But what was it about John that drew the crowds? Was it his startling message of repentance and baptism? Was it his strange appearance? Was it his emphasis on the Messiah and the hope he inspired? Maybe it was all of these.

John the Baptist was a trailblazer. He was clearing a path and making a way into the hearts and lives of people. It is important to note that this highway was not intended to enable human beings to travel to God, but for God to reach us. God was coming to you in the person of **Jesus**.

John answered them all, saying, "I baptize you with water, but he who is mightier than I is coming, the strap of whose sandals I am not worthy to untie. He will baptize you with the Holy Spirit and with fire."

Luke 3:7-18 (Matthew 3:7-12; Mark 1:7-8)

JANUARY 23

Jesus was about to step on to the stage of his ministry among the people he came to save. If people were unprepared for him, it was not the fault of John the Baptist. John's message was loud and clear: One more powerful and worthy, One who will save and judge is coming after me! This was John's good news!

The people were eagerly awaiting someone who would be their deliverer. When they heard John's preaching, when they saw his passion, they thought it might be him. But John was quick to point them in another direction. The One coming would baptize with the Holy Spirit and with fire.

Naturally, the people wanted to know what to do. In a word: repent! Let your lives show that your heart is changed. Whether a tax collector, a soldier or an ordinary citizen, repentance meant living differently than before.

Of course, John anticipated those who would claim special privileges. He knew that there would be resistance from some who took pride in their heritage. Religious leaders claimed the right to refuse baptism because they were Abraham's children. In other words, they already had their ticket to heaven.

John was not simply trying to get people to see sin as some kind of social problem and feel badly about it. He was calling for people to confess their sins based on their genuine sorrow over offense to God and make real changes. Showing remorse over sin is essential to repentance. However, it is just the beginning. "Produce fruit in keeping with repentance." Being sorry is not enough. There must be evidence of change. We don't just think about living differently; we live differently.

John's passionate words came from his deep conviction that sin was very, very serious and that the Messiah was, indeed, coming. Then, as now, changing your heart and life is the best way to prepare for the coming of **Jesus**.

> ...and a voice came from heaven, "You are my beloved Son; with you I am well pleased." Jesus, when he began his ministry, was about thirty years of age...
>
> Luke 3:21-23a

JANUARY 24

Jesus always knew that day would come. He swept up the wood shavings on the floor of the shop, put the tools away, and walked out for the last time. He closed the door on his life as a carpenter and began focusing on the mission that was his alone.

He journeyed from his home in Nazareth of Galilee to the Jordan where he sought John and asked for baptism at his hands. John was humbled in the presence of Jesus. In fact, he felt the roles should be reversed.

What did John know about Jesus that prompted his response? How well did these two know each other? Did they ever spend time together in their youth? We do not know. This is the only time we observe them together.

So, why was Jesus baptized by John in the river Jordan? Perhaps, it was an opportunity for Jesus to put his seal of approval on John and his work. God was speaking and John was the voice.

Jesus expressed his own reason: to fulfill all righteousness. It was not a matter of having sins to confess but a matter of having a heart that wanted to be wholly submissive to the Father.

Maybe Jesus was baptized to identify with us and set an example for us. He waded out into the water to stand with us in our sinfulness. He was identifying with the sinners he came to save.

Whatever reason or reasons for Jesus' baptism, one thing we can say for sure: His baptism pleased the Father. As quickly as he arose from the water there was a dove (the Holy Spirit) and then a voice (from God). The message was one of absolute approval.

The baptismal account, though brief, is a very important part of his story. It marks the official beginning of a life to be lived before all the people. Even more, it reflects his priority: Pleasing the Father is the way of **Jesus**.

But he answered, "It is written, 'Man shall not live by bread alone, but by every word that comes from the mouth of God.'"
Matthew 4:1-4 (Mark 1:12-13; Luke 4:1-4)

JANUARY 25

Jesus was clear about his mission as the Messiah, but a question of strategy remained: How would his life be lived? How would he go about redeeming the world?

Satan arrived to make some strategy suggestions. Not surprisingly, his suggestions called for ignoring God's will in favor of one's personal needs.

The first temptation was a test. Would Jesus trust his Father to provide his basic needs? In time, Jesus would teach his followers to trust God and to pray to God for their daily bread. Would he live by the same requirements of faith and dependence on God as everyone else in the kingdom?

Satan wants you to believe that if you don't take care of you, if you don't provide for you, then you will live without those objects and pleasures that make life worth living. He wants you to believe that God cannot be trusted to provide them.

But is it possible that what we learn from Jesus is a new definition of *need*? That he was hungry is not under debate. That bread could be had is also not a question. However, Jesus' response indicates that the greater need for him was to listen to the Word of God, and that Word told him (and us) that bread was not his greatest need!

This is where faith rubs hard against the pains and urges, against the desires and wants of life. And it is here that the devil seizes upon our weakness of flesh to convince us that we are justified in trusting our own judgment about what we think we need.

The truth is: if you trust God, then you don't need to steal money, you don't need to take another man's wife, you don't need to get answers off someone else's exam, and you don't need to worry yourself sick. You don't have to follow Satan's advice if you trust God to provide all that you really need.

But you must be clear about what you need. If you are, it is much easier to look to the only One who can provide. Just like **Jesus**.

Jesus said to him, "Again it is written, 'You shall not put the Lord your God to the test.'"

Matthew 4:5-7 (Luke 4:9-12)

JANUARY 26

Jesus' second temptation was an invitation to instant attention. Just think of the sensation created in the city by someone who could jump from the temple and be caught by angels before he hit the ground! Instant popularity! All that was required was a small compromise: a dare on Jesus' part to make God rescue him. It would be a painless shortcut to grabbing the attention of the people.

Temptation. The word means different things to each of us. For some, it is the struggle with staying on a diet. For others, it is the daily battle with porn online or X-rated movies. For others, it is grappling with prescription drugs or secret sexual fantasies.

But whatever our weakness, one thing is sure: temptation is inevitable. There is no place to hide and no way to escape. Temptation is wherever you are. The devil will see to that.

Satan wants you to believe that you are special and that your will, your view, your understanding of the situation, your feelings, are just as important as anything God says. After all, who knows better than you what you need? And, surely God wants you to be happy.

Satan says, "If your goal is important, it is okay to break a rule here or there. If you have good intentions, it is okay to cut a few corners, to violate a commandment or two. If you think this will advance you in some way, it is okay to do what you think best."

Of course, Satan never tells the truth. And here is the part he always leaves out: Sin always diminishes your potential. You are never better, never richer, never healthier, and never happier when the devil is done with you. While there may be temporary "gains," you are never better as a person for having followed Satan's directions.

On this day the devil brought his lies to Jesus. "Give the people something that will excite them and then they will follow!"

"No. I will only do this God's way," said **Jesus**.

Then Jesus said to him, "Be gone, Satan! For it is written, "'You shall worship the Lord your God and him only shall you serve.'"
Matthew 4:8-11 (Luke 4:5-8, 13)

JANUARY 27

Jesus' third temptation was the devil's approach to getting a kingdom. "If you want to be a king and reign over a kingdom, I can make it happen. Better still, I will keep you from having to suffer and die for the sins of the world. I will give you a shortcut to glory."

Satan wants you to believe that everything important, everything worth having in life can be had without pain or sacrifice or patience. He tells you there is no need to wait until married for the joy of sex–there is no need to wait for things by hard work–there is no need to wait for advancement through integrity. He offers shortcuts, attractive and easy paths to all the things your heart desires. For most of us, the easy way is hard to resist.

For some reason, we have such short memories on this. We forget our own experiences and the experiences of others. Maybe it's because we believe it will be different with us. Maybe we think that our secret struggle with pornography won't hurt anybody....that our affair won't affect our family....that our weakness for alcohol isn't really that serious.... that stealing some small items from the office is really not that bad. At least, those are the lies we tell ourselves.

How much Jesus struggled with any of these temptations is not clear. But at day's end his decision was unmistakable. Whatever the plan might bring, he chose the way of God, the way of patience and purity, the way of integrity and love, and, if required, the way of suffering. God would be first in his life!

The subtlety of temptation is that it invites you to something that appears to be both attractive and advantageous. What is more, it can always be had at the end of any easy path.

But Jesus knew what each of us must learn: God's order is to bear the cross first and wear the crown later. How wonderfully blessed we are because the way of God was chosen by **Jesus**.

> The next day he saw Jesus coming toward him, and said, "Behold, the Lamb of God, who takes away the sin of the world!
> ...And I have seen and have borne witness that this is the Son of God."
>
> John 1:19-34

JANUARY 28

Jesus was not yet the name on everyone's lips, but it soon would be! Just now there were great happenings at the river and much talk about this dramatic new preacher named John who was baptizing all kinds of people.

His preaching called for the people of God to repent! And there were even rumors that he might be Elijah returned, or the Messiah, or the prophet. But John said, "I'm only a voice. I'm nobody. Only a voice."

And then there was the issue of baptism. Nobody had gone around baptizing as John did. He had even become known as John the Baptizer. "Why," they asked, "do you baptize?" The real issue was one of authority. "If you are no one in particular, who gave you the right to do this?"

Despite the apparent success of his preaching, John appears totally unaffected by it. In fact, John felt unworthy to loosen the sandal strap of Jesus. He was conscious only that he was a servant whose task was to prepare the way for the coming of the Messiah. His own ministry, by comparison, was insignificant. The focus must be on Jesus!

John may have seen his cousin, Jesus, when they were little boys, but John did not know him as the Messiah previous to the baptism experience. There had been no private collusion or arrangement between them. John needed a special revelation from God in order to perceive Jesus as the Son of God.

God cannot overlook sin. We ought to pay the price but are incapable. Only God could do that. So, God became man. God provided the Lamb for the sacrifice.

We had sin but no righteousness. He had righteousness and no sin. How could there be both judgment for sin and pardon from sin? Only by providing a substitute for you and me so that the substitute received the judgment and we received the pardon. John said, "This is the substitute. The Lamb is **Jesus**."

Andrew first found his own brother Simon and said to him, "We have found the Messiah" (which means Christ). He brought him to Jesus.
John 1:35-42

JANUARY 29

Jesus now occupied center stage. John knew that his role was to announce the Messiah, then step aside. He lost his audience because they believed his message, and they became disciples of Jesus.

Many of us are like John and Andrew. We want to know more. We have open and inquiring minds but we do not want to be pushed against our will. We need time to investigate and consider. No problem. Jesus invited them – and us–to come and see, and to learn and consider.

Ultimately, discipleship is expressed by action. We can't sit on the sidelines and be disciples. We don't just study about discipleship or meet in small groups to discuss it. We become disciples by following.

Also, no one comes to Jesus and stays the same. No one begins this walk without change. And you can be sure that where change takes place, there is a cost.

But what did you expect when you became a disciple? That good folks wouldn't suffer? That prayer would always bring a quick and pleasant answer? That all your doubts would go away? That obedience would be easy and the devil would leave you alone? That God would remove all the risks from your life?

Perhaps, we become disappointed disciples because we lose sight of whom we are following. If I asked you to tell me about yourself, about your faith, would you spend all your time telling me what you do? Would you tell me about your busy church life? Or, would you tell me about your relationship with Jesus? Would you tell me how he has your heart and how wonderful it is to know him? Would you say that following him is worth it no matter the cost?

With such exciting news in his heart, Andrew searched for that one person with whom he wanted to share such news; it was his brother, Peter. No two conversions are just alike. No two followers have identical experiences. Yet all true disciples are led by one Spirit and serve one Lord. We share in common what matters most: our relationship with **Jesus**.

Nathanael answered him, "Rabbi, you are the Son of God! You are the King of Israel!" Jesus answered him, "Because I said to you, 'I saw you under the fig tree,' do you believe? You will see greater things than these."

John 1:43-51

JANUARY 30

Jesus called several men to become disciples. Each one had his own experience with Jesus. But it made no matter: all were called disciples.

Some of us heard Jesus calling through the words of a hymn or the text of a sermon. Some of us heard his call in the voice of a parent, or a friend, or a minister. Some of us heard him calling us through experiences that touched our hearts. But no matter the means of his calling, each of us knew it was Jesus and that saying "no" would be our worst mistake.

Being a disciple is not like any other experience of life. We don't submit a resume' and hope that he will see something attractive about us and want us for his group. We don't "try out" for the team, either. We don't "sign up" because we have something to offer or because it is the best deal going around. Instead, Jesus calls us to walk with him every day.

The amazing thing is that he does that even though our story has "sinner" written across it in the boldest letters and we have nothing of value to offer him! Yet, he wants us!

Jesus knew about all of those he called. Jesus knows all about you, too. He knows where you've been. He knows all that has happened with you. He knows your character inside and out. He knows what you love and what you hate, what you fear and what excites you. He knows how your heart aches and what wounds you carry from life. He knows you. Still, he loves you and welcomes you as his disciple.

These men could not have imagined what kind of experiences lay ahead or how dramatically their lives would be changed by their decision to follow. But that's the way it is with all who become disciples of **Jesus**.

> This, the first of his signs, Jesus did at Cana in Galilee, and manifested his glory. And his disciples believed in him.
>
> John 2:1-12

JANUARY 31

Jesus' concept of serving God was not one of long face and constant seriousness. No one ever walked this earth with greater purpose and mission. But Jesus still believed you could have a good time. His life would not be lived on the fringe of civilization but in the center of it. He would accept invitations to many social events. Evidently, Jesus enjoyed conversation, laughter, and good food.

In Jesus' day, a wedding was a great celebration, and no small half-hour event. Following the ceremony there was a procession to the home of the groom, a joyous, noisy parade, with an open house and a party that went on for several days.

The wedding at Cana was a social disaster waiting to happen! There is nothing more embarrassing to host or hostess than running out of something.Whether the crowd was larger than expected, the hosts were poor, or the festival was in its final stages, the fact remained: "They have no more wine."

How Jesus' mother became involved in this wedding is not explained. Why did Mary approach Jesus about the matter? Did she actually expect him to do something special to meet the need? Was Mary concerned about the shortage of wine, or the glory of her son?

"My time has not yet come," he said. Jesus was not insensitive to the needs of others; but he was quick to discern how he could meet those needs in the context of the Father's will. He came for a definite purpose and definite task. That was his priority.

And what great counsel from his mother—"Do whatever he tells you." Sometimes we struggle to wait for the Lord, to trust him to provide. But we can make no demands. We are deserving of nothing. He understands our situation. How important to trust and obey!

The best wine saved until last! Isn't that just like him? No matter how good things appear to be, they are always made better by **Jesus**.

**In the temple he found those who were selling oxen and sheep and pigeons, and the money-changers sitting there.
…And he told those who sold the pigeons, "Take these things away; do not make my Father's house a house of trade."**

John 2:13-25

FEBRUARY 1

Jesus had been in Jerusalem many times during the years before his public ministry began. As a faithful Jew, he would have been to the temple on numerous occasions and, no doubt, had often seen the corruption there.

But on this particular day, the sight stirred his blood! He found the place filled with clutter and noise, dirty-smelling animals, money-changers and merchandise. No one in the temple seemed to be concerned that the House of God was itself in need of cleansing!

For the benefit of those paying the temple tax, money-changers provided an answer to the foreign coin problem, but charged exorbitant rates. To those needing an approved animal for sacrifice, there were temple merchants.

What Jesus found was the business of religion. The place of prayer had become a setting for arguments about prices, disputes about coins, and haggling about animals. No doubt, the priests would have argued, "We just want to make everything user-friendly."

We tend to think the same way. Gyms and coffee houses, bookstores and game rooms have become the norm in our efforts to attract outsiders as well as hold on to believers. A lot of "business" is conducted in the name of religion. Our intentions may be good but it is easy to lose focus.

For Jesus, the issue was simple: the honor of God in the place of worship. The honor of his Father fueled his zeal on this day and in this place, but it would continue to provide his motivation throughout his ministry. Later, after his resurrection, the disciples remembered the zeal and words of Jesus.

No doubt, your day will have its share of clutter and noise, people and business. Distractions can make it difficult to stay focused on your purpose. But recalling his passion for God's honor can be just what you need to stay on course. After all, today is all about being like **Jesus**.

Jesus answered him, "Truly, truly, I say to you, unless one is born again he cannot see the kingdom of God."

John 3:1-8

FEBRUARY 2

Jesus knew that beneath the long robe beat a searching heart. Jesus always welcomed searching hearts. Jesus welcomes–and still does–those who come with their doubts, their fears, and their struggles. In fact, he came looking for just those kinds of folks.

Perhaps Nicodemus had grown weary of the ritual and was hungry for something with more meaning. Maybe he was touched by the words of this peasant preacher. Perhaps he was curious from the many rumors circulating about the man from Nazareth. Maybe he was struck by Jesus' strange behavior.

We give Nicodemus a hard time because he came at night. But the real significance of this is not that Nicodemus came by night. The important thing is that he came at all! Maybe he was afraid. Maybe he was concerned about being seen with Jesus. Maybe he was lacking in faith and courage. But he came!

Born again. It has a wonderful sound for anyone longing for a fresh start, a new beginning. But Nicodemus did not understand. Many folks still don't. The words have become common, a part of the theological jargon of our time. People are frequently heard to refer to themselves as born again Christians. Of course, there is no other kind of Christian.

The new birth marks a change in you. When you are born of the flesh, you inherit the fleshly nature. But when you are born of the Spirit, you receive a new nature from God. As birth is the gateway to life, your life now has new meaning and purpose. Your desire, your will is no longer based or framed on what you want but on what God wants. But this change takes place in the unseen part: your soul.

Here is the most amazing thing: "born again" describes the action of God. Jesus was telling Nicodemus that God accomplishes in the heart what a man could never do for himself. We respond in love and faith but it is God who makes a person brand new. We can start anew because of **Jesus**.

> "And as Moses lifted up the serpent in the wilderness, so must the Son of Man be lifted up, that whoever believes in him may have eternal life."
>
> John 3:9-15

FEBRUARY 3

Jesus knew he was going to die. And he knew how and why.

Nicodemus was trying his best to understand. After all, he came to Jesus looking for some answers. But what he was hearing was probably too much too fast.

In time, Nicodemus would defend Jesus (John 7:51) and then take the unusual step of helping Joseph of Arimathea in caring for the body of Jesus (John 19:38-39). But that's later. Right now, Nicodemus is struggling to understand Jesus' words, to understand heavenly things. And who better to teach heavenly things than the only one who has come from heaven?!

In the wilderness journeys, the children of Israel grew impatient and complained, "There is no bread! There is no water! And we detest this miserable food!" So, the Lord sent venomous snakes among them. The snakes bit many of the people and they died. The rest then pleaded to Moses who prayed for them. The Lord told Moses to make a bronze snake and put it up on a pole. Anyone who was bitten could look at the bronze snake and live. The power was not in the bronze snake but in God. They were healed as they turned to God.

Twice more (John 8:28; 12:32-33) Jesus would speak of his being "lifted up" and the difference that would make to lives. He knew he was going to die. That was the heavenly plan!

You see, the cross was always in God's plan because you were always in God's plan. He planned for the cross because He planned for you. How remarkable and special is that?

Understanding heavenly things can be difficult. Furthermore, God's plan didn't include providing answers to your every question. Thankfully, His plan did include showing you how to live the life He intended for you. And He made that a reality by lifting up His Son, **Jesus**.

> "For God so loved the world, that he gave his only Son, that whoever believes in him should not perish but have eternal life."
>
> John 3:16-17

FEBRUARY 4

Jesus answered *our question* with words that we cannot forget. "Why did Jesus come and die?" Because God loved us. God took the initiative.

Later, Paul would write that this is a love that surpasses knowing. You just cannot understand it. It defies description. It is beyond the rational limits of intellect. Nothing makes a difference in a human life like the deep, genuine belief in the love of God.

Perhaps, it is His love that most confounds us. After all, we are accustomed to loving others in response to their treatment of us and we know something of the ebb and flow of love. Though we have doubted, denied, and deserted Him, there was never a moment when God did not love us. We have dismissed and forgotten Him, but there was never a moment when God did not love us. We have offered excuses and built barriers, but there was never a moment when God did not love us. We have never lived a day, a minute, or a second, when God didn't love us.

Even though we are accustomed to the idea of 'doing more' to influence the love of another, there is nothing we can do that would cause God to love us more or less than He already does. The things we do may be wonderful expressions of our love for Him, but they won't change His love for us in even the smallest way. God could never love you any more than He already does. And, God could never love you any less than He already does.

You awaken every morning to the love of God greeting you. You close your eyes every night with God's love watching over you. But if Jesus' words about God's love leave you still wondering and unconvinced, then look one more time at the cross. God wrote His love for you in the cross of **Jesus.**

> "Whoever believes in him is not condemned, but whoever does not believe is condemned already, because he has not believed in the name of the only Son of God."
>
> John 3:18-21

FEBRUARY 5

Jesus' words make far more sense to us than they would have to a first century Jew. The Jews looked for a Messiah who would sit in judgment on the rest of the world while exalting them to favored nation status. Saving the world was certainly not what they expected.

But his words are not disturbing to just a first century Jew. In a world that relishes the idea that there are many pathways to God and numerous ways to engage in religious expression, Jesus' words are more than a little troublesome. In fact, in our pluralistic society we might wonder why anyone should be condemned who chose not to believe in Jesus. But we would take such a view only because we understand neither the nature of God nor the seriousness of our own situation.

Condemned. It isn't a nice word. It doesn't conjure up pleasant thoughts. It isn't a term spoken in admiration or gratitude. It doesn't signal a noteworthy achievement or describe a meaningful accomplishment.

Condemned is all about rejection and pain. It is a word we associate with guilt and conviction. It is a word that makes us think of doom. If the thought saddens us, think of how God must feel.

We are without excuse. The Light came into the world so that we could see the greatness of our God and better understand the enormity of His love for us.

Tragically, we often seem bent on darkness. Naturally, we seek the cover of darkness to hide the evil we do. But the darkness never helps us, never renews us, and never gives us hope.

But the Light is so different! We walk in the Light, not because we are perfect, but because he is and we want to be near him and like him! The light exposes us for what we are and that can be painful, but it is worth it because the Light is all about forgiveness and salvation.

A Messiah saving the world may not have been what they expected but it was what they needed. He is what we need, too. **Jesus.**

"You yourselves bear me witness, that I said, 'I am not the Christ, but I have been sent before him.'
He must increase, but I must decrease."

John 3:22-30

FEBRUARY 6

Jesus' reputation spread and the crowds following him grew larger. As a result, more and more people were baptized. No doubt, this created much excitement in Jesus' camp. It had quite the opposite effect among the disciples of John the Baptist.

John's disciples were concerned about the success of Jesus. They did not like the fact that their leader was coming in second. They were confused and disappointed. How easy it would have been for John to take advantage of their concern. After all, he was teaching and baptizing first. Also, John baptized Jesus, not the other way around.

All this sympathy from friends and admirers could have encouraged him to feel sorry for himself. In answering his disciples' complaints, it would have been very easy for John the Baptist to express how he felt injured, neglected, or forgotten by this turn of events. But John would have none of it! He knew who he was. John's reply to his disciples was the response of a spiritual man who had found contentment and purpose because he knew his place in God's plan. What God wanted for John was far more important than anything John might want for himself!

Even preachers like to preach to a growing church. It is not easy to be second chair in the band, or the backup on the ball team, or the runner-up in a race. Coming in second is even more difficult to live with if we are accustomed to coming in first.

But John knew something that was helpful: Anything a person receives is given him/her from heaven. It is arrogant for us to resent someone whom God has blessed. Also, it fails to give God glory for His sovereignty.

John knew who should be first and he gladly accepted his role as a friend of the bridegroom. Perhaps his followers were decreasing in number. Maybe he wasn't baptizing as many as Jesus. But this was one time when coming in second was exactly the goal! After all, his purpose was to point people to **Jesus**.

> The Father loves the Son and has given all things into his hand. Whoever believes in the Son has eternal life; whoever does not obey the Son shall not see life, but the wrath of God remains on him.
>
> John 3:31-36

FEBRUARY 7

Jesus is special. Hardly anyone would disagree. After all, who else has time measured by their coming? Who else has millions who claim to be followers? Who else is the theme of so many songs or the subject of so many books? Who else has a name on so many buttons and badges, bracelets and backpacks in which people want to know what he would do?

John the Baptist wanted his followers to know that Jesus really was special. He wanted them to know that this man was *the one* people should follow. But why was Jesus so special? Why should anyone follow this Galilean? John had an answer.

"Jesus is the one who comes from heaven," John said. Earth and heaven are vastly different realities. We are very aware of how far we are from heaven. While we have immediate, first-hand knowledge of our earthly experience, we can only speak of heaven in words and tones that reflect our desires and longings. We have never known it, but we want to. We have never seen it, but we want to. And we have never talked with anyone who has been there. Until now.

Now there is an authentic messenger from heaven. Now there is someone who can verify the reality of such a place, who can tell us that such a life is real, and who can reveal to us the nature of the God who is there. Never before! Until now.

Also, John says, "Jesus is the one who speaks the words of God. Jesus is the one who tells the truth."

Truth. It seems harder than ever to find someone who really tells the truth. Jesus is only going to tell you the truth. He does not lie. If he says something, you can believe it. For the first and only time, a man walks this earth who has come directly from heaven and every word he speaks is true.

John was right. There is no one so special as **Jesus**.

Jesus said to her, "Everyone who drinks of this water will be thirsty again, but whoever drinks of the water that I will give him will never be thirsty again. The water that I will give him will become in him a spring of water welling up to eternal life."

John 4:1-15

FEBRUARY 8

Jesus was tired. So, about noontime on a hot day he sat at Jacob's well. His thoughts were interrupted by the sound of sandals on the path. Looking up, he saw a Samaritan woman approaching with a water pot on her shoulder.

She came in the heat of the day. But it was easier this way. No stares, no sneers, no taunts, no jokes, no scorn from the respectable ladies of Sychar. Her story was common knowledge. Five failed marriages. Now she lived with another man.

Life had been hard. She could handle the cutting words of the townspeople but she would fall apart when looking at herself in the mirror. And worse, she had lost all hope of anything ever changing. There was no way to begin anew, or so she thought.

Typical of human nature, she thought of life improvements in physical terms. "I could be really happy if I did not have to keep coming to this well….if my health improved……if I could just have that job you have…… if I had some friends……if I just had more money….."

When you follow Jesus, you still have to travel the path to the well. You still have to go to work and mow the lawn. You still have to wash the dishes and clean the toilets. You still get the flu and your kids still try your patience. You still get stuck in traffic and you still have to pay taxes.

But you don't have to ache in your heart over life on a dead-end street. You don't have to live with feelings of worthlessness. You don't have to live without love or hope. You don't have to go to bed with emptiness or greet the day with dread. You don't have to be afraid.

Like her, we are staggered by what must be the requirements to have such a life. And then comes the best news of all: this new life is a gift from **Jesus**.

> The woman said to him, "I know that Messiah is coming (he who is called Christ). When he comes, he will tell us all things."
> Jesus said to her, "I who speak to you am he." John 4:16-26

FEBRUARY 9

Jesus believed in her. He knew that beneath the cheap dress was a heart longing, aching for a higher, better life.

"Go, call your husband and come back."

What a strange request. It may even strike us as a bit irrelevant, even inappropriate.

But Jesus knew that she could not receive the gift of new life if she continued to hold on to the old way of living. He was helping her to face herself.

New life begins with the admission that the old one is going nowhere. Sadly, our pride often keeps us from admitting that we are living on a dead-end street. But we know it in our hearts!

Perhaps she was growing uncomfortable with this intrusion into her history. Maybe she felt the need to defend herself. Why not just change the subject? "What about worship?" she asked. "You say Jerusalem is the place; we claim Mt. Gerazim."

"Worship anywhere," Jesus said. "God is not confined to buildings or places on a map. Only be sure that He has your heart. God wants true worshipers."

She responded, "I know about the Messiah. I know he is coming."

Jesus said, "That's me."

Wow! I wish John would have recorded her facial expression. What was racing through her mind now? Could he really be the One? She left her water pot and ran to town!

Jesus knew all about her past, her prejudices, and their points of religious disagreement. Still, he showed her nothing but kindness.

Would we have been as willing to help her? Or, do we have our own ideas about who fits in the kingdom? What about the homosexual? What about the person with AIDS? What about the divorced, or those who have been married several times? What about those who live on government help?

Everyone had given up on this woman. She had even given up on herself. But who would ever expect her to change? Who would ever help her to change? Who would ever believe she could? Who would ever believe you could?

Jesus.

So the disciples said to one another, "Has anyone brought him something to eat?"
Jesus said to them, "My food is to do the will of him who sent me and to accomplish his work."

John 4:27-38

FEBRUARY 10

Jesus crossed the land of the Samaritans. He did not have to do so. In fact, most Jews would not have done that. So, why did Jesus?

Well, we might say, "for this woman." Every person was important to Jesus. And what about the people of the village? He came for them, too.

But perhaps the reason is found right here with the disciples. Maybe he wanted to open their eyes to the possibilities of their task. Perhaps, Jesus wanted to make them think about their role as his ambassadors.

The Samaritans were now coming to him from the village. In telling the disciples to lift up their eyes and look on the field, Jesus was probably directing them to look at the approaching Samaritans.

But couldn't Jesus have just told the disciples about the harvest without actually going through Samaria? Yes, he could have. Around an evening campfire in Galilee or Judea Jesus could have explained the need for someone to eventually make a mission trip into Samaria. Jesus could have described Samaritans thirsting for God and longing for news of the Messiah. But what an experience these disciples would have missed! Seeing the harvest was far more inspiring than just hearing about it!

There was that moment, though, when their attention was focused on more practical matters: food. But even here they met confusion. Had someone already given him something to eat?

"No," said Jesus, "but what sustains me, fills me up and energizes me is doing the will of the Father and completing the work He gave me to do."

Perhaps, Jesus crossed Samaria rather than go around because he wanted his disciples to learn that everyone matters to God, to face their prejudices and to get out of their own comfort zone, to see the doors of opportunity being opened by God, and to know that the time for work is now. And here in Samaria the disciples learned that doing the will of God nourished the life of **Jesus**.

They said to the woman, "It is no longer because of what you said that we believe, for we have heard for ourselves, and we know that this is indeed the Savior of the world."

John 4:39-42

FEBRUARY 11

Jesus did not come simply to inform, to educate folks about God and His ways. Jesus came to show people the Father. Jesus was here among us to change lives, not exchange ideas. He wasn't here to give us more or different or better religion to do. He was here to give us more than we could ever dream, to help us be different from the world, and to make us better than we could ever hope to be. So, it must have brought him enormous delight to see someone's face brighten up as the truth found a home in the person's heart! He must have wanted to shout with joy when people seemed eager to hear him and know him!

A most unlikely person had become a witness, an ambassador for Jesus. Her excitement translated into action! Exciting news, good news could not be kept in one's heart. It had to be shared!

Never underestimate the power of your words. Your testimony about Jesus as your Savior may arouse interest when you thought there wasn't any. Your words may stir hearts in ways you could not imagine. Your excitement over what you have found may rub off on those who are searching.

You do not convert the world. You do not convict the world. You do not save the world. Your total contribution to the salvation task is to make possible an encounter between Jesus and lost people.

Programs designed to help everyone become evangelistic typically fail because they are programs. Evangelism is not a program. It is a lifestyle. It is a way of thinking and living.

This woman opened the door with her excitement and, suddenly, an entire community wanted to meet Jesus and hear for themselves. Before long, their elation was equal to hers!

It is amazing what happens to us when we hear the best news! And it is also amazing what can happen when we share that wonderful news about **Jesus**.

Jesus said to him, "Go; your son will live." The man believed the word that Jesus spoke to him and went on his way.
John 4:43-54
(Matthew 4:12; Mark 1:14b-15; Luke 3:19-20; 4:14b-15)

FEBRUARY 12

Jesus moved in a world of sorrow, but he never saw people without being touched by their pain. Never did a morning come to evening but Jesus' heart ached for the misery and hurt he witnessed in human lives.

Jesus went to Cana, the place of his first miracle. At the same time that he was renewing friendships, just twenty-five miles away in the city of Capernaum, an anguished father was standing at the bedside of his young son, watching the boy slowly succumb to fever and disease. It is every parent's worst nightmare: feeling helpless to save your suffering child.

Then, someone mentioned Jesus. Maybe it was a servant, maybe a friend. It does not matter. Jesus the healer represented his last hope.

When he finds Jesus in Cana, he does something uncharacteristic for a man of his position: he begs. He begs for the life of his little boy. If he had any prejudices against traveling Jewish teachers, he laid them aside. If he possessed any concerns about what others might think of him begging, they no longer seemed to matter.

This father took Jesus at his word and departed for home. Do you suppose he had any doubts, any second thoughts as he traveled the twenty-five miles to home?

Here is the dilemma of faith — when we are asked to believe God before there is any evidence that what He has promised will happen. What will we do when we have no outward assurance?

But remember: genuine faith does not mean we don't have questions, but it does mean we obey. He may have had some doubts, but he kept on toward home. That's what Jesus told him to do.

Can you imagine his joy when the servants met him with the good news? And every day for the rest of his life, whenever he looked at his son, he would know that the best decision he ever made was when he went to **Jesus**.

> "The Spirit of the Lord is upon me, because he has anointed me to proclaim good news to the poor. He has sent me to proclaim liberty to the captives and recovering of sight to the blind, to set at liberty those who are oppressed, to proclaim the year of the Lord's favor."
> Luke 4:16-21 (Matthew 4:13-16)

FEBRUARY 13

Jesus walked to the raised desk; all eyes in the room were riveted on him. There was a buzz in the air. Sensational rumors had spread about this carpenter-turned preacher. A heavy scroll was brought to him and he carefully unrolled it while the people waited.

When he had found the passage he desired, he read the words of Isaiah. Puzzled looks began to appear on faces. What was his intention in choosing this passage?

Jesus handed the scroll back to the attendant, and sat down in his seat, as a rabbi would do when he was ready to teach. He looked into the faces of those who were watching him so carefully and he said, "Today, this scripture is fulfilled in your hearing."

Because they knew Isaiah's prophecy, they knew two things: those words applied to the Messiah and those words referred to the year of Jubilee. So, why was he using them?

Everything would be made right in the Year of Jubilee (Leviticus 25:8-17) and Isaiah promised a deliverer that would bring hope, healing and freedom. The principle of the Year of Jubilee had now become a promise of deliverance!

Jesus shocked the group by claiming the principle of the Year of Jubilee and the promise of a coming deliverer are found in a person, and that person is himself. The promised Messiah had finally arrived and he was sitting right in front of them! Of the texts he could have chosen, of all the sermons he could have preached, of all the ways he could have announced his mission to his family and friends, he chose a passage about sharing good news, proclaiming freedom, bringing healing, and releasing prisoners. It was clear: His mission was about people!

If you have ever wondered about his purpose, if you have ever wondered about what he came to do for you, here it is. This is the mission statement of **Jesus**.

**And they rose up and drove him out of the town and brought him to the brow of the hill on which their town was built, so that they could throw him down the cliff.
But passing through their midst, he went away.**

Luke 4:22-31

FEBRUARY 14

Jesus was not surprised by the reception in his hometown. Impressing those who know you best is never easy. It is even more difficult when others have their own preconceived ideas.

At first the people of Nazareth seemed to believe Jesus. They sensed an air of authority about him and he spoke unlike anyone they had ever heard. So, they hung on every word and they watched him carefully.

But then he started saying some pretty incredible things and some things they just did not like. Suddenly, his credentials did not look so good.

"Didn't we see this kid playing in our streets just a few years ago? Isn't he the son of Joseph, the carpenter? What makes him think he's so special?"

But when he reminded them of God's benevolence on the widow of Zarephath and Naaman the Syrian in the days of the prophets, they became angry. The inclusion of Gentiles in the kingdom was totally unacceptable.

What was the real problem in Nazareth? Why couldn't they see the real Jesus?

The box.

They had created a box for the Messiah. The box held their ideas about the Messiah: what he would look like, what he would say, what he would do, who he would bless. The box held their expectations for what life would be under the reign of the Messiah. There was definitely no room in the box for Gentiles!

Trying to place deity in a box is as old as humans. After all, what else is an idol but a vain attempt to impose our box ideas. But once we put God in a box (or some tangible form), the box becomes our world, too.

Jesus wanted them to know him. But their preconceived ideas about the Messiah and their familiarity with his family got in the way. He just was not right for their box. They did not know: there is no box for **Jesus**.

And when they had brought their boats to land, they left everything and followed him.
                                       Luke 5:1-11 (Matthew 4:18-22; Mark 1:16-20)

FEBRUARY 15

Jesus knew all about fishing. He also knew the hearts of these fishermen. But their skepticism was natural.

Consider it from their point of view. These fellows were tired from their night's work. The fishing was poor. Now they were busy with the irksome task of cleanup, never much fun when you're weary and unsuccessful. The time for fishing was past. They would enjoy some downtime and fish another day.

Yet, here was this carpenter-turned-preacher talking as though it was an excellent time to fish! What did he know about fishing?

But these guys were about to discover something fantastic about this Jesus! The guy knows about fishing!

Jesus knows all about you and your day. The projects and tasks. The interruptions and mistakes. The pressures and problems. The appointments and meetings. The phone calls and emails. The pickups and deliveries. The exercise and the diet. The vitamins and the medicines. The quick lunch and the late dinner. The soccer practice and the music lessons. And most important of all: he knows your heart. He knows what you love and where you hurt, when you are strong and why you are afraid. Jesus knows you.

This was all pretty unsettling to Peter. Humbled, he fell at Jesus' feet.

Can you imagine the village talk? A human fish finder! What an opportunity to make some big money!

And what a blessing it would be to the kingdom. The money could be used to finance those preaching campaigns. But just as quickly as they discovered that Jesus knew all about fishing, they discovered that Jesus was not really interested in fish. He was after a bigger, more important catch: people.

So, these fellows left it all behind. The fishing boats, the nets, and the biggest catch of their lives. They left behind a whole way of life. Why? Because this Jesus knew all about fishing — and them.

And why not follow? They could not and would not just go on living as though nothing was changed. They had to follow. They were changed...by **Jesus**.

And they were astonished at his teaching, for he taught them as one who had authority, and not as the scribes.
                              Mark 1:21-28 (Luke 4:31-37)

FEBRUARY 16

Jesus talked and people said, "Wow! Nobody speaks like this guy!" Jesus was probably more conversationalist than orator. In fact, the greater part of his teaching is presented in conversations rather than sermons. But he was a Teacher who amazed the listeners.

Perhaps, accustomed to the rabbis' approach, people were surprised by his various platforms: in the temple at Jerusalem, in synagogues of various towns, out in the open fields, along the shore of Galilee, and even in a boat.

Or, maybe the people were astounded by the nature of his audiences. After all, he included everyone!

Or, maybe it was what he talked about that so stunned them. Loving your enemies and praying for your persecutors. Turning the other cheek and going the extra mile. Not worrying, but trusting God. Not judging, but forgiving others. Being as concerned about what you think as what you do. No one ever said such things!

Or, perhaps it was just his manner of presentation. He didn't read from books or talk over their heads like the rabbis. He didn't quote other rabbis or refer to the traditions of famous teachers from the past. He spoke like a man who was confident and convicted about what he said.

But a word of warning is in order right here: many people are amazed by Jesus, but it makes no meaningful difference in their lives. Jesus' goal was not amazing people but changing them.

What he said and how he said it may be impressive to many but it does not always translate into change. As in Jesus' day, there are plenty who acknowledge that "no man ever spoke like that," but not so many who choose to follow.

What about you? Are you amazed by the way Jesus talks and by what he says? Do you hear the authority in his voice? When Jesus speaks, can you hear his passion for goodness and his love for everyone? When you listen, do you not hear the voice of God in the words of **Jesus**?

And the whole city was gathered together at the door.
And he healed many who were sick with various diseases, and cast out many demons. And he would not permit the demons to speak, because they knew him.

Mark 1:29-34
(Matthew 8:14-17; Luke 4:38-41)

FEBRUARY 17

Jesus silenced the demons even though they knew the truth about him. But why? Perhaps, Jesus was not ready for an open revelation of his deity.

The origin and exact nature of demons and demon possession are unknown to us. While modern-day claims are rare, opinions on the subject are many. In the Scriptures, demons took possession of people and afflicted them in body and in mind. Demon-possessed people appear as individuals who have little control over themselves and are, instead, ruled by the demon.

Admittedly, the Bible stories of demon possession foster all kinds of questions as they present some bizarre behaviors on the part of those possessed. These are not dramas produced by the movie industry but real-life stories of Satan's work.

The really good news is this: Jesus has authority over everything in our lives! Whether something is happening to us or something is happening within us, Jesus is in control.

We may not have to fear or grapple with demon-possession as in Bible times, but we certainly have to struggle with the devil every day. He never leaves us alone. Our failures and messy lives are evidence that he often wins the struggles and rules in us.

But it does not have to be that way! As Jesus ruled over the demons then, he rules over Satan now. Jesus came so that we might awaken every morning in our world knowing that we are safe in his care. We are never strong enough or smart enough to defeat Satan. We can, however, place our trust in the One who has defeated the devil by his life and death. By his power we live our lives without fear and with confidence that one day Satan will be sent away for good!

Maybe the best news of the day is right here: There is one person who has authority over everything that happens in your life and his name is **Jesus**.

And rising very early in the morning, while it was still dark, he departed and went out to a desolate place, and there he prayed.
Mark 1:35 (Luke 4:42a)

FEBRUARY 18

Jesus never tried to prove the reality of prayer by formal arguments. Nor did he endeavor to prove the benefits of prayer by cold logic. Instead, he chose to show the value of prayer by praying. He demonstrated its worth by making it an important and meaningful part of his life. His disciples could not fail to see that. In time, they would ask him to teach them to pray.

There is so much about Jesus that we do not know. His biographers chose to focus on his words and ways, not the details of his appearance or daily routine. If there is an exception to this, it is his practice of prayer. Scattered through the Gospels are these notes on his habit of slipping away from others to solitary places where he could pray. Often, he did so in the early morning hours while others slept.

Perhaps, the early morning was when it was easier to be alone. Or, maybe he chose that time because it was preparation for the day's demands. Whatever his reason, Jesus thought prayer was that important.

Many of us talk a lot about quiet time with God. Unfortunately, we usually excuse ourselves by explaining how busy we are. We know that spending a few minutes each day with God would be good for us. But, evidently, we don't believe that the good would outweigh what we can do ourselves if we keep on working. Prayer is our back-up plan, not the primary approach. We make time for God because we want or need something or because we're in trouble. Jesus made time to be with the Father because he longed to be with the Father.

Faced with the needs and demands of the crowds, confronted by the ever-watching critics of the Sanhedrin, and carrying the hope of humanity in his heart, Jesus sought time with the Father.

The picture is sketchy and the details are few but the message is clear: facing the day, time with the Father was priority for **Jesus**.

> And Simon and those who were with him searched for him, and they found him and said to him, "Everyone is looking for you." And he said to them, "Let us go on to the next towns, that I may preach there also, for that is why I came out."
>
> Mark 1:36-39 (Luke 4:42b-44; Matthew 4:23-25)

FEBRUARY 19

Jesus prayed. Simon and the others searched.

Simon and the others probably thought it strange that Jesus would be in seclusion when his popularity was soaring. They would, in time, have a greater appreciation for the value of getting away from the crowds. But for now, they are excited about all the excitement!

And who can blame them? There was plenty of opposition. But how wonderful to be among people who were receptive and liked what they were seeing and hearing!

Although faced with the temptation to stay among those singing his praises, Jesus chose to journey on to other places and spread the news of the kingdom. Jesus was on a mission: to preach to as many as possible in the time he had.

Jesus was, after all, a preacher first. He was a healer and miracle-worker. People came to him from other regions to be healed. Evidently, they brought to him every imaginable malady and he healed them all. But while those incredible displays of compassion and power spoke volumes about him, they did not provide the whole story. He was a man with a message, and not just any message. He came to bring good news.

Did you ever deliver really good news to someone? Exciting, wasn't it? The joy on the person's face told you everything. They may even have shaken your hand right off or hugged you so hard you could barely breathe, but it didn't matter.

And did you ever receive really good news? Overwhelming! It was like the sun just came out, all the colors in the world were suddenly brighter, and life seemed hopeful again. There is nothing quite like really good news.

God had good news for us. He sent His very best messenger with the news. In fact, the messenger and the message were the same: **Jesus.**

> And behold, a leper came to him and knelt before him, saying, "Lord, if you will, you can make me clean."
> And Jesus stretched out his hand and touched him, saying, "I will; be clean." And immediately his leprosy was cleansed.
> Matthew 8:2-4 (Mark 1:40-45; Luke 5:12-16)

FEBRUARY 20

Jesus was full of compassion. Whether he was looking out over a crowd or into the face of an individual, Jesus' heart ached for the people he came to save. Their suffering was his, too. So, when a leper came to Jesus and begged for help, his heart was moved.

His life was a nightmare. He knew only isolation and loneliness. He was repulsive to himself and to others. His leprosy kept him from his own family and friends and cut him off from the religious festivals and worship services of Israel. Worst of all: there was no cure.

When he walked down the street, he was shunned. Little children ran; older kids threw rocks and taunted. Adults walked on the other side of the street, shaking their heads in disgust. No one ever put an arm around him or hugged him or kissed him.

Somehow, he learned of Jesus and his words revealed his faith in Jesus' power. "You can make me clean." Where or how he came to this conviction, we do not know. But there was hope, if he was willing....

Like this leper, most of us do not have a hard time believing that God *can* work powerfully in our lives. We have a hard time believing that God *wants* to work powerfully in our lives.

This is a preview of the cross. Rather than being repulsed by our wretchedness, Jesus reached out to us. In fact, he took our uncleanness upon himself so that we might be clean.

Like this leper, there was absolutely nothing we could do to cleanse ourselves. Our only hope was Jesus. We come saying, "Lord Jesus, if you are willing, I know that you can make me clean."

The good news is: no one is so willing as **Jesus**.

And when Jesus saw their faith, he said to the paralytic, "Son, your sins are forgiven."

Mark 2:1-12 (Matthew 9:1-8; Luke 5:17-26)

FEBRUARY 21

Jesus could see their faith and determination. They would not give up. They were not easily discouraged by a crowded house. The four begin to tear away the roof and the pieces of the ceiling began falling on the people below. When they had made a hole big enough, they lowered the man on his mat.

We don't know why or how long this man was paralyzed. We also know that the paralytic's friends were willing to go to a lot of effort for him. Perhaps, the boldness of his friends came from having witnessed Jesus healing others. Or, maybe they had heard others testify to the miracles of Jesus. Perhaps, they were desperate to help their friend and Jesus represented their last hope.

Jesus looked up to see four anxious faces peering down through the hole. Then, he looked down into the hopeful face of the man on the mat.

Jesus addressed the man's greatest need first. But that only drew the criticism of the Jewish observers. So, Jesus said, "Which is easier?" It is easier to say, "Your sins are forgiven." Why? Because no one can tell if it's true. You can't see if someone's sins are forgiven. Anyone could say that, and you'd never know if it was true. But, if you told someone who was paralyzed to get up and walk, you could see if it was true or not.

These critics were right when they said that only God can forgive sins. Jesus was claiming power that only God could rightfully claim. So, at Jesus' word, the man got up and walked! Imagine the excitement of the four men on the roof!

Faith. How easy to discuss. How hard to possess. If all our decisions were based only on what our eyes see, if whatever we see was the total of reality, life would not seem so complicated. But because we believe in what cannot be seen with these eyes, because we are people of faith, life becomes more interesting, decisions more challenging. But life also becomes meaningful and adventurous.

"We have never seen anything like this!" You get that a lot with **Jesus**.

After this, Jesus went out and saw a tax collector by the name of Levi sitting at his tax booth. "Follow me," Jesus said to him, and Levi got up, left everything and followed him.
Luke 5:27-28 (Mark 2:13-14; Matthew 9:9)

FEBRUARY 22

Jesus' invitation to Matthew (Levi) was surely unexpected by everyone. But think how special Matthew felt!

There is something really fantastic about being specially chosen. It is wonderful when a church says, "Mike, we want you to be our preacher." Or, when a company calls, "Mary, we want you to come to work for us." Or, when a university writes, "Tom, we want to offer you a scholarship."

It is very unlikely that Matthew's parents were excited about his occupation. In fact, he may have been a real disappointment to them. Having given him the name Levi, his mom and dad may have envisioned their son in a life of service to his God and his people. Working for the enemy and making his living off his countrymen were not a part of their dreams for him!

His job was lucrative and steady. But his friends were few. Despised by the Romans for being a Jew, the devout and patriotic Jews viewed him as a traitor who had betrayed his own people for money.

Matthew may have been thinking about Jesus for some time. After all, Jesus had been preaching and teaching in the area. Whether Matthew had heard Jesus or only heard about him, something had touched his heart and wouldn't leave him alone.

What a heart-searching experience it must have been to leave the security of his most lucrative position, and follow Jesus with no prospect or promise of material support. Perhaps, no disciple had more wealth to forsake than Matthew.

In the most important opportunity of all time, the invitations have gone out. Your name is on one. It was specially inscribed. And it was delivered in person by Jesus. It says simply, "Follow me."

It is your personal invitation from **Jesus**.

> And Jesus answered them, "Those who are well have no need of a physician, but those who are sick.
> "I have not come to call the righteous but sinners to repentance."
> Luke 5:29-32 (Matthew 9:10-13; Mark 2:15-17)

FEBRUARY 23

Jesus was not bothered that the man was a tax collector. Jesus came to call people to follow. He looked into Matthew's heart and found a man who was ready to do exactly that.

Matthew and Mark simply mention that Jesus was having dinner at Matthew's house, but Luke tells us that Levi (or Matthew) "held a great banquet for Jesus at his house." Perhaps, it was Matthew's way of saying "thank you" for the invitation. Or, maybe he wanted to provide an opportunity for others to meet and to know Jesus as he did. Whatever his reason, it was a joyous occasion for a man embarking on a new life!

It probably did not take Matthew very long to compose his guest list. After all, whom does a tax collector hang out with after work? Other tax collectors. Naturally, he would have trouble getting a lot of folks to attend, especially those of good reputation.

Motivating folks to change can be challenging. Basically, there are two approaches: judging or loving. We often feel the need to convict people of their sins because we believe that only then will they recognize their need of redemption. But the truth is: we respond better to being loved than being judged.

Jesus' approach was to convince people of how much God loved them and wanted them in His family. Eating with them was one way to convey this loving acceptance.

Resist the temptation to decline his invitation by saying, "I am not worthy." You are right. But that is precisely why Jesus came. To call sinners. We do not say "yes" to his invitation because we are worthy to follow. We say "yes" because we are both unworthy and hopeless.

Also, remember that you are a follower. Everyone is a follower, a follower of someone or something. But that also suggest that you are being led somewhere. Do you feel good about that? You should if you are following **Jesus**.

> He also told them a parable: "No one tears a piece from a new garment and puts it on an old garment. If he does, he will tear the new, and the piece from the new will not match the old."
> Luke 5:33-39 (Matthew 9:14-17; Mark 2:18-22)

FEBRUARY 24

Jesus came to give life that was brand new and this disturbed those who thought the old life was fine as it was. To no one's surprise, this meeting of old and new ideas created enormous tensions. Such is often the nature of change.

Clashes with the religious establishment came frequently during the ministry of Jesus. His ways and words were constantly against the grain. Jesus did not fit. The Pharisees could see it, but they were frustrated that so many of the common folks could not.

The wedding imagery suggests both something new and something joyful. To fast would be inappropriate. The time for fasting would come. But this was not that time. They needed to recognize the presence of the Messiah and celebrate!

Putting a new patch on an old garment was also inappropriate. When the patch shrinks on the old cloth then the problem may be worse. Perhaps, Jesus wanted his listeners to understand that what he was bringing was not a patch for Judaism. Jesus was bringing a new garment!

Old wineskins became rigid and brittle with time. Lacking the necessary elasticity, these old wineskins could not handle the fermentation process and expansion of the new wine. Thus, one must pour new wine into new wineskins. Jesus would not put a patch on Judaism, nor would he pour his new teaching into the inflexible and rigid system of traditionalism developed by the Jews.

Jesus came to provide humanity with a new way of thinking and living. But, sometimes, he makes us uncomfortable, even irritable, by his words and his ways. He stretches our thinking and we do not always appreciate the stretching.

If today finds you bothered over the call to walk in his steps, then perhaps you should think of it for what it is: an opportunity to be stretched by **Jesus.**

> **This was why the Jews were seeking all the more to kill him, because not only was he breaking the Sabbath, but he was even calling God his own Father, making himself equal with God.**
>
> John 5:1-18

FEBRUARY 25

Jesus has all the power in the world to heal, but a person has to want to be well. Unfortunately, everyone does not.

The man in this story had been ill for thirty-eight years. But there are few details of his illness, and there is no explanation why Jesus chose him among so many. There is one thing we do know: the man did not seek Jesus' help. In fact, he did not even know who Jesus was.

"Do you want to get well?" It would seem an unnecessary question. But for thirty-eight years he has known a certain lifestyle. He has made it work for him. If healed, he would have to venture into the unknown and relinquish all his present securities. He would have to be responsible for himself, even get a job. There would be no more begging.

The same thing happens spiritually. Even though we know what we are doing is not helpful, we are afraid of what change might mean. Paralyzed in heart and mind, we settle for less because we are familiar with what we have, and because we want to avoid what we imagine are unwelcome changes.

Even though the man did not answer Jesus' question, Jesus did not dispute the man's theology or his ideas about an angel stirring the waters. He just helped him.

It was amazing! One moment he was the paralyzed man he had always been. In the next moment, because of Jesus, his life was transformed. Everyone celebrated! Well, maybe not everyone. The joy of the day was overshadowed by the legalism of these critics. But they were already envisioning a solution to their problem.

The question is not—Can you be well? The question is—Do you want to be well? The question would be easier to answer if you did not hold on to the world so tightly. Who knows what will happen if you let go of what you know, what works, what is comfortable? But then, isn't this what it means to trust **Jesus**?

> **The Father judges no one, but has given all judgment to the Son, that all may honor the Son, just as they honor the Father. Whoever does not honor the Son does not honor the Father who sent him.**
> **John 5:19-30**

FEBRUARY 26

Jesus' behavior had a logical explanation. Like Father, like Son. Because He was (is) God, he acted like God. He could act in no other way.

But if his claim to be the Son of God is troubling to us, his declaration that he is our judge is especially upsetting. In fact, he tells us that his opinion is the only one that counts! He decides what is right and wrong. He is what it means to be good.

Folks resent that. In a culture that gloats over its freedom to decide right and wrong and celebrates the philosophy that there is no single standard by which all are judged, Jesus is, at best, marginalized in matters of ethics and, at worst, scoffed at. We don't like anyone telling us what to do. We like even less someone judging us for what we choose to do.

The American version of Christianity prefers a God who is more open-minded, enjoys giving good advice, and encourages everyone to be nice to each other. We would prefer that sin be reframed as something that was 'inappropriate,' 'misguided,' or 'bad judgment.' Even more, we prefer to see Jesus as an outstanding man we can admire and quote, but not someone who has the right to lay claim to our lives. It is no wonder that people are always going on some journey to find the 'real' Jesus. Clearly, they don't like the one who appears in the Gospels.

Why did Jesus tell of his unique relationship to the Father? Jesus wants us to understand that deity is among us! He wants us to know that his voice is the voice of God and that his ways are the ways of God.

Write this on your heart: Response to Jesus is response to the Father. Today, the best way for you to walk in God's ways is to walk in the ways of the Son. The best way for you to love God is to love **Jesus**.

> "For if you believed Moses, you would believe me; for he wrote of me. But if you do not believe his writings, how will you believe my words?"
>
> John 5:31-47

FEBRUARY 27

Jesus made some amazing claims, but he appeared to be an ordinary man. Considering his humble beginnings and his rather plain lifestyle, what was there to set him apart from others? Why should anyone think that he wasn't just another man?

So, Jesus brought out the witnesses. The first witness was John the Baptist. John came declaring that Jesus is the Lamb of God, the Savior of the world. He pointed people to Jesus.

And what of the wonderful things Jesus did? People were amazed that the winds and waves obeyed him. They were amazed at how paralyzed bodies sprang to life and a mute man could suddenly speak. They were amazed at how the demons obeyed him and how he walked on water. His works were in the open for all to see. And his works were telling all who he was and who sent him.

Jesus' third witness was the Father Himself. Of course, God spoke from heaven declaring, "This is my Son in whom I am well pleased." But these people did not hear His voice. But what of God's revelation through the prophets? Did He not tell us about the Messiah?

And what about the fourth witness, those Scriptures? Jesus told them, "You go to the Scriptures as though they were the savior...but they testify concerning the Savior; they testify of me."

And the final witness was Moses. Moses was the man all Jews revered as leader and lawgiver. Jesus says Moses would not praise you but rather accuse you for failing to accept me. "Moses wrote about me!"

Jesus said, "Whenever you are reading your Bible, you are reading about me. When God is speaking, He is speaking about me. When your eyes are open to the lives that are transformed, you are seeing those who are witnesses to me."

Yes, he is the Father's Son. Your life says so. And the lives of thousands and thousands join in saying it is true.

The whole creation awakens each day declaring that the Lord of all is **Jesus**!

"And if you had known what this means, 'I desire mercy, and not sacrifice,' you would not have condemned the guiltless.
For the Son of Man is lord of the Sabbath."
                                    Matthew 12:1-8 (Mark 2:23-28; Luke 6:1-5)

FEBRUARY 28

Jesus and his disciples didn't break into a field and rob the owner of his grain. Unlike today, fields were not fenced. Roads or paths could go right through a field of grain. Equally important, stopping to pick a bit of grain when hungry was an acceptable practice (Deuteronomy 23:25).

But make no mistake: the issue for these Pharisees was not about picking grain in someone's field. Believing that God must need help communicating to the people exactly what constituted labor, the Pharisees came up with a few dozen different things that were prohibited on the Sabbath. So, to the Pharisees, these disciples were Sabbath-breakers! More importantly, this was a reflection on their master.

Although Jesus may have toyed with the idea of telling these critics to lighten up and get a life, he proceeded to show them why they were wrong. He reminded them of David's experience with the bread of the tabernacle. Reserved only for the priests, the loaves were given to David and his men because they were hungry.

Then Jesus appealed to the ministry of the temple priests who, in spite of the law regarding Sabbath work, labored in behalf of the people and were considered innocent.

He said, "If you had known what these words mean, 'I desire mercy, not sacrifice,' you would not have condemned the innocent." Through the prophets God revealed His heart of compassion for the weak and less fortunate, for the widows and orphans. He called upon His people to show mercy rather than simply engaging in ritual, to engage in service rather than ceremony.

Finally, Jesus tells them that He Himself has authority over the Sabbath – and if He says this is okay, then it is indeed okay. Now, this would have raised their neck hairs!

Just think: there is something greater than the rules. It is love. Caring for people has always been important to the Lord. It should be important to us.

And there is someone greater than the rules. It is **Jesus**.

And they watched Jesus, to see whether he would heal him on the Sabbath, so that they might accuse him.
Mark 3:1-6 (Matthew 12:9-14; Luke 6:6-11)

MARCH 1

Jesus was a marked man. He was a target and the Pharisees were taking aim. His words irritated them and his actions frustrated them. So, they came to Jesus looking for some reason by which they could accuse him before the people. His Sabbath behavior provided the perfect opportunity.

They asked Jesus, "Is it lawful to heal on the Sabbath?" Now, they were not seeking information, but accusation. The Pharisees had a rule that one could only heal on the Sabbath if it was a matter of life and death but, beyond that, practicing medicine was unauthorized work on the Sabbath. Of course, this was one of their many interpretive rules intended to help clarify things for God.

Jesus healed the man. In doing so, Jesus pointed out the hypocrisy of the Pharisaical rule – their Sabbath rules allowed a man to "lay hold of and lift out" a lamb that had fallen into a pit, even though that was "work." What about helping a fellow human? People are more valuable!

Rules or laws are good. They are given for the purpose of encouraging good behavior and restraining evil behavior.

But laws or rules can become a burden rather than a blessing if applied too strictly. For example, the library rule is intended to limit talking and when you have to speak, whisper. But suppose someone was having a seizure or suffering a stroke. Would you just whisper you needed help? Even though everyone knows the rules, mercy and compassion toward the person in need would take priority. We would shout that there is an emergency. The needs of the person would be more important than the rules governing library conduct.

So, where is your focus? Is it on keeping good rules? Reading your Bible, saying your prayers, being in church, contributing your money? Is your idea of being like Jesus to simply be someone who follows the rules?

Knowing law or rules is good and helpful. Even better is knowing the heart of **Jesus**.

> And whenever the unclean spirits saw him, they fell down before him and cried out, "You are the Son of God."
>
> Mark 3:7-12

MARCH 2

Jesus' astonishing authority over demons and his incredible healings of so many had awakened great interest in him from a wide area. People came from all over that part of the world, from regions east of the Jordan, as far south as Idumea and from the coastal cities of the Mediterranean.

Evidently, the crowds numbered in the thousands. For the first time in a very long time, incredible miracles were being performed in the land of God's people. There was a rumor of hope in the land. Expectations were revived. People were excited! So, the multitudes came.

No doubt, many were there out of curiosity. They came to see if the rumors were true. Others probably came just for the show. They never intended to take any of it seriously but they were looking for a good time. But many were there because they hurt and they did not want to hurt anymore.

It is not too difficult to imagine the crowd pressing to get closer, all the hands extended to touch him. After all, if you had traveled a great distance to be healed or had brought some friend or loved one to be healed, getting close to Jesus was essential. But desperate people can become unruly.

So, Jesus instructed his disciples to have a boat ready. It would be his way of creating a little space, a bit of breathing room between himself and the crowd.

And what about those evil spirits? Why did Jesus warn them not to make him known? Why not allow them to proclaim the truth about him?

Perhaps, Jesus knew that, in spite of their confession, they had no intentions of advancing his ministry. Their testimony would thwart his efforts, not help them. People might even begin to associate Jesus with demonic beings. So, he told them to be quiet.

Imagine the commotion around Jesus. Thousands of needy people. Pushing and shoving for position. Trying to get as close as possible. Begging to be healed. With hope in their hearts. They were, after all, just like you. People whose hearts and lives needed the touch of **Jesus**.

This was to fulfill what was spoken by the prophet Isaiah:
"Behold, my servant whom I have chosen, my beloved with whom my soul is well pleased. I will put my Spirit upon him, and he will proclaim justice to the Gentiles."

Matthew 12:15-21

MARCH 3

Jesus' unusual approach to ministry prompted Matthew to recall the words of a long-ago prophet. Isaiah's words were of a special servant. Clearly, Matthew saw Jesus as that servant and he believed that Jesus was the hope of the nations. But why?

God did not survey the inhabitants of the earth in search of candidates to be the Messiah and then choose the son of Joseph and Mary. Instead, Christ came into the world as the eternally chosen one of God. Had the burden of choosing some candidates been ours, we would have been in serious trouble. Not only would we have been unable to agree on one, we would have been unable to find one!

What does it all mean? It means that your hope is in the One God chose!

Surely, if any ruler ever had a right to advance his kingdom by whatever means necessary, it was Jesus. However, that is not the nature, the spirit of his kingdom or reign. This kingdom will not advance by violence.

The reed grows in the marsh or on the riverbank. It is a weak plant and easily bruised or broken. The smoking flax is the wick that is burning on an oil lamp and is practically extinguished. Each is descriptive of people, weak people. People that are bruised and broken, crushed by circumstances and their own failures. They are disillusioned and feeling hopeless because of life's hardships.

But this special servant does not trample them. His ministry is like his spirit: compassionate. He invites the weary and burdened to come to him for rest.

What does it all mean? It means that you have hope because his mission is to bring blessing and healing, not to condemn and destroy.

Isaiah wrote of broken reeds, but Matthew was thinking of broken people. These people now had the very best reason to hope. God was promising victory! Their hope – and yours–was in the one God chose. **Jesus.**

And he appointed twelve (whom he also named apostles) so that they might be with him and he might send them out to preach and have authority to cast out demons.

Mark 3:13-19 (Luke 6:12-16)

MARCH 4

Jesus sought the solitude of a mountain and there he spent the night praying to God. From that experience he emerged ready to name twelve men as his apostles. These men would become his body and his voice. That was the plan. There would be no second string, no backup players, no plan B. So, Jesus chose his men.

Although they could hardly imagine it then, they would be the first preachers of the new covenant and the foundation stones of the church. They would turn the world upside down!

At first glance, they were not particularly impressive. In fact, they were very ordinary men in every way. Not one was well-known, or well-read. Several of them spent more time with fish than people. They had no experience as public speakers, much less theologians. They didn't even share the same political views; one was a tax collector and another was a Zealot. Other than their willingness to follow Jesus, there was not much to say about them.

In time, they would argue among themselves, display wrong attitudes, speak without thinking, experience ministry failures, and have lapses of faith. More than once, Jesus found it necessary to rebuke them for their behavior.

But in the selection of such men, Jesus was showing that the source of power for this ministry was not in their skills or collective wisdom but in the power of God!

No doubt, he selected them for what he saw in them. Sure, they had some wrong notions about the kingdom, some prejudicial views about Samaritans and they would spend too much time arguing about who among them was the greatest. But they had hearts that were open to his words and ways.

That is the key! What Jesus could do with fishermen and tax collectors he can do with you. Who can imagine what's possible if you open your heart to **Jesus**?

Seeing the crowds, he went up on the mountain, and when he sat down, his disciples came to him.
And he opened his mouth and taught them, saying: "Blessed..."
Matthew 5:1-2 (Luke 6:17-19)

MARCH 5

Jesus had their attention from his opening word: "Blessed!" But did anyone leave early because company was coming for dinner? Were there any crying babies? Did anyone constantly glance at the sun to know the time?

Regardless of the answers, it is difficult to imagine anything other than a multitude captivated by the man from Nazareth. Whether they listened in rapt attention with their eyes riveted on him, we do not know. But there is no question that he made quite an impression. They were filled with amazement!

We are still fascinated by Jesus. But, like his listeners long ago, our amazement is rarely translated into discipleship. We recognize in his words an extraordinary way of living, but it seems as impractical in the age of spaces shuttles as it did in the time of chariots. Jesus' assessment of the human condition is too simplified, too idealistic for our scientific and technological age.

Being morally upright, going the second mile, loving our enemies, traveling opposite the majority —- the Sermon on the Mount does not sound like happy living. The lifestyle is challenging! Most of us find the words tough and the way difficult. Little wonder this path has so few travelers.

To most of us, happiness is getting what we want when we want it. Happiness is living as we please, grabbing all the gusto. To Jesus, happiness is living like God.

From the Beatitudes that opened the sermon to the story that closed it, Jesus was telling us who God is. The blessedness promised by Jesus is nothing less than the life of God himself! The only people who will experience this blessedness are those who partake of the divine.

This is more than a collection of wise sayings or practical rules for living. This is the Lord's portrait of life as it is meant to be lived. This is his word.

Let no one be deceived. The way of Jesus does not represent a natural tendency. The only people who can live this way are those who know they cannot live this way — without **Jesus**.

> "Blessed are the poor in spirit, for theirs is the kingdom of heaven."
> Matthew 5:3 (Luke 6:20-26)

MARCH 6

Jesus begins with us where we must begin with him. Until we acknowledge and confess our spiritual destitution there is little point in talking about living like God. Incredible though it seems, God-like living begins precisely at the point where we realize how unlike God we are.

In an age of assertiveness training, books on the art of intimidation and self-promotion, and cult followings for whoever flexes the most ego muscle, Jesus' words sound alien! So, why does Jesus start here? Because this is the foundation, the first thing which must occur.

If turning the other cheek, going the second mile, loving one's enemies, or forgiving others are to become daily expressions of this unique life, then poverty of spirit must precede. Unless we recognize our own spiritual bankruptcy, we are helpless to live such a distinctive life.

Blessed are those who humbly realize that they are spiritually bankrupt without Christ, who cringe and cower because of their shame and helplessness. Theirs is the kingdom. This, says Jesus, is blessedness. Our response: "You must be kidding."

Our reaction may be an attempt at reform. Convinced of our wretchedness, we set out to reshape ourselves so that the Lord will find us worthy. We put spiritual sayings on the refrigerator, attend church regularly, engage in various church works, and refrain from certain unhealthy habits. Although we are trying hard, the joy and peace of Christianity seem to elude us. But we find comfort in knowing that we are doing something about our condition.

This attempt at reformation is futile. The only way to become poor in spirit is to adore Jesus, the Savior. To confess that we are spiritual paupers is the beginning. Resignation from sin is not the result of our self-discipline but his welcome sovereignty in our hearts. Only Jesus can affect the change. Suddenly, the spiritual pauper is rich!

When we glimpse the matchless love and beauty of the Lord, we realize how great is our need. As spiritual beggars, we confess our hopelessness but for him. This is not the end of living but the beginning. And this is the hardest thing we will ever do. Thus, it was placed first by **Jesus**.

> "Blessed are those who mourn, for they shall be comforted."
>
> Matthew 5:4

MARCH 7

Jesus' words must have come as quite a shock! To people interested in getting rid of life's aches and pains, linking a better life to sorrow must have caused some confusion. Like them, we find it difficult to believe that happiness and mourning could be linked in any way.

We know that Jesus' presence in our world was, among other things, to bring us to a state of mourning over our sin so that we might be comforted. His perfect life, his spiritual message, and his sacrificial death declared that God was reaching down to offer comfort to beggars. Unfortunately, few saw themselves in that way then; few see themselves in that way now.

The infrequent use of the word sin is indicative of human efforts to get away from acknowledging sin or even thinking about such. Like beggars who refuse to be serious about their condition, too many avoid facing the spiritual realities. Seeing ourselves as we are and facing squarely the change that must occur requires honesty and courage. Neither comes easily for us.

Jesus called us to the highest life. The nearer we get to him the nearer we are to that life. The closer we get to that life the more sensitive to sin we become. If we choose to avoid such sensitivity to sin, then we avoid Jesus.

Comfort is not found merely because we mourn but because, in our sorrow, we seek God. The comfort is in His love. It is the courageous beggar, desperate for spiritual comfort, who knows no barriers to the change required. And it is into such a heart and life that Jesus comes bringing comfort and joy

Blessed are they who, seeing the loveliness of Christ, mourn their unworthiness and their helplessness. To these whose hearts go out to God comes the comfort which only God gives.

For hearts broken over sin, for lives anguished by the devil's lies, there is a comfort that fills the soul with peace and hope. Such comfort has proven costly. Jesus' crucifixion was heaven mourning over sin. But after the darkness came the brilliant light of the exalted Lord. Our path to heaven must travel a similar road. No surprise there. We follow **Jesus**.

"Blessed are the meek, for they shall inherit the earth."
Matthew 5:5

MARCH 8

Jesus certainly knew of their expectations. The times were hard and Jews were looking for relief. They were searching the horizon for a leader, a commander, someone who would liberate the people and restore a kingdom. Imagine their surprise when Jesus spoke of meekness instead of might!

Meek is not a word we employ very much. For one thing, it is not commonly linked to happiness. Too many people associate happiness with material possessions, and believe that the way to gain them is through ability, strength, hard work, self-assurance and even self-assertion and conquest. Meekness is noticeably absent from the list. Furthermore, the way to survive and hold on to what one possesses is to be aggressive, heavy-handed, hard-hitting and self-assertive. After all, if you don't look out for number one, who will?

Also, meekness does not seem like a necessary ingredient to victorious living, unless one enjoys being pushed around. Unfortunately, the popular understanding of meekness is probably voiced this way: "Blessed are the meek: for they shall become doormats." But weakness and cowardice have nothing to do with meekness.

Meekness is power under control; it is disciplined strength. Weakness is yielding to our nature; meekness is mastery over it.

People have become monks to make themselves meek. It cannot be done. We can never make ourselves meek. One cannot fast, pray or sacrifice his/her way into meekness. It is not outward, but inward.

The promise, the inheritance is a bit troublesome. We know that the world appears to belong to the men and women of ambition, power and wealth. Also, we have learned that to possess the earth in an outward sense does not bring happiness.

The meaning is this: The meek will get everything there is to get out of life. They live in accord with the very purpose of their existence. Their lives are true and genuine. They inherit the earth and all that belongs to their Father. They are rich for they possess all that is truly valuable.

The meek are possessed of God and thus find the true meaning of life. Their concerns are spiritual. Their desire is to be like **Jesus**.

> "Blessed are those who hunger and thirst for righteousness, for they shall be satisfied."
>
> Matthew 5:6

MARCH 9

Jesus' words are penetrating. How much do you want goodness? Blessed are those who long for goodness more than anything else! Genuine joy is the possession of those who hunger and thirst, ache and yearn, pant and long for God!

Jesus does not urge us to desire spiritual things because it is our duty. Instead, he teaches that genuine joy is the possession of men and women who have acquired a hunger and thirst for spirituality. In truth, we do not go in search of happiness but of God. When we have found Him, we have found incomparable joy.

Perhaps one additional thought is important here: this is a continuing pilgrimage. Jesus did not say 'have hungered.' It is not a one-time experience that results in a single filling. Instead, Jesus presents the most fascinating idea! The Christian is one who, at the same time, is hungry and thirsty, yet filled. The more he/she is filled, the more he/she hungers and thirsts. He/she finds it impossible to get enough! It isn't that he/she is not thoroughly satisfied. In fact, he/she has never known such satisfaction. It is not his/her satisfaction that propels him/her onward. It is God who draws him. The blessing is upon those who desire goodness, not satisfaction.

It is more than difficult to be filled by our world – it is impossible! It is in our weakness that we long for what the world would offer, believing that this would satisfy us. It is an illusion. Try as we may to be filled, we inevitably find that satisfaction never comes and the hunger remains. A larger house, a vacation condo, an expensive car, a prettier companion, a bigger salary, a club membership – it is a hunger than never stops but neither is there any filling.

You were made to be filled by God, filled not because of what you own but because of who owns you, satisfied not because of what surrounds you but because of who is in you. You hunger and thirst for all that is truly good because you have learned that this is when you are most satisfied in life. Today, you know that you require nothing more than **Jesus**.

"Blessed are the merciful, for they shall receive mercy."
Matthew 5:7

MARCH 10

Jesus presented the very thing they needed most. But could they see it? Jesus' listeners were looking to receive mercy, not show it! To do so they would need to think beyond their own misfortune, beyond themselves. That was hard for them. It is hard for us.

Mercy is a lovely word, but it is frequently misunderstood. Perceived as lacking toughness, mercy is often applied to situations or people in which indulgence or leniency would be more accurate.

Mercy is not excusing or smiling at those who violate the law. It is not leniency to criminals, rebellious children, or to the hungry who refuse to work. It is not looking the other way, refusing to prosecute, or feeling sorry for another. Mercy is not merely sympathy or pity.

Mercy is compassion plus action. No one is really merciful who stops at pity. You must both feel and act to be merciful. In fact, our faith (James 2:14-17) and our love (1 John 3:16-18) are evident by our mercy.

Whatever we may decide as to the meaning of mercy, it is true of God. It is God who is "rich in mercy" (Ephesians 2:14). Thus, Jesus does not merely call us to higher living but to divine living; not simply to be better people, but to be like God! "Be merciful, just as your Father is merciful" (Luke 6:36).

Mercy, not always easy, demands personal involvement. We can hire no stand-in, no substitute. What is felt must come from our hearts. What is done must be by our hands.

The promise of this Beatitude is both lovely and fearful. This seeming paradox is found in the fact that mercy shown is linked to mercy received. If the merciful can rejoice in the knowledge that they will receive mercy, those lacking merciful spirits can only be in dread knowing they will receive none.

We are such utter failures. So, we long only for mercy. Therein is our hope and comfort. May we grant to others that which is so exceedingly dear to us. May the Father of mercy find His likeness in us as He did in His Son, **Jesus**.

"Blessed are the pure in heart, for they shall see God."

Matthew 5:8

MARCH 11

Jesus came seeking the hearts of the people. Never was there a more beautiful promise; never was there a greater task. What could be more exciting than seeing God? What could possibly be tougher than living with only pure thoughts and affections?

But the possession of a pure heart is not of our own doing. We lack both the strength and wisdom to accomplish such holiness in our lives. However strong may be our desire, purity remains forever beyond our reach and we search in vain when we look within ourselves for the secret.

How then do we acquire this new heart? The answer was given in beautiful language long ago. "I will give you a new heart and put a new spirit in you..." (Ezekiel 36:26). Purity of heart is the result of God's work. With a penitent and submissive spirit, we open ourselves to the creative hand of God. New hearts come in no other way.

What a wonderful blessing follows this change! While the unrighteous appear to possess little or no sensitivity to His presence, those with pure hearts see and know their God.

You see things as they really are; your eyes and ears and heart are open to the real world. You see your Father in the sunrise and the sunset, in the smile of a friend, in the love of a mother, and in people. You see God in the movement of nations and kings, in prosperity or adversity, and in the ebb and flow of human life. Seeing God, you know the meaning of death as you understand the purpose of life. Sensitive to His presence, you know you are safe and you live with confidence.

If the real battles of life are fought here, if this is where life's greatest questions must be answered, and if here the destiny of every man and woman is decided, then nothing is more important than the character of one's heart.

God wants to be seen and there is so much of God to see. But no one sees so much so clearly as the one whose heart is home to **Jesus**.

> "Blessed are the peacemakers, for they shall be called sons of God."
> Matthew 5:9

MARCH 12

Jesus knows that the trouble with our world is in the hearts of men and women. Until hearts are changed the problems will remain.

So, what is a peacemaker? Are we to compromise or yield for the sake of peace? Does he mean that we should be marching in some peace movement?

To avoid all trouble out of "love for the quiet life" is not the way or spirit of the peacemaker. Nor is the peacemaker a compromiser of truth. Peace at any price is not really peace at all; it is only pretension. Merely getting people to shake hands and let "bygones be bygones" is not the sole aim of the disciple of Jesus.

What makes the peacemaker unusual is his view of peace. He is not out to change the world but to change hearts. He knows the adversaries of peace are not guns and bombs, but envy and greed. While the world has its share of professional negotiators, arbitrators, and mediators, only the Lord's peacemaker puts hearts ahead of circumstances. So, when he sees the distressed and harassed, the anxious and depressed, the fearful and uncertain, he knows what is necessary. He may attempt to lighten the load or alter some circumstances but his energies will largely be spent on the heart.

Be a peacemaker. It is not so difficult. Did you ever return good for evil? That's what a peacemaker does. And when you share the story of peace with others...and when you face up to struggles to solve problems and unite people...and when you exercise care over your words and actions so as not to offend...and when you forgive quickly.... Peace is spread through the lives of godly people. It moves about in no other form. Wherever it goes, a lovely harvest remains.

Those who return good for evil, break down walls of division, help in bringing contentment to troubled lives, and sacrifice all so that God might be known are children of God. How do we know? They are like their Father. The peacemaker acts like God. He looks like God. He reminds people of God.

Do you remind people of God? If you do, you are like **Jesus**.

> "Blessed are those who are persecuted for righteousness' sake, for theirs is the kingdom of heaven."
>
> Matthew 5:10-12

MARCH 13

Jesus never left any doubt about the cost of discipleship. What these Jews thought of Jesus' words can only be imagined but their thoughts probably resemble ours. How can persecution be associated with the blessed life? In fact, why should the righteous be persecuted at all?

Although we struggle to see why righteousness is rewarded so, Jesus wants us to know what happens when we choose to follow him. "If the world hates you, keep in mind that it hated me first." (John 15:18)

It is right here that a hard truth must be faced. When your life is changed, the world does not understand. The ideals of each are totally incompatible. The world is utterly baffled by Christian living. The irritation is further enhanced by the message of your life: "I have found something in Christ that is superior to the world." Whether you verbalize it or not, that is the meaning of your changed life. When one is truly righteous, he or she condemns an unrighteous society — even though one need not speak a single word of condemnation.

Righteous living will draw response from the world. Disciples will be made. But enemies will be aroused. It is important to remember that Jesus told us this would happen.

This persecution calls for an unusual response. It is not so important that we are persecuted, nor does it matter how we are persecuted. It is our response that matters. Jesus said, "Rejoice and be glad." No retaliation. No resentment. No despair.

This Beatitude is the natural result of the others. Persecution is the logical outcome. The world is at odds with the godly. The natural man feels condemned by the spiritual man. Good and evil are eternal enemies.

If you follow Jesus, you may expect to be insulted, avoided, rejected, falsely accused and persecuted in other ways. You ought not to be surprised. If the distinctive goodness of the Master was unacceptable to the world, then the distinctive goodness of the disciples will not be acceptable either. But such is the price you gladly pay to be with **Jesus**.

> "You are the salt of the earth, but if salt has lost its taste, how shall its saltiness be restored? It is no longer good for anything except to be thrown out and trampled under people's feet."
> Matthew 5:13

MARCH 14

Jesus knew that following him would create some disturbing situations for us.

So, what do we do? Live in seclusion? Should we retreat to the wilderness so as to remove ourselves from an evil society?

Having described a way of life so different from the norm, Jesus immediately explained the disciple's relationship to the world. He said, "You are the salt of the earth."

This unique life is to be lived amidst the lovely and the ugly, right up against the good and the evil of this world. This was Jesus' way. He said it should be ours, too.

Salt is essentially different from the object it contacts. If it is like the object, nothing meaningful happens. Salt which renders no change to the food it contacts is merely salt in name only. It is ineffective and useless.

In the same way, the goals and ways of the Jesus-follower are different from the goals and ways of the world. So, contact with the world will cause things to happen. Pleasant things happen. Unpleasant things happen. But always change takes place because of the essential difference between the spiritual and the worldly. If the Christian is like the world in his goals and ways, then nothing happens. Our effectiveness says something about our character.

Sadly, many followers of Jesus are Christians in name only. They may yet have the look but they have lost their spiritual energy and power.

Perhaps, the most exciting thought to come out of this is Jesus' expressed belief that we can make a difference in this world. By being rubbed in and poured on, we can influence others. Actually, we can't help it. It is our nature.

In a world so antagonistic to the spiritual, where do you go to live your faith? Jesus says you live right up against those who seem opposed to goodness. But why expose yourself to criticism and persecution? The answer: Because the power that changed your life can change others. It only needs to be displayed in its genuine beauty. That happens when you imitate **Jesus**.

> "You are the light of the world. A city set on a hill cannot be hidden. Nor do people light a lamp and put it under a basket, but on a stand, and it gives light to all in the house."
>
> Matthew 5:14-16

MARCH 15

Jesus was light in the midst of darkness and he knew how important was his presence. Now, as his followers, we are light. Our charge is not to hide or evade, but to live like Jesus — to live in the open so that all can see the Light.

Our responsibility to shine before the world is not the result of who we are but who he is, not the result of what we have done but what he has done. Jesus intended for the unbeliever to recognize him — in you and me! We are the light of the world. If we fail, there are no others. There is no Plan B.

All must be able to see that we are Christians. There is no such thing as self-contained light. It is the nature of light to shine. Even so, there is no such thing as secret discipleship. The secrecy either kills the discipleship, or the discipleship kills the secrecy.

Unfortunately, we often misinterpret what "letting your light shine" really means. It does not mean seeking to draw attention to self. Looking pious or carrying an over-sized Bible will certainly bring stares, but it is unlikely that these will be translated into changed lives.

The Beatitudes provide a clear statement of what it means to shine before the world. It's not the size of your Bible but the character of your heart that matters. It's not what you do in public but what you are in private that determines what you are in public. To shine before the world has little to do with door-knocking and church-going, but it has everything to do with the way you treat your husband or wife and your children, the way you serve your employer, the way you play, the way you drive, the way you talk, etc. Everything about you is to proclaim one clear message: your Light is **Jesus**.

"Do not think that I have come to abolish the Law or the Prophets; I have not come to abolish them but to fulfill them."
Matthew 5:17-19

MARCH 16

Jesus' preaching created questions. For many, there was a desire to know the relationship of his teaching to the Law of Moses.

But Jesus' attitude toward the Scriptures was one of reverence. He had no intention of violating, breaking or relaxing what was written in the Law or the Prophets. He said that he did not come to abolish the old Scriptures.

There is nothing smaller in the Hebrew language than the smallest letter or the smallest mark of a letter. So important are the Scriptures that not one letter, not even the most indistinguishable portion of one letter, should be relaxed. Such was the reverence of Jesus for the Law and the Prophets.

And if reverence described his attitude, obedience described his actions. Jesus said he came "to fulfill." Jesus meant that Scripture finds its fullest meaning and expression in him. Here was a man whose life displayed what the Scriptures were all about: not a list of dos and don'ts but affirmations of God's love and holiness; not a set of rules to bind but principles to set us free; not burdensome regulations but words to comfort and inspire us.

This was, however, a problem for the Pharisees and scribes. No one spent more time with the law than these fellows. By making the law less demanding and by emphasizing the act without regard for attitude, they lowered the standard.

While they were willing to settle for being "good men," Jesus was calling men to be like God. And nowhere was the difference between them any more striking than their respective views of Scripture. Where they saw commandments to refrain from certain actions, Jesus saw statements of God's holiness. While they were willing to compromise the Scriptures to make "righteousness" attainable, Jesus refused to compromise on any point and displayed the true righteousness that is of God. Thus, their eyes never rose above the level of human goodness. But Jesus was inviting men to see God Himself!

It wasn't a new teaching that people were hearing but that same ancient call to holiness. But now they could also see it...in **Jesus**.

> "For I tell you, unless your righteousness exceeds that of the scribes and Pharisees, you will never enter the kingdom of heaven."
> Matthew 5:20

MARCH 17

Jesus' words were intended to raise the bar, not lower it. But some of us would be gratified if the Bible gave a minimum mark. We would like to know the least we could do and still go to heaven. If we could just know the exact percentage of our income we must give or the precise number of church cuts we are allowed, we would rest easier.

No one was ever better on the outside than the Pharisees! They were the best givers, prayers, and fasters around. They did it better and more often than anyone. In our day a church full of Pharisees would be a remarkable institution. But Jesus could see through the facade. No wonder they hated him!

Jesus' teaching was marked by an emphasis on inner attitudes rather than rules on behavior. Thus, his words regarding murder or adultery were first given to discussing hate and lust. Before addressing the issues of alms, prayer and fasting, he raised the question of what motivated one to engage in these.

But to say that Jesus was only concerned about attitudes is wrong. Although emphasizing our motives, Jesus was equally concerned with how things were done. So, he told us what to do when giving, praying and fasting.

While human righteousness seems satisfied with an attractive cover, the surpassing righteousness of God could never be content with that. Or, while human righteousness finds contentment by emphasizing feelings, the surpassing righteousness of God requires more. God wants our hearts! The actions will follow. Each is important but inseparable in doing the will of the Father.

Many people probably stood in awe of these religious leaders and thought: "I could never do all that fasting, praying, studying, converting, attending and washing." Fortunately, no one has to.

Human righteousness lowers the standard instead of raising it. It makes righteousness easy and cheap. It simply calls upon humans to be better humans. But surpassing righteousness is a call to be like God. Or, to say it another way: Surpassing righteousness is the way of **Jesus**.

> "So if you are offering your gift at the altar and there remember that your brother has something against you, leave your gift there before the altar and go. First be reconciled to your brother, and then come and offer your gift."
>
> Matthew 5:21-26

MARCH 18

Jesus came preaching the righteousness of God. He not only addressed the action but also the attitude that fathers the act. This made him very unpopular with the Pharisees.

Knowing that holiness is more than merely the absence of certain actions in our lives, he expressed concern for the attitude that precedes murder. Both the one who is angry and the one who murders are subject to judgment.

Each of these words (Raca and fool) is a reflection of the contempt that is in the heart. To look with contempt upon any person is to hold a sinful attitude in the heart for one who is made in the image of God. Though stopping short of the action of murder, the feeling of contempt and hate is foul, nonetheless.

Our heart can condemn us. We may never murder with gun or knife, but if we hold someone in contempt, then we are as guilty as if we had shot that person. We may never attack with vicious language that wounds, but if we harbor hatred in our hearts, then we are condemned. God's righteousness is not merely the avoidance of certain sinful acts. Rather, it begins with a heart that loves and seeks goodness.

A broken relationship affects your relationship to God. Reconciliation must precede worship, public or private. It is absurd to imagine God will accept your worship when you mistreat or hate someone whom He has made in His own image.

Broken relationships require your immediate attention. There are two things especially striking about Jesus' illustrations. First, the responsibility to act is yours. You are the one who initiates a settlement. Second, you are to act immediately. Simmering anger usually leads to sad consequences.

Accepting personal responsibility and taking quick action — hardly the way the world thinks! That's alright. You are not called to be like the world but to be like **Jesus**.

> "You have heard that it was said, 'You shall not commit adultery.' But I say to you that everyone who looks at a woman with lustful intent has already committed adultery with her in his heart."
>
> Matthew 5:27-28

MARCH 19

Jesus' words are not so surprising as they are a bit perplexing, even discouraging. What is a lustful look? How can he expect you to control every thought that passes through your head? Doesn't he know that you are bombarded on all sides by sexual messages?

God created us sexual beings. In addition, He made us so that we are visually stimulated. Into this world God has placed attractive people, not hundreds but thousands of them! It is normal to notice them. Women enjoy looking at men; men enjoy looking at women. It has been so since Eden. To enjoy the beauty of another is not lust; to be stirred by an attractive person is not sin.

An interested glance is not wrong. But if that thought takes the soul captive and conceives a plan to use that person, then we have crossed the boundary from appreciative interest to lust. Let's face it: men don't turn the pages of pornographic materials because they are looking for a woman to care for. They are looking for a woman to use. Jesus' words condemn the deliberate decision to center our thinking on a particular person with the intent of sexual sin — even if no action takes place. It is a clear warning that purity of heart is as important as purity of the body.

It is not simply a physical action that brings condemnation — it is the heart's decision to love evil instead of good. The action is but the revelation of the heart! Jesus calls us to abhor the thought that fathers the act.

Jesus has not asked you to abandon your feelings or suppress your desires. He has asked you to examine and respond to your thoughts, feelings and desires in a way that glorifies rather than shames.

True words, noble actions, and pure thoughts are not easy in our world. But they are not impossible. We know that because the one who told us what is possible is the one who accomplished this among us. **Jesus.**

"If your right eye causes you to sin, tear it out and throw it away. For it is better that you lose one of your members than that your whole body be thrown into hell."
                                                                    Matthew 5:29-30

MARCH 20

Jesus wants us to know: Sin is terrible!
Terrible, horrible, disgusting, hideous, awful, sickening, repulsive, ugly, offensive, painful, abominable, atrocious, dreadful, damning. Even viewed collectively the words fail to fully describe sin or tell the whole story of our condition. It is left to God to do that.

A literal interpretation would miss the point. Such an action against the body would not eliminate sin. Our problem is not uncontrollable limbs but ungodly hearts. Jesus' words emphasize the gravity of sin.

Nothing is more important than holiness. This all or nothing approach to God is more than disturbing; it is frightening!

But we tend to balk. Such devotion, such commitment strikes us as too extreme if not downright impractical. We are in favor of goodness, but on our own terms. However, Jesus does not make deals.

Confession comes hard for us. Repentance–that action of gouging out or cutting off–comes only from a heart broken by godly sorrow. This is the character of the spiritual beggar who weeps not because his evil heart has been exposed but because he agrees with God about his condition. Painful, yes. But so necessary.

If we are unconvinced that sin is so terrible, or that holiness is so wonderful, then this world does not look so bad, God's love does not appear so great, and Jesus' death does not seem so important. But we know in our hearts that Jesus has told us the truth.

One day the war will cease and you shall go home to glory...and to wholeness. Until then, you must cut off and gouge out, you must demolish strongholds and arguments, you must take captive every action and thought, and you must fight Satan in every corner of your soul because nothing is more terrible than Satan and nothing is more wonderful than **Jesus**!

> "It was also said, 'Whoever divorces his wife, let him give her a certificate of divorce.' But I say to you that everyone who divorces his wife, except on the ground of sexual immorality, makes her commit adultery, and whoever marries a divorced woman commits adultery."
>
> Matthew 5:31-32

MARCH 21

Jesus' words were not some new revelation on marriage. He was not suddenly addressing an issue in which heaven had been silent. Nor was he contradicting God's earlier word on the matter. Jesus' words on marriage were not so much an effort to overturn the Law of Moses as they were intended to call people to God's plan. What was permitted was not best. What was allowed was not a blessing.

A wedding is one of life's most beautiful and exciting moments: two people standing and declaring their love and devotion for one another before a gathering of family and friends. The service is lovely, the music is pretty, and the couple has never seemed happier. Then, it is the time to promise. "I promise you that I will love you..."

Just think how many times those words, or words like them, are said each year. Many thousands of people make those promises and most have every intention of keeping them. Sadly, many won't.

God joined them! Marriage is the result of God's initiative, and it is not surprising that He has something to say about it. Defining the nature of marriage is not a matter of general consensus. Determining the boundaries of marriage is not a matter of public opinion. There is a divine standard.

God must smile broadly when He observes the love between a man and woman as they make promises to one another. After all, this was His idea. What is accomplished in the wedding is an act of God, not humans. In marriage, two people enter a totally new relationship. A new family has been created. That is the work of God. The rings they exchange are a symbol of what God has accomplished in their lives.

Potentially the most rewarding of all human relationships, marriage unites two people who seek a gift that comes from God. It is really no surprise that serious words about the gift would come from the Giver's Son, **Jesus**.

"Let what you say be simply 'Yes' or 'No'; anything more than this comes from evil."

Matthew 5:33-37

MARCH 22

Jesus was not trying to undo a valid and beneficial system under Moses' Law but he was confronting the effort to circumvent honesty. Any Pharisees under the sound of his voice could not have missed the point. They had sought to create a loophole in oath taking by shifting the focus from honesty to the way in which the oath was worded. Jesus denied them this escape.

Oaths were a part of daily interaction in Bible times. Swearing was heard in legal proceedings, in daily commerce, and in religious matters. The oath was the means by which one sought to verify the truthfulness of words and the faithfulness to perform them.

Typical of their legalistic approach to God, the Pharisees had developed some very special rules for oaths. An oath was valid only when worded in a certain form. As usual, the rules were endless and burdensome, and represented their attempt to avoid the principle of honesty.

Like the Pharisees, we tend to play down the seriousness of this matter. We do that by lying to ourselves. We want to believe that just because we lie, it does not mean we have something wrong on the inside. We even try to justify our lies. We lie on our income tax form and reason that our taxes are too high. We lie about our expenses to the company by concluding that they can afford it and we are underpaid, anyway. Such disregard for truth, such perversion of honesty to serve our own desire is self-deception.

Let your YES be YES! Let your NO be NO! When you speak, others should know that your word is good, you say what you mean, and you are faithful to your promises. Your behavior should reflect your love and devotion to truth so that no one would think it necessary to put you under oath.

It is an exciting surprise to find a fair merchant, an honest lawyer, or a truthful leader. However, there should be no surprise in finding honesty among the followers of **Jesus**.

"And if anyone forces you to go one mile, go with him two miles.
Give to the one who begs from you, and do not refuse the one who
would borrow from you."

Matthew 5:38-42 (Luke 6:27-30)

MARCH 23

Jesus knew that, in order for people to live surpassing righteousness, they must get past their concern for rights. While the 'eye and tooth' approach sounded fair and equitable, and made good sense to most of us, it lacked that single, vital element which Jesus came to provide: healing.

Before us are little cameos of life situations. Each is easy to imagine. It's just like Jesus to speak to our hearts when we are most vulnerable: outside the church house! It is there—in the street, the shop, the house, the gym—that discipleship is tested and shown for what it is.

"If someone strikes you...." We never forget being slapped! It's the ultimate physical insult. Very degrading. Our instant desire is to strike back!

"If someone wants to sue you...." How modern! Bringing legal action against someone has become the national pastime.

"If someone forces you...." No one likes to be forced, especially if it means doing something we would never choose to do.

"Give to the one who asks you...." How do we respond to needs? Do we lend our tools, books, sugar, mowers, tablecloths, punch bowls, cars and card table?

Turning the other cheek, giving up our cloak, going another mile, and sharing with others — this is Jesus' portrait of very unusual people. Such people the world cannot understand. It isn't that disciples of Jesus don't have rights. Our rights have been consumed in a higher purpose: displaying the righteousness of God. Placing the needs and desires of others ahead of your own is not easy. In fact, it is as tough as anything you are asked to do. You have been injured, deceived, used, taken for granted and neglected. Do you give insult for insult, blow for blow? Or, do you return good for evil? Do you argue your rights or relinquish them?

Christians dare not demand their rights, guard their possessions, drive stakes in the ground, or refuse needs. An unbelieving world is waiting and watching to see if this way really works. After all, we are ambassadors of **Jesus**.

"You have heard that it was said, 'You shall love your neighbor and hate your enemy.'
But I say to you, Love your enemies and pray for those who persecute you, so that you may be sons of your Father who is in heaven."
Matthew 5:43-48 (Luke 6:32-36)

MARCH 24

Jesus' words were probably considered unrealistic by some and they found in this command sufficient reason to dismiss him entirely. If there is any single command in this sermon which sets Christianity apart from other religions and quickly divides the half-hearted from the devoted, then this is it: love and pray for your enemies and persecutors. It is a strange way to behave. If the pathway of surpassing righteousness has seemed uphill, then this must surely be the summit!

This unnatural response is the result of a transformed life, a renewed mind that has a clearer perspective of everything and everyone.

The sun's rays touch those who love God and those who do not. The rain enriches the fields of those who love goodness and those who do not. The innumerable blessings of God's creation are experienced daily by saint and sinner. His actions are governed by His love rather than the worth or character of the people.

To overcome our stubborn hearts and rebellious ways, to bring us to Him by bridging the chasm that separated us, and to empower us to be like Him, God chose love. While we behaved like an enemy, He loved us (Romans 5:8, 10). His refusal to retaliate to insults or threaten when he suffered was so that we might be healed (I Peter 2:23-24). Only love closes the breach in a relationship; only love heals broken hearts. The cross says so. We are his witnesses.

Determining who is to be loved by what they offer the relationship may be natural, but it is not godly. This pan-scale approach to love is not God's way. Thank God that it is so! We had no hope of ever offering anything to this relationship that would balance the scales.

As Jesus reconciled God and man through his loving sacrifice, so we, too, serve as his ambassadors of reconciliation. As the love of God was his message, so it is ours. As love was his way, so we follow in the steps of **Jesus**.

> "Beware of practicing your righteousness before other people in order to be seen by them, for then you will have no reward from your Father who is in heaven."
>
> Matthew 6:1-6, 16-18

MARCH 25

Jesus knew that where there is the genuine there, too, will be the counterfeit, that where there are sincere followers there will be phony ones. Those who masked their true identity (called hypocrites) were often the recipients of his stinging words! The temptation to excel for men's praise had moved their benevolence to the streets and church houses, brought their prayers to synagogues and street corners, and caused their fasting to become a public show. His focus was not on what we do but on what we are, not on **doing** righteous acts but on **being** righteous.

Righteousness is not a part we play in a church building or a Bible we display on a shelf. We don't wear righteousness about the neck like a chain with a cross. It is not something we bake, sew, share or carry. Righteousness is not related to how early, how long, how much or how often we do something. It does not rise and fall with the attendance, the prayers or the contribution. It does not sound horns or shout for attention but neither is it confined to secrecy. And words, such as "more" or "most", do not apply to righteousness because it is not available in varying quantities. And most important, righteousness does not originate with us.

The Father sees everything. Sitting by the bed of one seriously ill, preparing a dish for those in need, cleaning the house of one who is bedfast, mowing the lawn for an elderly couple, babysitting so that young parents can have a night out — these quiet deeds are seen by the Father.

And surpassing righteousness will be rewarded. The Father will see to it. So also, will human righteousness. But the rewards are so different. Surpassing righteousness enjoys the limitless possibilities of God's storehouse of blessings; human righteousness is limited to what man can do for man. The reward reflects what we are.

This is about righteousness that flows from a heart whose only desire is the Father's pleasure and praise. This is about being like **Jesus**.

> "And when you pray, do not heap up empty phrases as the Gentiles do, for they think that they will be heard for their many words."
> Matthew 6:7-8

MARCH 26

Jesus prayed because he knew that his deepest need could be met only by God. Nothing less than communion would suffice.

Prayer appears to be a poor form of communication — a one-sided conversation. Few of us find such conversations very meaningful in everyday life. To define prayer as "talking to God" may be the best we can do but we soon discover that it seems more like we are talking to ourselves with the hope that He is listening.

But spirituality only makes sense to any of us if it is seen to work. Perhaps we hesitate to pray because we only half believe in it. Or, maybe we find ourselves doubting even the ability of God to override the obstacles. Maybe we feel it's foolish to spend time praying when we could be really doing something.

If prayer-life is separated from every day-life, then prayer will forever remain a meaningless duty. But when life is seen as something lived in God's presence so that every event of the day is viewed and interpreted from a spiritual perspective, then prayer becomes a meaningful, even vital, experience of communion with God.

Children seem to have a good grasp of prayer. Their prayers are simple and honest. They mention the most obvious things, things that are a part of their daily lives. Children appear to have the most direct line to the very heart of God. And that is what prayer is: the most direct line to the very heart of God.

Communion is the natural consequence of love. We do not love prayer; we love the Lord. Prayer is the result of that love.

Prayer is not about words but about hearts. It describes the relationship between the two most vital beings in the universe: God and a human. It is His incomparable greatness and our absolute and complete dependence on Him that keeps life in focus and drives us to prayer. And it is in prayer, in this unique communion, that we experience the indescribable delight of access to the very heart of God. We learned that from **Jesus**.

"Pray then like this: 'Our Father in heaven, hallowed be your name. Your kingdom come, your will be done, on earth as it is in heaven."
                                                             Matthew 6:9-13

MARCH 27

Jesus gave his listeners a model of prayer. Having criticized the meaningless practices of the unrighteous, his prayer was not simply a model of how to pray but also how to live.

"Our Father In Heaven" Jesus captures the essence of spiritual living, the dynamic which makes not only prayer but everything come alive with meaning and excitement — a personal relationship with God. "Father" was (is) an expression of an intimate relationship with God.

"Hallowed Be Your Name" It was the passion of Jesus' life to glorify God. His every word and action reflected that desire. God is God and must be recognized as God. God's name is to be exalted above all names. His name is to be held in reverence in every part of life.

"Your Kingdom Come" The kingdom Jesus proclaimed was (is) larger than any one nation, yet so personal in its nature that each citizen might approach the king. Jesus was not espousing a new doctrine for the rabbis to dispute but a new way for men to relate to God.

"Your Will Be Done On Earth As It Is In Heaven" The test of faith as expressed in prayer is not that we have wants but that those wants are swallowed up in the greater passion of living in the Father's will.

"Give Us Today Our Daily Bread" Jesus linked our physical concerns to the interest of God. Incredible! God is involved in our daily bread!

"Forgive Us Our Debts, As We Also Have Forgiven Our Debtors" The act of confession underscores the nature of prayer: communion. Like beggars clutching the ankles of a passerby we cast ourselves at Jesus' feet. Forgiving others is testimony to that penitence.

"And Lead Us Not Into Temptation, But Deliver Us From The Evil One" This is a cry for freedom! To be pulled out, to be dragged away, to be rescued from the tyranny of Satan. Our prayers reflect our awareness of that danger.

This is more than a prayer. It is the plan for those who would live like **Jesus**.

> "For if you forgive others their trespasses, your heavenly Father will also forgive you, but if you do not forgive others their trespasses, neither will your Father forgive your trespasses."
>
> Matthew 6:14-15

MARCH 28

Jesus' words on forgiveness are tough. But the standards of the kingdom are the highest.

This is another of those sandpaper commands! The kind which rubs and irritates because the action required is often the very opposite of our feelings. Stinging words seem to call for verbal retaliation. Unkind actions seem to require revenge. The world is constantly reminding us that we don't have to take anything from anybody because we have our rights!

The pious attitude of the Pharisees was reflected in their treatment of society's unacceptable sinners: publicans and prostitutes. Lacking any sensitivity to God's grace in their lives, these religious pests possessed no grace to display to others. Therein is a tremendous lesson for us. **The greater our sensitivity to God's amazing grace in our lives, the greater our capacity to show such grace to others.** Overwhelmed by His love, we cannot keep it to ourselves; overwhelmed by His grace, we must show it to others. We forgive because we have been forgiven. It is in forgiving that we are forgiven.

Forgiveness is not about rights or who makes the first move. Our forgiving is not linked to their confessing. Our forgiving is linked to our rejoicing — rejoicing in the grace of God. Knowing our need, we can understand theirs. Knowing that we are in His image, we realize that they are, too. Remembering Jesus' death for us reminds us that he died for them, also. And we are never more like our Lord than when we are forgiving those who mistreat us.

The wounds of mistreatment can be deep and we may feel a great urge to fight back, to prove our point, even to inflict pain. Such is often the choice of the natural man. But Christians must choose differently.

As we forgive, we are forgiven. Moved by His amazing grace for us every day, we have fresh grace for others. And we have that because of **Jesus**.

"For where your treasure is, there your heart will be also."
Matthew 6:19-21

MARCH 29

Jesus did not come to make us loosen our grip on things, but to show us the difference between two worlds so we would choose to loosen our grip. He did not come to force our eyes away from earth's treasures, but to reveal life's real treasures so that we would choose to look away. He did not call us to poverty but to riches. He did not ask us to live without but to live abundantly. It isn't earth we are giving up but heaven we are gaining.

The answer to our dilemma lies not in forced poverty or some type of monastic lifestyle. The Bible places no ban on possessions and it does not condemn private ownership. There is nothing wrong with a savings account, an insurance policy, or a wise investment. Each may actually demonstrate good stewardship.

Jesus presents us with two worlds, two very different approaches to life. The issue is not how much money we have in the bank or how many items we have carefully displayed in the house. The issue is deeper and broader than that. It has to do with choice: our choice of two worlds.

The treasures Achan hid in his tent were of little consequence but what they said about his choice of worlds was the telling blow. Ananias and Sapphira were never required to choose between all or part of the price of the land but they were required to choose between two worlds, and they made the wrong choice.

Perhaps our great delusion is to believe we can store up treasures in both worlds at the same time, that we can choose both worlds at once. It is an impossible task. "For where your treasure is, there your heart will be also." It is our choice of two worlds.

But how can we know when we've got it wrong? The answer: when what we want to possess is more important to us than what we want to become; when what we have is more important than who we are.

Today, we have insecticides, rustproof paints, and burglar alarms, but our treasures are as temporary as theirs. It is time to listen to **Jesus**.

> "The eye is the lamp of the body. So, if your eye is healthy, your whole body will be full of light, but if your eye is bad, your whole body will be full of darkness."
>
> Matthew 6:22-23

MARCH 30

Jesus came so that we might see. He opened our eyes to the genuine and the fake, to the lasting and the temporary, to the lovely and the ugly, to the good and the bad. Until we saw his loveliness and felt his love, until we walked in his light and experienced his presence, we had no idea which way to go or how to get there if we had known. Jesus spoke of good eyes and bad ones because he knew that only the person who had life in focus could live the life of a disciple.

Just as our eye affects our whole body, so our heart affects our whole life. As physical light through the eye gives light to the body so that it can function properly, so spiritual light through the heart gives light to the soul that it might function in union with God. If spiritual light is absent from the heart, then the soul must function with an inaccurate view of life.

If our spiritual perspective is clear, then our lives are filled not only with purpose and meaning but with a clear sense of direction and destiny. But if our spiritual vision is distorted, then we lose the ability to properly distinguish between the genuine and eternal treasures and the false and temporary ones.

Make no mistake: you cannot fix it yourself! You cannot have such clear vision without God. Jesus' words are not some pep talk to get us to urge ourselves to more human effort, more positive thinking, or more reliance on religion. No, our view is changed because of God! Understanding what is truly valuable and investing in unseen realities is the product of our transformation, a transformation that occurs because of the redemptive work of our Lord. We are not blind to the beauty of gold and silver, diamonds and rubies, but our eyes are focused on a crucified Savior. There are but these two views and we have chosen the one illuminated by **Jesus**.

> "No one can serve two masters, for either he will hate the one and love the other, or he will be devoted to the one and despise the other. You cannot serve both God and money."
> Matthew 6:24

MARCH 31

Jesus says we have to choose. Our choice of worlds determines our treasure. Our choice of views determines our focus. Our choice of masters determines our servitude.

The great delusion is to believe that we can live in two worlds, live by two views, and serve two masters at the same time. **IMPOSSIBLE!** The whole idea is the devil's lie. But he is no fool and clothes his deception in the brightest colors.

The tension between these two diverse ways of life is so great as to be beyond our comprehension, yet we struggle to unite the two. Any effort to such unity only brings chaos to our lives. Different goals, contrary aims, and opposite directions mean that our commitment must be total and our allegiance unconditional. Reconciliation or compromise is unthinkable and neutrality is impossible!

Too many of us still measure life in terms of money and possessions, and covetousness is the sin of the masses, both rich and poor. Many fine church-going people bemoan the world's materialism while grappling with the problem. In truth, we want the treasures of both worlds.

The Lord and Satan are incompatible. While Jesus came to enrich us and save us, Satan is here to deprive us and damn us. And all that Jesus does in our behalf is because he loves us, but Satan only hates us. We may invite either one to dwell within and we may even try to make a place for both, but only one will lodge with us.

We don't like the idea, but it is true: We are all slaves. The very thought offends us. We struggle and fight to prove it otherwise, to prove that we are free individuals who must answer to no one. The question is not about slavery but about masters.

Only one must rule; only one can rule. Our choice determines destiny. It is our choice of two masters. Satan or **Jesus**.

> "Therefore, I tell you, do not be anxious about your life, what you will eat or what you will drink, nor about your body, what you will put on. Is not life more than food, and the body more than clothing?"
> Matthew 6:25-32

APRIL 1

Jesus knows us so well. He knows we worry. He knows we worry over the wrong things. He knows that we worry because our faith is small. So, he tells us the very things we need to hear. But do we believe him?

Three times Jesus says, "Do not worry" (verses 25, 31, 34). While a weakness calls for strength and a failure requires encouragement, sin demands removal. Worry is not explained as merely some weakness of temperament or some failure in character; it is sin.

In our effort to excuse ourselves, we are prone to say, "Oh, I know it's foolish to worry, but I just can't seem to help it." But Jesus believes we can choose something else: faith!

Absolutely useless — that's worry. Worry lifts no burdens, dries no tears, nor solves any problems. We never get richer, healthier, or happier from worry. Yet, like stubborn mules we seem determined to be the exception.

Underline this: <u>God cares for us</u>! Jesus' argument is simple and direct: If God is willing and able to care for things of lesser value (birds and flowers), then He is willing and able to care for things of greater value (you and me).

And our heavenly Father knows our needs. What a marvelous thought! Why wouldn't He know? He made us! We are engraved on the palms of His hands. He knows us inside and out. We are never out of His mind.

"O you of little faith." That says it all, doesn't it? The quite remarkable thing about many of us is that we have trusted God with our soul for eternity but we find it difficult to trust Him during this brief span on earth. God has not failed us; we simply haven't given Him a chance.

Like a child gripping his father's hand we cling to promises of Jesus. We know that our lives are in his hands. His words are for our hearts. Are we willing to trust the words of **Jesus**?

> "But seek first the kingdom of God and his righteousness, and all these things will be added to you."
>
> Matthew 6:33

APRIL 2

Jesus said there is an answer to our anxious hearts. **Seek the kingdom before everything else.** Get your priorities straight. Put first things first.

But that is so easy to say and so hard to do! There are so many things that want our attention. Our days are a constant barrage of needs and demands. Our lives feel pulled in a dozen directions. Trying to make anything or anyone a priority seems an overwhelming task.

Perhaps, we misunderstand him. Seeking the kingdom first doesn't require full-time ministry at the church building or twenty-four-hour commitment to a church program. And it is not some kind of project like reading your Bible through in a year or having a daily prayer partner. Seeking the kingdom first is more than a catchy saying on the fridge or a song sung around the campfire.

Seeking the kingdom first is devotion to your troubled marriage, obedience to the laws of the land, prayer for those who hurt you, attention to those who neglect you, and sacrifice for those who fail to notice. It is service when you are not in the mood, forgiveness for the eighty-seventh time, and honesty when no one else knows. It is giving even when it is inconvenient or seems unfair.

Kingdom living extends far beyond the boundaries of the church property to the offices and shops, hospitals and jails, schools and colleges, and apartments and houses. We go out as ambassadors with the King's words written on our hearts.

You don't need lessons on positive thinking but the firm conviction that God, and God only, is enough for you. Finally, when your heart is filled to overflowing with God, then there will be no room left for anxiety. When your every waking moment belongs to Him, then there will be no moments left for worry.

In essence, seeking the kingdom first is not some religious experience but a spiritual adventure on the road to heaven, not merely some alternate choice of lifestyle, but the only choice of life. Seeking the kingdom first is a way of life you choose because of the person you love: **Jesus.**

> "Therefore do not be anxious about tomorrow, for tomorrow will be anxious for itself. Sufficient for the day is its own trouble."
>
> Matthew 6:34

APRIL 3

Jesus said, we must live one day at a time. It sounds easy enough. After all, what else can a person do but live one day at a time. However, Jesus knew our tendency to live ahead and waste the day we had in hand. Although planning for the future is commendable, trying to live in the future before it arrives is something else.

Unfortunately, our worry over tomorrow is usually focused in one of two directions: at those things that will inevitably happen and at those things that will never happen. Some things are inevitable. If God blesses us with life then our children are going to grow up, we are going to grow old, and we are going to die. Our skin wrinkles, our hair thins, and our body aches. Some things are in the plan and our worry won't change it. Our anxiety can spoil our preparation.

We even worry about things that will never happen. We often expect the worst and choke today's joys in anticipation. Just think: if all our fears had been realized, most of us would be jobless, childless, spouseless, penniless and lifeless many times over!

The truth is that tomorrow may never come. If God grants us another day, the character of the day may be quite different from what we expected. Whatever the day brings, God is more than enough.

Some of us have the 'as-soon-as syndrome.' As soon as we get out of school...get a car...get a job...get married...get a house...get a bigger house...finish this next project...get the children through school...get this weight off...get a vacation...then we'll be happy. We are so busy worrying about what's to come, we forget about what's here!

Today is the only day you have. Yesterday is gone and cannot be reclaimed. Tomorrow is not yet here and may never come. This moment is all you have.

Getting life's priorities in order and living one day at a time is the counsel of the One who knows you better than you know yourself. Listen to **Jesus**.

> "Judge not, that you be not judged.
> For with the judgment you pronounce you will be judged, and with the measure you use it will be measured to you."
>
> Matthew 7:1-5 (Luke 6:37-42)

APRIL 4

Jesus does not forbid our efforts to discern between good and evil, truth and error. He is not asking us to ignore wrong or refrain from confronting sinners. He is not counseling us to shut our eyes to the facts or stop our ears from the truth.

Jesus employs the word "judge" in the sense of faultfinding. He forbids our seeking the worst instead of the best. He is condemning our fixation with and magnification of someone's faults while ignoring his/her virtues.

Jesus' approach to the subject of criticism is on a level we can understand: self-interest. Instead of warning us about the damage done to the one criticized, Jesus focuses our attention on the effects which criticism has on the critic.

We want a blanket of love cast over our foolishness and faults. We want others to assume the best about us when they know only part of the story. We want others to give us the benefit of the doubt when there is a question mark about us. We want others to measure us by our desire to do good, not merely our failure to do good. If understanding, mercy, forgiveness and acceptance are what we want, then understanding, mercy, forgiveness and acceptance must be the gifts we give to others.

If Jesus' speck-in-the-eye story is nothing else, it is about seeing correctly. Fixing our eyes on the worst means we miss the best. Intent on condemning, we fail to see anything worth commending. Unable to see hearts, we can't always be certain of motives. Unable to see the whole situation, we can't always be certain we have all the facts.

Jesus wants us to be helpers, not judges. He does not ask us to close our eyes to the truth, but he does plead with us to open our hearts to one another. He does not want us to ignore evil, but he does want us to love people. As his followers, we should want it no other way. After all, the gifts we share are those we received from **Jesus**.

> "Do not give dogs what is holy, and do not throw your pearls before pigs, lest they trample them underfoot and turn to attack you."
> Matthew 7:6

APRIL 5

Jesus' words seem strange. After all, who would ever give pearls to pigs or holy things to dogs?

Dogs have no appreciation for what is sacred. Holy things mean nothing to them. Just so, there are people who behave the same way. When spiritual truths are presented, they do not merely reject what is said but they treat the ideas with disdain and insult those who share such truths. These folks are both hardened and hostile.

Pigs are much like dogs. They have no understanding of what is truly valuable. They live for their stomach. If it doesn't go in the stomach, then it is worth nothing and left to be trampled. Unfortunately, there are people who behave the same way. Lacking an appreciation for the value of the gospel, they cast it aside and continue on. The dogs and pigs represent people who treat the most important matters with contempt. Their great tragedy is to miss all that really matters.

No one was more in favor of sharing good news than Jesus. He came so that everyone might know God. Yet, there were occasions when he refused to answer questions or engage in discussions because he knew the hardened attitude of his listeners. They were not seeking the truth but intent only in finding some flaw in him. They were not interested in knowing more about God's plan for humanity; instead, they were focused on finding something in his words that would serve their selfish purposes. Thus, he refused to engage them in meaningless conversation.

We want to be sharers of God's good news. But we are to be discerning. Many people do not value the gospel. So, zeal is to be guided by good judgment, enthusiasm is to be directed by common sense. We do not want to hide the treasure, but neither do we want to carelessly toss it to those intent on abusing it or us. Spiritual discernment is for our own good. More than that, spiritual discernment is the way of **Jesus**.

"Ask, and it will be given to you; seek, and you will find; knock, and it will be opened to you.
For everyone who asks receives, and the one who seeks finds, and to the one who knocks it will be opened."
Matthew 7:7-11

APRIL 6

Jesus' words leave us astonished and embarrassed. It sounds so fantastic and wonderful, and we want to believe him but our eyes struggle to see beyond the physical. Also, we may be uncertain about what he is actually offering. Jesus is not promising a new car, a mansion, a top-level job, a large bank account, or immunity from disease. Jesus is not speaking of so many wishes in a lifetime or suggesting that God is the grandfatherly sort who cannot say 'no' to His children.

Jesus is telling us that not even the sky is the limit! To everyone he offers this distinctive way of life. He offers us a return to the life we were created to live, the life where reality is better than fantasy.

The specific actions of this text do not suggest that we receive because we ask, find because we seek, or meet an open door because we knock. God does not owe us because we do something. Neither is Jesus suggesting that God is wholly limited by what we do. Instead, Jesus is teaching that our actions are our choice, the natural expression of our dependence on God, and that the response is God's choice, the natural expression of His love for us.

We are children of the King, yet we often live as though we have nothing. We are described as more than conquerors, yet we behave like the fearful. God has promised His presence in our lives, yet we wonder how we are going to make it.

Christians are God's unlimited people! We are not bound by possessions for it all belongs to our Father and He has promised us heaven. We are not limited by time for our God is eternal and so is His promise to us. We are not confined by space for the universe is our God's. We do not lack for strength because it is His power that works in us. This is the reality that came by **Jesus**.

"So whatever you wish that others would do to you, do also to them, for this is the Law and the Prophets."

Matthew 7:12 (Luke 6:31)

APRIL 7

Jesus did not call this the Golden Rule. How it came to be named or who is responsible for its naming remains a matter of some dispute. Golden it is, and it is probably the best-known statement in all of the teachings of Jesus.

The Rule, when understood comprehensively, allows us to keep all of the rules in the Law concerning how others should be treated. Furthermore, living by the Golden Rule prevents the need for laying down an endless list of little rules and regulations to govern conduct. One Rule says it all.

Jesus is not proposing that we treat others as they treat us. That approach makes good sense to the natural person. It appears to keep things even. Also, Jesus is not exhorting us to do for others so they will do for us. In fact, he promises the opposite will often happen (Matthew 5:11). What he is doing is reflecting the way of God.

Obedience to God's commands is not a burden but a delight when love is our motivation.

Law hammers a stake one mile from the house; love pulls it up.
Law keeps a notebook of wrongs; love keeps no records.
Law behaves out of duty; love acts of sincerity.
Law insists on equality; love puts the other first.
Law demands rights; love relinquishes rights.
Law consults the books; love consults the heart.

Jesus asks two things of you: one requires thought, the other action. First, you are to consider the way you want to be treated. What an easy command! Second, based on your response to the first request, you are to treat others accordingly. This is as difficult as the first is easy. But putting your thoughts into action is always challenging.

It may brand one as naive to suggest that this is the answer to the world's ills...but this is the answer to the world's ills. You cannot fashion a system of morality better than this. You cannot frame a better rule for life than this. In fact, it just does not get any better than the Rule of **Jesus**.

> "Enter by the narrow gate. For the gate is wide and the way is easy that leads to destruction, and those who enter by it are many.
> For the gate is narrow and the way is hard that leads to life, and those who find it are few."
>
> Matthew 7:13-14

APRIL 8

Jesus was not merely disseminating information, nor was he preaching to entertain. He was not trying to impress his audience with his knowledge of theology or prove that he was an unusually gifted rabbi. He was a preacher with a message on his heart and that crucial moment had come for him as it does for all preachers: decision time.

As the primary themes of his message were completed, Jesus urged it on his hearers. It was not enough to be hearers of his words; they must be doers of his words. Also, these people were discovering something about Jesus that would characterize his entire ministry: his words never permitted folks the luxury of indecision.

This simplistic either-or, black or white approach to life probably alienated many people then as it does today. But Jesus was not seeking disciples at the price of lowered standards or diluted truths. He called it like he saw it: two gates, two roads, two crowds, and two destinations. Each one was as different as heaven and hell.

Jesus was not offering cheap grace or easy believism. He wanted no disciples under false pretenses. Nor did Jesus hide the truth about the numbers: discipleship is not the pathway of popular choice.

Remembering Jesus as the healer of sick folks, the comforter of hurting people, and the friend of little children, we may forget that he was first a preacher. He came with a message that contained clear-cut options and definite consequences of our decisions. He was here because heaven and hell are real. He died for the same reason.

Jesus says that every person decides the way his/her soul shall go. Which road is it for you? Upward toward glory or downward toward shame? Indecision is not an option with **Jesus**.

"Beware of false prophets, who come to you in sheep's clothing but inwardly are ravenous wolves.
You will recognize them by their fruits."
                                    Matthew 7:15-20 (Luke 6:43-45)

APRIL 9

Jesus warned us: "Be alert! Be on guard! Watch out for the religious mountebank and his toady!"

The words may not be common but the experience sure is! A mountebank is an unscrupulous dealer or promoter. In 'olden days' mountebanks dealt in quack medicines. The word comes from the mixing of Italian words meaning "one who climbs on a bench." This fellow would climb on a bench to draw a crowd and from that perch he would endeavor to sell his phony wares.

The toady served an invaluable role as the usual crowd would have its share of doubters. In the midst of the mountebank's spiel, this hired friend, the toady, would rush up in a state of excited agitation and announce that he was dying for he had just swallowed a toad (or some other life-threatening thing). In the blink of an eye the mountebank would thrust the life-saving elixir at him. This toadeater would take a large swig and, lo and behold, he would suddenly be just fine. Naturally, any liquid that would bring life to a toad swallower must be good for what ails you.

Religious mountebanks. We have always had them. Each has his or her style. Some move from town to town like a traveling carnival, setting up the tent and folding chairs for the next "healing show" and contribution on Saturday night. Others preach for large churches with huge budgets. Some even have their own television program in which the message or elixir is beamed to the nation while inviting contributions.

Jesus is not trying to discourage us but to warn us: "Don't be misled. There are many impostors. Spiritual counterfeiting is big business. Vigilance is needed." The danger is real because the devil is real. Being on guard is vital.

In our world beauty must dwell side-by-side with ugliness, love must live next door to hate, truth must endure the presence of error, and goodness must abide next to evil. "But it will not always be so," says **Jesus**.

> "Not everyone who says to me, 'Lord, Lord,' will enter the kingdom of heaven, but the one who does the will of my Father who is in heaven."
>
> Matthew 7:21-23 (Luke 6:46)

APRIL 10

Jesus' words confirm the tragedy of misplaced confidence. Even religious folks can put their faith and hope in the wrong place.

Perhaps, they placed their confidence in holding to the right doctrine. After all, what a person believes is very important. They appeared to be right in doctrine. They said the right words, believed the right things.

But Jesus emphasized something more. The heart. What does it matter if you believe the right doctrine on murder but you are quick to anger and hold hate in your heart? What difference does it make that you oppose adultery if you secretly lust through pornography? So what if your doctrine on prayer, giving and fasting is correct if you do those things to be noticed by others?

What you believe is important. Sound doctrine does matter. But our confidence, our hope does not rest in simply being sure of what we believe.

Maybe their confidence was in their good works. These folks were fervent and zealous. Look at all they did!

Being busy for Jesus is certainly important. There are many passages that encourage us to be workers in the kingdom. But our good works are an expression of our relationship with the Father, not the basis of the relationship.

So, if the saved are not those who merely believe the right things or those who simply do the right things, who are the saved? Jesus identifies them: "...only he who does the will of my Father who is in heaven."

What you do is important. What you believe is important. But even more important is **who**. You are not saved because of all the good you do or because you are correct in all your beliefs. You are saved because of who has your heart.

Commendation in judgment is not the result of believing certain things or even doing certain things. Ultimately, acceptance is the eternal blessing of a relationship: Jesus knows you and you know **Jesus**.

> "Everyone then who hears these words of mine and does them will be like a wise man who built his house on the rock."
> Matthew 7:24-8:1 (Luke 6:47-49)

APRIL 11

Jesus closed his sermon with a story. And what a story...and song! We remember it well from childhood. Of course, the part about the wise man was merely the preliminary to the song's most exciting part: the noisy collapse of the foolish man's house!

And how do we explain the foolish man's behavior? Obviously, he did not want his house to collapse during a storm. And he did a lot of things right. Evidently, he was diligent and energetic, a hard worker. And he did it all without power tools or Home Depot. But in the end, all his hard work was for nothing. So, why did he build on sand?

Maybe he was in a hurry. After all, we have all tried to take shortcuts. Perhaps, he did not take advice very well even though others counseled him to build on more solid ground. Or, maybe he preferred to work with sand rather than rock. Perhaps, he wanted his house in a certain place. Or, maybe he just did not think through all the possibilities of living in a house built on sand.

And what shall we say of the wise man's decision to build on rock? Maybe he took the advice of others. Perhaps, he thought through the possible problems of building on sand. Maybe he preferred working with rock rather than sand.

While such details are lacking for both builders, the story is more than just the summation of his words; this is the final call to do something about those words, to see them for what they are: the words of the Lord. This is not about building houses. This is about building a life. He is talking about the house of your soul.

So, having shared the thoughts of his heart and the ways of the Father, he pressed for decision. My words make a difference, he said. You decide.

On that day long ago, some believed him, some didn't. People have not changed much. What about you – wise or foolish? Do you believe **Jesus**?

> **When Jesus heard these things, he marveled at him, and turning to the crowd that followed him, said, "I tell you, not even in Israel have I found such faith."**
>
> **Luke 7:1-10 (Matthew 8:5-13)**

APRIL 12

Jesus was amazed!

What would it take to amaze Jesus? If you wanted to amaze him, would you show him some beautiful, breath-taking place on the planet? Good luck finding one. He made the whole planet. Would you perform some incredible deed, some trick? Good luck with that one, too. This is a man who walked on water. What could you do that would bring amazement to the Savior?

Only twice in the Scriptures was Jesus said to be amazed. Once was when he began his public ministry in his hometown of Nazareth, and he was rejected by his fellow Jews – "he was amazed by their lack of faith." (Mark 6:6).

The other occasion was in Capernaum. This time he was amazed at the faith of a man. Think about that...the Son of God amazed by the faith of someone.

A centurion was a military officer of the Roman Army, corresponding to our captain. He was probably in charge of soldiers who were stationed in Capernaum, a city on the northwest shore of the Sea of Galilee.

But this was not your typical centurion. He had an unusual interest in the well-being of his slave and wanted to help him. Also, those who vouched for this Gentile soldier were Jews! But more than that, though a man of power and influence, he was humble and saw himself as undeserving of Jesus' presence.

As a soldier he understood authority and he saw a parallel between the way he commanded his soldiers and the way Jesus commanded diseases. He believed that Jesus need only speak the word and his servant would be healed. No wonder Jesus marveled at such faith!

Selfish and confused, we want God's blessings but only as long as it does not require us to take our hands off the controls of our lives. We want Jesus to be Lord, but just not Lord of us!

Jesus was amazed by the faith of a man who expressed complete trust in him. Wouldn't it be wonderful if you, too, amazed **Jesus**?

And when the Lord saw her, he had compassion on her and said to her, "Do not weep."

Then he came up and touched the bier, and the bearers stood still. And he said, "Young man, I say to you, arise."

Luke 7:11-17

APRIL 13

Jesus knew all about death. It was why he was here. He understood the heartache and tears. He knew all about the sense of loss. Jesus knew the hole was deep and the sorrow was great when people were separated from those they loved. He understood, all too well, what death meant to a relationship.

Death had come a second time to her life. First her husband; now her son. Her only son. When a child dies, part of a parent is buried...for this is our flesh and bone. You may know that feeling very well. Now, what you hold onto are the precious memories of your child and the precious promises of God.

Moved in his heart by the pain written all over her, Jesus told her not to cry. Then, to the astonishment of all, he touched the coffin and told the young man to get up. And he did!

To no one's surprise, this incredible event brought a reaction. "They were all filled with awe and praised God" and they said, "God has come to help his people." They were so right.

Did you read the stories of death this morning in the paper? Did you notice the length of the obituary section? Why doesn't God do something about all that grief?

And the answer from Scripture rings in clarion tones: He has! This is what Christianity is all about! What God has done!

When you see the cross, you are seeing what God has done! Look in the empty tomb and see what God has done! This is our hope!

You are going to die. Those you hold onto are going to be lost from your grip. No amount of pleading or tears can change what must be. The time is coming when your life will be measured in days, then hours, then minutes....and then seconds — four, three, two, one. And then you will be more alive than you have ever been. That is what God has done for you through the life and death of **Jesus**.

And Jesus answered them, "Go and tell John what you hear and see: the blind receive their sight and the lame walk, lepers are cleansed and the deaf hear, and the dead are raised up, and the poor have good news preached to them."

Matthew 11:2-6 (Luke 7:18-23)

APRIL 14

Jesus was not the Messiah that John the Baptist expected. He was a better Messiah than John the Baptist expected!

John had publicly condemned the marriage of Herod Antipas and Herodias. So, Herod had John arrested and thrown into prison.

After a few months, John may have thought, "this is not what I expected." He may also have wondered why someone, like Jesus, did not do something to get him out of prison.

After more than a year in prison, John called some of his disciples and asked, "what is going on out there?" They told him, "Well, the crowds are flocking to Jesus. But he's not like you. He is frequently at social events and even eats with tax collectors and sinners. He hugs little children and welcomes prostitutes as disciples. Also, Herod has not arrested him. John, are you sure He is the One?"

John said, "Go to Jesus and ask him if He is the One who was to come or should we expect someone else."

Why this doubt? Perhaps, John became discouraged while he was languishing in prison and needed assurance. Or, maybe he sent his followers to Jesus with the question for their benefit.

But another plausible explanation for John's question was that Jesus wasn't the Messiah he expected. Maybe Jesus wasn't carrying out his ministry the way John envisioned the Messiah should have. He was expecting a fire and brimstone Messiah rather than one who showered grace. Perhaps John was perplexed.

This raises an important question for you. What does your Christ look like? Is he a liberator or stern judge? Is he a distant or intimate Savior? Is he more like an acquaintance or a friend? More like a distant relative or a brother?

Sometimes it's good for us to doubt the image we have of Jesus, not because the image we have might not be the right one, but because our doubts cause us to look closer and seek a clearer and deeper understanding of **Jesus**.

> "Truly, I say to you, among those born of women there has arisen no one greater than John the Baptist. Yet the one who is least in the kingdom of heaven is greater than he."
> Matthew 11:7-19 (Luke 7:24-35)

APRIL 15

Jesus knew that John's role as a messenger of God was important to the preparation for the kingdom. He was the very special prophet foretold by Isaiah. He was the Elijah to come. He wanted the people to know that.

But Jesus' greater concern was not the role of John the Baptist but the vacillating attitudes and ways of the people toward those sent by God. Regardless of the ways of the prophet, the people struggled to believe.

This, Jesus said, was a generation that could not make up its mind. Whether the flute was playing or a dirge was sung, these folks never seemed to make the right response. They could not be pleased.

On the one hand, there were many who rejected Jesus because he didn't fit their idea of what the Messiah should be. His association with sinners and tax collectors and his lack of respect for the traditions of the elders were things they found difficult to accept. Feeling threatened by him, they rejected his message and they rejected him.

But, on the other hand, there were plenty of "sinners" who were pressing hard to enter the kingdom. The words and ways of Jesus gave them hope. They found comfort in his words about the Father, joyful relief in his words about forgiveness, and excitement when he spoke of the coming kingdom. They were ready to storm the walls of heaven in an effort to get in. They were willing to do whatever it took, make whatever sacrifices were necessary to forcefully lay hold of the kingdom. And Jesus says that they were the ones that were going to get in!

It is no surprise that the people that are commended by Jesus are so frequently individuals who are desperate for Jesus — a father with a dying child, a woman wanting to be healed, a blind man begging for sight. There is a lesson here. Their willingness to lay their pride aside, admit their need and do anything to reach him brought the praise and healing of **Jesus**.

> "Woe to you, Chorazin! Woe to you, Bethsaida! For if the mighty works done in you had been done in Tyre and Sidon, they would have repented long ago in sackcloth and ashes."
>
> Matthew 11:20-24

APRIL 16

Jesus was passionate about salvation. He came so that every person might know the indescribable joy of living with God. Yet, for all that we heard him say and for all that we saw him do, we were reluctant to trust him.

We know nothing of Korazin from the Gospels and only a bit more about Bethsaida. Evidently, Jesus spent some time there. Capernaum was more significant to the ministry of Jesus. This city served as his base of operations. But all three cities shared one thing in common: Jesus denounced them!

These people saw and heard wonderful things from Jesus, but they refused to change. Why?

Some probably thought that sin, their sin, was not really that serious and did not require repentance. Others may have felt that Jesus was overreacting and that salvation was not all that urgent. We tend to think we have plenty of time to make those needed changes. And some, no doubt, found it difficult to believe that God would really condemn anyone. After all, Jesus did talk about love, too. Some knew they should make some life changes, but they couldn't get over their pride. Honesty and confession come hard. Sound familiar?

But why did Jesus denounce these three cities while speaking more favorably of Tyre, Sidon, and Sodom? In a word: opportunity. The people of Korazin, Bethsaida, and Capernaum had watched God walk among them and had witnessed his incredible power in the miracles he performed. The other cities had never had the opportunity to see such things.

Today may afford you the opportunity of being a good listener to someone who is hurting or sharing your faith with someone who is searching. Perhaps, the day will present you with the opportunity to offer comfort or hope. But whatever the day may bring, it is an opportunity to follow **Jesus**.

"Come to me, all who labor and are heavy laden, and I will give you rest."
Matthew 11:25-30

APRIL 17

Jesus' invitation to all the weary and burdened to come to him and receive rest is more than a sweet invitation. It is a lifeline.

Jesus' invitation, "come to me," was not an invitation to church or to some new religion. This was more than an invitation to join a new group or assume a different lifestyle. Jesus was inviting us to him. And in him we would find rest for our souls.

Rest. How wonderful that sounds. Rest for your soul. Whoever offered you that?

Sadly, we are often like children who fight sleep and argue that we are not even tired. We resist the very thing designed to help us. But we are weary. Weary from the guilt we have for our sins. Weary from the heartache of shattered dreams. Weary from the pain in our hearts from relationships gone wrong. Weary from the fears and worries we drag through each day. Weary from the burden of trying to hold ourselves together when we feel like we are coming apart. Weary of trying to be good enough to go to heaven.

Augustine wrote, "Thou hast created us for Thyself, and our heart in not quiet until it rests in Thee." Jesus invites us to this quiet.

The Gospels contain many invitations from Jesus. Follow the good shepherd. Eat the bread of life. Choose the narrow way. Enter through the door. While you may be inclined to balk at someone seeming to order you around, Jesus simply invites you to the life you were created to live. You were created to be at rest in your Maker. You will never get another invitation like this one! This invitation comes only from **Jesus**.

And he said to her, "Your sins are forgiven."

Luke 7:36-50

APRIL 18

Jesus rarely refused an invitation. In fact, it seems he would go home with anyone. He loved people. So, when Simon invited Jesus for a meal, Jesus said, "Okay, I will come."

While the host and his guests were reclining at the table, they were interrupted by the boldness of an uninvited woman. Her actions probably created that discomforting mix of admiration and embarrassment. Rebuke her or praise her? It was difficult to know which was more appropriate.

Travel on dusty roads made for dirty feet. Therefore, foot-washing was one of the customs. A thoughtful host might also offer some oil for anointing. In a warm climate with a short supply of deodorant this was a refreshing gesture. Also, it was customary to greet with a kiss. This was not a kiss of affection but simply a polite acknowledgement of the guest's arrival.

As we soon discover, Jesus received none of these courtesies in Simon's house. Such rudeness did not go unnoticed.

Jesus told a story to help Simon. His problem was blindness.

The woman, on the other hand, could see clearly. She had lived a sinful life. Forgiveness was her concern. And Jesus spoke to that very thing. "Your sins are forgiven."

But Simon's view of sin was no clearer than his view of himself. Jesus told the story, not to emphasize greater sin versus lesser sin, but to help Simon understand that forgiveness was needed by every person. We are all sinners.

Both people in Jesus' story were in debt. Whether 500 or 50, both were unable to pay their respective debts. And the debts were cancelled for both. This was not about the amount of sin but the awareness of sin.

This unnamed woman humbled herself before Jesus. Perhaps, she had heard him speak or had been present when he healed someone. Maybe she had observed his kindness to others or had witnessed his care for hurting people. Whatever she believed about him, she honored him by her attention and sacrifice. In return, he gave her the one thing she needed and wanted most: forgiveness. This gift comes only from **Jesus**.

> And the twelve were with him, and also some women who had been healed of evil spirits and infirmities…
>
> Luke 8:1-3

APRIL 19

Jesus preached in the larger cities and in the smaller villages. Evidently, there were times when he and his disciples were on the move continually. We can only imagine what such a group looked like as they came walking into one of the small villages. Accommodations for so many would have been scarce!

Although we know about the male disciples accompanying Jesus from place to place, perhaps, we are surprised to discover that women were among those who traveled with him, too. Evidently, they supplied his financial needs again and again.

While their stories are largely unknown to us, Luke says they each had a story to tell. They had once been possessed by demons or afflicted with disease. In Mary's case, seven demons at one time!

These women were not following out of some sense of obligation or fulfilling some religious requirement. They were in love with Jesus! Their financial support of his ministry was their way of saying "thank you" for the transformation he brought to their lives.

Evidently, Jesus had no bias against women. While he did not lead a social movement to correct the injustices suffered by women in his day, he did provide an example for all to follow. His every encounter with the opposite sex showed his esteem and appreciation for women. He respected them and treated them as persons.

Whether he was speaking to a Samaritan woman at a well or a woman caught in the act of adultery, whether he was interacting with Mary and Martha in their home or was being touched by an unclean woman in the street, Jesus always showed kindness and respect to women. In light of attitudes and customs of first-century life, such behavior would have been judged remarkable in his day.

So, in what was definitely a man's world, in a world where women were often treated with no more respect than that accorded to cattle, in a world where they had few rights and their opinions seldom valued, these women found love and respect, cleansing and healing. They couldn't say "thank you" enough to **Jesus**.

> "Therefore, I tell you, every sin and blasphemy will be forgiven people, but the blasphemy against the Spirit will not be forgiven."
> Matthew 12:22-32 (Mark 3:20-30)

APRIL 20

Jesus had performed a miracle, healing a demon-possessed man. There were two responses. Some saw it as proof that Jesus was the promised Messiah. "Son of David" was a Messianic title. His actions gave them hope.

But others accused him of casting out demons by Beelzebub. In other words, Jesus was just a demon-possessed man himself, subject to the devil. Whatever powers he had did not come from God!

Interestingly, the Pharisees did not question the fact that a miracle had taken place. But unable to deny the miracle, they accused him of being in league with Satan. After all, if you cannot attack the message, then attack the messenger.

Jesus responded with three arguments of his own. First, he told them their accusation was illogical. Why would Satan cast out one of his own demons? Since when did Satan do something that would only hurt Satan?

Second, Jesus said they were inconsistent. Did they intend to level this charge against everyone who drove out the demons? Or, were they just focusing on him?

Third, Jesus argued that their accusation against him was impossible. The strong man is Satan. How could Jesus—according to this logic—receive his power from Satan and then also be stronger than Satan?

We can only imagine how they wrestled with his logic. But there was more to come. Jesus said, "There is only one thing that is unforgivable."

Numerous volumes have been written and countless sermons preached in an attempt to identify this unpardonable sin. Was the sin in what they said about Jesus' works or was it their continuing attitude of rejecting the Son of God?

People often worry about whether they have committed the unpardonable sin. If you are concerned about your relationship with God, then you have not committed something unpardonable. When it comes down to it, the only sin that God won't forgive is the sin for which forgiveness is not desired.

One of the sweetest experiences of today is the knowledge that God's forgiveness is yours. It is His gift to you because of His Son, **Jesus**.

> "I tell you, on the day of judgment people will give account for every careless word they speak, for by your words you will be justified, and by your words you will be condemned."
>
> Matthew 12:33-37

APRIL 21

Jesus said that your words matter. More than that, he said you have to account for what you say, and that what you say makes an eternal difference. Sobering thoughts for people who have trouble with words.

We may not like the sound of it but it is true: What we are on the inside spills out. Our words reveal what is in our heart.

You are known by your words. So, what do they say about you? Are you an encourager? Do your words convey acceptance, kindness and forgiveness? Are others always better for having heard you speak?

Or, would your words mark you as a gossip or a liar? A grumbler or complainer? Would your words reveal anger or impurity within?

Sadly, our tendency is to dismiss this as being unimportant in the greater scheme of things. After all, an angry outburst here or a dirty joke there is hardly the same as murder or adultery. Our reasoning misses the point entirely.

God wants your heart! The call to holy living is not simply a call to practice or avoid something but to **be** something! Jesus did not come just so you would do good things but so that you, by his power, might be good. Not good as God is perfect, but good as one who loves and longs for what is good.

Your heart is revealed by the words you use. What you say reveals what you think, and what you think is what you are. If your heart is good, then so are your words. If your heart is bad, then so are your words.

Take heed: your soul is judged by your words. You better take your words seriously because the Lord certainly does!

Your words are important because they help identify you as a follower of **Jesus**.

> "For just as Jonah was three days and three nights in the belly of the great fish, so will the Son of Man be three days and three nights in the heart of the earth."
>
> Matthew 12:38-45

APRIL 22

Jesus had performed many miracles and signs. He had done mighty works and wonders for all to see, more than sufficient for them to believe. Still, they wanted something special that would settle the matter. They wanted some kind of defining miracle that would remove all doubt.

Jonah's story was certainly special! He was swallowed by a huge fish and, after three days, the fish spit him out on the land. Jesus said he would do better than that!

And when it came to good judgment, Solomon's reputation was rock-solid. The Queen of the South could testify to that. However, Jesus said Solomon is a distant second to me.

Sometimes, we miss what is right in front of us. We become so busy looking for our own idea of what God will do that we miss what God really does. We can become so focused on what we want God to say that we never hear what He actually says. We can become so sure of who God is that we fail to see Him altogether.

Often, we seek signs when we need help or reassurance. We want a "sign" in order to know that God really loves us and approves of us. We seek a sign that guarantees God cares and we are not alone. Our memories are so poor! We already have that definitive sign. There is no greater sign, no greater proof of God's love than the cross. There is nothing God could do to you or for you to prove His love that would be greater or better than what He has already done.

Does God work in your life? No question about it. But He does so because He loves you, not because He feels like He needs to prove Himself to you. The signs have always been there. Seeing is believing.

Love for you was written in blood at Calvary. Today is a perfect day for you to show Him you got the message – and that you trust **Jesus**.

And stretching out his hand toward his disciples, he said, "Here are my mother and my brothers! For whoever does the will of my Father in heaven is my brother and sister and mother."
Matthew 12:46-50 (Mark 3:31-35; Luke 8:19-21)

APRIL 23

Jesus was the oldest of at least seven children born to Joseph and Mary. He had four brothers, James, Joseph, Simon, and Jude, plus unnamed sisters (Matthew 13:55-56). Wouldn't it be great if we had a family portrait?

We have much curiosity about Jesus' youth in the home of Joseph and Mary. What kind of boy was he? What was his favorite thing to do? Did he like to play games? Did he get along with his siblings? Did he have many friends? Did his brothers and sisters notice anything different about him? How did he handle a scraped knee or a cut finger? What was his favorite food? Could he run faster than everyone else? What kind of kid was this son of Joseph and Mary, and what was his home like?

While we might wish for more information, it seems reasonable to believe that his home was like other Jewish homes and that his childhood was typical of that experienced by Jewish boys. Evidently, his youth was so typical that, later, both his family and the hometown folks found his fame difficult to understand.

So, what do we make of his comments about his family? There is no doubt that Jesus' response surprised his hearers and his family. But Jesus was not dismissing the importance of his earthly family; instead, he was giving priority to his spiritual family. Jesus is not saying that our earthly family relationships are unimportant, only that they are not all-important. Doing the will of God is all-important.

Make no mistake: our obedience to the Father's will does not make us deserving of a place in the family or entitle us to a place at the table. Our obedience is our way of saying "thank you" for inviting us into this forever family.

"You are my family!" This could be the best news you hear all day! There is nothing better than being in the family of God and being related to **Jesus**.

> "As for that in the good soil, they are those who, hearing the word, hold it fast in an honest and good heart, and bear fruit with patience."
> Luke 8:4-18 (Matthew 13:1-23; Mark 4:1-25)

APRIL 24

Jesus told common life stories with word pictures to connect with people and teach God's truths. In a world where the economy was based primarily on farming, nothing was more fundamental to their existence than the planting and harvesting cycle. The picture of a farmer, his pouch slung over his shoulder, scattering the seeds evenly in his field would have been of interest to everyone.

Some of the seed fell on the little walkways that were between the fields. Beaten down by human feet and the passage of animals, the soil was not inferior but it was hard. So, the seed just lay there for the birds. That hardness also happens in hearts that lose their sensitivity to spiritual things.

Some of the seed fell on good, rich soil; at least, it was good on top. But rocks lay just beneath. This made it difficult for plants to develop a good root system and to get needed moisture. They couldn't survive. Good beginners, poor finishers. Superficiality cannot sustain us.

How we hate weeds! But sometimes the weeds grow up with good plants. Some of the seed fell on fertile soil and good plants grew up. However, those plants were not alone and the soil could not support both plants and weeds. But isn't it just like us to try and make a life of mixing good and bad?

Then, some seed fell on good ground and produced a wonderful crop! This is the good news of the parable. There are those who are open to the words of Jesus. People can change!

God speaks. God whispers in my deepest pain, speaks in my perplexing problems, and shouts in my most delightful moments. I may fail to listen but He never fails to speak. He wants me to know His heart.

God is speaking to you right now. Are you listening?

Is He not telling you to listen to His Son, **Jesus**?

> "So it will be at the close of the age. The angels will come out and separate the evil from the righteous and throw them into the fiery furnace. In that place there will be weeping and gnashing of teeth."
> Matthew 13:24-30, 36-43, 47-50

APRIL 25

Jesus' return is a theme fundamental to the Christian faith. A key component of that return is the separation of good and evil. But in a world where evil often seems to win, it is easy to forget the promises of God and easy to forget that Jesus' return will bring a judgment of evil that is beyond us.

Weeds are a curse to any farmer or serious gardener! We hate them!

Perhaps, as Jesus related this story, he pointed to a nearby field where the weeds were growing thick with the crop. This, Jesus said, is the devil's doing. Interesting idea! Whatever happened to the devil? The devil was once real and frightening...but few folks seem to be afraid or take him seriously anymore. We have rendered the devil a non-factor by no longer identifying sin. After all, we don't have to have the devil if actions are only inappropriate or misguided.

"Leave it to us, Master. We will rid the world of evil." Did you ever notice what happens when humans decide to take this matter into their own hands. We end up with the Crusades or the Salem witch trials. We have a poor record doing things our way because it requires a wisdom we do not have.

So, what are we going to do with these weeds? Jesus says, "Be patient." Judgment is coming.

It may not come as quickly as we would like, but it is coming. From our vantage point, it may appear that the wicked always seem to escape the consequences, that the guilty always get by...but there is a day of reckoning. And when it comes...it is God who will be judging, not humans.

There is a final separation. The time will come when the good and the bad will be in each other's company no more. It will happen with the return of **Jesus**.

> This was to fulfill what was spoken by the prophet: "I will open my mouth in parables; I will utter what has been hidden since the foundation of the world."
>
> Matthew 13:31-35 (Mark 4:26-34)

APRIL 26

Jesus spoke of many things. Perhaps, few things excited him any more than talking about the kingdom. After all, from day one he announced it is coming. He envisioned something unlike anything the creation had ever seen. This was no ordinary kingdom as we think of kingdoms. This was a kingdom in which the spiritual transcended the physical universe. Neither boundary markers nor armies determined the size or extent of this kingdom. This was a kingdom without buildings or a capital city. This was a kingdom in which God reigned in the hearts of His people.

Jesus wanted others to be excited, too! He wanted people to understand the unique nature of this new kingdom. So, he told them stories, or parables, to provide pictures from different angles.

The kingdom, he said, will start small, but it will grow big. Just think about mustard seeds and yeast.

Mustard seeds were very small. From this very tiny beginning came a bush, and then the bush became a shrub the size of a tree, a tree that birds could nest in. A mustard seed would not give you reason to expect much. But in God's hands look what happens!

This is a picture of God at work. Planting a seed in Bethlehem. So small and inconspicuous. From a baby in a manger to a movement that would change the world.

And God's work is often quite unseen! Does He take action to grab the attention of people? Absolutely. But not always. The kingdom is not all noise and activity. There is so much that happens within...like leaven.

This parable is about God's work on the inside. Transformation.

Leaven was a little piece of dough, the starter. When it was ready to be kneaded into a new batch of dough, an amazing change took place. Although impossible to see how it worked, the resulting change was obvious.

This is your God at work. Start small, start slow. No matter. Something wonderful is inevitable. And it is all for you. No wonder the kingdom put a smile on the face of **Jesus**.

> "The kingdom of heaven is like treasure hidden in a field, which a man found and covered up. Then in his joy he goes and sells all that he has and buys that field."
>
> Matthew 13:44-46, 51-53

APRIL 27

Jesus told two stories which emphasized the supreme worth of the kingdom. In the first, the finder of the treasure seems to have come upon it unexpectedly. But in the second story, the merchant was earnestly looking for a pearl of great value. Each found something beyond their dreams!

Banks were uncommon in Jesus' day. For ordinary folk, the best and easiest way to guard your valuables was to hide them. A hole in the ground would be a natural choice in a world without bank vaults and safety deposit boxes.

Perhaps, he was plowing and unearthed this treasure. It did not take him long to realize that this was a special find. Hiding his treasure, he hurried off to buy the field. This would make it official. Knowing what he knows, the cost of the field is unimportant. What he has found is so much more valuable!

On the surface, he may have looked the part of a fool to those who knew him. Perhaps, he had always appeared to be a levelheaded, common sense kind of fellow. Now, all of sudden, he wants to trade everything for a field of dirt!

And what shall we say of a merchant who would sell everything for a single pearl? Whatever happened to diversifying? What about not putting all your eggs in one basket? What if he made a mistake and misjudged the quality of the pearl?

Recognizing the value of what they had found, each man, farmer and merchant, was willing to pay whatever price, willing to give up everything for what was truly valuable. Each man, having experienced the immense delight in possessing something of true value, could not be satisfied with anything less. That's the way it is when we truly discover the wealth of the kingdom. Nothing else will ever do.

What about you? If you win whatever it is you are chasing, what will you have? If you find whatever it is you are looking for, what will it be? And, will it be truly valuable?

There is a way you can know. Listen to **Jesus**.

And they woke him and said to him, "Teacher, do you not care that we are perishing?"
                           Mark 4:35-41 (Matthew 8:18, 23-27; Luke 8:22-25)

APRIL 28

Jesus had spent a busy day with people and was exhausted from the crowds. In his weariness he had fallen asleep in the stern of the boat. The disciples, on the other hand, were nowhere near sleep. They were panicked! They found themselves in the midst of a terrible storm on the Sea of Galilee.

We have all been there: caught up in some crisis, unable to sleep or so afraid we can't put two meaningful sentences together. All the while, it seems like God is off somewhere taking a nap.

Storms in life are inevitable. They find us no matter where we live. Also, storms are unpredictable. They come suddenly. They come unexpectedly. In Matthew's account of this story, he says, "Without warning, a furious storm came up on the lake." There was no opportunity to plan for this one.

Many of the storms that blow across our lives bring a sense of helplessness. We feel at the mercy of a situation that seems overwhelming. What often follows is confusion, even anger. "Lord, don't you care?"

It wasn't their fear Jesus was rebuking. It was the way they were reacting to this fear that brought his questions. "Why are you SO afraid?" Jesus was asking. "Why are you reacting to the situation this way?"

It's easy to believe in Jesus when the skies are clear and things are going smoothly, but when the storm gathers and the winds blow and beat upon our lives, it's then we discover how much we trust him. If we never had problems, we would never know what a difference faith really makes. We would never discover how very much the Lord cares.

Jesus didn't promise his disciples or us freedom from storms. Instead, he promised us freedom from discouraging and paralyzing fear. The promise was that we could trust him no matter what happened, and we could know that no one cares about us more than **Jesus**.

> And when he saw Jesus from afar, he ran and fell down before him. And crying out with a loud voice, he said, "What have you to do with me, Jesus, Son of the Most High God?"
>
> Mark 5:1-10 (Matthew 8:28-29; Luke 8:26-31)

APRIL 29

Jesus and his disciples stepped from their boat and were met by this ranting, raving lunatic. What must the disciples be thinking? They have just survived a great storm on the sea and witnessed the awesome power of Jesus. Now, he is talking to a crazy man!

This fellow was once someone's little boy. He sat in his daddy's lap; his mom tucked him in at night. He played in the streets with his friends and dreamed of growing up. In time, his childhood dreams gave way to the dreams of a young man: wife, family, career. But it did not happen for him.

Somehow, somewhere, his life became a nightmare! He was a prisoner of the dark side and powerless to resist. His behavior was often violent and out of control, unpredictable and extreme. Night and day he howled like a dog. It had been a long time since he wore clothes. He was filthy. His body bore the scars of many self-inflicted wounds. His wrists and ankles showed the marks where chains once tried to restrain him.

There was no place for someone like him. No hospitals or asylums. No place in the community. So, he lived in the tombs, on the edge of humanity.

The man's vexation by demons is the story of us all. This is a microcosm of our own sad, tragic story: living life the devil's way, hurting ourselves in the process, and powerless to do anything about it. But Jesus came to free us from Satan's grip! It is salvation full and free!

This is why Jesus came: so that our chaotic and miserable lives, our dark and hopeless souls might leave the tombs and find genuine joy in God's world. It is the moment of truth in the human heart. We seize it because this is our only hope!

It is amazing how often we see ourselves in the people of the Bible. Sometimes what we see reminds us of who we are and where we've come from because of God's grace to us in **Jesus**.

As he was getting into the boat, the man who had been possessed with demons begged him that he might be with him.
And he did not permit him but said to him, "Go home to your friends and tell them how much the Lord has done for you, and how he has had mercy on you."
Mark 5:11-20 (Matthew 8:30-34; Luke 8:32-39)

APRIL 30

Jesus' authority was unmistakable. Modern manuals on demon expulsion read like a chemistry book. Jesus just said, "Go!" Into the two thousand pigs nearby, down the steep bank, and into the water. No more pigs, no more demons.

A life is changed! A soul restored! Blessings from above! Everyone is thrilled, right? Wrong!

Those tending the pigs went to town and told the story. So, the people in town came out to see for themselves what had happened. They saw Jesus, and they saw the man who had the demons. He was dressed and behaving normally. This frightened them.

What were they afraid of? More healings? More pig deaths?

Of course, someone owned those pigs. Maybe they reasoned: if that could happen to one pig owner, it could happen to other pig owners. Pretty soon, the whole pig industry could be in jeopardy!

Besides, we have managed to put up with one lunatic in the tombs all these years. You start helping those kinds of people and, before you know it, the country will be full of them coming here for help. Think of the problems. The noise. The smell. Their unpredictable behavior. The inconveniences.

So, it's just better if this guy moves on. What a tragedy.

Do you think the fellow went back to living in the tombs after the demons were gone? Absolutely not! He was a different man! Like a new convert, he was overwhelmed with gratitude and awe. He begged Jesus, "Let me go with you!" Jesus said, "No." But Jesus did give him an assignment: "Go home and tell your family what God has done." That's a happy assignment.

Tomb living is life with the devil. You know it. You can feel it in your heart. You can see it in your life. But what you cannot do is free yourself.

Then and now the only answer to the devil and the tomb-life is **Jesus**.

> Then came one of the rulers of the synagogue, Jairus by name, and seeing him, he fell at his feet and implored him earnestly, saying, "My little daughter is at the point of death. Come and lay your hands on her, so that she may be made well and live." And he went with him.
>
> Mark 5:21-24a (Matthew 9:18-19; Luke 8:40-42a)

MAY 1

Jesus responded so naturally to calls for help. If he was ever inconvenienced, he did not show it. If he ever felt interrupted in his mission, he gave no sign of it. Although he found it necessary to retreat from the crowds to quiet places from time-to-time, he welcomed the requests of people.

But asking for help is rarely easy, especially for many men. We fellows have a strong need to demonstrate our "mastery" of situations, our "fix it" qualities for any circumstance. But we cannot fix everything or make everything right. Being honest about that is very important. So is asking for help.

Enter Jairus. As synagogue ruler Jairus enjoyed a position of authority as leading elder in this local fellowship of Jews. He was very important and very respected. But none of that brought immunity from life's tragedies.

As a whole, the religious leaders of the Jewish community were not very accepting of Jesus. Evidently, Jairus saw Jesus differently. Maybe Jairus had heard one of Jesus' sermons or watched him as he healed someone. Perhaps he was acting on the basis of Jesus' reputation. Whatever his knowledge of Jesus, he was now pleading as a father rather than as a religious leader. "I beg you, please!"

Our children are very special to us. We delight to see their smiles and joy. We ache to see their pain. Most parents can imagine themselves being willing to do anything if it would save their child.

We are not told how long the little girl had been sick when Jairus came seeking the touch of the Physician. Had he tried other options? Were his financial resources drained? Was Jesus his last hope for his daughter?

While we may have more questions than answers about Jairus, we do know that in this moment of deep heartache he came to the right person. Jairus came asking the help of the one person who could make a difference: **Jesus**.

And he said to her, "Daughter, your faith has made you well; go in peace, and be healed of your disease."

Mark 5:24b-34 (Matthew 9:20-22; Luke 8:42b-48)

MAY 2

Jesus and Jairus were pressed on all sides by the large crowd. Everyone was wanting to see and to hear, to be a part of the happening. Except one. Her reason for being there was different.

She had been bleeding for twelve years. According to the Levitical law, this made her unclean. She was a social outcast, an untouchable. She was barred from any social occasion, any religious assembly.

In addition to the loss of her physical strength, she was now bankrupt. She had tried every doctor, every promising remedy. None worked. Her condition had only worsened. Now, her money was gone, and her hope, too.

Somehow, somewhere, sometime, she heard about Jesus. Summoning her courage, she weaved her way through the press of the crowd. She feared that at any moment someone might recognize her, rebuke her and send her away. If only she could get close enough to just touch his garment. That's all an untouchable can hope for.

The moment had come. She was close enough. She touched his garment. Instantly, she could feel a change. The crowd continued walking but she was fixed to the spot as she tried to understand what had happened!

What an incredible moment! Twelve years of misery and pain. Twelve years of exclusion. Twelve years of doctors and remedies. Twelve years of hopes dashed time after time after time. And now, to be well, to be whole again!

But she wasn't the only one who knew something incredible had happened. "Who touched my clothes?" Jesus asked.

In that moment it seemed that no one else was there. Just her and Jesus. Trembling, she fell at his feet and told him everything. Her words rolled off her lips as easily as the tears rolled off her cheeks.

And what did Jesus say to her? "There is nothing magical about touching this garment. It is your faith in me that brings healing."

There is nothing magical about the water, or the emblems, or the Book. The power of the transformed life is found when you place your trust in **Jesus**.

Taking her by the hand he said to her, "Talitha cumi," which means, "Little girl, I say to you, arise."
Mark 5:35-43 (Matthew 9:23-26; Luke 8:49-56)

MAY 3

Jesus was not popular with the religious leaders of the Jewish community. So, this story of Jairus, a synagogue ruler, is a refreshing change from what usually happened as Jesus journeyed from one town to another.

Perhaps, Jairus saw Jesus differently because he was so desperate for help. Desperation will do that. His only child, a 12-year-old daughter, was dying. Jesus was his last hope. But that hope seemed to vanish when the news came from home: "your daughter is dead."

Jairus had sought Jesus out of his deep heartache. He came believing. Maybe not fully understanding everything...but he came believing that, if there was any hope, any chance, any blessing, any healing, Jesus was it.

The wailing flutes, the screaming mourners, the rent garments, the torn hair...expressions of grief greeted Jesus and Jairus when they arrived at his house. The sounds of hopelessness.

Jesus sent everyone out of the room except mom and dad and some of his disciples. Then, Jesus took the child's hand and, in Aramaic, said, "Little girl, get up!" Immediately the girl stood up and walked around. Those present were completely astonished. After this, he told them to tell no one about it. Now that would be a hard secret to keep!

Faith does not always mean 'winning' in this world. The story of Jairus is not a story about how trusting God means we get what we want. The story is about Jesus, the one and only one who is worthy of our trust.

So how do you deal with a hopeless situation? What do you do when the circumstances are bleak? You turn yourself, your life, your plans, your future, and all of its outcomes over to Him. You trust Him.

We most often pursue the Lord when we realize that our situation is hopeless and only Jesus can save us. But what does that really tell us? That we should have been seeking him from the start! And we will never find it easier than it is right now to reach out to **Jesus**.

> Then he touched their eyes, saying, "According to your faith be it done to you." And their eyes were opened.
>
> Matthew 9:27-34

MAY 4

Jesus must have delighted in healing people. Bringing such joy and excitement to the lives of folks burdened by physical problems, some of them for a lifetime, must have produced a very broad smile across his face. Jesus was all about joy in the hearts of people.

Even so, his own heart must have found special delight when people expressed faith in him. While there were many who sought healing, there were few who recognized him as the Son of David. But two blind men did.

They were following Jesus. How could blind men follow him? Perhaps, someone was assisting them, leading them along.

And why do they possess such faith in Jesus? Being blind, they have had no opportunity to see anything that he has done. Evidently, they are depending on what others have told them about Jesus.

In one incredible moment they went from seeing absolutely nothing to seeing everything around them! How could they possibly keep this to themselves? In fact, they didn't. Jesus warned them sternly about it but it made little impression. This was just too wonderful to keep to yourself!

Jesus touched their eyes and said to them, "According to your faith will it be done to you." What if they had doubted Jesus? Would they see?

Few subjects receive as much attention in the Bible as the subject of faith. Yet, it is often misunderstood. Faith is not something magical; nor is it mind over matter. Faith is about God. And the power to heal comes from God!

The blind men believed in Jesus. They believed that Jesus could heal them. Then they acted on their belief. They asked Jesus to heal them.

You want to know what faith is? There it is: trust + action = faith. But the men always knew where the power came from. Jesus! Neither their trust nor their actions produced the power, but the power was the result of their faith in the one who was able to heal.

The power of God to do great and wonderful things in your life is still available to you....according to your faith in **Jesus**.

> "Is not this the carpenter, the son of Mary and brother of James and Joses and Judas and Simon? And are not his sisters here with us?" And they took offense at him.
>
> Mark 6:1-6a (Matthew 13:54-58)

MAY 5

Jesus was not what people expected of the Messiah. They were not expecting someone who looked so ordinary, so common. So, believing in him was difficult for them. And this was especially true in his hometown.

Evidently, as he grew older in front of them, there seemed to be nothing special about him. He didn't walk around with a halo over his head or perform special tricks as a youngster. His ordinary looks and his seemingly ordinary life made it difficult for his hometown folks to imagine that he was in any way extraordinary. In fact, they were offended by his commonness!

For thirty years they knew him as the oldest son of Joseph and Mary. In a family of at least nine, there was nothing to suggest that he was destined for greatness. The people of Nazareth thought they really knew him. But this may have been the first time that many had heard Jesus teach. Certainly, many of them were amazed at how he had changed. And many of them were skeptical.

We are much like those Nazareth folks. We live in a world that worships the grand, the great, the outstanding, but has little time for the ordinary. We faithfully follow the lives of the celebrities and want the details of the rich and the famous. The routine is rarely exciting to us, the familiar doesn't usually bring inspiration, and the ordinary has difficulty holding our attention.

God wanted to get as close to us as humanly possible. So, He got in our skin and lived with us. But He wanted us to be drawn to Him, not by His looks or the tricks He could perform, but by His indescribable love for us. He wanted us to come to Him with hearts open to His goodness and seeking His righteousness. That common-looking man on the streets of Nazareth was God! You know him as **Jesus**.

> And Jesus went throughout all the cities and villages, teaching in their synagogues and proclaiming the gospel of the kingdom and healing every disease and every affliction.
>
> Matthew 9:35-38 (Mark 6:6b)

MAY 6

Jesus was all about people. He wanted to be with the people he came to save. Although there were occasions when he withdrew for privacy and prayer, most of his time was spent with people.

Although we are not told the names of the towns and villages, his presence must have created quite an excitement in each one. As his reputation spread, crowds gathered to hear his words about the kingdom and to witness his miracles.

As Jesus departed one village on his way to another, we can easily imagine that he left behind many lives which were forever changed by his hopeful words and kind actions. All manner of sick people were brought to him and he healed them all. Never had these villagers witnessed anything or anyone like this man!

But his motivation was not fame or fortune. He wasn't trying to gain a political following or become the leader of some social movement. While some probably envisioned how a man with such abilities could turn all this into a tidy profit, no money was changing hands and no deals were being made.

His real motivation was simple: compassion. Jesus loved people and he cared about them. Seeing the crowds, Jesus was moved with compassion. Jesus' heart went out to people who were hurting and in need.

Perhaps, Matthew's description of the people provides an indication of why Jesus was particularly moved by what he saw. "They were harassed and helpless, like sheep without a shepherd." Jesus could see in their faces and hear it in their voices, and it touched his heart. If only they had someone, a shepherd, to follow. If only they had someone they could believe in, someone who could give their lives meaning and purpose. Now, they did.

We don't really need more time or money. We don't really need more things or more pleasures. We need hope and direction. We need acceptance and love.

Jesus journeyed to towns and villages changing lives – inside and out! Sometimes his words renewed their spirits and sometimes his actions restored their bodies. But always people were better for knowing **Jesus**.

And he called the twelve together and gave them power and authority over all demons and to cure diseases, and he sent them out to proclaim the kingdom of God and to heal.
Luke 9:1-2 (Matthew 10:1-4; Mark 6:7)

MAY 7

Jesus' mission always required people. Knowing that death awaited him, others were needed to carry his message and expand the borders of his kingdom. So, choosing some helpers was inevitable.

It was certainly an odd assortment of men. While some shared a similar vocation, like fishing, other than Jesus, they seemed to have little in common. For example, Matthew collected taxes for the Romans while Simon was a Zealot against Roman authority. That must have made for some interesting campfire conversation!

While their vocations, interests and personalities may have raised questions, their lack of education and training for such a mission would have even more! Had any of them ever made a speech, argued a point of Scripture, or confronted a wrong-doer? How could men who had spent their lives catching fish or collecting tax money be expected to take a stunning message to a doubting world with the result being a kingdom over all the earth? What sense did that make?

Yet, for all the ways they were different, Jesus chose them for the one mission that would forever change humanity. They stood on the threshold of the greatest experience of their lives! Where they were going was all new territory. No one had ever traveled this way before. They were heralds of a king with a fresh announcement for every person on earth!

Of course, now we know the story. Judas Iscariot would dishonor himself by his betrayal of Jesus. The others would find their way around the Mediterranean world until the gospel had reached and changed thousands and thousands of people.

But on this particular day, with Jesus' instructions ringing in their ears, they could not imagine how their lives were about to change. But, of course, that is how it always is with those who are called by **Jesus**.

He charged them to take nothing for their journey except a staff—no bread, no bag, no money in their belts—but to wear sandals and not put on two tunics.
Mark 6:8-9 (Matthew 10:5-10; Luke 9:3)

MAY 8

Jesus told the twelve, "I have something I want you to tell people. This is it: The kingdom of heaven is near."

What must the disciples have thought? They hardly understood the nature of the kingdom themselves!

But Jesus also told them, "I have something I want you to do. I want you to take care of people. I want you to serve them."

What exactly goes through your mind when you are told that you are going to cleanse lepers or drive out demons?! They haven't exactly had a lot of experience with this sort of thing.

And then, if this was not enough to think about, he told them, "I want you to travel light. Don't take stuff."

Their reaction to his words is not recorded so we can only imagine what ideas were flooding their minds as they contemplated their assignment. Admittedly, it was a lot to take in.

But it shouldn't sound so strange to us. "Speak a word for Jesus. Serve people. Lay your treasures up in heaven." We have heard this before. We know this mission.

Just think of all the words you spoke last week. How often did you speak of things that really, truly mattered? How often did you speak of Jesus or his kingdom? How often did your words reflect your devotion to the way of Jesus?

And what about all you did last week? Did you share yourself with others? Did you give freely your time and energy to those who needed help?

What about your investments? Were you busy collecting for here or did you act with a view to your eventual departure from this world?

Something to say, something to do, and traveling light. Doesn't that sound like the call you accepted?

Each day is an opportunity to say something and to do something that brings glory to God while making a difference in the lives of people. Your mission, like the twelve apostles, is straight from the heart of **Jesus**.

> "Whenever you enter a house, stay there until you leave that town. And if any place will not welcome you or listen to you, shake the dust off your feet when you leave, as a testimony against them."
> Mark 6:10-11 (Matthew 10:11-16; Luke 9:4-5)

MAY 9

Jesus wanted his followers prepared for the best and the worst. He knew exactly what they were up against: he faced it daily. Jesus' ways and words made indifference difficult. People loved him or hated him. He knew that his disciples would find a similar reception.

So, he told them, "search for some worthy person there and stay at his house." The disciples could expect to find acceptance among some. And when the disciples found those who were receptive to the kingdom message, they were to bless these people because their support was a blessing.

When the disciples met rejection, they were to waste no time. There were other people in other places. "Shake the dust off your feet" and start in a new direction. Time was precious and Jesus wanted them to go to as many villages and towns as possible.

The conflict between sheep and wolves was familiar to them. That they were to be sent as sheep among vicious, deadly wolves was Jesus' way of graphically illustrating the dangers of confronting a skeptical world with the message of the kingdom and the Messiah. How did that imagery make them feel as they pondered their mission? How does it make you feel when you consider your mission in an unfriendly world?

Jesus sends us to our friends and neighbors as well as to those in distant places on our globe. Being salt and light, we want people to know the Lord we serve. We dream of seeing scores of people experiencing new birth. But the reality is often very different.

As it was with these disciples of Jesus in century one, we face every kind of reaction to our words and works: from excited acceptance to violent rejection, from those who would be partners to those who would be enemies. But none of this should come as a surprise. This was exactly the reaction we were told to expect whenever we begin to tell people about **Jesus**.

> "Brother will deliver brother over to death, and the father his child, and children will rise against parents and have them put to death, and you will be hated by all for my name's sake. But the one who endures to the end will be saved."
>
> Matthew 10:17-25

MAY 10

Jesus' honesty is refreshing, even if it is also troubling. He did not want his disciples caught by surprise! "It is a tough world. Be on guard. Be prepared for pain."

Discipleship doesn't make friends of all! Following Jesus faithfully comes at a cost! Speaking the truth in love does not automatically mean receptive hearts! Doing what is right and best does not guarantee gratitude on the part of others!

This seeming inequity is distressing. We want so much to believe that truth will bring confession, that kindness will produce good, and that love will result in change. Sometimes those things happen. But sometimes your honesty only makes another angry. Sometimes your kindness is misinterpreted. And sometimes your love is rejected.

Jesus knew that the presentation of a message calling for repentance and confession of sin, humbling oneself and thirsting for righteousness, would find enemies as well as friends. He knew that this was a lifestyle change that would pit family members against one another. And he also knew that the disciples would bear the brunt of all this hostility that was stirred by their words about him.

The temptation in every age is to soften the approach, water down the demands, and tone down the consequence of decision. Our fear is that anything unattractive or negative will drive people away. Unfortunately, what often occurs is that followers only see Jesus as the pathway to friendships, promotions and an enjoyable lifestyle. They are quite unprepared for disappointment and suffering.

While his words to the disciples hardly strike us as an inspiring call to action, sandwiched among his warnings is a single phrase that makes all the difference to those who love and trust Jesus. "...but he who stands firm to the end will be saved."

That's it! Today's assignment is not to be successful in changing the world. You are called to be faithful to **Jesus**.

"And do not fear those who kill the body but cannot kill the soul. Rather fear him who can destroy both soul and body in hell."
Matthew 10:26-31

MAY 11

Jesus knew their minds were racing and their hearts were pounding. After all, he had just told them they were going to be hated and persecuted!

But he also told them, "Don't be afraid. Don't be afraid. Don't be afraid." Three times he spoke the same words.

Did you ever notice how easy it is to tell someone to not be afraid? And did you ever notice how slow we are to take our own advice? The problem is one of vision. We seem to be able to view the problems of others with greater clarity than we view our own.

Knowing that human hearts struggle with the need to be in control, Jesus calmed their concerns by reminding them that their heavenly Father was in control. Regardless of what others may do to you, God has the final word. You can trust Him. Nothing happens apart from His will.

And equally important to who is in charge is the matter of who cares. God does! As surely as God knows what happens with each bird, so He knows what happens with you. You are valuable!

Jesus' words were not going to change the animosity his disciples would face or the persecution they would have to endure. His words were not going to spare them what must be experienced. But his words did give them reason to go, and to go with confidence and boldness.

Inevitably, we find ourselves facing things we cannot control. We feel helpless and imagine the worst. The resulting fear is to be expected. What we need is perspective. Jesus provides that by reminding us that, no matter our situation, nothing has really changed. God is still in control and He still believes we are valuable.

"Don't be afraid." Whether dealing with bodily pain or struggling with a broken heart, whether facing an uncertain future or working through loneliness, these three words bring calm to our souls because they come from the lips of the one who knows us and loves us best: **Jesus**.

> So everyone who acknowledges me before men, I also will acknowledge before my Father who is in heaven, but whoever denies me before men, I also will deny before my Father who is in heaven.
>
> Matthew 10:32-33

MAY 12

Jesus sent his disciples forth with an unmistakable message: Jesus is the Son of God. Whatever else they might say about the kingdom, they could tell people the king had come!

So, the disciples spread out across the territory with these remarkable words ringing in their ears. No wonder Jesus told them they would find hostility, even persecution. No wonder he told them that people would betray one another over him. Either-or claims tend to draw strong reactions.

In our religious buffet-kind-of-world, the thought that acceptance by God must come by listening to a single voice is not a popular idea. We prefer choices. We like options. We want to find what works best for us. We value our freedom to choose. We want to be open and accepting to those who choose differently. In other words, we don't want to hear any either-or messages.

This confession is not private or secret. Instead, it is an open affirmation of trust, allegiance and belonging. It is made boldly and unashamedly before others, whether they are friend or foe.

To acknowledge one's faith in Jesus in the face of adversity is not about behaving stubbornly for the sake of making a point, but rather to joyfully confess the reality of a relationship that is life-changing. We want people to know that Jesus is our Lord and that we live only to please him. We want people to know him.

We stand in relationship to Jesus as a servant to a master, a disciple to a teacher, a sinner to a Savior. Our confession comes not from fear of people but fear of God. We confess, not because we love the facts about him, but because we love him.

The greatest joy will be to hear Jesus say, "Father, he/she is one of mine. Invite this one into the joys of heaven." The most frightening thought would be to hear him say, "I never knew you. Depart."

But it is one or the other. We know because the one who decides is **Jesus**.

> "Do not think that I have come to bring peace to the earth. I have not come to bring peace, but a sword."
>
> Matthew 10:34-37

MAY 13

Jesus' words are not what we expected. We DO associate him with peace on earth! After all, wasn't that part of his birth announcement from the angels? Where was anything said about a sword coming out of Bethlehem?

Filled with enthusiasm for their task, the disciples were about to discover for themselves that kingdom news does not necessarily unite people. It often divides them, even those in the same house.

Changing our life because of Jesus sometimes creates rubs and irritations with others. They don't always appreciate our new way of looking at life and our new basis for making choices. Without a word being spoken, they may feel judged. Now, they face a decision because it is not possible to live happily in this way. Sadly, they may blame us for their discomfort.

Differences among family members are not uncommon. From music genres to movie choices, from clothing styles to reading materials, people don't always see eye-to-eye. Generally speaking, such individual tastes may make little difference to the overall interaction of family members. But when one becomes a Christian, what one hears and sees, the way one dresses and what one reads are no longer simply individual tastes but choices made with Jesus in mind. Family members may not always appreciate or understand this new you.

For most folks, family is everything. Home is a refuge and the people there top our love list. What they think is very important to us. How they feel about us has a tremendous influence on our health and happiness. To be at odds with them is very unsettling, practically traumatic.

Yet, the gospel does divide families. People who love each other don't always love the same things.

Jesus had no desire to divide family members. Yet, he did call us to an unqualified allegiance, to an undivided loyalty. He wanted us to know that discipleship meant loving him above all others.

So, there is a sword. It is the Word of the Lord. And wherever it goes, people are divided because it always forces a decision of what to do with **Jesus**.

And whoever does not take his cross and follow me is not worthy of me. Whoever finds his life will lose it, and whoever loses his life for my sake will find it.

Matthew 10:38-39

MAY 14

Jesus knew exactly what he was talking about when he used the word 'cross' in connection with discipleship. But what were the disciples thinking? A cross was an instrument of torture and death. They had seen Roman soldiers march many a poor soul to his death by crucifixion. Everyone knew about crosses. Now, Jesus was talking about voluntarily taking one!

Soon, Jesus would show them (and us) exactly what he meant. Jesus presented himself to those who came to arrest him. Having struggled with the decision in the garden, he now made the conscious choice of choosing suffering over safety, death over escape. In other words, he chose the righteousness of God over any other alternative. His motivation was love beyond understanding.

In like manner, he calls upon each of us to choose righteousness and to do so willing to accept whatever may result from that decision. Taking up our cross is placing his will above our own, choosing his path, not ours.

It is popular in our time to speak of 'finding oneself.' Usually, that means we want to live without restraints and do what we want to do. Interestingly, we always make it sound like we have to go somewhere else to make this discovery.

Jesus had a different idea. You don't actually have to go anywhere to find yourself or the life God offers you. You simply have to lose or relinquish your life to him and what you receive is the very thing you were seeking. You can only find the real you in the pathway of God.

Our problem isn't understanding his words. Our problem is believing them. We have been taught to pursue in order to gain, to sacrifice and work hard in order to have. Dependence on another runs against the grain, as well as common sense.

For his disciples, the message was clear and simple: Without a cross there is no following Jesus. And there is no real life without following **Jesus**.

"Whoever receives you receives me, and whoever receives me receives him who sent me."

Matthew 10:40-42

MAY 15

Jesus had given his disciples their marching orders: "As you go, preach this message: 'The kingdom of heaven is near.'" But he sent them forth with more than simply a message. He warned them of what to expect. They would encounter rejection and persecution. They could expect to be arrested and required to defend themselves before officials. Their words would set family members against one another. They would be hated because of Jesus and, like their teacher, they would be accused of being disciples of the devil! All things considered, not much to look forward to!

Yet, they were to be unafraid. Their heavenly Father knew all about them and they were in His hands. Their faith would sustain them and their good deeds would be rewarded.

And while they would experience rejection in many places, there would be some who would receive them with kindness and extend to them a most desired cup of cool water. How welcome such would be in an arid land. Both the giver and receiver would experience the reward of being refreshed.

Living in a land of showers and toilets, water fountains and swimming pools, we find it difficult to appreciate how precious water really is. Water is basic to life. It is a necessity. Historically, communities developed around water sources. Wells or cisterns became gathering places for residents and sojourners. Sharing water was a lovely expression of hospitality.

At the same time Jesus spoke of the unpleasant expectations of their mission, he wanted them to know that moments of refreshing lay ahead. Good souls would welcome them and, in doing so, would welcome him, too.

Children were powerless. There was little to be gained by showing kindness to them. In a way, they represented the grieving who were looking for comfort, the discouraged who were seeking hope, and the suffering who were wanting relief. Yet, to show even the smallest kindness, to give a cup of cool water to a thirsty disciple, would not go unnoticed.

It is good to remember that everything you do today is about **Jesus**.

> And they departed and went through the villages, preaching the gospel and healing everywhere.
> On their return the apostles told him all that they had done.
>
> Luke 9:6, 10a (Matthew 11:1; Mark 6:12-13, 30)

MAY 16

Jesus had given them a lot to think about. He had also given them a lot to do! So, off they went.

How did they decide who would go where? Did they get to pick or did he tell them? How long were they gone? Did he give them a set date to return? How many people did they teach? How many became believers in a coming kingdom? How many times did they get run out of town? Were they ever afraid for their lives?

Imagine the experience of actually healing someone! Or, think about the moment that a demon came out of someone because they commanded it to be so. Also, these were not trained orators, yet they had a primary task of preaching the gospel. What kind of preachers were they? And what kind of response did they get when they told people that they should repent?

Evidently, they told it all to Jesus. We can only imagine the constant chatter of stories shared about wonderful people who blessed their efforts and exciting things that changed the lives of many. But several would have told of difficult and discouraging days in which it seemed that no one would even give them a fair hearing, and how they grew disheartened, even afraid.

It was, to be sure, an early introduction to their future ministry when Jesus wasn't there to report to; at least, not as he was now. In brief and limited fashion, they experienced something of what lay ahead for each of them. How did they feel about it? Were they thrilled by the possibilities or concerned for the wisdom of this endeavor?

Following Jesus is often challenging. He told you that himself. Likely, there will be times when you even doubt the wisdom of following. But while there are those days of discouragement because righteousness is not appreciated, there are so many other days when love and joy break forth in hearts and lives and remind you of why you said 'yes' to **Jesus**.

> King Herod heard of it, for Jesus' name had become known. Some said, "John the Baptist has been raised from the dead. That is why these miraculous powers are at work in him."
>
> Mark 6:14-20 (Matthew 14:1-5; Luke 9:7-9)

MAY 17

Jesus is the focus of Mark's writing. He's going to put his primary theme on pause and bring us up to speed on what has happened with John the Baptist.

News of Jesus spread. Herod heard the reports and immediately jumped to the conclusion that John the Baptist had returned to life. That he felt responsible for John's death is evidenced in his own admission: "John, the man I beheaded, has been raised from the dead."

Herod the Great (who tried to kill baby Jesus) had three sons (Philip, Antipas, and Archelaus) and, at his death, divided his kingdom among them. Antipas married the daughter of King Aretas IV of Nabatea. Philip married his niece, Herodias, daughter of Aristobulus, another son of Herod the Great. But, in time, Antipas and Herodias became romantically involved. They eventually divorced their spouses and married one another. John condemned the marriage for what it was: adultery.

Herodias wanted John dead. But she could do nothing because her husband would not consent to it. In an odd way, Herod had a certain respect for John. Maybe it was a superstitious fear. As a compromise to his wife's demands Herod had John imprisoned.

As so often happens with us, Herod had two choices before him. He could please his wife and put an end to John's humiliating assault on their relationship. Or, he could do what was right and put an end to his sinful relationship with Herodias. Not surprisingly, he did not like his choices.

Faced with undesirable choices, we often look for some way to find the middle ground. We want to get out from under the condemnation of sin without actually giving up the pleasures of it. We want to hold on to what we want without suffering any of the consequences of selfishness. We want to have our own way and feel justified in our own eyes. Herod discovered, as we do, that there is no negotiated middle ground for sin. We choose our master but we don't negotiate with him. Today, choose **Jesus**.

> When his disciples heard of it, they came and took his body and laid it in a tomb.
>
> Mark 6:21-29 (Matthew 14:6-12)

MAY 18

Jesus without John the Baptist as part of the story is hard to imagine. We have never known it any other way.

To John was given the challenging task of preparing the way of the Lord. And, as we might expect, some found his words wonderfully refreshing and hopeful. Many repented and were baptized after hearing his preaching. Others found him to be a source of constant irritation and resented him for stirring up the people. Herodias fell into the latter group.

When our hearts are set on evil, isn't it amazing how opportunities to *do* evil seem to present themselves? The devil can be so accommodating at times.

Herod's birthday arrived and it was time to party. Being a king, it must have been an impressive affair. The party was attended by all the important people. Plenty of wine was consumed and Herodias sent her daughter to dance in front of the guests. She was probably a teenager and her dance probably had strong sexual overtones.

Herodias knew her husband well. Herod's pride and lust got the best of him. Wanting to impress his guests, he offered the girl anything she wanted, even up to half his kingdom. It was a foolish offer that he would soon regret. To his surprise and sorrow, the daughter quickly returned at her mother's urging and asked for John's head on a platter. Suddenly the party had taken a somber tone and all eyes were on Herod.

Again, Herod was faced with choices. Execute John or repent of his rash offer. But his pride was going to decide. How he looked to those watching was more important to him than doing what was right.

It happens all the time. We attempt to ride the waves between good and evil, trying our best to avoid having to choose. Then, when forced to make a choice, we make it based on what others think.

John spent his life preaching a message of repentance only to die at the hands of man who would not. No wonder Herod was afraid of **Jesus**.

When he went ashore he saw a great crowd, and he had compassion on them, because they were like sheep without a shepherd.
Mark 6:31-34
(Matthew 14:13-14; Luke 9:10b-11; John 6:1-3)

MAY 19

Jesus knew all about being busy. He knew all about people making demands on your time and energy. He knew what it was like to be surrounded by noise and see the needs of people. He felt the pressure of their expectations. He also knew the importance of quiet and rest.

Perhaps, the boat provided him with some respite. Whatever quiet and rest he found was short-lived. The people were determined to be with him. Wonderful things happened in the presence of Jesus. They didn't want to miss anything he said or did. So, they were waiting for him when the boat landed.

It is not very complimentary of us, but it is a common image in the Bible. We are like sheep. We often behave as though we were without a shepherd. Not smart enough to know which way to go, we are easily lost. Not strong enough to protect ourselves from harm, we are frequently in trouble. Unable to provide for ourselves the basic needs, we are prone to go looking in the wrong places. Quickly inclined to follow the flock, we often find ourselves in situations we soon regret. What can we say? We are sheep!

The picture painted by Mark is a microcosm of the 'good news' story. We are the sheep in need of a shepherd. And in his great compassion, the shepherd came and he brought us everything we needed for life, not merely surviving but really living. All we needed to do was follow.

Wouldn't you like to know what Jesus taught them? Maybe it was about the Father or heaven. Perhaps he rehearsed the Beatitudes or told them some parables. Or maybe he simply told them about himself. But whatever he taught, it was exactly what they needed to hear. The shepherd always knows the needs of the sheep.

Sheep probably isn't the image you would have chosen for yourself. But it is okay. After all, the shepherd is **Jesus**.

> So they gathered them and filled twelve baskets with the pieces of the five barley loaves left over by those who had eaten.
> John 6:4-15 (Matthew 14:15-23; Mark 6:35-46; Luke 9:12-17)

MAY 20

Jesus really does understand what it is to be pushed and shoved by the pressures of daily life, to reach the point where you just need to get away for a little while and regroup. He tries to get a little rest by slipping away up the hillside with his disciples, but the crowd allows him no respite.

The disciples suggested that Jesus send the people away so they could go to the village and find food. But Jesus is too good a shepherd to do that.

Instead, he seizes the moment to ask Philip, "Where shall we buy bread for these people to eat?" Philip grew up just a few miles away in the town of Bethsaida. If anyone knew where to buy bread, it was Philip.

But there's an even more important reason why Jesus put this question to Philip. Jesus "asked this only to test him, for he already had in mind what he was going to do."

Philip quickly put his pencil to the problem and calculated the cost. He concluded that the expense was beyond their budget. He put his pencil down murmuring, "Impossible. Can't be done."

It was not that Philip was unaware of Jesus' presence; nor would it be right to assume that Philip doubted Jesus' ability or power. More accurately: Philip simply never considered the Lord's involvement in the matter.

That's our crime! It isn't that we doubt the Lord's power or presence. We just don't imagine he cares enough to be involved!

Andrew goes to a little more effort for a solution and finds a lad with loaves and fishes. It is not much. But what Philip and Andrew don't see is that impossible situations are not solved by how much we have in our hands.

Impossibilities are solved by the Lord of heaven. In fact, God is glorified in the impossibilities of life!

Who would have thought that Christianity could begin with fishermen and tax collectors? Who would have believed that people could love their enemies or pray for their persecutors? The impossible becomes reality with **Jesus**.

He said, "Come." So Peter got out of the boat and walked on the water and came to Jesus.
Matthew 14:24-29 (Mark 6:47-50; John 6:16-20)

MAY 21

Jesus means power to your life. This great and incredible idea is interwoven in the themes and stories of the New Testament, ordinary people living in an extraordinary way because of their connection to Jesus.

The miracle of Jesus feeding more than five thousand with the loaves and fishes was now a memory. When the evening came, the disciples went down to the shore where they got into a boat and set their sails for Capernaum. Jesus, however, went up into the mountains to pray. The wind became strong and the seas became rough and the disciples were not making good time.

Then, to their astonishment, they saw a figure moving across the surface of the water. They rubbed their eyes and squinted into the darkness. They could hardly believe what they saw. Even though they saw Jesus walking on the water, they were terrified and cried out in fear. But Jesus identified himself and told them, "Don't be afraid."

Never in his entire life had Peter said to anyone, "Tell me to come to you on the water." But he could say it now because of Jesus! In the presence of Jesus, Peter could say the unbelievable!

Wow! Peter walked on water! Can you imagine what the others were thinking as he vaulted over the side? Can you imagine what he was thinking? Was he startled not to sink? Peter's whole history of water walking was one of failure! But in the presence of Jesus he was willing to try the impossible!

Who gives you the power to forgive those who mistreat you or show kindness to those who are your enemies? Who gives you the strength to surrender your desires to those of another or to do the extra work for someone who is unfair?

Every day there are people saying the most unbelievable things and doing what once seemed impossible! All of this happens because of their faith in Jesus.

How would Peter ever explain what he did? How could he ever have imagined himself doing that? Only because of **Jesus**.

But when he saw the wind, he was afraid, and beginning to sink he cried out, "Lord, save me."
Jesus immediately reached out his hand and took hold of him, saying to him, "O you of little faith, why did you doubt?"
Matthew 14:30-36 (Mark 6:51-56; John 6:21)

MAY 22

Jesus' invitation to Peter to walk on the water came at Peter's request. Jesus was not unaware of Peter's impetuousness and had witnessed it often enough to know that Peter may not have thought the matter through before making his request.

But Jesus also knew that Peter was capable of great things and possessed a courage that others lacked. Jesus knew Peter, and Peter was gradually coming to know Jesus.

So, over the side he went! Perhaps, the others gasped fearing for his life, or maybe even laughed at another of those 'act before you think' actions of Peter. But the one thing that none of the others did, the one thing that none of the others even tried was to join him. In this, they were perfectly willing for Peter to go it alone.

Trusting Jesus often means doing something you have never done before and doing it without others. But then, Jesus told us that at the beginning of his ministry. Go the extra mile. Turn the other cheek. Love your enemies. Pray for your persecutors. Forgive those who mistreat you.

While these actions may not sound as thrilling as walking on water, they still require us to take Jesus at his word. And, as Peter discovered, others may not be too anxious to join us.

But as the cold mist hit his face and he took his eyes off Jesus, he began to think about what he couldn't do instead of what Jesus could do. His faith gave way to fear and, suddenly, he was sinking and yelling for help. Jesus reached out and saved him.

Watching Peter sink into the water and hearing Jesus' rebuke about little faith, we may be unfairly critical of Peter. Peter's walk on the water was not easy. Sure, his faith would grow. But even in weakness he was daring to believe and willing to try something he had never done before. Even in your weakness, amazing things happen when your eyes are fixed on **Jesus**.

Then they said to him, "What must we do, to be doing the works of God?" Jesus answered them, "This is the work of God, that you believe in him whom he has sent."

John 6:22-29

MAY 23

Jesus' reluctance to be their king may have surprised them but it did not discourage them. Perhaps, he had some conditions they had to meet before he would agree to lead them. So, they asked him, "What must we do to do the works God requires?"

Now, don't miss what Jesus says: The "real food" is not had by work but comes as a gift.

Like them, we are often confused about God's will for our lives. God has a marvelous plan for you and me. From our vantage point, He has literally spent thousands of years on it. And the heart of the plan is His incomprehensible love and grace.

Yet, it is often difficult for us to be convinced that hard work won't win the day. We just believe that if we will work hard enough and do our best, then the goal will be ours. Jesus says what you want and need is a gift God gives. In fact, it is not a work that originates with man at all. It is the work of God, the work of grace; it is food that cannot be earned, only received.

They were confused about what is truly important in life, as well as how to acquire it. It is an easy mistake to make. After all, the world appears to hold so much for us and all we have to do is work hard enough.

But did you ever notice that all the things which come from our hard work always lose their value and cease to satisfy. But whatever God gives only grows in value to the soul. The Bible tells us over and over, in hundreds of ways, that God's gifts are forever, but the things of the world pass away.

When we understand that there is more to life than bread, we are open to the gift of God, living bread: **Jesus.**

Jesus said to them, "I am the bread of life; whoever comes to me shall not hunger, and whoever believes in me shall never thirst."
John 6:30-40

MAY 24

Jesus had just fed over five thousand people with two fish and five loaves of bread. Now, of all things, they were asking him for a sign! "Perform a miracle and we will believe," they said. "After all, Moses could provide bread!"

Centuries ago, the whole Israelite community had grumbled against Moses. "You have brought us out into this desert to starve us to death!"

The Lord said to Moses, "I will rain down bread from heaven for you." Every morning the Israelites awakened to find thin, white wafers on the desert. This bread was called manna.

Now, hundreds of years removed from that event, Jesus had taken the loaves and fishes and fed thousands. Unfortunately, they missed the point: God did it! It was God who graciously provided food for hungry Israel and it was God who provided food for these thousands.

Typical of the narrow, fleshly view of humans, they interpreted both past and present events in light of their physical needs. It does not seem to have occurred to them that there was any spiritual significance to what was happening. And it does not seem to have crossed their minds that this Jesus might be more than a political leader or a Galilean holy man.

It is very difficult for us to think beyond our physical concerns. After all, they are daily. Beyond the basics, it would appear that everything about our world seems focused on making our experience here as pleasurable as possible.

Perhaps, this explains our resistance to Jesus' call to discipleship. We interpret that to mean sacrifice, devotion, commitment, and discipline. In other words, it sounds a lot like doing without!

As Jesus nudged them along toward a more spiritual view of things, he spoke of true bread, of never being hungry or thirsty again, and of the Father's will. But mistaken about what really satisfies and misguided in their attempts to find God, they failed to see that all they would ever need to be truly full was standing right in front of them in the man called **Jesus.**

"Everyone who has heard and learned from the Father comes to me—not that anyone has seen the Father except he who is from God; he has seen the Father."

John 6:41-47

MAY 25

Jesus now had their attention. They could admit that his teachings were captivating. They could even acknowledge that something unusual had happened with the loaves and fishes. They might even be able to bring themselves to confess that he must be a man from God. But that was as far as they could go. After all, look at him.

Claiming to have come from heaven was a little much, especially since they knew his family. So, they talked among themselves about his words and wondered why he had gotten so carried away.

Sounds a lot like us. We don't mind Jesus being born in Bethlehem or raised in Nazareth. We don't mind that he helped people and taught them how to love one another. We actually like the fact that he promoted peace and goodwill among people. His unfair treatment and his cruel death at the hands of an evil empire only makes us want to hold him up as an example of what a single man can do when he is willing to be a leader, challenge the system and sacrifice for the betterment of others.

But from heaven? That requires us to go somewhere we just as soon not go. Let him be a man. Let him be the best of men. Let him be someone we can admire. We can live with that. But being God totally changes things.

If he is simply a wonderful person, then we can weigh his words against what other wonderful people have said. If he is a man with extraordinary wisdom about life, then we can consider his wisdom in the same way that we consider the wisdom of others. And if he is a marvelous example of how life ought to be lived, then we can select from his life what we choose to emulate.

But if he is from heaven, then his words and his wisdom and his ways require much more from us. If he is from heaven, then no one compares to **Jesus**.

> "I am the living bread that came down from heaven. If anyone eats of this bread, he will live forever. And the bread that I will give for the life of the world is my flesh."
>
> John 6:48

MAY 26

Jesus came from heaven to satisfy the deepest needs of humanity. He was not unmindful of our physical needs, such as food and water, but those were not his priorities. The work of reconciliation was foremost.

Unfortunately, we are far more focused on our immediate, physical needs. So, too, were those who experienced the miracle of Jesus feeding five thousand with just a few loaves and fish. In a harsh land where getting food was literally day-to-day, the miracle created enormous excitement and hope. Full bellies looked to him as the answer to their problems. They were so focused on the food they received that they seemed oblivious to the source of it.

Jesus guided their thinking away from the physical bread to the true bread that comes from God: himself! "I am what you need. As the Father sent manna for those who would still die, the Father has sent me so that you might never die!"

By referring to himself as the bread of life, Jesus was claiming that he was essential. People could not do without him.

Even more, his statement was bold in claiming that the real hunger in their lives could only be satisfied by him. Nothing has changed. He is the only food for our souls.

It is not surprising that people would find his words difficult to swallow. Even now, we like believing that we are in control of our lives and we don't need someone else telling us what will satisfy us. After all, who would know better than us what we need?

Jesus came to fill our lives with meaning and purpose, and to help us learn how to value our souls as God does. Knowing that our hunger would take us in all the wrong directions, Jesus came to show and to tell us how we could be filled with what our hearts truly seek.

We are hungry people and there are many breads, but only one bread is the bread from God that fills us forever: **Jesus**.

"As the living Father sent me, and I live because of the Father, so whoever feeds on me, he also will live because of me."

John 6:52-59

MAY 27

Jesus created plenty of excitement by his actions (feeding the five thousand), but his words were equally stirring. Using Israel's wilderness experience with the manna, he contrasted worldly bread with spiritual bread. As he had spoken with the Samaritan woman about living water, so he spoke to these Jews about the bread of life. Now, the Jews began to argue among themselves about the meaning of his words.

Jesus used metaphorical or figurative language on occasion. Such language often created questions and this time was no exception.

But eating his flesh and drinking his blood were descriptive of what he had already told them: believe in him. As bread and water were basic staples of physical life, so his flesh and blood were necessary to spiritual life. In other words, he was necessary to spiritual life, to real life!

Although they did not grasp the fullness of the imagery, they understood very well the gist of the metaphor. Even if they thought he was speaking crudely, they knew he was calling them to be followers, even insisting that they accept his words as the words of God. They understood that he was requiring them to acknowledge him as the Son of God, the very one God sent from heaven.

This was too much for them. They were thrilled at his miracles, especially when their stomachs were full, and they liked the fact that he spoke with authority and gave such wise counsel. But they were not ready to fall at his feet and call him Lord. They were not ready to believe he was heaven-sent.

And particularly troublesome was the way he left no room for anything or anyone else. He used that word "unless." "Unless you believe in me you have no life."

Like these Jews of long ago, our tendency is to want the blessings without the sacrifice, to desire the benefits without obedience. In other words, we want Jesus to serve us rather than Lord us. It does not work that way.

"Unless." It is Jesus or no salvation! What a difference a word makes, especially when that word is spoken by **Jesus**.

> "It is the Spirit who gives life; the flesh is no help at all. The words that I have spoken to you are spirit and life."
>
> John 6:60-65

MAY 28

Jesus offended folks because he emphasized the spiritual above the temporal. Do you remember how all this started? Feeding five thousand with the loaves and the fishes. On the other side of the lake the discussion focused on food. But from the start Jesus told them to work for a different kind of food, to eat the food of real life. Jesus was emphasizing the spiritual, not the temporal.

He was not unconcerned about daily bread. After all, he fed them. But he wanted them to think deeper, to live richer, and to cast their eyes toward heaven when they considered their meaning and purpose. He wanted more for them than they wanted for themselves.

Jesus gave the soul pre-eminence over the body and the kingdom of God precedence over earthly governments. At the same time, he condemned those who gripped their riches more tightly than their faith, those who loved the world more than the Father.

Jesus offended them because his words were hard to accept. He said he was the bread of life....that God was his Father....that he had come down from heaven....that life was in eating his flesh and drinking his blood....that failure to do that meant death.

These were hard words to believe. People still struggle to accept them. We don't like an either-or approach. We prefer options. We don't care for commitment, sacrifice, or obedience. We like to be free to live as we want.

And we certainly don't like the idea that we are dependent on someone else for life! We want to believe that we can take life by the scruff of the neck and make it turn out as we want.

Did you ever notice how every story of Jesus finally winds its way to the same conclusion: you have to make a decision. Sooner or later a choice must be made and it is usually at that place that the offense becomes apparent. After all, if you never had to decide about Jesus, his words and ways would be of little significance. But you do. So, for today what did you decide about **Jesus?**

So Jesus said to the Twelve, "Do you want to go away as well?"
Simon Peter answered him, "Lord, to whom shall we go? You have the words of eternal life, and we have believed, and have come to know, that you are the Holy One of God."

John 6:66-71

MAY 29

Jesus came from heaven with words that would forever change the course of history. People were amazed at his words. They marveled at what he said and how he said it.

Words have the power to create change, sometimes tremendous change. Words have inspired nations, started wars, initiated reformations and cost men and women their lives.

But sometimes, words can be tough to hear. The very words that would give life were also the very words that some people would not accept. Some found his words too hard, too difficult to believe. It wasn't as though they found newer or better words with another, or that his words were no longer interesting. No, they left because his words were not easy. That often happens when someone tells us what we need to hear.

At this point, Jesus turned to the Twelve and asked them, "Do you want to go away as well?"

They were free to go. Jesus never holds anyone by force, never holds anyone against their will. He does not hold you. But where will you go? To whom will you go?

Perhaps, we should ask this another way–Why would you leave? Jesus has the words we need to hear, the words that supply the answers and provide the hope. Jesus has the words that confront and conquer our fears, the words that rescue and restore our spirits. Jesus' words are urgent because our situation is desperate, yet his words are kind because he loves us. And Jesus always tells us the truth. No one ever spoke to us like Jesus.

We have huge bookstores that can carry only a share of the books actually coming from the publishers. The airwaves are filled with people giving financial counsel, relationship advice, health tips, etc. All of these words are to help us live happier, healthier, longer, more productive lives.

In the midst of this barrage of words, who really has the words we need to hear? Only Jesus, Peter says. Only **Jesus**.

And he said to them, "Well did Isaiah prophesy of you hypocrites, as it is written, 'This people honors me with their lips, but their heart is far from me; in vain do they worship me, teaching as doctrines the commandments of men.'"

Mark 7:1-13 (Matthew 15:1-9: John 7:1)

MAY 30

Jesus was now accustomed to being the object of scrutiny. The religious leaders were watching his every move and listening to his every word. Naturally, they were also watching his disciples.

To the people of the first century, the Pharisees were heroes, not villains. While misguided in their application of the Law, at least they were passionate! Religiously, they demanded much of themselves and endeavored to teach the common folks the importance of keeping the Law. But the Pharisees tended to expand the requirements of the Law; thus, adding laws to laws.

Jesus was not impressed. "You have been careful," he said, "but careful about the wrong things." Their mistake was to confuse their ideas for God's ideas.

Then, Jesus illustrated how they set aside God's will for their own purposes. Under the Law supporting one's aging parents was important. But the Pharisees and scribes tried to create a "loophole" by declaring that if one was to announce those assets as a gift to God, then the person was no longer expected to use those assets to care for his parents. This evasive behavior had become their tradition.

This tendency to fixate on less important things and create our own rules for holiness is not limited to long-ago Pharisees. We, too, may decide that dressing a certain way, abstaining from certain things, or using a certain version of the Bible leads to holiness even though God never spoke of such things. What begins as simply a functional way to accomplish something may become a tradition that we employ as a mark for determining righteousness.

Perhaps, we choose to do this because it permits us to be in control. There is something attractive about believing that we can make ourselves godly by what we do. After all, we thought of it.

But godliness is not the result of making and keeping our own rules. We walk with God as we listen to and obey His Son, **Jesus**.

And he said, "What comes out of a person is what defiles him.
For from within, out of the heart of man, come evil thoughts, sexual immorality, theft, murder, adultery, coveting, wickedness, deceit, sensuality, envy, slander, pride, foolishness.
All these evil things come from within, and they defile a person."
Mark 7:14-23 (Matthew 15:10-20)

MAY 31

Jesus and the Pharisees agreed that the problem with the human race was sin. Yet they differed radically on how to get to the heart of this problem.

The Pharisees who questioned Jesus had the wrong idea about addressing sin because they had a false concept of what holy living was all about. To them, holiness simply had to do with performing the right "spiritual exercises." Their religious practices came from habit, not heart. They thought if it looked good, it was good.

The Pharisees were trying an outside-in approach to solve the sin problem. They thought sin could be rooted out by doing outward actions, such as watching what you eat.

Instead, Jesus focused on the heart. Jesus said, "If you are trying to do something about sin, you're starting at the wrong place!" The kind of food you eat doesn't matter nearly as much as the kind of person you are.

Legislating more laws against sinful practices, spending more money to fight sinful habits, or educating more people about the dangers of sinful ways are just the kinds of things that make us feel good about ourselves, that we are actually doing something about sin. But while focusing on the symptoms may give us a lot to do and improve our feelings, we are not actually addressing the problem. Transformation of the human heart is required and that change is accomplished only by Jesus.

Make no mistake: You only get to the heart of your problem with sin when you deal with the condition of your heart.

King David prayed to God, "Create in me a clean heart." He knew his heart was the problem and he knew that a clean one comes only from the work of God.

It is impossible to become a Christian without a change of heart. But it is a mistake to believe that faithfully living the Christian life requires something extra. Your heart was always the goal of **Jesus**.

> Then Jesus answered her, "O woman, great is your faith! Be it done for you as you desire." And her daughter was healed instantly.
> Matthew 15:21-28 (Mark 7:24-30)

JUNE 1

Jesus heard the woman pleading for help but he seemed inclined to reject her request. In fact, we find Jesus doing exactly the opposite of what we would expect. He did not rush to her aid. He did not agree to follow her home to see her daughter. He offered no soothing words of encouragement for her heart. Instead, "Jesus did not answer a word." Having watched Jesus in so many different situations in which he was kind and compassionate, this seems to be out of character.

The disciples seemed to care more about this woman than Jesus did. But their interests in her may not be as genuine as it appears. They may have seen her more as a nuisance. If Jesus would give her what she wanted, she could be on her way.

Even though Jesus seemed not to care, he cared very much. And, it would have been easy to grant her request. But this provided another of those teachable moments for his disciples. More than that, Jesus cared about this woman's deeper needs.

Like a mother who identifies with the pain of her child, the woman pleaded for her daughter. "You don't have to help me, you don't owe me, but I plead for your mercy and grace for my child."

She did not care if she was making a spectacle of herself. Even though Jesus ignored her, she did not leave. She was persistent—she had nowhere else to turn. Jesus was her hope. She would not accept the rejection.

"Yes, I am a dog—I am not worthy to be your child, but you are so rich in blessings and goodness, that even a crumb will be enough to heal my daughter."

Her words delighted him! Her faith thrilled him! "Your request is granted." And this unnamed woman of great faith returned home to a daughter who was made whole by **Jesus**.

> And looking up to heaven, he sighed and said to him, "Ephphatha," that is, "Be opened." And his ears were opened, his tongue was released, and he spoke plainly.
>
> Mark 7:31-37 (Matthew 15:29-31)

JUNE 2

Jesus, right in the middle of healing a deaf man with a speech impediment, gazed into heaven and sighed. It may have been a sigh that went unnoticed by most standing nearby. But, perhaps, no sigh ever said so much. Jesus really does care.

We all do our share of sighing. We sigh over what happens with our children. We sigh over what happens to our country. We sigh about those things that hurt but we don't understand why. We sigh when life gives us something that we did not expect. We sigh when we lose those who mean so much to us.

Long ago, Isaiah had the unenviable task of telling the people of the coming judgment of God. But Isaiah also had good news! The day was coming when God would come to the people. That was God's promise! But how would the people know? Isaiah's answer: When the deaf hear and the mute speak!

The day of good news had arrived! Jesus was the good news!

When Jesus looked into the face of this man, Jesus sighed. If he had not felt the burden of the man, if he had not been sensitive to the misery of his life, if he had not listened to the pleas of those who had brought the man to him, then he never would have sighed.

Because our bodies hurt and our hearts break, Jesus sighs. Because we wound one another and our pride gets the better of us, Jesus sighs. Because we are often selfish and separated from the Father, Jesus sighs.

Healing the man is another display of Jesus' awesome power. We are always impressed by his power! But we need more than knowing what he can do. We need to know what he wants to do. It is the sigh that warms our hearts and reminds us of the compassion of **Jesus**.

And they all ate and were satisfied. And they took up seven baskets full of the broken pieces left over.
Matthew 15:32-39 (Mark 8:1-10)

JUNE 3

Jesus' came to us with the clearest sense of purpose: to address the sin problem in our lives and save us from the certain eternal death we deserved. But Jesus also cares about those everyday issues that bring us heartache and worry: such as finding food.

Not surprisingly, the disciples appeared skeptical that much could be done for so many in this remote place. But they discovered once again that Jesus was not limited by the surroundings.

The miracle recorded here is not to be confused with the feeding of the five thousand in Matthew 14:13-21. The feeding of the five thousand took place in Galilee, near Bethsaida. The feeding of the four thousand was in The Decapolis, an area composed of ten cities on the east side of the Jordan River.

When Jesus fed the five thousand, he did so with five loaves and two small fish. The feeding of the four thousand involved seven loaves and a few small fish.

Some in the larger crowd, primarily a Jewish audience, wanted to make Jesus king. No one in the crowd of four thousand seemed interested in that.

More than four thousand people walked away from this remarkable occasion. What did they tell their friends? How did they describe the miracle?

You can be sure that each one told the story from their personal perspective and offered their own ideas on all they had experienced. But for all the differences in their accounts, there was one constant in every telling: Jesus. No matter how they described the special events of the day, Jesus was the one who made it all happen!

When you hear believers speak of how their lives were changed, of how they quit some sinful practice, or of how they began treating someone differently or started using their time and money to help others, their stories reflect such different circumstances and experiences, as you would expect. But for all of the differences, their stories share one thing in common: Jesus.

No matter how long or how much, no matter how many or how often, the details of our stories always arrive at **Jesus**.

> "An evil and adulterous generation seeks for a sign, but no sign will be given to it except the sign of Jonah."
> Matthew 16:1-4 (Mark 8:11-12)

JUNE 4

Jesus had a way of drawing the fire of both the primary religious parties of the Jews. As a rule, the Pharisees and Sadducees were two groups at odds with one another. But they were unanimous in their opposition to Jesus.

So, these religious leaders came to Jesus asking for a sign. But not just any sign—a sign from heaven. Perhaps, they pretended that they were willing to be satisfied and convinced if he would just provide such a sign. But Jesus knew they were deceitful men. After all, he had performed many miracles, yet they refused to believe. In fact, they had claimed that his work was by the power of the devil!

There is an old adage: "Red sky at night, sailor's delight. Red sky in morning, sailor's warning." Red sky at night means good weather is coming. Red sky in the morning means foul weather is coming. These are common rules drawn from observation and experience.

Jesus said, "You are pretty good at figuring the weather by reading the signs. But when it comes to reading the signs of God, you are blind."

Such blindness is still with us! It is sad that we are so good at understanding the way our world works—in anatomy or biology — in engineering — in computers and technology — but are blind to the signs of God! Research and subsequent discoveries ought to bring clearer vision about the fantastic God who made this world. Unfortunately, those discoveries are often used to argue how wonderful man is!

These religious fellows were looking at and talking with God in flesh. Yet, they could not see the truth. So, he left them scratching their heads and wondering how Jonah figured into all this.

Jesus knew the intent of their hearts. So, he withdrew from them. But you must know that he walked away with a heavy heart. They could read the signs in the sky but they could not read the signs of God as revealed in His Son, **Jesus**.

Then they understood that he did not tell them to beware of the leaven of bread, but of the teaching of the Pharisees and Sadducees.
Matthew 16:5-12 (Mark 8:13-21)

JUNE 5

Jesus issued warnings to his disciples for the same reasons that we warn others: we believe they are in danger and we want them to be safe. Admittedly, the Pharisees and Sadducees did not appear to be dangerous, but Jesus knew their teachings were misleading. So, Jesus put his disciples on alert.

The disciples did not understand at first. But after Jesus revisited the past events and focused their attention on what really mattered, they caught on. "Be on guard against the teaching of the Pharisees and Sadducees."

Their doctrine contained a mixture of God's truths and man's traditions. The result was error in beliefs and corruption in practices. Jesus knew that mixing a bit of truth with error could deceive even well-intentioned souls.

We live in confusing and disturbing times. Many argue that what we believe is not so important. Further, they maintain that everyone is right in their personal views and everyone has his/her own truth, so we simply need to allow for many different expressions of truth. This view runs counter to the Bible's warnings against false teaching and Scripture's encouragements to believe and practice what is true.

Evidently, Jesus thought it made a difference what a person hears and accepts as true. While Jesus taught that everyone was free to decide for themselves what they would believe, he emphasized that they were not free to simply call anything truth.

But why did this matter to Jesus? Why was it important to believe the truth? Jesus knew that, if his disciples believed these men, they would soon be acting like these men.

What we believe about marriage shows up in the relationship. What we believe about worship shows up in our worship. What we believe about honesty shows up in the way we conduct ourselves in even the smallest details of life. It does matter what we believe!

What you believe is important because it determines how you live. Because he came to show you and tell you the truths of God and, thus, to effect an eternal change in your life, what you believe is important to **Jesus**.

Then Jesus laid his hands on his eyes again; and he opened his eyes, his sight was restored, and he saw everything clearly.

Mark 8:22-26

JUNE 6

Jesus always acted with purpose and plan. Miracles were no exception. Whether feeding thousands with a few loaves and fish or walking on the water to his disciples, Jesus knew what he was doing and why. He never acted with uncertainty or in confusion, and he never found himself powerless to accomplish what he needed to do.

The blind man must have had some good friends who truly loved him. Some folks brought the blind man to Jesus and begged Jesus to touch him and heal him. That is evidence of much love and faith!

Previously, the people of Bethsaida had not been impressed with Jesus or his disciples. Although privileged to see many of Jesus' miracles in that vicinity, they refused to believe. Perhaps, this is the reason Jesus led the blind man out of the village to a more private place.

What we do know is that Jesus put his hands on the man's eyes a second time and he could see clearly. What joy must have filled his soul! How excited he must have been as he thought of all the people with whom he would love to share such wonderful news! But Jesus sent him home and told him not to return to the village. Why? Only Jesus really knows the answer to that question.

Some stories about Jesus seem to generate more questions than answers. This is one of them. Who are the friends of this blind man? What do they believe about Jesus? What did the blind man know about Jesus? Why did Jesus take him outside the village? Why did Jesus spit on the man's eyes? Why didn't the man have clear vision immediately? Was Jesus affected by the man's faith? And why did Jesus tell him not to go into the village?

There are so many questions to consider. But isn't it amazing how we can get bogged down in all the questions and miss the most important one: Who is this guy that can make a blind man see? This was Jesus' purpose and plan: to make us ask the question, "Who is this **Jesus**?"

He said to them, "But who do you say that I am?"
Simon Peter replied, "You are the Christ, the Son of the living God."
Matthew 16:13-16 (Mark 8:27-29; Luke 9:18-20)

JUNE 7

Jesus and his disciples ventured into the region of Caesarea Philippi, an area about 25 miles northeast of the Sea of Galilee. Although the stay was temporary, this area would provide Jesus with more private time with the disciples.

By this time in his ministry there were signs that the tide was turning against him. He had been a disappointment to many who had expected more from him. Their hopes for some kind of national movement, maybe even a revolt against Roman rule, had simply not happened. Gradually, they were sensing that this was not Jesus' plan at all.

Of course, there had been critics from the beginning. Now, they were secretly plotting his death.

In the meantime, rumors were flying. Some compared him to great men in Israel's history. Others thought he was one of those great men returned to life!

Jesus had two questions for his disciples. Question one: "Who do people say the Son of Man is?" Their reply placed Jesus among the famous in Jewish history: John the Baptist, Elijah, and Jeremiah.

Question two: "Now that's what everyone else thinks. What do you think? Who do you say I am?"

"You are the Christ, the Son of the living God." While we thrill to the courageous truth uttered by Peter, it would be interesting to know what answer would have been given by some of the others, like John or Thomas, Matthew or Judas.

Peter's answer has not satisfied everyone. Critics and skeptics continue to write books arguing that Jesus was no more than a social or political reformer, no more than a holy man or sage, or even a magician or con man. Such views share one thing in common: Jesus was only a man. If so, Peter was mistaken.

"What do you think?" It is one of those questions that requires an answer. Believe him or not. Follow him or don't. But everyone must answer the question.

And when we have answered it, we decide not only the way we will live but also the way we will die. Everything rests on the question of **Jesus**.

> "And I tell you, you are Peter, and on this rock I will build my church, and the gates of hell shall not prevail against it."
> Matthew 16:17-20 (Mark 8:30; Luke 9:21)

JUNE 8

Jesus said he was going to build his church. What must his disciples have been thinking? What was a church? And when did he plan to start construction? What would it look like and how big would it be? How much would something like that cost and where would the funds come from? And most important of all: what was it going to do?

'Church' has been around for a long, long time. Unlike the disciples, we have never known a day without church. Churches have been on our street corners and highways for as long as we can remember. Many of us have been 'going to church' since birth. We can't imagine life without church!

But on this day Jesus was promising something to his disciples which was not only beyond their vision, it was also beyond their understanding. In time, they would become the very building blocks for what Jesus had in mind. For now, they had to be content with just wondering.

However, there were two things in his words that they could not miss. First, this church was built on one incredible but undeniable truth: Jesus Christ is the Son of God! The rock upon which this church would rest was the truth spoken by Peter. From the moment these men went forth declaring this truth churches began to form. And wherever churches formed were people whose lives reflected their deep faith in this truth. The deity of Jesus and the church are inseparably linked. Jesus said so.

A second yet equally important truth is the power of this church he would build. Not even the gates of Hades will prevail against it! Jesus wasn't simply talking about longevity but about power. The power of the church lay not in forts and armor, generals or soldiers but in the Spirit that would possess those who put their faith in Jesus.

Church has never been important because of what we think about her. The church is important because she belongs to **Jesus**.

Then Jesus told his disciples, "If anyone would come after me, let him deny himself and take up his cross and follow me."
Matthew 16:21-28 (Mark 8:31-9:1; Luke 9:22-27)

JUNE 9

Jesus spoke the most incredible words. In a world of conflict and rivalry, Jesus said the way to get ahead is to put others first. In a world of greed, Jesus said the way to gain all is to give up everything. In a world that insists on independence and rights, Jesus said the way to freedom is to make yourself a slave. In a world of selfishness, Jesus said the way to live is to die. In a world that values only winning, Jesus said the way to win is to surrender.

Surrender is synonymous with defeat. Losers may surrender. Winners never do. The British surrendered to the colonies; Japan surrendered to the Allies. When surrender occurs, everyone knows who gained and who lost. Most would say that surrender is never a goal.

Surrender is synonymous with defeat. Losers may surrender. Winners never do. The British surrendered to the colonies; Japan surrendered to the Allies. When surrender occurs, everyone knows who gained and who lost. Most would say that surrender is never a goal.

Jesus is on his way to Jerusalem to die. The cross is on his mind...and he wants to talk about it. He wants it to be on the minds of his disciples.

"If any would...he must...." Few of us like being told what to do. The word "must" is not a popular word. It immediately creates within us a desire to express some level of defiance. We like options, choices, and variety. But Jesus says that surrender is the imperative of our discipleship. If you won't surrender, you won't be a disciple.

Jesus' words are particularly remarkable because they are an invitation...an invitation to follow. But who would issue such an invitation? Listen to him! Deny yourself. Carry a cross. Not exactly our idea of an invitation to great things. "Go with me to surrender."

The goal of surrender is to be conformed to the image of Christ. Sadly, too many of us want him to save us but we don't want him to Lord us. We don't want to surrender. The irony of this surrender is that it ends in victory, not defeat.

Discipleship begins with this powerful, incredible love bond between the Savior and sinner. It is a relationship forged because Jesus willingly carried a cross for us. Jesus surrendered to the will of the Father and we surrender to **Jesus**.

> He was still speaking when, behold, a bright cloud overshadowed them, and a voice from the cloud said, "This is my beloved Son, with whom I am well pleased; listen to him."
>
> Matthew 17:1-13 (Mark 9:2-13; Luke 9:28-36)

JUNE 10

Jesus seemed to find a special connection with three of his disciples; at least, they seemed to have shared several experiences with him when the other disciples were not included. This day, Peter, James and John were chosen to accompany Jesus to a high mountain.

Jesus was there to pray. He often sought such secluded spots so that he might pray. But as he was praying, his appearance changed. His faced turned brilliant as the sun and his clothing as white as pure brilliant light. To make his point, Mark adds that his clothes were whiter than anyone could actually bleach them!

And if this was not incredible enough, suddenly two men, Moses and Elijah, "appeared in glorious splendor." One a lawgiver, the other a prophet, talked with Jesus. And what did they talk about? Luke said, "they spoke about his departure." Just imagine! Jesus talking with Moses and Elijah about his earthly journey and the cross that lay ahead! Perhaps, they offered him words of comfort and encouraged him to be faithful in the Father's will.

As so often happened, Peter was the first to speak. As usual, he would have done better to have said nothing. He wasn't trying to be irreverent by his suggestion. Peter loved Jesus and he was willing to do anything for him. But, after all, what did Moses and Elijah need with a tent?

Now, for only the second time, the silence of heaven was broken by a divine voice declaring the Father's pleasure in His Son. The Father loved His Son! The voice from the cloud said, "Listen to him!"

Peter, James and John may have replayed this day numerous times in later years. They may have talked about the way Jesus looked, or actually seeing Moses and Elijah, or Peter making a foolish suggestion. But most likely, they talked about that moment they heard God Almighty say, "Listen to **Jesus**!"

And Jesus said to him, "If you can'! All things are possible for one who believes."

Immediately the father of the child cried out and said, "I believe; help my unbelief!"

                              Mark 9:14-29 (Matthew 17:14-20; Luke 9:37-43a)

JUNE 11

Jesus specifically gave his disciples authority over demons. They had even had some success. But, for some reason, their best efforts failed to help in this situation.

Obviously, the behavior was extreme–robbed of speech, thrown to the ground, foamed at the mouth, gnashed his teeth, became rigid and thrown into fire and water. But, in a sense, isn't it the same old story? If anything of the devil is in your life, suffering follows. The devil just makes life miserable.

The father was desperate and he asked the disciples for help. They tried. They wanted to help. But they could not. And to make matters worse, the teachers of the law were present. What an embarrassing time to fail!

In his desperation, the father made his appeal to Jesus, ".... if you can do anything, have compassion on us and help us." "'If you can'?" said Jesus. "Everything is possible for him who believes." Immediately the boy's father exclaimed, "I do believe; help me overcome my unbelief!"

What honesty! "I believe! But it may not be enough! I want to believe more!"

Did you ever notice that it is only after a time of questioning and doubting, only after a time of uncertainty and pain that we grow in our faith. With no answers in hand and maybe fear in our hearts we go to searching and reading, praying and reflecting. Amazingly, what grows is our trust in the Lord, even when we can't see an answer or make sense of what's happening. It is in our pain and grief that we discover again His amazing love and that only He can help us. Only later do we realize that without that valley our faith would not have grown so.

The demon is cast out, never to return. The son is saved and the father is grateful and joyful beyond words. And the disciples have learned something about themselves. All that was needed was **Jesus**.

> "However, not to give offense to them, go to the sea and cast a hook and take the first fish that comes up, and when you open its mouth you will find a shekel. Take that and give it to them for me and for yourself."
>
> Matthew 17:22-27 (Mark 9:30-32; Luke 9:43b-45)

JUNE 12

Jesus told his disciples of his coming death. Afraid of looking foolish or fearful of facing the reality of what his words might mean for them, they chose to be silent rather than ask for help. We can understand their reluctance to speak.

Shortly after Jesus and His disciples arrived at Capernaum, Peter received a visit from the collectors of the temple tax. While there is debate as to whether this tax was voluntary or obligatory in Jesus' day, it seems to have been taken seriously by some, including Jesus. The revenue from the tax was used to pay for the many supplies used in the temple and for the many people who worked in the temple. Matthew, being a tax collector himself, was perhaps more likely to be interested in this subject and perhaps that explains why he is the only one of the Gospel writers to tell us this fish story.

Peter wanted to defend Jesus to his critics. At the same time, he felt awkward raising the matter to Jesus. Jesus took care of that. Rather than claim exemption from the tax since his Father owned everything, including the temple, Jesus chose instead to accept that which was part of our lot, to identify with us in every way.

If Jesus had refused to pay the tax on any grounds, he would have opened the door to his critics to charge him with being unfaithful to the Jewish people, a rebel to the traditions of the elders, and disrespectful to the authorities. Jesus gave his critics no opportunity by paying the tax for himself and Peter.

"Peter, go catch a fish!" What a wonderful way to come up with your tax money: fishing! And what excitement and anticipation must have filled Peter when he hauled in that first fish. And the coin in the fish! Peter would not soon forget this tax year!

Humility – the quality more important than any right. We would expect nothing less from **Jesus**.

> "Whoever humbles himself like this child is the greatest in the kingdom of heaven."
>
> Matthew 18:1-6 (Mark 9:33-37,42; Luke 9:46-48)

JUNE 13

Jesus walks ahead of them in silence. In the meantime, his straggling disciples push and shove, trying to establish the order of the processional behind him. The disciples still have visions of grandeur and they do not fantasize about becoming servants. So, they begin to argue with each other about who would be the greatest.

It isn't a scene too difficult to imagine. Peter probably spoke first and argued for his being one of the first disciples, walking on the water, and making the great confession. Impressive resume, he would argue. But with that, each one could chime in and recite their accomplishments or special connections to Jesus. This was not the only time they fussed about who was the best and it would not be the last (Luke 22:24).

But did you notice the disciples' reaction when Jesus asked, "What were you arguing about on the road?" They were ashamed and embarrassed that Jesus had caught them fighting for position and greatness. They knew they were wrong. So, "they kept quiet."

How do we measure greatness? Is it how long we live, how famous we become, or how rich we are at retirement? Our world defines greatness in terms of power, money, intellectual brilliance, athletic ability, and good looks. But Jesus defines greatness in an entirely different way. It is no surprise that his words are not exactly what we want to hear.

"If anyone wants to be first, he must be the very last, and the servant of all."

While they all stood around scratching their heads, trying to figure out his words, Jesus scooped up a toddler and tenderly held the child in His arms. He was saying that the greatest person is the one who serves others the way an adult serves a child. You have to receive one of these little ones to be big with God.

Greatness doesn't reside at the top of the ladder but at the bottom, not at the front of the line but at the back. Who then is the greatest? The person who chooses to be a servant of others is the greatest in the kingdom of **Jesus**.

John answered, "Master, we saw someone casting out demons in your name, and we tried to stop him, because he does not follow with us." But Jesus said to him, "Do not stop him, for the one who is not against you is for you."

Luke 9:49-50 (Mark 9:38-41)

JUNE 14

Jesus came among us to invite everyone to come join the family of God. No one who desired entrance would be excluded. However, not everyone caught the idea.

In your childhood, did you and your friends ever form a club? Did you have any rules, such as "no boys allowed" or "no girls allowed"? Did you have any secret signals or code words? One of the great things about all that was the feeling that you were a part of something and you felt special. After all, everyone did not get to be in on this.

Jesus' disciples had been their own little club now for some time. They felt pretty special. They felt possessive of Jesus and proud of their special relationship with the man who was the talk of the land. Perhaps, that's the reason for John's words. Some unauthorized person was moving in on their territory!

John was upset because this unnamed individual was acting in Jesus' name. He did not say the man was guilty of any wrong or that he was teaching anything false. John did say: "He is not one of us." That was the rub: he is not in our club!

This certainly has a modern sound to it. Church jealousy shows itself when we dismiss the good others do because they are not in our group. In other words, we are not going to give them full credit because they are not in the right camp—ours!

This story does not mean that you accept people who do good regardless of what else they might believe and practice. Nor does this story mean that you pretend that differences do not matter. However, this story does emphasize the danger of failing to recognize and appreciate the good work of other believers.

Being thankful for all the good you see doesn't mean you are blind to the imperfections of people. However, it does mean that your heart rejoices at every sign of **Jesus**.

> "And if your hand or your foot causes you to sin, cut it off and throw it away. It is better for you to enter life crippled or lame than with two hands or two feet to be thrown into the eternal fire."
>
> Matthew 18:7-14 (Mark 9:43-50)

JUNE 15

Jesus just wants us to know the truth, to know what we are up against, to know how very, very serious sin really is. His words sound extreme, and they are! His tone is that of a passionate man who can see it no other way!

" Cut it off and cast it aside!" Get rid of it! It's deadly! Jesus' words are a call to decisive action! Anything that would cause us to sin is to be cut off!

Sadly, the human condition is that we do not always believe it. When viewed in the modern context of an enlightened and technological age, his words sound like an overheated alarmist out of touch with the new, real world.

Make no mistake: his message is extreme, but so is our condition. He does not suggest compromise or settlement, truce or reprieve.

Nothing is more important than holiness. Not an eye or a hand. Not a relative or a friend. Not a job or a career. Not a recreation or a vacation. Not a house or a car or a boat. Not social standing or position. Not health or life. Nothing!

To Jesus, there is an inseparable link between sin and hell. Our refusal to be rid of the one makes it impossible to be rid of the other. That is how terrible sin is.

Sin is terrible. The war is real. And the victory cannot be gained without sacrifice and pain. But you are not alone. In fact, no one wants your salvation more than the Father. Like a tireless Shepherd pursuing a lost sheep, He never quits where you are concerned. And no matter what you must cut off or gouge out to be faithful to Him, He promises that you will never regret it.

When God dealt with our greatest problem, sin, it meant pain to His heart, and pain to His Son. But from that pain came the best news you have ever heard. The victory is ours through our Lord **Jesus**.

"If your brother sins against you, go and tell him his fault, between you and him alone. If he listens to you, you have gained your brother."
Matthew 18:15-20

JUNE 16

Jesus' proposes something that is not easy. Most of us do not like being the bad guy, especially with people we love. Also, if we are sincere and honest, we realize that we are not without sin ourselves. So, we feel uncomfortable speaking to someone about their sins. Furthermore, we are often afraid of the other person's reaction.

So why do this? Because sin is that serious and people are that important.

The action of becoming involved in another person's life to the extent of confronting them, even lovingly, is not popular today. Minding your own business is the prominent view of our time. And in the event that you believe someone is doing wrong, don't judge them but be tolerant. After all, we are told, what's right for you may not be what's right for them.

Such a philosophy runs counter to Jesus in every way. Jesus charging into the temple area and overturning tables and driving out money-changers and animals is hardly the picture of man minding his own business. Jesus confronting the Pharisees and calling them snakes and whited tombs is hardly the picture of a man who believed they had their truth and he had his.

When we go, we go to the person in private. No one wants to be confronted about their shortcomings in front of others. Both our attitude and words should affirm the relationship.

Sadly, in spite of your best efforts, the response may not be what you'd hoped. Then, take one or two witnesses with you. The purpose of taking witnesses is not to gang up on someone. So, why? To confirm what was said and done, and because sin is that serious and people are that important.

Finally, in the absence of any sign of penitence, the matter should be taken to the church family. While this action is exceedingly difficult for everyone involved, people are that important.

Our actions and words reflect our belief that sin is a serious matter and that this person is worth our every effort. In this we are like **Jesus**.

Then Peter came up and said to him, "Lord, how often will my brother sin against me, and I forgive him? As many as seven times?"

Matthew 18:21-35

JUNE 17

Jesus came from heaven to teach and to show us all we needed to know about living for God. Some things made sense; some did not. Forgiveness was among the latter.

The Jewish rabbis taught that a man was to be forgiven three times, no more. Perhaps, Peter thought he was being generous in suggesting seven times. Many of us feel like we are benevolent if we give someone a second chance. We are grateful God did not attach a number limit to His forgiveness.

The situation was hopeless. The debt was overwhelming. The man, deserving whatever the king decided, fell to his knees and begged for mercy, and promised to pay all back. The king knew that was not possible. So, the king cancelled the debt and took the loss himself.

But what had been so freely received was not freely given. Hearing of this despicable behavior, the master called the fellow back. "Where was your mercy?" he asked the servant. Then, the unmerciful servant was cast into prison.

Then, Jesus said, "This is how my heavenly Father will treat each of you unless you forgive your brother from your heart."

If we are honest, we can do nothing but fall to our knees and beg for mercy. God extends to us His grace in spite of all we have said and done. We are free of the debt by the blood of Jesus. We do not deserve this but God loves us. What we have freely received, we freely give.

Contrary to what many believe, forgiveness is not a weakness but a sign of true inner strength. Forgiveness doesn't depend upon who hurt us, what they did, or whether or not they are sorry for their actions. Forgiveness is not something we just do for others; it is what we do for ourselves and for the God who forgives us.

Whatever the wounds and however they have come, healing is found in forgiveness. We forgive because we have been forgiven. For that, we thank **Jesus**.

We forgive because we have been forgiven. For that, we thank **Jesus**.

**As they were going along the road, someone said to him, "I will follow you wherever you go."
And Jesus said to him, "Foxes have holes, and birds of the air have nests, but the Son of Man has nowhere to lay his head."**
                                            Luke 9:57-62 (Matthew 8:19-22)

JUNE 18

Jesus was not your typical recruiter. He often sounded more like a man dissuading others from following. Actually, Jesus just wanted people to understand what they were getting into if they did follow.

Three men engaged Jesus in conversation. They were all potential followers. The first man said, "I will follow you wherever you go." That is a pretty bold statement! Not many of us would say that. At the very least, we would want a little information before we just embarked to wherever.

What a great opportunity for Jesus to welcome someone voicing such confidence! But Jesus told this potential recruit that he did not travel by chariot or stay in the finest inns. This was no comfortable ministry.

To another man Jesus said, "Follow me." But the man felt it necessary to take care of family matters first. Specifically, the man wanted to bury his father. Jesus' reply seems a bit shocking. Doesn't the man's request seem reasonable?

The third recruit made a most reasonable request. "I will follow you, Lord; but first let me go back and say good-by to my family." Now, what could be wrong with that?

Jesus' words are strong, especially when you consider that the three individuals are potential followers expressing future interest in following. But that's the problem: future interest. There is danger in delay.

How many have said—"I'll follow Jesus later. Now I need to focus on my education, or my career, or my family." The mistake is to equate all of these with the invitation of Jesus, to act as if discipleship is no more important than the various interests of life. It is this attitude which makes one unfit for the kingdom. If the Lord is calling you to follow Him, his call comes first. Whatever is slowing your decision, whatever is getting in the way, whatever is consuming your interest, leave it behind so you can follow **Jesus**.

For not even his brothers believed in him.

John 7:2-10

JUNE 19

Jesus, along with his disciples, did set out for Jerusalem, but he did so in secret. What emotions must have filled him as he bade farewell to the land of his youth and the base of his ministry. But the "right time" was almost here and Jerusalem was the place to be.

Jesus' situation with his brothers and sisters can only be imagined since the Scriptures provide very little detail. Surely, Jesus' heart ached over the fact that those who knew him so well were unbelievers. Perhaps, it was the nearness that blinded them.

James, Joseph, Simon and Judas, along with sisters that are not named, were the children of Joseph and Mary. Because of a desire by some Christians in later centuries to venerate Mary as a perpetual virgin, numerous theories developed to explain these sons and daughters. One popular notion was that these children were Joseph's by a former marriage. Another explanation was that these brothers and sisters were actually cousins. But in spite of such attempts, early Christian writers wrote in convincing language that these were the children of Mary and Joseph and, thus, the half brothers and sisters of Jesus.

While no explanation is offered for why his siblings did not believe in him, a partial answer may lie in their sarcasm. They spoke of his disciples who might see his miracles and appealed to his natural desire to show such works to everyone. Whether they denied the validity of his miracles or rejected the claims that accompanied them, his miracles may have been the point of greatest tension.

Sarcasm or not, his brothers had their own ideas about what Jesus should be and do. We are prone to the same. Uncertain of how effective his way might be or simply wanting things our way, we attempt to set the agenda for Jesus. We want him to work on our schedule and in a way that makes sense to us. Like the brothers, we tend to prefer leading rather than following.

The brothers encouraged Jesus to seize the festive moment in Jerusalem and make himself known. However, walking in step with the Father's will was the only plan of **Jesus**.

And when his disciples James and John saw it, they said, "Lord, do you want us to tell fire to come down from heaven and consume them?" But he turned and rebuked them. And they went on to another village.
Luke 9:51-56

JUNE 20

Jesus turned his face toward Jerusalem one last time. The disciples might be uncertain of what lay ahead, but Jesus was not. It was for this that he had come into the world.

Traveling through Samaria would have enabled him to make up any time lost by the delay in departure. Also, it would be easier to maintain secrecy since most Jews would travel around Samaria rather than through it.

Some of the disciples were sent ahead to find lodging but found an unwelcome response instead. Whether these Samaritans were rejecting Jesus specifically or this group of Jews going to Jerusalem, James and John believed that an angry response was justified. They wanted Jesus to 'zap' these inhospitable people. Instead, Jesus rebuked the two disciples.

Jesus "set his face to go to Jerusalem." Luke's words reflect the determination of Jesus to see this through no matter the cost. And the cost would be great.

Jesus went knowing what awaited him. He set his face to the suffering ahead because of his love for us and his desire to do the will of the Father.

Jesus went knowing that he was our only hope and that there was no 'Plan B.' This was **the plan**! He was the plan!

Jesus went knowing that angels could deliver him but only he could save us.

Jesus set his face toward Jerusalem with the full knowledge that his labor and death for us would not be in vain. However defiant our attitude, however shameful we treated him, his sacrifice would not be ineffectual.

Jesus went knowing the way it would all play out, knowing that he was made to be sin for us. He knew, but still he went.

Jesus went, not because he had to, but because he wanted to. His love compelled him to take each step toward Jerusalem just as it would compel him to stretch out his hands for the nails at Golgotha.

He was thinking of you. You were etched in the resolute face of **Jesus**.

So Jesus answered them, "My teaching is not mine, but his who sent me."
John 7:11-20

JUNE 21

Jesus had become front-page news. Jerusalem was buzzing with rumors about him. Not all of the talk was complimentary, but he was on everyone's lips. Opinions were divided.

When Jesus arrived in Jerusalem, he began teaching. But his critics could not understand how he possessed such learning without the proper education. After all, he did not go to their schools and he was not taught by their teachers. They did not understand the nature or motive of his teaching.

There was a lot of confusion and division about Jesus. But their questions were certainly genuine: Is this man for real? Is this guy a fake Messiah, fooling even the best religious scholars? Is it possible he was groomed by his parents for this or was he a part of some well-planned conspiracy to become the long-promised king that Israel had been looking for? They had hoped for so long and they wanted to know if he was the real thing.

What did Jesus tell them? First, listen to what I say. "My teaching is not my own but it comes from the one who sent me." To this he added, the one sent "is a man of truth and in him there is no falsehood." If people would only listen and think, Jesus said.

Second, apply my words and find out for yourself. "If anyone wills to do God's will, he will know whether the teaching is from God or whether I am speaking on my own authority." Practice what he says and you will know he speaks the truth!

Think about it. Is this not the best way to test the claims of Jesus? There is no higher authority; there is no court of appeals or supreme court. No lab experiment, national survey, or voter support can help us here. Only by submitting in complete willingness is there an opportunity to evaluate Jesus and the words he has spoken. He welcomes this because he knows what we will discover when we trust him.

The words and ways of Jesus are not subject to the usual methods of evaluation. But they can be tested. Try his words. Practice the ways of **Jesus**.

"You know me, and you know where I come from? But I have not come of my own accord. He who sent me is true, and him you do not know."

John 7:21-31

JUNE 22

Jesus was in Jerusalem for the Feast of Tabernacles, a joyous festival that ran for seven days. It was a time when the people gathered to thank God for their material blessings.

Among this throng Jesus' presence only stirred questions and accusations. While most seemed uncertain what to make of him, some defended him as a good man against the critics who claimed that he was demon-possessed.

Having already defended himself by appealing to the truthfulness of his words, Jesus then argued for his actions. "I did one miracle, and you are all astonished. But let a man be made whole on the Sabbath and you do not see beneath the surface. You are so caught up in your rules that you cannot see the truth. You are so fastened to law that you cannot see grace."

It is true today. Too often, we can't seem to get to Jesus for the laws that get in the way. Captivated by the external, the superficial, we cannot see the deeper meanings of life. Thus, we interpret faithfulness only in terms of keeping the accepted rules. It is easier that way and it makes sense to us.

Some did put their faith in him because of the signs. But many did not. In their minds, they knew all about Jesus. Evidently, there was a kind of legend surrounding the Messiah. No one would know where he came from and he would suddenly appear. But there was no seeming mystery to this man. We all know about him, they said.

Isn't it incredible that God walked among us and we did not recognize the words as being His? Isn't it astounding that God walked among us and we did not recognize His extraordinary ways? For some reason we thought we were capable of determining what God would say and how God would act. But not knowing the Father, neither did we recognize His Son.

The greatest mystery in our lives is why God would become flesh, suffer and die for people who only meant to do Him harm. That is the mystery that is **Jesus.**

**Jesus then said, "I will be with you a little longer, and then I am going to him who sent me.
You will seek me and you will not find me. Where I am you cannot come."**
John 7:32-36

JUNE 23

Jesus was on everyone's lips. People were sharing what they knew about him. Everyone had a story to tell, an opinion to offer. Had there been a Jerusalem newspaper, his presence in the city would have been front-page news. No doubt, the editorial section would have carried an article or two and the 'letters to the editor' section would have been filled with people offering all kinds of opinions on the man.

When Jesus stepped out of the Judean desert to begin his ministry the Jews were eager to put their hope in a Messiah. As the prophets had foretold, so they envisioned a new and brighter day dawning for the Jewish people. Maybe Jesus was the man to lead them!

But certain things bothered them. For one, he did not look like a Messiah. He was rather ordinary. His birthplace was a stable in an insignificant place called Bethlehem. His father was a carpenter by trade. By all appearances the family was simply another peasant family in Palestine.

Also, there was his ministry. For approximately three years he traveled the land, preaching his message of repentance and a coming kingdom. His ministry was marked by miracles, huge crowds, sermons, and vicious critics. Some followed him, believing he was God's anointed one, while others dismissed him as a pretender and a troublemaker. He said virtually nothing about the Jews overthrowing the Romans and he talked more about loving your enemies than conquering them.

His words could be reassuring and hopeful, but sometimes they only created more questions about what was to come. Sometimes, his statements only created more questions about him. This was one of those times.

Why was he talking about leaving? Why couldn't we find him? In fact, where could he go that we couldn't find him? What sense did any of this make?

Was Jesus trying to create confusion? Was he intentionally tying to be mysterious? Perhaps. But he did want people to think. And people were thinking. After all, the name on everyone's lips was **Jesus.**

On the last day of the feast, the great day, Jesus stood up and cried out, "If anyone thirsts, let him come to me and drink.
Whoever believes in me, as the Scripture has said, 'Out of his heart will flow rivers of living water.'"

John 7:37-44

JUNE 24

Jesus seemed to create divided opinions wherever he went. Whether delivering a sermon, performing a miracle, or simply choosing to go home with someone, Jesus generated followers and critics. Nothing much has changed since that first century. Today, he remains one of history's most controversial people.

The Feast was in its final day when Jesus extended an invitation to the thirsty. "Come to me and drink," he said. Trust in him would forever change a person's life and bring a satisfaction unlike anything else. That was his promise.

In a land and time where getting water was far more difficult than now, the imagery would have struck a responsive chord. Humanity was settled around the primary bodies of water for a reason.

Jesus wasn't suggesting that some people are not thirsty. Everyone is thirsty. Unfortunately, our search for satisfaction often takes us in wrong directions. That's why we chase pleasures and drink from different wells. We are thirsty and are looking for something that will satisfy.

But Jesus was announcing that if anyone is thirsty for God, "let him come to me and drink." As Jesus was the bread from God that fills us, so he was the water from God that satisfies us.

Faith is required. "Whoever believes in me..." And the gift for that trust is the Spirit of God. What an incredible promise!

But then, as now, people debated whether he was really able to keep that promise. While some allowed that he might be a prophet, and others believed that he was the Christ, some were very skeptical. He just didn't look the part. So, the people were divided over him.

But what if he is the Christ? What if the Pharisees had it all wrong? What if the promise is real? What if Jesus is all you will ever need?

Knowing you are thirsty is easy. Knowing where to drink can be more difficult. There are many invitations but the only one who satisfies is **Jesus**.

> The officers then came to the chief priests and Pharisees, who said to them, "Why did you not bring him?"
> The officers answered, "No one ever spoke like this man!"
>
> John 7:45-53

JUNE 25

Jesus' time had not yet come. The temple guards returned empty-handed.

When questioned about their failure to accomplish their mission, they explained, "No one ever spoke the way this man does." While they may have been impressed with his oratorical skill, it was likely they were also amazed by his teaching.

As might be expected, the Pharisees were very perturbed. After accusing the guards of being easily deceived simpletons, these Pharisees were quick to point out that they were too smart to be taken in by Jesus. The people were duped because they were ignorant of the law and under a curse!

Pride can be a terrible thing. It tends to close our eyes to reality and our ears to what we need to hear. Instead of looking to God for direction, we trust our own abilities. Instead of respecting the thoughts and feelings of others, we regard others as inferior and unworthy. Our prideful heart neither seeks nor welcomes truth if it clashes with our own ideas.

But there was one voice of reason among them. Nicodemus spoke up. Although we may be uncertain as to his level of faith in Jesus at this point, at least he continues to be open to hearing the man. Having visited Jesus at night and listened to the Teacher then, Nicodemus argues for the decent and fair thing: letting the man be heard before he is condemned. But pride will not hear of it!

Perhaps, the answer to courage is not so much a matter of what we have come to fear as it is a matter of what we no longer possess. In the beginning we were filled with Jesus and could not but speak of what we had seen and heard. Like a new bride full of love or a new father filled with joy, being quiet was impossible! What was inside of us had to get out! But isn't that the way it always is: what fills your heart is what comes out? So, fill your heart with **Jesus**.

Jesus stood up and said to her, "Woman, where are they? Has no one condemned you?"
She said, "No one, Lord." And Jesus said, "Neither do I condemn you; go, and from now on sin no more."

John 8:1-11

JUNE 26

Jesus spent the night at the Mount of Olives.

At dawn he was in the temple courts teaching folks about the Father and the kingdom. It was while he was sharing his message that he was interrupted by a noisy group shoving their way through the crowd.

The Pharisees had caught a woman in the act of adultery. This was a serious crime punishable by death. The Law of Moses said so. But before they took any action, they wanted to know what Jesus would do. Of course, they were not really looking for truth or searching for answers.

But in this tense moment, with her fate in the balance, Jesus did the unexpected: he bent down and began writing on the ground with his finger. The silence must have been deafening. All craned their necks to catch a glimpse of what he was writing.

Then Jesus said, "Stone her." But he added: "But let those who throw stones be free of sin." Judge her, but judge yourself first. In just minutes they were all gone.

Jesus did not minimize the sin, nor did he try to cover it up. But he did help her to catch a glimpse of heaven's grace. He was as eager to save her as these fellows were to stone her.

His words gave her hope. He offered her a new beginning. He knew that she had a future as well as a past. He saw her in terms of what she could become rather than just what she was right then.

Hopefully, in months and years to come she would remember the day when those who kicked in her door actually introduced her to the man who changed her life. Perhaps, she would think of how close she had come to death at the hands of so many angry men only to be rescued by just one man whose heart was full of love. And maybe when she would share her story with others, she would recall how no one had ever treated her like **Jesus**.

> "I am the light of the world. Whoever follows me will not walk in darkness, but will have the light of life."
>
> John 8:12

JUNE 27

Jesus cannot be adequately described by any single metaphor. But each one helps us understand a little bit more about him.

It is hard for us to imagine a world without light. Unlike those who heard Jesus, we are accustomed to merely flipping a switch. How differently we might see his words if we lived in a world of candles and campfires.

But regardless of our time, we all know about darkness. We know about being lost and needing direction, we know about a broken heart and deep sadness, we know about making bad decisions and doing evil things. We know about being in darkness!

We live in a world that has two very distinct spiritual spheres. Each is quite the antithesis of the other. Each sphere has its own nature and ways. Each sphere possesses its own destiny; one leads to death and one leads to life. One is of the devil; the other is of God. So different are these two spheres that God called one darkness and the other light.

Scripture is consistent. Good can have no fellowship with evil. Truth cannot be a companion of error. Light and darkness can never be friends.

Perhaps, our struggle with the darkness is the result of our failure to see it for what it is. After all, we like the darkness if our deeds are evil. Maybe the fact that the darkness is sometimes our friend deludes us into believing that it really isn't so bad.

Jesus had a different view. He came so that we would no longer be confused about our purpose or uncertain as to the meaning of life. He came so that even in the midst of sadness and heartbreak we could feel hopeful. He came so that even though the darkness beckoned us to hide our deeds, we could resist because of the desire to walk only in the light that is God.

"I am the light of the world" is the second "I am" in John's Gospel. There are seven. But it is more than simply a nifty way for Jesus to speak of himself. Jesus is describing a choice we all make. Everyone chooses to live in the darkness or in the light. Those who would choose light must choose **Jesus**.

Jesus answered, "You know neither me nor my Father. If you knew me, you would know my Father also."

John 8:13-24

JUNE 28

Jesus had been on the lips of the prophets. Still, his arrival took everyone by surprise. Centuries of prophetic utterances, generations of planning, finally the long- awaited Messiah was here. Yet, very few even noticed. God walked among us but we couldn't see Him

Jesus told them the problem: they judged by human standards. He did not appear to be anything more than a man. His clothes and companions, his family and hometown certainly did not mark him as anyone special.

They asked Jesus about his father. They thought they knew them both. But they did not really know Jesus or his Father.

Now, they knew he was Jesus. They knew his parents and his family. They knew his hometown of Nazareth. They knew what he looked like and what he sounded like and who his friends were. So, what does he mean by know?

They did not know his heart. They didn't know how he felt about them and what he wanted for them and how much he loved them. They did not know that every word he spoke and every deed he did were accomplished with their good in mind. They did not know just how far he had come to bring them the best news ever. They did not know just how far he would go to accomplish the will of his Father.

They knew some facts, but not him. It is the same today. Most folks know some facts about Jesus. The Christmas season provides those. But they do not really know his heart and they have no relationship with him. Sadly, that means they do not know the Father. You'll never know God, you'll never have a relationship with the Father, until you know His Son, Jesus.

Now, is this important? Does it matter that we believe? Evidently, Jesus thought it did. He said, "I told you that you would die in your sins, for unless you believe that I am he you will die in your sins."

The failure to know Jesus cannot be dismissed as just some unfortunate oversight. The best and most important thing that happens in your life, or in any life, is knowing the man called **Jesus.**

> So Jesus said to them, "When you have lifted up the Son of Man, then you will know that I am he, and that I do nothing on my own authority, but speak just as the Father taught me."
>
> John 8:25-30

JUNE 29

Jesus knew who he was. His listeners, however, were not so sure about him. "Who are you?" It was the most important question they could have asked.

They were clearly puzzled by Jesus. But they judged him by human standards. Naturally, he did not fit neatly in any category. They were ignorant of his real mission and they struggled to make sense of his words.

Sadly, when Jesus spoke of his Father, they were still bewildered. The irony is that these Jews were the stewards of God's Word. For centuries, they enjoyed the blessing and privilege of hearing God speak through prophets and they had been the recorders and keepers of God's revelation of Himself. Yet, for all of this exposure to His heart and will, they did not know Him.

Now, living in front of them was deity in the flesh! But they did not recognize him or the truths he spoke from the Father.

Trying to explain who Jesus was (is) continues to be a challenge for people of every time and place. The centuries are littered with the writings of those who espoused the deity of Jesus and those who denied it. While today's bookshelves hold many volumes written to uphold Jesus' unique claim, there are an equal number of books written suggesting that Jesus was nothing more than a man. Some are kind in their portrayal of him as a man, but many are not. After all, if he wasn't who he claimed to be, he was a liar and fraud.

How could anyone ever really be sure? What explanation could he give that would change our minds? How could any of us ever know and see the truth about him?

Jesus answered the questions for us. The cross. "When you have lifted up the Son of Man, then you will know..." What a strange place to learn the truth.

All the truth that really matters to you cannot be known apart from the cross of **Jesus**.

> "If you abide in my word, you are truly my disciples, and you will know the truth, and the truth will set you free."
>
> John 8:31-36

JUNE 30

Jesus told them the last thing they expected to hear: You are not free unless the Son makes you free. They could not imagine it! As descendants of Abraham, Jesus' listeners could not conceive the idea that they were slaves to anyone. But Jesus was not speaking of the freedom to come and go as one wants, but the freedom to become the person God created one to be.

Jesus dared to say that we could be free from sin and live new lives! Jesus said that we don't have to be bound by our past, confined by our nature or limited by our sins.

We are free, not because we stood our ground, demanded our rights, or refused to yield, but we are free because we surrendered ourselves to the one true Ruler.

We are free, not because we fought to live on our own terms or to live for ourselves, but because we chose to die to ourselves and live only for the one true King.

We are free, not because we deserved it as some reward for our goodness or gained it as a prize for our service, but because the Lord is gracious to those who put their trust in Him.

But the truth does not free us simply because it is truth. It is wonderful to know the truth about God but such knowledge of itself is neither liberating nor transforming. Truth sets us free because we love it with our hearts and embrace it with our lives. Jesus said that those who "are really my disciples" are those who "hold to my teaching." Freedom comes not by simply knowing what is true, but by living what is true.

We may move freely about the planet and exert our will as we choose but, apart from Jesus, we lack the freedom to ever rise above our human nature and to become sharers in the divine nature. Only by being set free are we blessed to experience the life for which God made us. Amazingly, this freedom is a gift to those who would surrender to **Jesus**.

> Jesus said to them, "If God were your Father, you would love me, for I came from God and I am here. I came not of my own accord, but he sent me."
>
> John 8:37-47

JULY 1

Jesus told them: "You do not belong to God." They could hardly believe their ears! In fact, Jesus said that was precisely their problem: they would not hear. But they would listen to their father!

It was to be expected that they would counter by making appeals to their history. After all, who were the Jews without their history?

First, they argued that they were Abraham's children. But Jesus told them, "You sure don't look much like him. You don't have his mannerisms or expressions. You don't display his spirit or attitude. You certainly don't have his faith. No, I don't see how Abraham could be your father."

Then, they claimed that God was their father. Again, Jesus told them, "No, I don't think so. When I look at you, I sure don't see God. The truth is: If God were your father, then we would be brothers. Thus, we would know each other. But it is clear that you don't know me."

If they felt a bit shell-shocked at this point, the worst was yet to come. "But," he said, "I have identified your father. Your father is the devil. How do I know? Because you are just like him. It's his desires you carry out."

It is quite common for us to bear some resemblance to our parents. Physical features (eyes, ears, nose, etc.) may be there but, even more, there can be certain traits that reflect their influence on us. We may have their laugh or smile. We might walk in a certain way or gesture as they did. We may have their skills and/or interest in music or sports. And we might simply do a lot of things routinely that we later realize were their habits, too.

Two families. Two fathers. We all bear the traits of our father. Our words reveal the identity of our father. Our ways tell people that we are like our father. We know we belong to God because our Father has our heart and we long for nothing more than to be like our brother, **Jesus**.

**So the Jews said to him, "You are not yet fifty years old, and have you seen Abraham?"
Jesus said to them, "Truly, truly, I say to you, before Abraham was, I am."**
John 8:48-59

JULY 2

Jesus wasn't even fifty years old. There was no way he could have seen Abraham, much less precede him. He must be playing us for fools, they thought. Actually, this only proved what some already thought: he was demon-possessed!

Today, we are much too intelligent and sophisticated to say Jesus was possessed by a demon. When Jesus tells us to go the extra mile or turn the other cheek or love our enemies, we would kindly explain that he doesn't really understand how the world works and his ideas are not always practical but the thought is really sweet.

And when Jesus tells us not to worry about food and clothes, to forgive as we have been forgiven, and not to judge others, we would not accuse him of being mentally unstable. We would just dismiss his words by explaining that he doesn't intend for us to take him so literally.

We may stop short of insisting that he is demon-possessed, but there are other ways to show that we are unable or unwilling to accept him or his words. We are just as skilled as the ancients in finding ways to explain and dismiss what we do not wish to believe or practice.

Finally, exasperated by his claims and irritated by his accusations, they delivered the ultimate blow. Even though they stood in the very presence of God, they asked him, "Who do you think you are?"

It was not a sincere question as if they were seeking truth. It was a sarcastic, mocking kind of question intended to attack his perceived notions of superiority. After all, how could his words keep people from death?

It was a question of ridicule intended to expose him as an obvious fraud. How could he have lived before Abraham?

Unlike these religious leaders, we don't need to ask Jesus who he thinks he is because we know who Jesus thinks he is. He is the one the Father glorifies. Instead, the question of the day is 'who do we think we are' that we should be so blessed to know this man, **Jesus**.

And his disciples asked him, "Rabbi, who sinned, this man or his parents, that he was born blind?"

John 9:1-12

JULY 3

Jesus saw a man blind from birth. He grew up in a world of darkness. He never saw the faces of his mother and father. He never saw a dog or a fish or a frog. He never saw a sunrise or a sunset, or a flower or a tree.

There wasn't much he could do. So, he begged. He was a crumpled-up man on the side of the road listening for the sound of a coin, listening to the feet of humanity shuffling along to home or work or play.

Did he ever dream of what might have been? Did he ever wonder why?

To his neighbors he was only a blind beggar on the side of the road. The disciples, on the other hand, looked at this man and saw a big theological question. Who caused his blindness? Who was to blame for this?

Even today, we try to identify the culprit. We seek the hidden cause for cancer, a car accident, or a deformity at birth. We persist in wanting to know who is responsible, who is to blame. We discuss the matter endlessly, trying to figure out the why. Is God punishing me? What did I do wrong?

The truth is: the man was blind because he was born into a world of suffering, a world where bad things can happen to innocent people. But Jesus sees the moment for what it is: an opportunity for God to be glorified!

Any kind of suffering is an opportunity for us to display God in our lives. The loss of a job, the death of a mate, the battle with pain, the struggle with depression, the reality of death......these are the moments when the most eyes are watching to see who we really are.

Can't you just see him all the way home? Shouting: "I can see! I can see!" Can you imagine it? "There's the sun! There's a tree and a flower and a dog and a bird! Wow! Look at those clouds! Look at that blue sky! Look at all the different faces!"

After life in the dark, there is sight because of **Jesus**.

And he said to them, "He put mud on my eyes, and I washed, and I see."
John 9:13-23

JULY 4

Jesus made a blind man see. Unfortunately, that action only served to magnify the blindness of others.

Those who knew this former blind man thought the Pharisees might be able to help resolve the matter. Sadly, the Pharisees' sight was no better than those who brought the man. They immediately concluded that Jesus could not possibly be from God as he did this healing on the Sabbath day.

Their religion was getting in the way of faith! "He does not do it the way we believe it." These guys were holding on to their traditions. They made laws God never made. They insisted that loving and serving God had to be done their way.

Sadly, religious folks can make the same mistake today. Traditions become laws and opinions become rules. When others don't comply, the judging begins. Inclusion becomes the goal and performance becomes the priority.

But there's more. They were skeptical of the good done by someone else. How could anybody not of their group possibly do anything to bless someone's life? They were the only ones sanctioned (by themselves) to receive the praise of others for good deeds.

Today, there are people who believe the only truth preached is that preached in their building...the only good done is that done by their church...the only folks saved are those who see every point exactly as they do. Pharisees are still alive and well, and they are still as blind as ever!

Unfortunately, his parents were not able to rejoice with their son over his sight because they were afraid. Do you see it? Forced conformity. When religion becomes nothing more than keeping rules, the resulting system seeks to make everyone conform. Leaders start looking for ways to make everyone look and sound alike. No openness. No discovery. No learning. Just do it the way you're told or you'll be kept out of the inner circle!

Blindness! This was far more serious than being unable to see trees, flowers and faces. This was about closing eyes to **Jesus**.

"If this man were not from God, he could do nothing."

John 9:24-34

JULY 5

Jesus had healed a blind man, but the Pharisees would have preferred that the man continue in his blindness. His new sight was a problem for them. Searching for answers, they called him before them one more time. He was not very helpful to their cause. Insulted by the man, they gave him the boot. More than that, they admitted that they were only going to accept what fit in their own frame of reference, only what they knew from their own experience. Jesus, they did not know.

We may be quick to condemn them for their attitude but we are more like them than we want to admit. We like the familiar and comfortable. We value our position and feel threatened by change. We like things to make sense to us, to have reasonable explanations.

But Jesus never fit in any of the usual categories. He wasn't easy to evaluate and even harder to classify. He was intimidating, not because he was big and strong, or rough and harsh, but because he was so manly in a striking sort of way.

He loved little children and he was kind to women. He could be gentle with those who hurt and stern with those who were foolish. He touched lepers, complimented Samaritans, put people ahead of rules and loved those who had made a mess of their lives. And if any were inclined to think he lacked those strong masculine traits of courage and toughness, time would reveal that he could endure pain like no other, and do so without saying a word.

You might think that we would be drawn to such a man. But that was the problem. He wasn't your usual kind of man. Such a man didn't fit into any of our categories. And if he didn't fit like the rest of us, how could we be sure about him, how could we trust him?

"If this man were not from God, he could do nothing." The brightest religious minds conducted interviews, weighed the evidence and came away holding on to their pride. It took a former blind man to see the truth about **Jesus**.

> Jesus heard that they had cast him out, and having found him he said, "Do you believe in the Son of Man?"
>
> John 9:35-38

JULY 6

Jesus found him. For the man who was born blind, this would prove to be more significant to his life than the miracle of sight!

No word is given on how Jesus learned of the man's situation, but he did. And Jesus found him. There is so much to consider in that short statement.

Jesus cared about him. He knew that so much had happened in a short space of time and the man would be struggling to put the pieces together. At the same time, his life had been turned upside down by the prideful treatment of the Pharisees. We can only imagine the emotional state of the man as he tried to make sense of it all.

Jesus actually went to the effort of searching for the man. Isn't that just like God? How long he looked or where he looked is not so important. But the fact that he looked is very important!

Jesus didn't come just to make blind men see or lame men walk. His compassion was apparent and, because of it, thousands were healed. But he came so that the eyes of the heart might be opened to God. We were the lost ones and he came to find us!

"Do you believe in the Son of Man?" It was the moment of truth. His answer revealed the character of his heart. He wanted to believe.

Jesus said, "I am he," and the man said, "I believe." And then he worshiped.

What do you suppose he did when he worshiped? What would you do? Maybe he fell to his knees and praised God! Maybe he kissed Jesus' feet and offered many expressions of gratitude for the grace he had received!

Worship is the most natural result of faith. The heart cannot contain the joy and the mind cannot contain the awe! So, the mouth breaks forth in praise and gratitude, in joy and adoration!

It is our story. A man in need met the Savior. His life was changed. The experience brought him to faith. And from his faith came his worship of **Jesus**.

Jesus said, "For judgment I came into this world, that those who do not see may see, and those who see may become blind."

John 9:39-41

JULY 7

Jesus wanted people to see, but he couldn't make them. He could tell them and he could show them, but the decision to believe had to be theirs.

With but a few exceptions, the Pharisees never seemed to take Jesus seriously until he became a threat to their favored status among the people. After all, he wasn't the first leader of some movement and there was little reason to think he would be the last. But as time went by, the multitudes were getting bigger and more vocal. And now there was this former blind man who claimed that Jesus gave him sight. So, they were forced to act, not for noble reasons but for selfish ones. Now, who was blind?

No searching hearts. No inquiring minds. No looking for answers. Just too much pride to admit that they could learn anything from someone else. These guys had life and God all figured out and that was the end of it! Amazingly, their only hope lay in the confession of their blindness.

Real blindness is not missing out on seeing the sun or stars, faces or animals. Real blindness is not the inability to see trees or flowers, mountains or rivers.

Real blindness is making tradition sound like God said it...and missing out on what God did say.

Real blindness is stressing programs and methods...and failing to focus on the One who makes all things possible.

Real blindness is accepting only what we can understand or what makes good sense to us...and thereby limiting God.

Real blindness is being too proud to admit our own weaknesses and failings...and missing the experience of God's wondrous love and grace.

Jesus said, "I came so that you could see." And our lives are forever different. We no longer see a sunset, but we see the wonderful artistry of God. We don't just witness a birth, but we marvel at what God has done. We no longer observe the struggle of a dying friend, but we behold the victory that God gives.

That is what it means to see. And that sight comes only from **Jesus**.

"The sheep hear his voice, and he calls his own sheep by name and leads them out. When he has brought out all his own, he goes before them, and the sheep follow him, for they know his voice.

John 10:1-6

JULY 8

Jesus' imagery would have made instant connection with those who first heard these words. The picture of the shepherd tending his sheep would have been one of Judea's most familiar.

The shepherd and his sheep are deeply woven into the language and the imagery of Scripture. The language is abundant and the picture is both comforting and inspiring. We know what it is to be cared for, guided and rescued.

The Shepherd is so familiar with the sheep that he knows every trait, habit and characteristic of each one. He understands all their peculiarities. He knows you...your trials and temptations, your weaknesses and strengths, your sorrows and joys, your fears and needs. You have the Shepherd who knows you by name.

Unfortunately, sheep have the reputation of being one of the earth's dumbest animals. Without help, they are inclined to wander away and become lost. In Isaiah's familiar picture of sheep, he writes, "All we like sheep have gone astray; we have turned everyone to his own way" (Isaiah 53:6). Straying seems to be one of the primary characteristics of sheep. Obviously, they need someone to help them stay on the path.

That sure sounds like us. Easily deceived. Quick to wander. Soon lost. Unsure where to go. Uncertain what to do next.

We need a shepherd. We need someone who knows which way to go. We need someone who can show us how to live. That's Jesus. Following Jesus, the Shepherd, means living with confidence. We know he knows us, he knows about life, and he knows which way to go. That's really good news for folks who are prone to wander.

If the ultimate measure of a good shepherd is how well he knows his sheep, how well he tends his flock, and his ability and willingness to defend them when they are in danger, then we have the Shepherd who has no equal. There is no shepherd like **Jesus**.

> "I am the door. If anyone enters by me, he will be saved and will go in and out and find pasture."
>
> John 10:7-10

JULY 9

Jesus never left any doubt that his coming was for the purpose of saving humanity. Whether talking about God's willingness to give His Son for the whole world, or telling stories of a shepherd in search of a single sheep, Jesus was a man focused on a goal and his words reflected it.

The shepherd imagery was a natural. Shepherds often brought their sheep into one central sheepfold. So, several flocks would be together and guarded through the night by a gatekeeper. However, if the shepherd found himself out on the hills at sunset, he would bring them to a roughly constructed sheepfold. This corral-type structure would have a single opening. Once the sheep were safely in, the shepherd would become the door or gate as he would lie across the opening through the night. In this way, no predator could go in and no sheep could go out without his knowledge.

In the plainest language Jesus is claiming to be the one way into the place of safety. Jesus said, "I am the door." You must enter by him.

This rather narrow approach to reaching a safe refuge is irritating to many. Wanting to believe that Jesus couldn't be serious and that there are actually many ways to heaven, they simply reject the idea that salvation is found only in Jesus.

Sheep safety is priority one for the Lord. So, he does not mislead us. The sheepfold is the place of safety. You enter only through him. In this story the Shepherd is the Savior.

Behaving like wayward sheep, we often try to find contentment in the wrong places. We race from one experience to another, from one relationship to another, from one job to another. But our hunger remains. We are searchers who cannot find, pursuers who don't possess.

There is only one Shepherd who can deliver on the promise of a full and abundant life. There is only one Shepherd who can provide the basic needs for every individual sheep. There is only one Shepherd who literally lays his life on the line for the sheep. There is only one Shepherd who can save you. **Jesus.**

> "For this reason the Father loves me, because I lay down my life that I may take it up again."
>
> John 10:11-21

JULY 10

Jesus said it four times (vss. 11, 15, 17, 18). "You are safe with me." It is a message hard to miss and even more difficult to understand. This Good Shepherd chooses to lay down his life for the sheep. Because these are his sheep, he wants them safe. So, he will not abandon them in the face of any threats.

What is both amazing and disappointing is the reaction of the Jews. Although his shepherd/sheep imagery would not have been lost on them, they seem unwilling or unable to read the deeper meanings. They certainly missed the part about "laying down his life."

It is a common mistake. Excited by the stories surrounding his birth, inspired by his words for life, and thrilled by his miracles that so dramatically changed the lives of people, we may actually miss the reason for his coming: to die for us. Without his sacrifice, the birth stories, the words from his lips and the miracles simply become more lines in the history books. We can add them to all the other stories we know but they make little lasting difference. But it is the sacrifice that changes all of that!

This was not a sacrifice that grew out of some deal or bargain. It wasn't a negotiated or contractual arrangement. The motive was not getting more or having the most. Nor was this an attempt to impress anyone. And make no mistake: we were not some impressive prize to be won! No, this was the sacrifice of one's life based on the one thing that defines God: love.

Jesus did not die for some great philosophy or principle, nor did he sacrifice himself to simply show the meaning of self-sacrifice. No, Jesus died for people. For you and me.

Whether nurturing or protecting or saving us, the primary characteristic of this remarkable Shepherd is that he loves and loves and loves... all the way to the point of death. There is not, nor has there ever been, a Shepherd like **Jesus**.

> "Go your way; behold, I am sending you out as lambs in the midst of wolves."
>
> Luke 10:1-16

JULY 11

Jesus did not leave the ministry to just the twelve. Seventy-two disciples were sent out with the message of the kingdom. We don't know their names or how they were selected. We don't know their hometowns or their vocations. We don't know where they went or even how that was decided. We don't know the details of their methods or how people responded to them in each place. But we do know this: their labor excited them and brought joy to the heart of Jesus!

And these messengers carried a very important and very urgent message. So important that rejection of the messenger was, in fact, rejection of God Himself! They would find receptive hearts in places and they would meet those who were stubborn. Woe to those who rejected the message! The consequences were serious. It would be more tolerable for that ancient, wicked city of Sodom than for those who rejected these messengers of Jesus.

So, what did Jesus tell them when he sent them out?

"You have to be committed. It's a lot of work. Pray for more workers.

"Be courageous. You are going to meet a lot of opposition. The wolves outnumber the sheep.

"Travel light. Don't get caught up in the things of this world or you'll never get the job done. Don't live cluttered lives so that you forget your spiritual purpose. Trust God to provide. Stay centered on the mission. Stay focused.

"Be wise. Everyone will not receive you and you only have so much time. Don't waste it. Don't take it personal. Rejecting your message is not a rejection of you but a rejection of me."

People may live at a faster pace and have more choices in daily life, but the problems of sin and suffering and the need for peace and contentment are still with us. So, if we ask Jesus for instructions on living well today, would our instructions be any different from those he gave the seventy-two? Would he not speak to us of commitment and courage? Would he not tell us to live uncluttered lives and to trust God to provide?

So, today you have your instructions from **Jesus**.

And he said to them, "I saw Satan fall like lightning from heaven."
Luke 10:17-24

JULY 12

Jesus was full of joy! How exciting to see the Master smiling over good news!

His ambassadors had returned with excitement in their hearts and on their lips! We know that feeling. Perhaps, it was a summer camp experience or a spring break mission trip. Maybe it was a one-on-one Bible study or a weekend seminar. We were inspired by what we saw and what we heard. Lives were changed, including ours. Hope and love were shared in wonderful ways. That's what happened to these seventy-two. They would never be the same again.

It is very important to appreciate this truth: we are now those disciples that Jesus sends out. The commission is now ours.

We might argue that times have changed. The world is different now. Connecting with people is not as easy as it once was. There are so many more distractions, so many more time demands. In fact, most people don't even seem all that interested in religion.

But what makes us think it was so easy for these seventy-two? What they were doing was hard work. They had to be committed. They had to get out of their comfort zone and away from the familiar. They had to speak to people who had other interests and concerns.

And because they went, Jesus could say that he "saw Satan fall like lightning from heaven." When you reach out in Jesus' name to help a friend or neighbor, Satan takes another tumble. When you forgive someone who has wounded you, when you go the extra mile for another, when you show kindness to those who would do you harm, Satan falls like lightning from heaven.

So many people long to know what you know. They want to know if it's possible to be forgiven after awful things have been done. They want to know if life can ever be meaningful and full. They want to know if good and right really can triumph. They want to know if these fears and worries will ever go away. They want to know if there's anything after the grave.

People need to know **who** you know. They need you to tell them about **Jesus**.

> "You shall love the Lord your God with all your heart and with all your soul and with all your strength and with all your mind, and your neighbor as yourself."
>
> Luke 10:25-33

JULY 13

Jesus wasn't really telling the man anything he didn't already know. After all, the questioner was an expert in the law. But Jesus' answer did make him squirm a bit. The reason: Jesus tells him nothing he does not already know, but something he is not doing.

Isn't that just like us? Our problem is rarely knowledge but usually action. We already have a pretty good idea about right and wrong, and we are clear about what God wants us to do. But we are not so good about putting all that into action. As it was with him, so it is with us: it is not the knowing but the doing that makes us squirm.

The road connecting Jerusalem and Jericho was famous for its many danger spots. The distance was about seventeen miles. It was a rocky and desolate terrain. The lonely, narrow road twisted through the Judean hills and those hills provided excellent cover for bandits waiting to fall upon the travelers.

The failure of the priest and the Levite to stop and render aid is very disappointing. After all, these are religious figures among the people. We would have expected better from them.

The Samaritan, on the other hand, was both a half-breed and a heretic in the minds of the Jews. The hostility and bitterness between these two groups went back several centuries.

The law expert was trying to separate his relationship with God from his relationship with his fellow man. He wanted to know whom he had to love and whom he didn't have to love! He tried to "justify" not loving certain people. We should be careful lest we fall into the same temptation.

This story began with a very important question about eternal life. The question was answered with "love God with your whole being and love others, too." He asked the right question and got the right answer from **Jesus**.

"Which of these three, do you think, proved to be a neighbor to the man who fell among the robbers?"
He said, "The one who showed him mercy." And Jesus said to him, "You go, and do likewise."

Luke 10:34-37

JULY 14

Jesus knew how to tell a good story. He used imagery common to the people and plots that the listeners could easily envision. But most of all, his stories often had a twist or turn that left the listener pondering on what they had just heard.

Samaritans were despised by Jews. Because of intermarriage with foreigners, the Samaritans were seen as half-breeds. Some probably wondered why Jesus included a Samaritan in his story at all.

But the racial prejudice was only part of the problem. There were theological matters at stake here. The Samaritans limited the Scriptures to the five books of Moses and rejected the rest. Also, they set up their own temple for worship on Mt. Gerizim.

While the Samaritan could have sized up the situation and come up with a number of excuses to avoid any involvement, his compassion would not allow it. His help was not based on whether the man deserved his assistance but on the man's need.

Perhaps, the difference in the three men who saw the injured man can best be explained by remembering this: What you do is determined by what you see, and what you see is determined by what you are. The priest, the Levite and the Samaritan saw the same thing. But, in another sense, they didn't see the same thing at all. Only one of the three actually saw a fellow human in need and took helpful action. But what he saw and did was the result of what he was.

Do you see need or inconvenience? Do you see opportunity or hindrance? Do you see blessing or interruption? Seeing comes from the heart.

The expert in the law knew the answer to his own question. We usually do, too. But knowing what God says and doing what God says are two different things.

What we do is determined by what we see and what we see is determined by what we are. That's why we want to be like **Jesus**.

> But the Lord answered her, "Martha, Martha, you are anxious and troubled about many things, but one thing is necessary."
> Luke 10:38-42

JULY 15

Jesus loved this family in Bethany. The little village was located only a couple of miles from Jerusalem. From the Gospel of John, it would seem that Jesus often visited the home of Mary, Martha and Lazarus. Evidently, Martha owned the home and so we assume that she was the oldest sister.

Naturally, Martha wanted everything to be just right. Like any good hostess, she wanted him to be impressed with the meal and impressed with the cleanliness of the house. But as the last-minute details were being handled, Mary remained at the feet of Jesus, listening to him, focusing on him, concentrating on his words.

Martha was beginning to feel some irritation, even anger, with her sister. After all, Martha was doing all the work. Perhaps she had already done everything she could think of to attract Mary's attention and signal her that she needed help. If so, Mary was missing the signals, or ignoring them. Finally, Martha took her irritation to Jesus.

Jesus did not fault Martha for being responsible. Martha's fault was that she was too busy to listen, too distracted to focus on his presence, too involved with all her concerns to give time to her guest. Martha was so busy preparing for Jesus that she forgot to be with Jesus.

Is it possible that we could get so busy with the things we think are important that we could actually miss what is most important? Perhaps, those things we think are important are only distractions from what is really important. After all, isn't that what Luke said about Martha?

Jesus said, "Mary has chosen what is better." The "better" is the presence and the words of the Master. Martha, however well-intentioned and busy being a good hostess, needed to put first things first.

In a world of so many distractions, we must remember that "only one thing is necessary." That one thing is **Jesus**.

> Now Jesus was praying in a certain place, and when he finished, one of his disciples said to him, "Lord, teach us to pray, as John taught his disciples."
>
> Luke 11:1-4

JULY 16

Jesus' disciples could have asked him to teach them on many subjects. After all, they had seen his miracles, heard his sermons, and watched his interaction with people. But through it all, one thing seems to have captured their imagination above all others: prayer. They wanted Jesus to teach them to pray. John taught his disciples. So, why shouldn't they receive some instruction?

Perhaps the disciples were struck by the prayer life of Jesus. Or, maybe they just sensed something lacking in their own prayers. Most of us would admit that our prayer life could use some work.

It is important to remember that the disciples said, "teach us to pray" not "teach us a prayer." It's one thing to read or deliver a prayer; it's something else to know how to pray.

Jesus gave his disciples a prayer designed to reflect their awareness and understanding of their needs, not to bring God up-to-date on their lives. Since God already knows our needs, we pray so that God may see that we know our needs!

Also, Jesus' model prayer was a reflection of priorities. Here, before God, we show what matters most to us, what dominates our thoughts, what we consider most important. Prayer is a reflection of what we are.

Perhaps, Jesus used their request as an opportunity to answer a question they did not ask: Why pray? One reason is that prayer is the place where we can express to God our desire for Him to work in our lives. Prayer opens new doors of opportunity for God to move. Since He respects our freedom of choice and free will, prayer enables Him to step into our lives. Prayer gives God the permission to do what He has been desiring to do all the time.

The disciples wanted to know how to pray. They certainly asked the right person. No one enjoyed a better relationship with the Father. No one knew the Father's heart better than **Jesus**.

> "If you then, who are evil, know how to give good gifts to your children, how much more will the heavenly Father give the Holy Spirit to those who ask him!"
>
> Luke 11:5-13

JULY 17

Jesus' approach to the subject of prayer may strike us as odd. After all, the images are a bit negative. The first is of a grumpy man awakened in the night. The second is the acknowledgement that fathers are evil. What was Jesus trying to say?

Can you imagine dealing with human requests all day long? Even more, can you imagine dealing with human requests all day long and every day?!

Yet, God never tires or gets irritated or becomes angry that thousands and thousands of people are asking him for something every minute of the day! If you think about it, the sheer volume of requests staggers the imagination!

Still, we can pray with confidence. After all, God is **not** like the grumpy neighbor.

Travel at night was not uncommon due to the heat. But a late evening visitor would have created problems for any first century family. Food was not readily available as it is today. There was no 24-hour convenience store on the corner. Food needs were daily. But hospitality was considered a duty, a very important one.

Jesus was not comparing God to this sleepy, irritated neighbor. This is a parable of contrast: this is what God is not like.

We say 'yes' or 'no' to our children because we want the best for them. Still, we don't always get it right. As parents, we have plenty of regrets, no matter how much we love our children.

Now, here is some wonderful news: God never regrets. He always gets it right. If earthly fathers, imperfect though they are, want to give the best to their children, yet sometimes make mistakes, just imagine what's possible with the heavenly Father who wants to give the best and never makes a mistake!

The disciples wanted to learn how to pray. Jesus gave them a model prayer. But he also wanted us to know that the God of all creation, the God who is sovereign over all, is never too busy or too weary to hear what's on our heart. Certainly, if anyone would know this, it is **Jesus**.

> "But if it is by the finger of God that I cast out demons, then the kingdom of God has come upon you."
>
> Luke 11:14-26

JULY 18

Jesus never presents the luxury of neutrality. We may choose him or reject him, follow him or go our own way, but we are never given a third option or some middle ground.

Jesus cast a demon out of a mute man. As soon as this man opened his mouth and spoke there was an immediate impact on the crowd. All who witnessed this event concluded that a great miracle had been performed, but from this point on there is a great difference of opinion as to what it all means. Same event, but different views.

Perhaps, there were some believers among those amazed people. But some in the crowd concluded that Jesus did this through the power of Beelzebub. This is the third time his enemies accused him of being in partnership with Satan. But if Satan was responsible for the demon being the man, why would Satan act in union with Jesus to cast out the demon?

Perhaps, typical of many groups, the majority were the undecided voters. These undecided or at least uncommitted, asked for "a sign from heaven." They were not quite ready to acknowledge that Jesus was the Messiah, but neither were they willing to deny it. They probably saw themselves as open minded and willing to be convinced. But they also believed that more evidence was needed before any conclusion could be made with confidence. Evidently, they thought a sign would help.

What about those who wanted to take a wait-and-see approach? But Jesus warned those who wanted to take a wait-and-see approach that neutrality was not an option. The kingdom of God had come upon them and that called for a decision! With him or against him. No middle ground. In fact, an attempt at neutrality would lead to a latter state that was worse than the former.

Everyone decides which side they are on—God or Satan- by their response to **Jesus**.

> "Your eye is the lamp of your body. When your eye is healthy, your whole body is full of light, but when it is bad, your body is full of darkness."
> Luke 11:27-36

JULY 19

Jesus knew their faith was weak and they wanted a sign. Their reluctance to accept him was driven partly by fear. That fear of what others might think and what lifestyle changes would be required still keeps people from accepting him.

But what's wrong with hanging back to see how things work out? Better yet, why not ask for a sign that will settle the matter? Isn't this the "scientific method?" Shouldn't we withhold a decision until all the facts are in?

Instead of a sign, Jesus told them of the Ninevites and the Queen of the South. Two things are noteworthy about Jesus' choice of stories. First, in each instance the blessed are Gentiles and, because of their belief, will condemn the unbelief of this generation of Jews.

The second is that both parties believed with much less evidence than that which this generation had seen. One greater than Jonah and greater than Solomon was standing before them!

But the real problem was not the evidence. The problem was sight. Just as our eyes (or sight) affect our whole body, so our heart affects our whole life. Physical light enters the eye and gives light to the body enabling it to function properly. If that light is denied entrance through the eye, then the body must function in darkness.

Even so, spiritual light enters the heart and gives light to the soul that it might function in union with God. If spiritual light is absent from the heart, then the soul must function with an inaccurate view of life.

Jesus came so that all might see. The Pharisees clashed with Jesus because their eyes were bad. They were religious but they had a distorted view of life.

Knowing that our vision affects our behavior, Jesus confronts us with the need to see clearly, to see beneath the surface. His words are a call to a new and different view of the life and, thus, to a new way of living. We only come to the right view of life by looking with the eyes of **Jesus**.

> "But woe to you Pharisees! For you tithe mint and rue and every herb, and neglect justice and the love of God. These you ought to have done, without neglecting the others."
>
> Luke 11:37-44

JULY 20

Jesus did not hate Pharisees. He loved them. But he did not love their distorted views about God and His Word, or their arrogant attitude.

Like many of us, they were concerned about doing the right things. They tried to be careful about keeping the accepted traditions received from those before them. They fasted and prayed, assembled and tithed, and studied and evangelized. In short, they were really good church folks!

But Jesus was not impressed. Regardless of their beliefs and practices, they still had it wrong. Something was missing.

An unnamed Pharisee invited Jesus for a meal and Jesus accepted his invitation. But what the Pharisee noticed was that Jesus did not wash before dinner. While he said nothing, he could not hide his heart from Jesus.

The matter of washing hands had nothing to do with cleanliness. It was ceremonial cleanliness that was the issue. There was nothing in Moses' Law that required one to wash their hands before a meal. What was tradition with the Pharisees had been elevated equal to Scripture.

But this situation well illustrates the ongoing tension between Jesus and the Pharisees — they were more concerned with form than substance; more interested in appearance than reality. The Pharisees focused on what a man did; Jesus was equally concerned with what a man was. Thus, Jesus insisted, "You should offer to God your inner self; that would make you really clean."

Like church members fussing about how to use the foyer, how early to unlock the building, how to stripe the parking lot, or which classroom should belong to the sixth graders, the Pharisees often majored in the minors. Jesus was not condemning good stewardship or thoughtful giving. But he was condemning their neglect of what was most important.

Something was missing – a heart centered on God. But now we knew what such a heart looked like when we saw **Jesus**.

And he said, "Woe to you lawyers also! For you load people with burdens hard to bear, and you yourselves do not touch the burdens with one of your fingers."

Luke 11:45-54

JULY 21

Jesus came for people. So, it was no surprise that those who made life difficult for others would draw his fire.

The experts in the law were likely well-intentioned as they developed their own set of guidelines for pleasing God. After all, these guys were devoted to doing things right. They were careful about God's laws to the point of being obsessive compulsive! But at some point, their guidelines for living turned into rules for living. What once was a suggestion became a requirement.

These fellows took the joy out of serving God. In fact, they made it a burden by their extra rules. They had lost the joy of serving God and had taken away the joy of others, too.

Their kind is not gone. Church folks can be bad about making rules God did not make. There are no laws about mission trips in the summer. There are no requirements about Wednesday nights, small groups or parenting seminars. The church may offer many opportunities for learning and growth, but these are not the ruler for determining faithfulness to the Savior. The church is about encouraging Christians to make good decisions about service, not berating them because they fail to choose what another has decided is a duty.

In misguided zeal, the Pharisees created the extra. Whether it meant more fasting or giving, more evangelizing or praying, they added to what God said. But their additions did not make better people, only burdened people.

The Pharisees focused on details. They emphasized what could be counted and measured. They concentrated their energies on matters of less importance and neglected matters of greater importance. And they did all this at the expense of others. They attended to their interests, not the interests of others. They were not helping others in this spiritual journey; they were discouraging them! "Woe to you!" Jesus said.

Jesus condemned their wrong priorities. To them, appearance mattered more than the inside and their own interests took priority over people. They were wrong on both. Today, be sure that what matters to you is what matters to **Jesus**.

"Beware of the leaven of the Pharisees, which is hypocrisy."
Luke 12:1-3

JULY 22

Jesus' view of hypocrisy is reflected in his words to the disciples. Having encountered the hypocrisy of the self-righteous leaders, he warned his disciples of being two-faced in their own kingdom labors.

Hypocrisy is universal. We don't always practice what we preach. But hypocrisy is more than simply failing. Hypocrisy is dishonesty about our failing. From the most famous to the least known, humans often pretend to be something they are not.

"Hypocrisy" originated as a theatrical term in the Greek language. An actor, playing multiple roles in the same play, would disguise himself by wearing different masks. This actor was called a hypocrite, someone with two or more faces. As words do, the meaning changed over the years and took on negative connotations. To be a hypocrite, then, was to be "two-faced," describing someone who said one thing and did another.

Now, let's just go ahead and say what we already know: No one tricks God. If we are pretending, God knows it. And God hates all forms of dishonesty. He will not tolerate our attempts to live callous and thoughtless lives of pretension, especially when we are pretending to be right with Him.

Hypocrisy is like a slow-acting poison. The more we pretend to be what we're not, the easier it is for us to do so. But that pretending has a price: the loss of our real self. Hypocrisy kills what is genuine within us. Pretending never makes us better or happier, never stronger or wiser.

The moment we start to think that we are better than others...the moment we begin to pass judgment on other people...the moment we think that we can hide our sin without consequences...that is the moment we become hypocrites. And it is in that moment that we begin pretending that we start poisoning our lives.

We usually pretend because we are afraid. Wearing a mask often brings temporary comfort. It is important to remember that no one hides from God. What you hide now will be seen, what you whisper now will be heard. From Adam we learned to hide. Living open before God we learned from **Jesus**.

"I tell you, my friends, do not be afraid of those who kill the body and after that can do no more.
But I will show you whom you should fear: Fear him who, after the killing of the body, has power to throw you into hell. Yes, I tell you, fear him."

Luke 12:4-7

JULY 23

Jesus said, "Fear God." But people don't. We are afraid of many things, and people — what others will think, financial ruin, the dark, heights, enclosed places, snakes and spiders, illness or disease, old age, and death. But very few folks seem to fear God.

There are no words sufficient to describe the profound respect that we should give to our God. Typically, we use words, such as, awe, reverence, respect, veneration or adoration. There are times when the Scriptures show the depth of that fear. "Do you not fear me? declares the LORD. Do you not tremble before me?" (Jeremiah 5:22)

This godly fear is a respect and awe so strong that it causes us to tremble before His majesty and holiness. It is a fear born of the knowledge of who God is. The fear of God is a healthy, restraining fear and a force in our lives. It motivates us to do right. We make decisions and choose our course in life because we fear God. This fear is the beginning of wisdom.

We are commanded to fear God. And as long as we fear God, we need fear nothing or anyone. Either we fear God and fear nothing else, or we don't fear God and fear everything else.

When we possess a deep respect for God, when our hearts are in awe of who God is, we want to live so that He is pleased and honored. We seek to please the one we fear. No wonder Jesus encouraged his disciples to fear God rather than men.

Then Jesus had one more word of encouragement for them (and you): Never think that God will forget you. He won't. He can't. The sparrows are pretty cheap, yet God does not forget them. You are of great value to Him and He knows every detail of your life. He misses nothing that happens to you.

You are special. Proof of this is the presence of **Jesus**.

"And I tell you, everyone who acknowledges me before men, the Son of Man also will acknowledge before the angels of God, but the one who denies me before men will be denied before the angels of God."
Luke 12:8-12

JULY 24

Jesus knew that his own experiences were only a forecast for what lay ahead for his disciples and for all who would eventually follow. They would not escape the wrath of people who refused the kingdom message. Standing up for him would make all the difference in this world and the next.

It is an old song, a standard in churches. "Stand Up, Stand Up For Jesus." It is a song about soldiering in courage and duty against dangers and unnumbered foes. But mostly it is a song about vanquishing every foe and receiving a crown of life. It is easily sung. It is not so easily lived.

This last week, did you stand up for Jesus? Did you stand up for Jesus by the way you treated people, by the way you did your job, or by the way you handled difficulties and disappointments? Did you stand up for Jesus by the way you responded to conflict, by the choices you made about television shows to watch or magazine articles to read? Did you stand up for Jesus when you socialized with others, or when tension broke out in the office, or when someone mistreated you?

In other words, could people tell that you belong to him? Could people see that you know Jesus?

But standing up for Jesus is not always so obvious or dramatic. Being a peacemaker in a tense room, returning kindness for mistreatment, or showing forgiveness when you have been wronged are also opportunities to show the way of Jesus when another response might have been easier, even expected. Insisting on honesty with your children, driving the speed limit, and being generous with your gratitude and praise are ways we stand up for Jesus.

How can we know that standing up is worth it? "If you live in such a way that people can see that you know me, then one day before the Father I will say I know you." That is the promise of **Jesus**.

And he said to them, "Take care, and be on your guard against all covetousness, for one's life does not consist in the abundance of his possessions."

Luke 12:13-15

JULY 25

Jesus was in the middle of his teaching when he was interrupted by a man unhappy over the settlement of his father's estate. Rather than ask Jesus what he thought was fair, he demanded that Jesus should instruct his "brother to divide the inheritance with me!"

But Jesus' response was, no doubt, disappointing to this fellow. Jesus told him that the very best thing in this situation was to change his heart. Did you ever notice that most of the time we come to God asking him to change our situation rather than asking him to change our heart?

Greed is one of the most socially acceptable sins in our fallen culture. If an individual works hard and makes a fortune, we call that person a success, even if they have sacrificed their family, friends and faith in the process.

Greed deceives us. It motivates us to try to earn more than we need, own more than we can use, and ache for stuff that never satisfies. Greed promises a better day, more friends and fewer problems, more money and less difficulty. Greed lies to us and promises that we will be happy if we only acquire what we desire.

We have to decide at what lifestyle level we will live. Unfortunately, too many of us allow the culture to make the choice, and the choice is always for more, more, more. We are restless and more of something sounds like the answer.

We were made to glorify and honor the Creator, not the creation. Reversing the process is only a sign that we are out of touch with reality.

How can we know when we have got it wrong, when our desires are misplaced? The answer: when what we want to possess is more important to us than what we want to become; when what we have is more important to us than who we are.

"More" is usually perceived as the answer to our inner restlessness. But the answer is not "more." The answer is **Jesus**.

> "But God said to him, 'Fool! This night your soul is required of you, and the things you have prepared, whose will they be?'"
>
> Luke 12:16-21

JULY 26

Jesus never hinted that the man had come to his wealth dishonestly or that he was the miserly sort. Also, Jesus never said the man made a mistake by making plans about what to do with his grain.

In our day, the fellow's face and story would be on the Profiles page of the Sunday paper. His success would draw the admiration of many.

But the troubling part of the story comes in a single word: fool. Jesus called him a fool.

Why? The story is about making a decision as to the kind of life each person really wants. He made the wrong decision. Sadly, it is the one most folks make.

There is no evidence that he trusted God at all. His security seemed to be in his full barns. He sounds like a guy who thinks he did it all by himself. Enamored with his own success, he doubtlessly viewed himself as a self-made man. His wealth created a false sense of importance and security.

But he had forgotten God. He forgot that God furnished the soil, the seed, the sun and the rain. He forgot that God gave him life and health. He forgot that God gave him talents, abilities, and opportunities.

He confused ownership and stewardship. He mistakenly thought that because it was in his possession for a time, he was the owner. He was always just a steward...a temporary steward. A temporary steward who starts acting like the owner is a fool.

If this wealthy man ever saw beyond this world, we cannot tell it. While he planned for years in this world, he made no plans for the next. His arrogance made him believe that tomorrow was a given.

Death doesn't care how important you are to your family, or how many good things you are involved in, or how much you have tucked away in savings. Your tomorrow—or mine—can be cancelled at any moment. To live this life without making plans for the next is to be a fool.

Being wise is making our plans with **Jesus**.

" And which of you by being anxious can add a single hour to his span of life?"

Luke 12:22-31

JULY 27

Jesus must have been utterly captivating as a teacher. They had never heard anyone speak like that. He didn't just make sense to the mind, he made sense to the heart.

While it is right for us to care, it is wrong for us to worry. A distortion has occurred. No longer confident that God will be present or able, we feel bereft and helpless to change the course of events we fear the most.

Self-help books on the subject of anxiety and various coping strategies are innumerable. Their popularity is not so much an indication of successful hints and proven methods as our gullibility to believe we can handle this on our own. Our history says otherwise. Perhaps, we are slow learners, or maybe we are just stubborn, or both.

"O you of little faith." Our problem is not related to inherited temperament, health problems or insufficient bank accounts. It is not solved by vacations, pills or counseling sessions. Afraid of trusting God, we cling tenaciously to the idols made by our own hands. We want to believe, but find it easier to trust the visible than the invisible and easier to rely upon the simple than upon what seems mysterious. And what good thing comes from all our anxiety? Nothing!

Although we feel the force of his words, "O you of little faith," we still find hope in them. Jesus is reminding us that we have a choice. We do not have to be bound by fear; we do not have to be seized by worry. What we seek is freedom from anxiety. Trust in God is the answer.

But undergirding this emphasis on trust is the most important fact of all: God cares for us! Jesus illustrates from the animal kingdom (birds) and the plant kingdom (flowers). His argument is simple and direct: If God is willing and able to care for things of lesser value (birds and flowers), He is willing and able to care for things of greater value (people).

Write it on your heart: God loves you! Knowing that, what do you have to worry about? After all, to show how much, He gave His only Son, **Jesus**.

"For where your treasure is, there will your heart be also."
Luke 12:32-34

JULY 28

Jesus never misses us. When he speaks, he is always on target with just what we need to hear.

We sometimes seek the wrong treasure. Instead of casting our eyes heavenward, we don't look beyond the earth's horizons. Confined by only what we can see, we have every reason to be afraid. Locked in a world of possessions, we fall apart when the society of dishwashers, automobiles, and computers don't work. Limited by our bank account, our joy is retarded by the ups and downs of a market we cannot control. Closer to home, we dwell in a body destined to wear out.

But if our eyes are heavenward, we have every reason to live life with joy and excitement! Able to see beyond the physical, our happiness is not determined by what works or how the market moves or the condition of the body. The treasure we seek is not found here!

The appeal of the world is strong and constant. Promises of more pleasure, greater happiness, and increased financial gain are hard to ignore. All we have to do, we are told, is be willing to invest ourselves in order to enjoy the benefits. It always sounds like a great deal. We can have what we love. But what if we love the wrong things?

And did you ever notice how easy it is to lose what you love? Somehow, we never seem to be able to hold on to the things we love. Businesses go under, health deteriorates. objects are stolen or decay, and people die. No matter how hard we try, we cannot hold them tightly enough. The things we love all abandon us sooner or later. Then, we have nothing. Not even hope.

But what if we love God? Then, no matter who or what abandons us, we are not alone! God doesn't close or decay. He can't be stolen or die. He is always here! Our hope is never lost!

Treasure can be anything. It is what we value, what excites us and makes our heart beat fast. Treasure is what we love the most, and we know that the only real treasure is **Jesus**.

> "You also must be ready, for the Son of Man is coming at an hour you do not expect."
>
> Luke 12:35-40

JULY 29

Jesus left no doubt to those first century listeners that he would return. And if, after all this time of studying his words, we have a difficult time getting our minds around the idea, just think about those who heard him say it! What must they have been thinking?

There are few Bible topics more fascinating than the second coming of Jesus. Although the Bible provides only sketchy details, hundreds of books have been written providing specific details of what the second coming will look like and even when it will occur. Many issues surrounding the Lord's coming have been debated for centuries. We seem no closer to resolving those issues today than when they were first addressed.

The return of Jesus is a doctrine so fundamental to Christianity that it stands on the same plane as the virgin birth, the incarnation, the resurrection and the ascension. If Jesus is not coming back, then he is a terrible liar and fraud, and we are fools.

But Jesus wasn't simply making a promise; he was giving a warning. The warning was: be ready! To make his point, he told a story.

The master had gone to a wedding banquet. It was impossible to know precisely when the master would return. So, the servants were to be dressed and ready for service. They were to be ready, to be alert, to be at their post for the master's return.

What does it mean to be ready for his return? Peter answered that question. He said that, while we await his return, we "ought to live holy and godly lives." (2Peter 3:11)

But think about it this way. What would it say about us if we were not ready? We don't appreciate the sense of urgency! Or, that we don't view his coming as very important. Or, maybe we just assume that it does not really make any difference.

While the details of the second coming of Jesus are few and our questions are many, we are told exactly what to do as we wait. It is all the instruction we need: be ready for **Jesus**.

"Everyone to whom much was given, of him much will be required, and from him to whom they entrusted much, they will demand the more."

Luke 12:41-48

JULY 30

Jesus says, "I am coming and I want you to be ready." But when is he coming? It has been a very long time and still he has not come. So, could it be today?

A common notion is that the coming of Jesus is imminent; that is, his coming is about to happen because the signs are right. There have always been plenty of folks to argue that the signs of our times are just right and Jesus is about to come.

It is probably not the news we want to hear but the signs are deliberately ambiguous. The descriptions are general enough to allow any Christian living in almost any era of church history to survey the world situation and identify certain circumstances that would appear to be the fulfillments of Bible signs. It is important to remember that God is more than capable of communicating to us the specific time if He so desired. The fact that He did not would suggest that it is a mistake for us to become very dogmatic over this issue.

Jesus is not warning us of the serious consequences of merely being surprised but of being unready for his arrival. What is his point? Since you do not know when the thief is coming, you lock your house every night. Since you do not know when the inspector is coming, you do your job faithfully every day. Since you do not know when the Son of Man is coming, you live godly every day.

Do you believe that Jesus is coming back? Perhaps, we believe it in our heads, but not our hearts. After all, he has not come in all these centuries, so why would we believe there is anything special about today?

Evidently, Jesus believed that life should be lived with an eye on heaven; more specifically, with an eye on him. It actually helps us. We stay focused on the priorities, keep a sense of urgency about us, and remain watchful for the return of the one we love the most: **Jesus**.

> "Do you think that I have come to give peace on earth? No, I tell you, but rather division."
>
> Luke 12:49-53

JULY 31

Jesus did not come wanting a father to be against his son or a mother to be against her daughter. However, this was the effect of his coming and he knew that it would be.

Jesus' ministry began in his hometown synagogue but it was a rocky start. Jesus read from the prophet Isaiah that day, but both the prophet's words and his own brought no peace to the occasion. The people were so angry with Jesus that they drove him out of town and attempted to throw him off a cliff (Luke 4:16-30). This was but a foretaste of what his teaching would bring.

Jesus knew that people would divide over him. He knew that the decisions of some would split families. Three against two, two against three. And you will notice that always people were divided into just two groups. There would always be those who were with Jesus and those who were against him. There was no third option.

But why did Jesus affect people like this? How could a peaceful, loving man generate such a divisive and hostile response? Why did this poor teacher stir such strong emotions in those who heard and observed him? Why were some drawn to him while others were repulsed by him?

Jesus said things that some found hard to believe. "I am the way, the truth and the life; no one comes to the Father but by me." "I am the Son of God." Since he looked like other men, it was inevitable that his words would create debate.

Jesus' ways were equally divisive. He refused to honor the social traditions and ate with publicans. His kindness to Romans and Samaritans angered many of his own countrymen. His respectful treatment of women and children, beggars and lepers was confusing and disturbing to observers.

Divided opinions and different responses surround him but today is another opportunity for you to choose **Jesus**.

> "You hypocrites! You know how to interpret the appearance of earth and sky, but why do you not know how to interpret the present time?"
> Luke 12:54-59

AUGUST 1

Jesus might be viewed as a sign that was missed or a promise that was not believed. He may be considered an answer that was not heard or a solution that was not found. But however we may choose to explain it, the bottom line is: we did not know him.

The signs were there. For centuries there were plans and promises. There was a certain man, a certain nation, a certain tribe, and a certain family. God told us where and when, and He told us who and why. Still, because we missed the signs, we missed him.

It is rather amazing what human beings can do in predicting the weather. We can find out what is happening and what is going to happen for weeks in advance, and not just where we live but anywhere in the world! And if we are really hung up on weather, we can just sit around and watch the Weather Channel!

Of course, the people who lived in Palestine in the days of Jesus were not able to know the weather as we do. Although they lacked the modern scientific equipment we use, they did have the ability to watch the skies and determine the conditions. By such observations the farmers planted their fields and the sailors sailed the seas.

Jesus acknowledged that they were rather good at reading the wind, the clouds and the sun. They could tell when the weather was changing, a front was coming through or rain was on the way. However, he asks, why can't you read the spiritual signs around you? How could they be so sharp in earthly concerns and such dunces in spiritual matters?

Not much has changed. People still pay far more attention to the weather forecast than they do to their eternal destiny.

What do you see around you? Are you missing the signs of God? Let's hope not. Nothing could be worse than missing **Jesus**.

"No, I tell you; but unless you repent, you will all likewise perish."
Luke 13:1-5

AUGUST 2

Jesus knew what they were thinking. It just made sense. These Galileans must have been doing something wrong to meet such a violent end. In fact, they may have been very wicked people.

It was an old view. But it was an answer that helped make sense of what sometimes was a senseless world. After all, how else could people explain why things happened to some people and not to others? Simply put: suffering was the result of doing wrong. God punished the wicked and blessed the righteous. Even the disciples were given to accepting this conclusion. They thought the blind man must be blind because either he or his parents had sinned (John 9).

So, when the news came from Jerusalem that Pilate had just killed a number of Galileans while they were offering sacrifices in the temple, Jesus seized the moment to teach an important lesson. "Don't think that you are without guilt because the same thing hasn't happened to you! Everyone should repent!"

Repentance. There is no way to read the Bible and not be impressed with the frequency of the command. Perhaps, it is mentioned often because it is so very difficult. Repentance calls for soul-searching honesty and that can be very hard after we have worked so hard to hide our failings. Repentance means changing our ways and that could bring great unrest to our life. Repentance demands that we confess our sins and that means we have to get over our pride. Repentance requires our admission of complete dependence on God and we don't like to be dependent on anyone. And repentance calls for our willing submission to the way of another and we much prefer to have our own way. So, who wants to sign up for all that?

Godly sorrow is the genuine, deep-down grief that comes because we have offended God and broken His heart, and that matters to us. Repentance is not simply being sad about what we've done; it is desiring to be entirely different.

No more hiding, no more blaming, no more denying. It is time to repent. It is the path to **Jesus**.

"And he answered him, 'Sir, let it alone this year also, until I dig around it and put on manure.
Then if it should bear fruit next year, well and good; but if not, you can cut it down.'"

Luke 13:6-9

AUGUST 3

Jesus came to bring the essential change to our lives. Without his effort we were hopelessly lost. His words encouraged us and his ways showed us. He came all this way for us. Even so, we resisted him.

The meaning of the parable is not difficult, especially coming on the heels of the tower story. The owner of the vineyard who rightly expects to see fruit on His tree is God. As the owner it is certainly within His right to destroy the tree if it fails to bear fruit. After all, bearing fruit is its purpose. The gardener, or keeper of the vineyard, is Jesus. The fig tree represents Israel (and you and me).

To this point, the fig tree has been only a failure. That sounds a lot like us—failed lives, broken homes, ruined marriages, rebellious and disobedient—failures all around. God could have given up on us a long time ago, but He didn't. Instead, we are presented the opportunity to live and accomplish the purpose for which we were created.

But this opportunity is not without end. God's patience has a limit. In the parable, the fig tree is granted another year. Perhaps, God will give us another day, another month, or even another year. But this extra time is so that we might repent and become the bearers of good fruit. Failing to bear fruit means certain destruction!

Even now God is working in our lives to bring us to repentance. Through the story of His Son He seeks to break through that prideful exterior and penetrate our heart with His love and forgiveness. He is patient. But He will not be patient forever. We have to decide.

Is there any part of your life where you are resisting the Lord? Time is shorter than you think. Today is a gift and your opportunity to live for **Jesus**.

> "It is like a grain of mustard seed that a man took and sowed in his garden, and it grew and became a tree, and the birds of the air made nests in its branches."
>
> Luke 13:10-21

AUGUST 4

Jesus noticed her and called her to come to him. There is no indication that she approached him about her condition or made any request for help. But Jesus knew her life.

Eighteen years is a long time to be bent over. Although she may have grown accustomed to people staring and children laughing, she still hurt. She couldn't look anyone in the eye. Her condition made others uncomfortable. She may have felt like an embarrassment to her family.

Although we have learned not to be surprised by Jesus, this was not a typical synagogue service and his actions must have startled many who observed all this. But Jesus did not respond to her simply because of her gender. Tax collectors, prostitutes, lepers, widows, and women were often the people to whom Jesus ministered most. He genuinely cared about those who were the most oppressed and ignored, those who were hurting and hopeless.

The synagogue ruler was more focused on religious rules and maintaining synagogue order than people needs. Instead of rejoicing that this woman was healed, he railed about keeping the law and informed those present that there were other days for healing. Jesus rebuked him by saying, "Even for the sake of your rules you wouldn't be so heartless to an animal!"

Difficult life experiences can bring a lot of tough questions. Why is God putting me through this? Why did God take my child? Often, people believe that God is behind it all and that He must be working out some master plan. Suffering does not always come with explanation, but Jesus said that Satan was responsible for her pain and suffering.

But a new day has come! The reign and rule of Jesus! As surely as a mustard seed grows into a tree, this kingdom will triumph over everything! The healing of this woman was only a taste of the change coming into the world. As surely as Jesus defeated Satan in the life of this woman, Satan would be defeated in the lives of all who were ruled by **Jesus**!

"My sheep hear my voice, and I know them, and they follow me. I give them eternal life, and they will never perish, and no one will snatch them out of my hand."

John 10:22-39

AUGUST 5

Jesus' identity, more than two thousand years later, remains a subject of controversy. Much of the debate rages over what we can know for sure about him. Believing the gospel stories of Jesus to be the prejudicial views of uneducated and superstitious people rather than the result of divine inspiration, many have gone in search of the *real* Jesus. As a result, we are left today with various versions of the Galilean: a political change agent, a Jewish street preacher, a social activist, a magician, a moralistic prophet, or an outright fraud.

This quest to discover who Jesus really is goes all the way back to the days when he walked among us. Even then we wanted him to explain himself, to identify himself in a way that made sense.

The Jews seized this festive occasion to press him. They were insistent. "Are you or are you not the Messiah? Tell us plainly." In truth, they were not really so much interested in the answer as in gathering evidence against him.

Jesus replied, "I did tell you but you did not believe me. And I have shown you but it has made no difference."

Then they picked up rocks. "And you are going to stone me for which miracle?"

"No, not for that but making yourself equal with God when you are only a mere man."

That's it! That's the problem we have always had with Jesus: he looks like a mere man. And since a mere man could not possibly be the Son of God, we search for the real Jesus, for the real story behind the man.

Very little has changed since Jesus walked among us. Whether it is the Passover Plot or the Jesus Seminar or the Da Vinci Code, people are still trying to show that Jesus was not who he said he was, that his real identity will show him to be only a mere man.

"Tell us plainly." He did. Now, we just need to believe **Jesus**.

> "Strive to enter through the narrow door. For many, I tell you, will seek to enter and will not be able."
>
> Luke 13:22-30 (John 10:40-42)

AUGUST 6

Jesus knocking on a door, symbolizing the heart or life, is an image that has been captured in numerous paintings through the centuries. The door has no handle and thus cannot be opened except from the inside. That person on the inside is you. You must decide whether you will open your heart and life to Jesus or keep him waiting on the outside.

But what if you consider the door from the other side? What if, instead of the door being closed and waiting to be opened by you, the door is opened by Jesus and he is inviting you to enter? That is exactly the imagery used by Jesus.

Becoming a disciple of Jesus is the result of a conscious decision. We do not accidentally wander through the right door. We do not accidentally fall into the kingdom. Jesus did not invite us to stand near the door or to simply associate with those who enter it. The door must be entered.

And there is just one door. Not many doors. Just one. People want there to be many doors. Or, in our postmodern culture: just make your own door. It can look like whatever you want. Make the door that works for you. Make the door that makes you happy. Not!

At some point, the owner rises and closes the door. Time's up! The invitation has a limit. The door is only open so long. We want so much to believe that we have plenty of time to do all the things we believe are important. But our time is limited. The door is going to close. The very worst thing is to be left standing on the wrong side of the door pleading for another chance to enter. He says, "I don't know you or where you come from."

Jesus says, "I have opened the door of escape. But you have to want to enter and you must enter before the door closes!"

One day God will interrupt your day and say, "Time's up! The door is closed!" Then, only one thing will matter: Being on the side of the door with **Jesus**.

"O Jerusalem, Jerusalem, the city that kills the prophets and stones those who are sent to it! How often would I have gathered your children together as a hen gathers her brood under her wings, and you would not!"

Luke 13:31-35

AUGUST 7

Jesus was not crying for himself, although his heart ached for what might have been. He was certainly no stranger to rejection and the ultimate rejection was still ahead. For now, he spoke like a parent groaning over a rebellious child whose stubbornness was costing more than could be imagined. Jesus said, "This is what I wanted for you, but you would not."

Jesus felt great compassion for the people of Jerusalem and his imagery demonstrated it. A mother hen is a provider and protector for her chicks. She will find food and call them to it. At the first sign of danger, she'll spread her wings and they will come running to safety beneath them.

Jesus looked over this city and said, "I want to be the one who provides for you. I want to be the one who protects you. I want to be the one who guides you. I want to be the one who comforts you. But you would not have it!"

But isn't this just like Jesus? Jesus came with his arms and his eyes wide open. He knew exactly what we were like. He said, "I love you. If you follow me or if you don't, if you believe in me or if you don't, if you love me or if you don't...I love you."

But it remains the greatest mystery: Jesus offers his very life for our eternal safety, yet most will say, "No thanks. I'm not interested." Like Jerusalem, far too many of us reject what we need most.

In danger, chicks run to find safety under mother's wings. Where do you go? Unfortunately, we often don't even sense any danger...or, we foolishly think we can handle and survive it on our own. We are wrong. So, write this on your heart: In the universe, the only safe place is under the love of the **Jesus**.

And Jesus responded to the lawyers and Pharisees, saying, "Is it lawful to heal on the Sabbath, or not?"
But they remained silent. Then he took him and healed him and sent him away.

Luke 14:1-6

AUGUST 8

Jesus often left people speechless. His unique approach to life was baffling, even shocking. His openness and vulnerability, his honesty and love were qualities that drew admirers and critics. But neither group knew exactly what to do with him.

Jesus frustrated the Pharisees. His lack of respect for their rules and his indifference to their traditions were more than simple irritations; this was blasphemy! Politically correct he was not.

While the common folk seemed to welcome his words of love and hope and faith, those with misguided notions about the nature of the kingdom found him hard to take. His idea of kingdom did not match theirs.

It appears that not much has really changed. Many times, we are resistant to the way of Jesus for those same reasons.

Sabbath laws were intended as good laws, designed to assist the people in focusing on God. But people were more important than the Sabbath laws. And focus on God was not lost because people received love and care.

Folks will reason, "Yes, but if you let it happen this time...if you grant this request...if you help these people...." The implication is always that if you put people ahead of your rules and laws, then someone will abuse it or it will lead who knows where. But that is our fear speaking, not our love. You can hide behind law, but love requires openness. You can excuse yourself from responsibility or involvement because the law says so, but love requires personal involvement.

Jesus never set aside God's law; but he did set aside the established laws of men. He loved God's way and he loved people. We ought to be like him.

Also, Jesus never felt compelled to do the same thing with everyone. He dealt with people on the basis of their respective needs. Under the guise of having to follow the rules, we make the mistake of lumping everyone together and excusing ourselves from having to help. Whatever else this may be, this is not loving others and it is not the way of **Jesus**.

> "For everyone who exalts himself will be humbled, and he who humbles himself will be exalted."
>
> Luke 14:7-11

AUGUST 9

Jesus watched them jockey for positions around the table. The places of greatest honor would be those closest to the host. Sitting near the host would suggest a special familiarity with the host, and that might translate into status and power. Perhaps, James and John were thinking along those lines when they tried to arrange for the best seats next to Jesus (Mark 10:37).

It is only human nature for us to want to sit in the best seat in the house. At sporting events it's the skybox seat, or the seat on the 50-yard line or the courtside seat at a basketball game. Those are the places that put us nearest the action or give us the most comfortable view, and the seats that carry the highest price. They also carry the greatest bragging rights. It impresses people when we tell them we have those seats.

Jesus' response to all this competition for seats was a call to humility. It was just one more occasion when Jesus reversed the usual rules governing social situations. Humble yourself and be exalted. Exalt yourself and be humbled.

Go to a bookstore and ask to be directed to the section on how to increase humility. No such section exists! There are plenty of books and videos on how to be more aggressive, how to succeed, how to win, how to intimidate, and how to get what you want.

Nobody wants the last seat. We deserve better. We deserve more attention. We deserve to be noticed. Besides, how will we ever advance if we are virtually out of sight in the last seat?

Do you want to be first? Go to the end of the line. Do you want to be the greatest? Become the least. Do you want to be in charge? Try serving. Do you want to be big? Become like a little child. Of course, this is not the way of our world but it is the way of **Jesus**.

> "And at the time for the banquet he sent his servant to say to those who had been invited, 'Come, for everything is now ready.' But they all alike began to make excuses."
>
> Luke 14:12-24

AUGUST 10

Jesus was so out-of-step with the social and cultural norms of his day that he offended people. In fact, he irritated them so much that they began to consider removing him altogether. His unusual perspective on how life should be lived and how that clashed with the typical thinking of his day is well illustrated in this story.

In a time without telephones or email, it made perfect sense to issue two invitations. The first was given well in advance so that people could make plans to attend. Then, when everything was ready, the servants were again sent out telling the invited folks that it was time to come.

These fellows did not reject the invitation because they were involved in bad activities. They simply thought they had more important things to do. Most of us don't reject God's gracious invitation because we are involved in some kind of terrible evil. We are just too involved in the business of life and too busy to think seriously about our soul. And even when we do, we always believe there will be other opportunities.

Jesus is not suggesting that God will accept any of our lame excuses. He is saying that God will not accept <u>any</u> excuses. How could any of us justify ourselves before God?

Now, how does the host respond to these excuses? The invitation to the banquet was extended to the most unlikely people. Isn't it just like Jesus to tell a story about an invitation to unlikely people?

But these fellows missed their opportunity. How many more opportunities do we have to accept the invitation of the Lord? Unknown. But we know this: there is an end to those opportunities. And when it comes, those who have repeatedly said, "I intend to...I'm going to...I just need a little more time...I'm still thinking about it...I will one day..." are going to be left begging for just one more chance.

Now, what is it that God wants you to do? What invitation is He extending to you? Now is the very best time to say "yes" to **Jesus**.

"Whoever does not bear his own cross and come after me cannot be my disciple."

Luke 14:25-27

AUGUST 11

Jesus knew that a crowd was not a sign of success. They were enthusiastic, but was their excitement based on an understanding of what it meant to be a disciple?

The call of discipleship is, fundamentally, a call to allegiance. Jesus refuses to be simply a diversion or a hobby in the lives of those who claim to be his disciples. Disciples do not volunteer on their own terms or at their own convenience.

Jesus' words are shocking! But did Jesus really want the people to hate their spouses, or their children, or their siblings?

Jesus is using hyperbole, an overstatement in order to make a point with maximum impact. They challenge us and make us think. No earthly tie, however close, must take precedence over our allegiance to Jesus. He is Number One! No one else is a close second.

But being a disciple is more than just loving Jesus above all others. It is loving Jesus more than one's own life!

Carrying our own cross doesn't mean much to us. We can talk about crosses...draw pictures of them...wear them about our neck... But we have never actually watched a crucifixion. (Hollywood movies don't count.)

But these people knew all about crosses. And they knew that anyone who picked up a cross was on a one-way journey. That person would not be back. They understood that when someone picked up a cross, he or she would finish with it.

So, they knew what Jesus was talking about. He was calling for a total abandonment of selfishness. He was speaking of the utmost in self-denial. We must not only be committed to Jesus more than to our loved one, but we must also be committed to him above even "our own life."

Twice in these verses, Jesus said, "he cannot be my disciple." Let no one be uncertain about the identity of "he." "He" is the person who would love anything or anyone, even self, more than Jesus.

Discipleship is not about an organization or cause. Discipleship is about a person: Jesus.

Time would reveal whether these were genuine followers or whether something else held their hearts. What about you? Is your heart only for **Jesus**?

> "So therefore, any one of you who does not renounce all that he has cannot be my disciple."
>
> Luke 14:28-35

AUGUST 12

Jesus wanted people to follow him. But he knew that many would follow for a time without really understanding the true meaning of discipleship. Then, when they became disillusioned by the difficulties or unwilling to make the sacrifices required, they would fall away. He wanted no one to follow under misconceptions. Jesus demanded full commitment; nothing less would do.

So, Jesus told the story of a man who desired to build a tower. Since this was a major undertaking, not to mention an expensive project, it was essential to plan wisely. What good is a half-built watchtower?

Most of us have a number of unfinished projects littering our past. We began some of them with the very best of intentions, but then other things distracted us and we lost interest or just gave up. Too often, we are good beginners and poor finishers.

But this isn't good enough for discipleship. The finishing is every bit as important as the beginning!

The second story involved a king contemplating the wisdom of going to war or asking for terms of peace. Could he win with an army half the size of the opposing forces? His thoughtful deliberations led to his decision to seek peace.

While both parables emphasize the importance of counting the cost before advancing, there is one striking difference between them: their perspectives. In the first parable, Jesus wants the people, like a builder, to consider whether they can afford to follow him. But in the second story, he calls the crowd to consider, like a king, whether they can afford *not* to follow him. Failure in the first would be failing to count the cost before trying to build (follow). Failure in the second would be making the wrong decision (not following) after counting the cost.

This discipleship was not to be taken lightly. Jesus wasn't inviting people to volunteer some of their time, money and energy to the latest "good idea." And he certainly wasn't inviting them to sign-on just for a time. No, this wasn't just any decision. This was an invitation to live and to die. Like **Jesus**.

"Just so, I tell you, there will be more joy in heaven over one sinner who repents than over ninety-nine righteous persons who need no repentance."

Luke 15:1-10

AUGUST 13

Jesus' love and acceptance of others attracted people from all walks of life. Even his stories touched them. While each story has its lost "object," the emphasis is clearly on the one who is searching. The passion to restore is beyond all bounds and nothing can hold back the celebration! This is the heart of our God!

Once a part of the fold, the sheep had somehow become separated from the group. What an aggravation! Just when you thought you were done for the day you discover that you are one critter short.

Of course, the coin did not wander off. Still, it was lost. Perhaps the coin, a day's wage, was a matter of sheer necessity. Poor people could not afford to lose even a coin. Or, maybe the coin possessed sentimental value to the owner. Whatever the reason for its value, it was lost and finding it in a small room with dirt floors and few windows would not be easy.

If you had one hundred sheep and lost one, would you leave the others to find the lost one? Not likely. Good business sense would suggest that you simply cut your losses, forget about the lost one, and continue with the ninety-nine. So, what is Jesus saying? That God is *not* like us!

When Jesus told the parable of the lost coin, he changed the image. The God character was no longer a shepherd but a woman, a very strange woman. She called her whole world to a stop to find a coin. And if that wasn't silly enough, when she found it, she called her friends and neighbors to come have a party over the recovery of the coin. Now, who would do that? No one but God!

But that is the point! No one but God would search for one and then celebrate as if He had found the entire herd! No one but God would search for one and then celebrate as if He had found a great treasure! No one but God!

Given the numbers and the values we wouldn't search or celebrate. But God will. No matter the cost to Him. Just ask **Jesus**.

"And he said, 'There was a man who had two sons.
And the younger of them said to his father, 'Father, give me the share of property that is coming to me.' And he divided his property between them."

Luke 15:11-16

AUGUST 14

Jesus wanted his critics to know that his ways reflected God's, his heart mirrored the Father's. So, he told them of a father forgiving a prodigal.

So, why did he leave? He wanted to please himself, to live his own life. Happiness was somewhere out there in greener fields and he wanted to find it. And he really believed that he could not find what he wanted at home.

Perhaps, he was tired of coming to the breakfast table and having to answer his father's question, "Where were you last night?" Maybe he was weary of the same old routine and longed for something different, more exciting. Or, maybe he just realized that he deserved to be free, that he was entitled to life as he wanted without answering to anyone, including his father. Especially his father.

Today, the talk-show psychologists would heartily applaud his actions. They would praise him for flinging away restraints, casting aside inhibitions, and engaging in free self-expression. He was doing his own thing. He was being his own man. He was simply being true to himself.

But things did not go as planned and he made a mess of his life, and he knew he had broken the heart of someone who loved him. He never meant to do that...and he always envisioned that one day he would go home...after he had made his fortune, established his reputation, proven himself to the world. But life just did not go according to the plan. The greener grass wasn't all that green. Does that sound familiar?

In search of having his way and being really free, he found himself more a slave than ever before. In search of a better, more exciting life, he found himself feeding pigs. In search of the world's pleasures, he found himself longing for nothing greater than pods.

What shall become of him? Of us? The answer lies with **Jesus**.

> "I will arise and go to my father, and I will say to him, 'Father, I have sinned against heaven and before you.
> I am no longer worthy to be called your son. Treat me as one of your hired servants.'"
> And he arose and came to his father.
>
> Luke 15:17-20a

AUGUST 15

Jesus said, "When he came to his senses..." Now he did not suddenly realize he was in a hog pen. He knew that all the time. No, he was now seeing himself, his condition in a different way. He knew that this was no way to live!

Although God's invitation is always open to us, it is often not enough. It takes a famine. We have to be driven to God because we are so stubborn and full of pride. The famine did not come by chance. God sent the famine to bring us home.

He knew that going home was the right thing to do, but it could not have been an easy decision. After all, going home was humbling. What would people think? How would his father react?

And he knew it meant confession. There is no restoration of joy until the confession is made. We just don't feel good until we have said what needs to be said. There must be that admission to the Father that we were wrong and we just want to be home.

Honesty is the first step on the journey home. Until a person faces up to the foolishness of their actions and feels the despair of how far they have fallen, there is no possibility of going home.

The young man offered no excuses to cover his guilt or any justifications for his waywardness. He admitted that he was in trouble. He was starving to death! He recognized the cause of his problem was his own sin. And he acknowledged that he no longer had a right to be called his father's son.

"When he came to his senses...." But what if he hadn't? What if he remained stubborn? What if his pride got in the way of the truth? What if...what if we would not go home?

Yes, this is our story, too. In trouble. Because of our own sins. Deserving nothing. But full of hope because of **Jesus**.

> "For this my son was dead, and is alive again; he was lost, and is found." And they began to celebrate.
>
> Luke 15:20b-24

AUGUST 16

Jesus moved through society seemingly oblivious to the fact that there are people you do not touch, folks with whom you do not associate. He shunned no one and sought everyone.

Perhaps the Pharisees might–if reluctantly–have tolerated the coming of sinners to Jesus. What they could not bear was that he welcomed them — worse still, he sought them out. And worst of all, he ate with them!

So, Jesus told them about God, our Father. And he did it in a story.

In time, the prodigal realized the one thing he had to do. He probably practiced his speech all the way home. And when face-to-face with his father, he confessed what they both knew: "I have sinned...and I am not worthy..."

When the father saw his son, he ran to meet him. He could have stood where he was and made the son come all the way to him. We might have done that. He had every right to demand an apology and penance before accepting his erring son. We probably would have done that, too.

But the words of unworthiness are lost in the exuberance of the Father! The crushed spirit of the son is overwhelmed by the immense joy of the Father! To be so loved! Why did he ever leave? Why did he wait so long to come home?

Jesus is not saying that God is just like we are. God is not like we are. We wouldn't leave ninety-nine to go find one. We would cut our losses and go on with what we have in hand. We would not spend the day hunting for a single coin and then throw a party when we had found it. We wouldn't cast aside our dignity and run to a rebellious child. We wouldn't celebrate without insisting they prove themselves. We wouldn't lavish gifts upon them; we would want them to earn them. We would not extend a welcome like this to such a child; we would not stoop for a son or daughter who so grievously offended us.

But God would. Our Father would give everything for the joy of receiving us home. In fact, He did. He gave **Jesus**.

> "...but he answered his father, 'Look, these many years I have served you, and I never disobeyed your command, yet you never gave me a young goat, that I might celebrate with my friends."
>
> Luke 15:25-32

AUGUST 17

Jesus said there is something worse than being lost like the prodigal, something far worse than finding yourself away from home. It is worse to be at home and still lost but not even realize it!

This older brother had remained at home, stayed out of trouble, obeyed the rules, worked hard, and perfectly positioned himself in the family. But the older did not really love and respect his father any more than the younger did at the beginning of the story. His years of working and toiling for his father were not out of love, only duty and obligation. Evidently, he overlooked the blessings, felt sorry for himself, and believed he was entitled to something better than he got. He may have been at home in one sense, but in reality, he was no more home than the prodigal. He was geographically near his father but he certainly did not share his father's heart.

Consider what Jesus is saying to his listeners, and to us? The older son is lost. Why? This good son is not lost in spite of his good behavior but because of it. His good behavior is his confidence; it is the basis of his relationship with his father. He isn't home because he loves his father. He is home because of what his father can give him as a reward for his good work. It is his work that entitles him, not the relationship.

The younger brother wanted the father's wealth, but not the father. So how did he get what he wanted? He left home. The older son wanted the same thing. But he stayed home to get what he wanted.

But the father loved both sons and, as he went out to the younger, he went out to the older. He lovingly pleaded with his son to recognize the error of his words and ways and to come inside to celebrate. Those hearing the story must have recognized a tender invitation in the words of **Jesus**.

> "One who is faithful in a very little is also faithful in much, and one who is dishonest in a very little is also dishonest in much."
>
> Luke 16:1-13

AUGUST 18

Jesus commended shrewdness. It's one of those words that almost sounds sinister, but it really isn't. The shrewd person is someone who has looked at the options and decides upon the wisest and best choice.

The master called for a complete audit of the books. Facing unemployment, the steward began to look at the alternatives. He said, "I cannot dig; I am ashamed to beg." In other words, "I have limits."

What he needed was a place to go and someone who would want him when his master threw him out. Perhaps someone would even provide him with another job. He decided that his best option was to make friends of his master's debtors. That way, he could smooth the path for a new job. So, he gave each of his master's debtors a generous discount.

The owner's praise of the steward didn't mean he was pleased with what he had done, but at least he was impressed with his wise and thoughtful planning. Besides, the master came out ahead in reputation and standing even if he lost some money.

Now it may look as though our Lord is commending a crook. Jesus is not telling us that we should imitate the dishonesty of the steward. He is, however, suggesting that we can learn from the clever and resourceful way "the children of the world" operate. He is pointing out the obvious: in worldly financial matters, unbelievers are often more astute or shrewd than God's children.

Jesus told this story to explain the importance of making the wise and right use of the money and possessions we have. While we have the opportunity, we must be wise and faithful stewards who invest our money in kingdom priorities. If we are trustworthy with worldly wealth, God can trust us with true riches. But this calls for some sobering questions: Are we a good investment? How are we doing with what we have? Are we good stewards?

Everything we have is ours to use only for a time. Eventually, each of us must give an account of ourselves to **Jesus**.

The Pharisees, who were lovers of money, heard all these things, and they ridiculed him.

Luke 16:14-18

AUGUST 19

Jesus' emphasis on the spiritual over the temporal was a constant irritation to the Pharisees. It is painful to be found out. So, they sneered at him.

The Bible has plenty to say about the dangers of money. From the prophets who warned the rich to the proverbs about stewardship, from the parables of Jesus about rich folks to Paul's warning about money being "a root of all kinds of evils," the Scriptures reflect God's desire that we love what is genuine and eternal and not be deceived by the fake and temporary.

Our world runs on money. Whoever has the most gets the last word. Money is power. Money allows pleasures. Money accumulates things. Money influences people. Money usually gets its way. In other words, money appears to do for us all that we might want or dream. It is not difficult to love it!

So, we chase after it in order to have all that life can give us. In the meantime, we feel compelled to justify our pursuit so we can live with our conscience. Big giving always helps ease the mind.

Jesus could see through that. Giving is not about the size of the gift but about the heart that gives it. No one fools God.

The problem is an old one. We tend to value what we can see with our eyes and touch with our hands. Because that's what seems real, we desire it most. The car, the house, the boat, the clothes, the land, the vacation, the corner office, and the tickets on the fifty-yard line all seem especially valuable because everyone else is trying to get them, too. Besides, they make us feel and look important, people praise us, and we are free to enjoy more of life.

Taking a vacation or having a corner office is not really the issue. Believing that this is what is truly valuable in life is.

God does bless us with many wonderful things. We should be grateful. But He never once said that those things were truly valuable for real life. However, He did say that about His Son, **Jesus**.

> "The poor man died and was carried by the angels to Abraham's side. The rich man also died and was buried, and in Hades, being in torment, he lifted up his eyes and saw Abraham far off and Lazarus at his side."
>
> Luke 16:19-24

AUGUST 20

Jesus never taught that it was wrong to be rich. He spoke often of the dangers of misplaced affections and wrong priorities, but he never condemned the rich for being rich. Thus, he did not tell stories designed to cast wealthy people as always being evil or poor people as always being virtuous.

There is not the slightest hint that the rich man gained his wealth dishonestly. There is no suggestion that he committed any crime or cheated anyone. He may have been a hard worker and a wise investor. He may have been the kind of guy who could turn anything into a profit. However, he did not use his wealth wisely.

Perhaps, like us, he was sold on the idea that one is what he or she possesses. Or, maybe he set out to buy happiness. Whatever he was trying to do with his own life, he missed Lazarus.

Every morning when he went to the office, there was Lazarus, seeking only compassion. Every evening when he returned home, there was Lazarus, asking only for crumbs. Every time he looked out his window, every time he took the dog for a walk, every time he greeted visitors at his front gate, there was Lazarus, desiring only some kindness. Lazarus was a daily, living opportunity for the rich man to show love and kindness, to use his wealth to bless another. But he missed Lazarus. He never really saw him. Wealth will do that.

Reminders are all around us. Whether you read the obituary, attend a funeral, or just follow the daily news, the message is constant. No matter who we are, no matter what we have done, no matter whom we know and no matter how much money we have...death awaits us.

Two lives, vastly different. Two eternities, vastly different. We know that what we do with what we have can make an eternal difference. We know it because we heard it from **Jesus**.

"He said to him, 'If they do not hear Moses and the Prophets, neither will they be convinced if someone should rise from the dead.'"
Luke 16:25-31

AUGUST 21

Jesus responded to the sneers of the Pharisees, who loved money, by telling them, "God knows your hearts." Regardless of how they might appear unto others, there would be no escape from the judgment of God!

For those squeamish about the thought of hell, this story isn't likely to be popular. But why would it? It violates several of our most coveted beliefs.

For example, the rich man and Lazarus were separated by a great gulf and no one could pass from one side to the other...and there was no invitation from Abraham's side to the other side! But we want so much to believe that a second chance must await all who made poor decisions in life.

Also, the reversed situations of the two men shreds our prejudicial views so often based on appearances. At a glance, whom would we have selected as the most likely candidate for heaven? The established and successful community man or the shameful homeless man begging for food? Who would we have chosen as the more religious? The man whose life reflected the blessings of God or the man who had little to show for a lifetime on the planet?

And then comes a moment in the story we could not have anticipated! The rich man wants Lazarus to return to the world of his five brothers and warn them about this place! Perhaps, he knew it would do no good to ask to go himself. So, he would do the next best thing and ask for the beggar to go. His brothers would surely remember Lazarus.

His words make sense. After all, who wouldn't believe a man returned from the dead? Who wouldn't believe a man who died in front of everyone and then walked out of his tomb with a message from God? Who wouldn't believe a man who came back from the world of the dead to tell people about life after death?

There will come a second when all stops. But in this moment, you can still hear and heed the messengers. Right now, you can still listen and decide. Right now, you are still free to follow in the steps of **Jesus**.

And he said to his disciples, "Temptations to sin are sure to come, but woe to the one through whom they come!"

Luke 17:1-6

AUGUST 22

Jesus always viewed sin as a serious matter. Most of us understand why: our sin is an offense against God. But Jesus said if you cause someone else to sin, it's even worse. And if you should dare lead a little child into sin, then you'd be better off to take a short rope attached to a really big rock, tie the rope around your neck and toss the rock into the deepest part of the ocean! Sin is that serious!

Perhaps, Jesus was reminding his disciples that people are always watching. Our carelessness may give someone the rationale for sinning. If so, we share the responsibility for that sin.

Then, Jesus confronts us with two of life's most difficult tasks: rebuking and forgiving. Neither comes easy for most of us.

We must rebuke sin whether we want to or not. Much of the time we would just prefer to ignore it if we can and stay out of trouble. We have so little success or good experiences when rebuking that we would prefer to just let others alone. After all, this is the age of tolerance.

And forgive. Not just once, but over and over and over. And don't keep count. Just keep forgiving.

We can all agree that this is difficult. But remember: Forgiveness is a choice we make. It is our decision to cancel the debt and set another free of any obligation. In doing so, we become a reflection of the forgiveness God offers us. Forgiving is a blessing to us as well as to them.

Maybe the disciples found this a little too difficult to take. Perhaps, their cry for increased faith was based on their belief that what Jesus was asking was impossible! Of course, it was if they tried to manage it on their own.

But Jesus said that even small faith can do amazing things! Already you have shown kindness to strangers, forgiven those who mistreated you, guarded your tongue, served others who needed help, and shown love to people whom others forgot. And how did you manage all this? With your eyes on **Jesus**.

> "So you also, when you have done all that you were commanded, say, 'We are unworthy servants; we have only done what was our duty.'"
> Luke 17:7-10

AUGUST 23

Jesus did not come to make life fair! Although it is a common complaint – "life is not fair" – this was not the issue that consumed him or drove him toward the cross.

In our age, there is considerable emphasis on 'rights' and 'equality,' what one receives and deserves. Even though life isn't fair, we seem determined to give our best effort to make it so. It isn't surprising that the idea of being a slave to Jesus is not very inviting to many.

But why did Jesus tell this story? It wasn't as though the listeners were unaware of how the system worked. They knew all about slavery. They understood that masters don't serve slaves.

Perhaps, Jesus directed his story at those self-righteous souls who felt God owed them something for their acts of piety. Maybe he was sending a warning to his own disciples that following him was not about earning some reward or gaining recognition for a job well done. Discipleship was not about special treatment or entitlement. No, discipleship was about loving him who first loved us.

Or, maybe Jesus wanted all who heard him to think once again of who is God and who is the servant. God does not owe us anything. He gives to us freely and He is continually gracious to us. But He does so because He is God.

Take a moment and look around you. What do you have that you deserve? What do you see that did not come from the gracious hand of God? What brings you the greatest joy just now that is from some source other than God?

Jesus' story is not about unfairness or inequality at all. His story is about our unworthiness before our gracious God.

But we are not slaves to a tyrant or servants to a despot. We serve the One who first served us, the One who died for us! Thus, we serve with gladness because we have been saved and we love **Jesus**.

So the sisters sent to him, saying, "Lord, he whom you love is ill."
John 11:1-16

AUGUST 24

Jesus received the news about Lazarus but did not rush to his bedside. He knew there was no need. Something quite remarkable was going to happen. There was no reason to hurry.

Whatever Lazarus's symptoms, it became apparent to his sisters that the situation was deteriorating rapidly and his condition was very serious. Desperate for Jesus to know their brother's condition, Mary and Martha sent a message to Jesus. They surely expected that Jesus would come soon.

And what do we make of the disciples' attitude about this? Initially, they considered a return to Judea to be unwise, even dangerous. After all, the Teacher's most recent trip there had been scary enough! They had barely escaped with their lives! Returning a few months later would be like inviting a stoning!

Then, Jesus gave them a fuller picture. "Lazarus is dead. We must go." When Thomas saw the inevitable, he voiced what others were thinking: "We'll all go die together."

God does not always act as we expect. He disappoints us. He takes too long. We come seeking direction or relief. We come seeking answers to how or why, when or where. When He delays, we wonder if He heard us or if He cares or if He can really do anything.

Mary and Martha must have been greatly disappointed. They may even have concluded that Jesus didn't care as much as they thought. Instead, he delayed because what he had in mind was greater than anything they could have imagined!

God's delay in answering our prayers is not an indication of God's indifference toward our concerns or a sign that He just doesn't hear us. What appears to us as a delay is only God's plan unfolding as it should. We view things only from the single page we read, but God knows the whole story!

So, we trust Him. Whether He comes immediately or He delays, we trust Him. And by doing so, we honor Him, and we see such wonderful things.

Jesus delayed. But who could have imagined that before this story was over, they would see both the tears and the incredible power of **Jesus**.

Jesus said to her, "I am the resurrection and the life. Whoever believes in me, though he die, yet shall he live, and everyone who lives and believes in me shall never die. Do you believe this?"

John 11:17-27

AUGUST 25

Jesus and his company arrived in Bethany to a very emotional scene. In a culture where mourning a death was a week-long event, often characterized by loud wailing, beating of breasts and casting dust over one's person, much had already happened when Jesus appeared.

One of the most difficult things we do in all of life is to say goodbye to those we love so much. Whether their departure was expected or comes as a surprise, it is still one of our greatest heartaches. While we may eventually return to the normal routines of life, life itself is never quite the same again. Such is the force of a life and the effectual power of death.

We all die eventually—all that remains to be settled is the date. So, if we are thoughtful about life and serious about our relationship with God, we live with the awareness that each day is a gift and each day may be our last. Such is the force of life and the power of death and we are not in control of either.

While she wondered what might have been if only Jesus had arrived earlier, Martha did believe in the resurrection. Jesus confirmed her faith and identified himself as the very one who makes that resurrection and life possible!

I miss my mom and dad. At times, I would give almost anything for just a few minutes of their counsel. My mom was a soft and gentle person who became my after-school confidante. My dad was always larger than life to me. I think I lived only for his praise. As a little boy, I remember in the evenings crawling into his lap as he sat in his big over-sized chair and he would wrap his large arms around me. Then, I would wake up the next morning in my bed.

That's death for the child of God. Larger than life itself, the Father wraps His arms around us and we wake up to a new morning. It happens because of **Jesus**.

Jesus wept.

John 11:28-37

AUGUST 26

"**Jesus** wept." How I used that verse as a kid! But what theology beyond understanding is framed in those two words!

Death is the inevitable invader that would take away those most precious to us. We are powerless before this enemy. There are no words that will wipe away our grief. No amount of well-intentioned logic or carefully selected Bible verses can assuage the pain of our loss. If such words or logic or verses could be found, no one could have presented them better than Jesus, but he didn't even try. He made no speech on the problem of suffering and he never told the mourners not to be upset. He understood their heartache.

Jesus did the one thing that would best convey his love and concern for their aching hearts. He cried.

But what made Jesus cry? Was he heartbroken over the death of his dear friend, Lazarus? Was he saddened by the lack of faith that he saw on the faces of those standing around?

Or, maybe the real reason is as simple as his sharing their heartache. Jesus wept. Their sadness touched his heart and the tears came naturally. Perhaps, he is more connected to us than we first thought!

Jesus mingles his tears with yours, just as he wept with Mary and Martha. Because it is you, he cares.

What an incredible Savior! Weeping not just for us in our sin but with us in our suffering. Here is the unmistakable connection between deity and humanity. Our distressing situation brought Him to us. Our pain summoned His tears. Our pain was important to him.

While some spoke of his love for Lazarus, others seemed less sure. Evidently, they felt that if Jesus could enable a blind man to see, he should have been there to keep Lazarus from dying. But think about it: Which is more incredible? That a man would open the eyes of a blind man or that God would weep?

Did you realize he loved you that much? Did you know that your pain would put tears on the face of **Jesus**?

When he had said these things, he cried out with a loud voice, "Lazarus, come out."

John 11:38-44

AUGUST 27

Jesus possessed unspeakable power to bless people. And he often did in the most remarkable ways.

Whatever the mourners and interested observers were thinking or expecting, they certainly didn't think or expect him to do this! In fact, they may even have thought that Jesus was momentarily disoriented. Maybe he had lost track of the days and did not realize how long Lazarus had been dead. Surely, there had to be a reasonable explanation. So, they asked him. "Lord, do you know what you are doing? He's been dead four days."

There was no magic, no shouting, no pealing thunder or bolts of lightning. There was just a simple word of command. That's power.

Now, here is the really good news: Death doesn't have the last word; Satan doesn't have the last word. Jesus does.

Wouldn't it be terrible if, after so many centuries of lies and deceit, the devil escaped accountability for his actions? Wouldn't it be awful if, after so many centuries of ruining the creation of God, Satan avoided any consequences? No way! Satan does not have the last word! Jesus does!

Every death is a reminder of our frailty; every funeral is a reminder of what awaits. Death is not optional. It is inescapable.

Death is a dreaded word. It stops most people in embarrassed silence. It is hard to talk about. We don't talk about what scares us and death scares us!

God never meant for us to stay here. Admitting our frailty comes easier once we believe that. In fact, our passing takes on a whole new meaning when we understand that death is but a doorway to where the party is actually taking place.

To Mary and Martha, and to Lazarus, and to all who witnessed this miracle, Jesus said, "Death doesn't get the last word. I do." And that's what Jesus is saying to you. "Don't be afraid. Trust me."

We don't understand his power any more than we understand his love, but both are given to bless us. Never could we grasp this. And neither in our greatest moments could we have imagined walking out of our tomb at the voice of **Jesus**.

So the chief priests and the Pharisees gathered the Council and said, "What are we to do? For this man performs many signs."
John 11:45-54

AUGUST 28

Jesus' miracles often brought two very different and remarkable responses. This miracle was no exception. First, there would be those who saw what he did and believed on him. They had much to learn about him and his way, but their hearts were open and, thus, they began the journey of faith. Second, and equally remarkable, there would be those unable to see the truth. Blinded by their prejudice, holding on to their power, and hardened by their pride, the Pharisees found themselves unable to embrace the man, even if they could not deny his miracles.

So, they huddled together to strategize. Their conclusion was inevitable. Better that he die than our lives be disrupted with his message and ways. "So, from that day on they plotted to take his life."

What do we make of this story? A man dead four days walked right out of his tomb! But what did the Pharisees miss? Is it not the continuing story of the Bible's two greatest and most important themes? How much we need God and how much God wants us.

Every one of us carries hurts and wounds in our heart, grief and heartache in our soul. Every one of us struggles with fear and worry, anguish and disappointment. We have made so many bad decisions and wrong choices and the consequences have taken away our joy. But ultimately, we discover that we possess nothing within ourselves that can bring hope and change.

Jesus always knew that he was going to die. Amazingly, we had never been nearer the heart of God but we were determined to push Him away even further in order to protect and hold on to our miserable, worthless, defiled world. Blinded by our pride and in love with ourselves, we could not see or hear the truth.

In one sense, we got our way. We killed him. But fortunately for us, his way prevailed. His love prevailed over our hate. His grace prevailed over our sin. And now we know that the only one who restores life is **Jesus**.

> Then one of them, when he saw that he was healed, turned back, praising God with a loud voice; and he fell on his face at Jesus' feet, giving him thanks. Now he was a Samaritan.
>
> Luke 17:11-19

AUGUST 29

"**Jesus**, Master, have pity on us!" What else could they do? They were the "walking dead." No physician could heal them; no medicine could cure them.

The disease was terrible, but the stigma that accompanied it made it more than terrible. The Mosaic Law declared a leper "unclean." They were prohibited from entering a place of worship, dwelling with their families, or living within the city. They were required to cover their faces and, whenever anyone came close to them, they were to shout "unclean." And, on top of all this, leprosy was regarded as a mark of God's displeasure.

So, from a distance they shouted to Jesus. He was their only hope.

In his compassion for them, he gave them an order to go present themselves to the priest. At some point in their journey they noticed something amazing had happened. Ten lepers discovered that they were lepers no more. What incredible conversations must have followed this discovery!

Nine of the ten now disappeared from the story. Maybe they went on to the priest. Maybe they ran home to their families. But one, a Samaritan, returned and fell at Jesus' feet and thanked him. This man, Jesus said, was giving praise to God.

Make no mistake: whatever your problem, the only one who can fix it is Jesus. Whether lonely or angry, whether afraid or hiding some secret sin, you cannot rescue yourself. You will try because that's what we all do. But you will fail. Like these lepers in hope of healing, your heart and soul cannot be rescued unless the rescuer is Jesus.

And did you notice when the healing came? It is when people trust God, when they even go against their own desires or ideas, when they can't see where things are going and they don't know what will happen, but they put their trust in God and His way, that's when God does His greatest work.

Ruined and helpless by a terrible disease, they called to the only one who could help. Ruined and helpless by sin, we, too, cry out to **Jesus**.

> Just as it was in the days of Noah, so will it be in the days of the Son of Man.
> They were eating and drinking and marrying and being given in marriage, until the day when Noah entered the ark, and the flood came and destroyed them all.
>
> Luke 17:20-37

AUGUST 30

Jesus' return is one of the most fundamental doctrines of Christianity. It stands on the same ground as the virgin birth, the incarnation, the resurrection and the ascension. If Jesus is not coming back, then he has made fools of all who call themselves his disciples.

If we found out that Jesus was going to return tonight, there would be a mighty scramble to get right with God. As it is, most of us don't feel a great sense of urgency. We just believe that we will eventually get around to taking care of our spiritual business. Unfortunately, the common thread in the two stories would suggest something else. Surprise!

Noah preached to his neighbors. Why were his neighbors so hard to convince? They were just too busy eating and drinking, marrying and burying, and buying and selling. They were caught up in the details of the present.

In spite of Lot's warnings, the people of Sodom were too busy with life to be concerned about death. Their interests trumped the interests of God. Even Lot's wife struggled to get her priorities right. She did not look back because she was curious but because she found it hard to let go of what was behind. Instead of looking ahead to what God had for her and her family, she looked backward at what she thought she was losing.

How tragic that we can become so engrossed in the material affairs and activities of life that we give no real thought to the Lord's return. How sad that we lose touch with the spiritual and eternal by giving our attention to the physical and temporal. With our spiritual senses dulled by earthly distractions we live as if the Lord was not going to return at all!

If we had more signs, would we be more faithful? Would more reminders help us live more like Jesus? If we had more details, would we be ready?

Actually, we have enough. We have the promise of **Jesus**.

Then Jesus told his disciples a parable to show them that they should always pray and not give up.

Luke 18:1-8

AUGUST 31

Jesus has carefully chosen his characters. In the Bible world, as one considered those who had power and those who did not, it would have been difficult to find two extremes greater than those used by Jesus in this story: a judge whose decisions determine the fate of people and a widow who is powerless and vulnerable in a man's world.

Why pray at all? Jesus said to. After all, prayer was God's idea, not ours. God wants us to pray. We do not pray to give God information. We pray because of who we are and what we seek. We are His children and we seek a continuing relationship with our Father. We have a need to speak what's on our hearts. We pray not because we love prayer but because we love the Lord.

Also, prayer does make a difference to life. If nothing else, the story reveals how asking can make a difference. But the reason for that difference is God!

Jesus was convinced of the Father's desire to help, and he was equally convinced that God was able. God is not like this judge! Jesus says the Father wants to hear and answer! God loves you and wants what is best for you. The saying is true: "Prayer is not overcoming God's reluctance but laying hold of His willingness."

The reason we are not better with prayer is not because we don't know what to say, or we are too busy. We fail in prayer because we do not hunger for God as He hungers for us. We do not long for Him as He longs for us. Prayer is not wanting something from God; prayer is wanting God.

The blessing of prayer is that we can feel complete freedom to ask our gracious Father the desires of our heart. We do so with hearts willing to set aside our concerns for the higher and better ways of the Father. Our ultimate desire is not to get what we want but to become what He wants. It is in this way that we are most like **Jesus**.

> "For everyone who exalts himself will be humbled, but the one who humbles himself will be exalted."
>
> Luke 18:9-14

SEPTEMBER 1

Jesus' parables were not missives sent forth without direction. They had targets. This time, the target was "to some who were confident of their own righteousness and looked down on everybody else."

The story focused on a couple of fellows who walked into the temple for their prayer-time. At a glance, one clearly looked better than the other.

One man was a Pharisee, respectable in appearance, highly esteemed by his countrymen, and faithfully religious in his practices. Fasting, giving, attending, praying, sacrificing–check to all of these. He took the Law seriously and it showed. He had divided the world into the good guys and the bad guys and had no trouble identifying each.

The other man in the story was a tax collector. Compared to the good Pharisee, he was the scum of the earth. He was a traitor to his own people and morally bankrupt. Even he had a sense of his inadequacies. He didn't feel worthy to stand very close or lift his eyes. His prayer made no attempt to explain his ways. In fact, he admitted being a sinner and asked only for mercy.

The listening crowd could easily see the distance between these two. But what would Jesus say about them?

In the final analysis, the only thing that saves any of us will be God's forgiveness, not our 'righteous' lifestyle. However our resume looks, it was never enough.

So, how did the Pharisee miss his way? He confused doing good things with being good. He came to trust his abilities rather than trusting God. He began measuring himself by those around him. He thought of God as a stern judge rather than a benevolent father. Ultimately, he possessed a distorted view of people and God. Sound familiar?

The parable is not about prayer. It is about humility, and the Father's acceptance. Pride comes easy. Humility is always difficult. But it is humility that allows us into His presence and grace. We learn that from **Jesus**.

> He answered, "Have you not read that he who created them from the beginning made them male and female, and said, 'Therefore a man shall leave his father and his mother and hold fast to his wife, and the two shall become one flesh'?"
>
> Matthew 19:1-6 (Mark 10:1-9)

SEPTEMBER 2

Jesus said marriage is God's idea, not ours. It was God who brought the man and woman together. He envisioned something wonderful for them! When people marry, God must surely smile broadly. After all, this wonderful and beautiful experience was His idea! The new family that is formed is His work. Every day that a couple honors their vows to each other is a day they honor the God who united them.

Then, so as to remove any doubt about God's intentions, Jesus declared, "what God has joined together, let man not separate." There it is: permanence. God intended marriage to be one man and one woman for life.

The fact that marriage is divinely sanctioned does not mean guaranteed success. Love doesn't guarantee a smooth journey. In fact, the love and patience of these two will be tested many times.

But there is the promise. You commit yourself to a lifetime of devoted effort to make your marriage be all that God wants it to be. Your vows are your bond and your rings are the symbols of your commitment.

Marriage is far less about romantic love and far more about integrity. Our culture is quick to champion the former but consistently silent on the latter.

Divorce always involves an act of covenant breaking. Divorce always involves sin—by either one person or both. But marriage itself is not to blame. The unhappiness in many marriages is directly the result of failed people, not a failed plan. Marriages fail because the persons in them fail as persons.

Although the consequences can be tragic, divorce is not the unpardonable sin. Penitent people find that God is always full of love and compassion.

God has a plan for His own idea. Our failure to follow His plan has brought us great heartache. The only hope we have of discovering the joy of marriage that God envisioned for us is to listen and obey the words of **Jesus**.

He said to them, "Because of your hardness of heart Moses allowed you to divorce your wives, but from the beginning it was not so."
Matthew 19:7-12 (Mark 10:10-12)

SEPTEMBER 3

Jesus knew it was a trap. While the Pharisees certainly possessed some interest in the subject of marriage and divorce, their primary goal was to ensnare him in his words. So, they asked him about this very controversial matter.

Jesus took them back to the very beginning, back to the creation and God's original purpose and plan: a man and woman leaving their respective families and being united. The two becoming one flesh. God being the One who joins them. Permanence written all over their union.

But God's design was interrupted by the sin of people. Although not the ideal, God permitted divorce. People were getting divorced, so Moses regulated it.

Whether you study from the Old or New Testament, the message is the same: divorce is contrary to the divine intent and God takes this very seriously.

While the tendency of our culture is to make light of getting married while downplaying the significance of divorce, the reality is something else. At the very least, divorce is the declaration of failure and sin. There is no such thing as 'no-fault' divorce. The term is in keeping with the mood of a culture in which fewer people are willing to accept responsibility for their actions. But there is nothing wrong with God's plan; it is people who fail.

Divorce has long been a difficult issue for churches. Christians want to hold firm to the teachings of the Scriptures regarding God's plan for marriage. On the other hand, Christians are personally affected by the large number of people experiencing divorce. Situations are often complex and emotions tend to run high. There is a great need for truth and a great need for understanding and compassion.

Sometimes our dreams don't come true. Sometimes both people are not equally committed. Sometimes people just don't need to be together because they hurt each other. There are many "sometimes" to talk about. But remember: whether married or unmarried, anything less than God's way means we have settled for less. For you, settling for less was never in the mind of **Jesus**.

But Jesus called them to him, saying, "Let the children come to me, and do not hinder them, for to such belongs the kingdom of God."
Luke 18:15-17 (Matthew 19:13-15; Mark 10:13-16)

SEPTEMBER 4

Jesus was at home with everyone. Whether sharing a meal with a Pharisee or a multitude, whether sharing a private conversation with Nicodemus or teaching his disciples, he seemed at ease in all circumstances and with all people. That included children.

It was common in Bible times for people to bring their children to a prophet, priest, or rabbi so that the little ones might receive a blessing. Perhaps, these people realized that Jesus was a holy man who could bless their children. Maybe they wanted Jesus to pray for them, or tell them how much God loved them, or even give them a special blessing from God.

The disciples probably thought they were just doing their job. They were, after all, protecting the Master from the unimportant, the insignificant, the powerless. Children seemed totally unnecessary to the mission. He had so many important people to see, so many sick people to heal, and a whole world to save. The children were a bother.

Indignant! That's quite a word, especially when it is used to describe Jesus! Indignant!

Jesus rebuked his disciples for hindering the children, for failing to appreciate their value. "Let them come to me and don't hinder them," Jesus said.

Adults are the windows to impressions formed by children. Through adults, children gain impressions of God and Jesus, church and life. We are the ones who introduce them to the world. Our views quickly become theirs. Jesus knew his disciples were sending the wrong message!

Interestingly, he turned the tables and told his disciples that the children were the examples of kingdom living. Imagine that! Not the disciples but the children!

Perhaps, Jesus was thinking of the way children are so trusting and possess such a simple faith. Or maybe he thought of the way children are so teachable, so full of questions and always curious. Or perhaps Jesus was talking of the way children love, the way they forgive and forget so quickly.

Amazingly, when Jesus wanted to impress upon his disciples the character of the kingdom, he chose children. They were the ones most like **Jesus**.

And Jesus, looking at him, loved him, and said to him, "You lack one thing: go, sell all that you have and give to the poor, and you will have treasure in heaven; and come, follow me."
Mark 10:17-31 (Matthew 19:16-30; Luke 18:18-30)

SEPTEMBER 5

Jesus never questioned the young man's statement. He just "looked at him and loved him." Then, he told him, "You've got the religion part down. What you are missing is me."

Even now, it happens. You can keep rules and still be lost. You can obey commands and miss the joy. You can get the religion part down really well and still feel as though something is missing.

He came to Jesus knowing something was missing from his life. He was a religious man doing all the right things but not feeling the pleasure of God. Sound familiar? And just like us, he thought the remedy was something else to do.

Jesus helped him focus by calling him to remove the obstacle to devotion, to remove that which hindered him most. Jesus targeted that little pocket of self, a little place that meant so much to him. Sometimes God calls us to do what we least want to do in order to reveal our heart—to reveal what's really in our heart.

"Strip yourself of every possession and cut away every affection. Let it be just you and your God. Reduce yourself down until nothing remains but you, and then give you to God!"

No person who comes so close to Jesus can go away happy. When you draw close enough to see the loveliness of Jesus, when you are near enough to hear his good news for you, when you are near enough to know how much he loves you, you cannot walk away with a smile on your face and contentment in your soul.

To see this young man so close, so near...and then to see his back as he moves away from Jesus...this is sad. So close to joy. So close to God. So close...so very close to the life he truly wanted. And now, too close to leave without Jesus and still be happy.

All that is needed is just you and **Jesus**.

> "For the kingdom of heaven is like a master of a house who went out early in the morning to hire laborers for his vineyard."
>
> Matthew 20:1-16

SEPTEMBER 6

Jesus told another story to help his listeners see a bit more of this kingdom, and to remind them that God is God. For some reason, we tend to get confused about that.

The situation was common in the ancient world. A man needed workers so he went to the place where he could hire some day-laborers. In fact, he hired men at four different times during the day, even hiring some when they could only work one hour.

Naturally, when payment came at the end of the day, those working the longest felt as though they had been treated unfairly. Most of us would tend to agree. After all, they put in the most time; they ought to get the bigger paycheck. For all the workers to receive the same does not seem fair.

But the owner reminded them that he paid them exactly the amount they had agreed to. They had not been misled or cheated in any way. And wasn't it his right to be generous and pay all the same if he so desired?

So, what was the problem? Those hired first expected to receive even more than they had agreed to. They were envious. They believed that others were getting what they did not deserve and they were not getting what they did deserve!

The temptation to "play God" is always with us. We want to judge for God and decide for God. We want to tell God who to love and who not to love, who is right and who is wrong. We have "fairness" all figured out. We know who is deserving and who is not.

Mark it down: there is nothing "fair" about this kingdom. The Lord took upon himself that which he did not deserve so that we might receive what we did not deserve. What's fair about that?

In God's kingdom, we enjoy blessings that come because of the generosity of our Father. There is never any place for complaining because what we receive is so incredibly far better than what we deserve. Thank you, **Jesus**.

"See, we are going up to Jerusalem. And the Son of Man will be delivered over to the chief priests and scribes, and they will condemn him to death and deliver him over to the Gentiles to be mocked and flogged and crucified, and he will be raised on the third day."
Matthew 20:17-19 (Mark 10:32-34; Luke 18:31-34)

SEPTEMBER 7

Jesus never kept the truth from his disciples. From the beginning he had tried to help them see exactly who he was. Also, he had tried to help them understand what lay ahead.

So, once again, Jesus tells them what is about to take place. He gives them the clearest and most detailed statement about His impending death. Luke writes, "The disciples did not understand any of this."

But Jesus knew all too well what lay ahead as he and his band of men drew nearer this special place. The city of Jerusalem was impressive enough, and it would be especially busy as thousands filled her streets for Passover. There would be so much happening. The place would be alive with energy and excitement as it always was when there was a reason for Jews to gather in the City of David.

But Jesus wasn't thinking so much of the sights and sounds of a city celebrating a special event. No, Jesus was thinking about a little piece of ground just outside the city gates. It was a special place where people died. It was Golgotha.

And he thought about people, the people he came to save. With their minds filled with visions of an Israel victorious over her enemies, the disciples found it hard to see the true nature of Jesus' kingdom. With their hearts excited over the salvation of a nation, they failed to see that Jesus' mission was to save souls. But he was always here for people! All people!

So, when he told them one more time of the things that lay ahead, they listened as they always did. But the words made no sense. How could he speak of a kingdom in one breath and talk of death in the next?

So, they followed him down the road as sheep follow a shepherd. They did not understand but still they knew they wanted to be with **Jesus**.

> "But whoever would be great among you must be your servant, and whoever would be first among you must be slave of all."
> Mark 10:35-45 (Matthew 20:20-28)

SEPTEMBER 8

Jesus must have had those moments when he simply shook his head in amazement. Amazed that his disciples just didn't get it. Amazed that after so many lessons on humility and service, becoming like little children and being a watchful servant, amazed that after so many examples of selflessness and service from his own life, they still didn't seem to grasp the nature of his kingdom. Perhaps, all he could do was shake his head.

James and John were the sons of Zebedee and two of the better-known apostles of this group. They have been with Jesus from the beginning. Their previous career was as fishing partners on the Sea of Galilee. Perhaps, had they really understood the true nature of Jesus' kingdom and the real nature of the life to which he had called them, they might have returned to their boat.

Failing to grasp that their leader was headed to a cross, they were envisioning an entirely different scene. In their minds they could see a glorious occasion in which Jesus would be seated in the place of highest honor. They were all for that. They just wanted to be beside him—one on the right and the other on the left.

Not surprisingly, the other ten were upset. James and John had gone behind their backs to get a special favor from Jesus. Not only that, their actions indicated that they felt they were more deserving of special honor.

But James and John had missed something. To this point in his ministry, where did Jesus say that there would be places of honor at his table? Where did Jesus even hint that kingdom glory was available to anyone?

As we are inclined to do, James and John had it all wrong because they underestimated the cost of following Jesus and they overestimated their own importance to the kingdom. They did not ask for work but for glory, not service but honor. It is an all too common mistake.

The only one deserving a seat of honor is **Jesus**.

And Jesus said to him, "Go your way; your faith has made you well." And immediately he recovered his sight and followed him on the way.
Mark 10:46-52 (Matthew 20:29-34; Luke 18:35-43)

SEPTEMBER 9

Jesus and his disciples were making their way to Jerusalem...for the last time. Passover was coming and Jesus was on his way to die. The road took them through the very old city of Jericho. Jerusalem was now about 15 miles away.

Suddenly, a man's voice was heard above the crowd and street noise. It was a man shouting for Jesus. It was the blind beggar sitting along the road. Bartimaeus shouted, "Jesus, Son of David, have mercy on me!"

Some of the locals were probably embarrassed for their city, and some of those traveling with Jesus probably assumed their protection mode. So, Bartimaeus was rebuked and told to be quiet. But he didn't listen and shouted all the more: "Son of David, have mercy on me!"

What he knew or believed about Jesus is uncertain but there was no doubt what he wanted. Bartimaeus had never seen a river, or a flower, or the face of another person. He had never witnessed a sunrise, or observed the fruit on a tree, or watched people in their daily activities. Even more, he had lived his life very much at the mercy of others.

Perhaps, it is true that the blind have a better grasp of faith than most of us. They are, after all, forced to live a life that requires a willingness to trust others. But actually, we are all blind. So, we need someone we can trust, someone who really knows the way. Jesus says, "That's me. You can trust me."

Like Bartimaeus, we carry in our lives the hurts and wounds, the sorrows and fears of our earthly existence. We seek relief and comfort; we seek peace and healing. We long for sight, for someone we can trust to show us the way and give us hope. The answer or solution to our brokenness is always the same. It never changes. Trust the Lord.

What's thrilling is not that a blind man can see but that a blind man knows whom to trust and is following Him! He knows to follow **Jesus**.

"For the Son of Man came to seek and to save the lost."
Luke 19:1-10

SEPTEMBER 10

Jesus' arrival brought folks together. He was not an easy person to ignore. The numbers swelled. Folks strained to see and hear Jesus.

Zacchaeus strained, too. He wanted to see who Jesus was. He wanted to see this strange holy man. Maybe he was just curious.

Maybe Zacchaeus had heard that this Jesus was a friend to tax collectors. He had even changed the life of Levi, the tax collector at Capernaum. Wow! What an incredible thought: A holy man who is a friend to the tax collectors!

So, he strained with everyone else. But he was too short!

So, Zacchaeus ran ahead and climbed a sycamore tree, a rather undignified thing for a wealthy man to do. Perhaps he was way past the point of caring any more what people thought. Or, maybe he was simply determined to see Jesus.

Zacchaeus was a publican, a tax collector. In fact, Zacchaeus was a chief tax collector, and he was quite successful. He had reached the top of his profession at the expense of his own countrymen. The Romans farmed out the business of collecting taxes to locals. Respectable men would not do it. It was unpatriotic, the work of traitors.

But Zacchaeus loved his money. He loved it better than his own country. He loved it more than the respect of his countrymen.

Jesus stopped beneath the tree and, to everyone's surprise, summoned Zacchaeus down and said he was going to the house of this tax collector. People were stunned! Doesn't Jesus know what this man does for a living?

It would be wonderful if we had a record of their conversation. But whatever was said, Zacchaeus emerged a changed man.

This is the Good News: you can change! If you're neglecting your family, you can change. If you're struggling for control of your temper or tongue, you can change. If you're full of envy or jealousy, lust or hate, you can change. Whatever is wrong, you can change! By the power of God, you can change!

We belong with God. Anywhere else is lost. The only person who can save you, who can lead you to where you belong is **Jesus**.

> "And he said to him, 'Well done, good servant! Because you have been faithful in a very little, you shall have authority over ten cities.'"
>
> Luke 19:11-28

SEPTEMBER 11

Jesus now shifted directions while he had their attention. As he so often did when teaching, Jesus told a story. In the story, all the servants received the same amount. But while two of them acted in behalf of the king, the other one only acted in behalf of himself. His faithlessness brought the wrath of the king.

This condemned servant was not faulted for cheating, lying or stealing. It wasn't dishonesty that did him in. It was his failure to use what was given to him. He was blessed with opportunity and something (a mina) to work with.

If, as the story suggest, we must give an account for what we receive, then the key question becomes: What are we doing with what God has given us?

We spend our lives collecting, and then gripping it tightly as if it were ours and we could prevent anyone from taking it from us. But everything you have—your spouse, your children, your job, your health, your hobby, your collection—everything is going to be taken from you. Then, it will be just you and God. And God is going to ask you, "What did you do with what I gave you?"

Often, our struggle with stewardship is the result of our confusion over ownership. We start to think of ourselves as the owners and then naturally assume that our will is all that really matters. It is very important that we understand who owns what. What do you own? Nothing! What does God own? Everything! Jesus said the secret to life is to hold everything loosely for it is not yours and to handle it well because you must answer for your stewardship.

God says, "Everything I gave you was mine. You had nothing. Because I love you, I gave to you. And you knew my heart on all this. Now, I call you before me to answer this question – 'What did you do with what I gave you? And especially, what did you do with the gift called **Jesus**?'"

> So the chief priests made plans to put Lazarus to death as well, because on account of him many of the Jews were going away and believing in Jesus.
>
> John 11:55-12:1, 9-11

SEPTEMBER 12

Jesus' arrival in Jerusalem was certain to create a sensation! The question was: would he actually show up? The Sanhedrin considered him Public Enemy No. 1. They had put a contract on his life and everyone seemed to know it. Would Jesus dare defy the authorities and show himself in Jerusalem?

Jesus' arrival at Bethany was no surprise. He had good friends here. The city's proximity to Jerusalem was perfect for allowing him to go in and teach in the day and then return to Bethany in the evenings. But it didn't take long for the news to spread: Jesus was at Bethany.

Part of the crowd's curiosity was focused on Lazarus. Who can blame them? They wanted to see a guy who had been dead four days and then restored to life.

In our day, Lazarus would be an international celebrity. He would be hounded by the press and probably appear on virtually every top-rated talk show. Everyone would want to interview him. In short time, he could get a book deal about his experiences, authorize a movie of his life (and death and life again), and run for some public office. The opportunities would be endless for a man returned from the grave! If he had a good agent, he could be set for life.

But that popularity did not go unnoticed by Jesus' opponents. They could hardly afford to have Lazarus going around as living proof of Jesus' power. So, Lazarus was now No. 2 on the list.

The great irony here is that the very men who served as custodians of the Law and ministers to the people were the very ones conspiring against God's messenger. The people might see him as some prophet of hope, but the Jewish leaders only saw him as a troublemaker who had to be stopped.

So, the Passover was almost here. It wouldn't be long before it would be time to slay the Passover lamb. But this lamb had a name and his name was **Jesus**.

> So they took branches of palm trees and went out to meet him, crying out, "Hosanna! Blessed is he who comes in the name of the Lord, even the King of Israel!"
> John 12:12-15 (Luke 19:29-35; Matthew 21:1-7; Mark 11:1-7)

SEPTEMBER 13

Jesus' instructions regarding the donkey were very clear: the donkey must be one that has never been ridden. This donkey was special, consecrated for a specific use: to carry the King.

It was not uncommon for kings, mounted on their stallions, to parade into a city amidst all the fanfare that goes with being a king. People would naturally gather to see it all.

But what may we say of this? A peasant riding a donkey! He has no army and has conquered no enemy.

And yet, as he drew near to the city, the news spread and the crowds became excited at the prospect of someone to be their deliverer.

"Praise the one who comes in the Name of the Lord!"

Perhaps, the picture says as much about the people as it does about Jesus. They were desperate for a leader! For poor people feeling hopeless and having little to be excited about, Jesus brought hope to their despair. He gave them reason to believe that things might change for the better.

But they did not wave palm branches or shout "Hosanna" because they saw him as a spiritual prince. Rather, they viewed him as a temporal deliverer. Later, when they found they were mistaken, they were as quick to shout, "Crucify him!" as they had been to cry "Hosanna."

But on that Sunday morning, the people were looking for the one who gave them new reason to hope. When Jesus came riding on a donkey, they could not restrain that hope. They began the chant, "Blessed is He who comes in the name of the Lord! Hosanna!"

Finally, someone had come who could give them relief from their misery, freedom from their oppressors, and honor among the nations. At last, someone had come who cared about their concerns and their burdens.

Maybe the donkey didn't matter. Maybe being a peasant didn't matter. Maybe being a warrior in battles was not important. Maybe it was just that sense of hope and love that always surrounded **Jesus**.

The reason why the crowd went to meet him was that they heard he had done this sign.
So the Pharisees said to one another, "You see that you are gaining nothing. Look, the world has gone after him."

John 12:16-19

SEPTEMBER 14

Jesus rode the donkey on a road littered with cloaks from the people and branches cut from the trees. There was an excitement in the crowd! Some went ahead of him and others followed him but all of them praised him and shouts of "Hosanna" filled the air.

What were his disciples to make of all this? The people were shouting "Blessed is the King of Israel!" and Jesus was gladly acknowledging them. What did this mean? Where was this leading?

Only later, John says, did they realize what all of this meant. Just now it was difficult to understand but later it would become clear and they would know that this was the work of God.

Evidently, the crowd was comprised of many people who had shared the experience in Bethany when Lazarus was restored to life by Jesus. No wonder they were excited! They had witnessed something so incredible that it was impossible to ignore. In fact, they couldn't be quiet about it. They told everyone they met about how this dead man was brought to life by Jesus.

Not surprisingly, this kind of news only created more excitement and brought out more people. The disciples may have thought the kingdom movement really is going forward! Look at how many people are joining the cause!

The Pharisees had a different take on all of this. They admitted that things were getting out of hand. "Look how the whole world has gone after him!" We tend to exaggerate when our emotions get charged.

Some people were celebrating what Jesus has done in lives while others were irritated because of what he had done to theirs. Not much has changed since then. Always just these two groups. Jesus leaves us no other options.

Today would be a great day for celebrating **Jesus**!

... saying, "Blessed is the King who comes in the name of the Lord! Peace in heaven and glory in the highest!"
Luke 19:36-38 (Matthew 21:8-9; Mark 11:8-10)

SEPTEMBER 15

Jesus came riding on a donkey. Now, a man riding on a borrowed donkey using a donated coat as a saddle may not appear very impressive, but in the minds of the disciples and the people of Jerusalem, he was—for the moment—a King. In hard times he had become their hope of better days. For so many, he was the answer to prayers and he was the One that they had long expected. Life in God's country was about to change and they believed that this was the man who could make it happen.

But why would people applaud him at all? The miracles. They had witnessed the blind receiving sight. They had seen the crippled walk. They had watched as lepers became clean. They had even watched as a dead man was raised. They had seen with their own eyes what Jesus could do.

This was, of course, not the first time the Jerusalem crowds had become excited over a potential leader, and it would not be the last. But Jesus did seem different. He was a holy man who was at home with the common people. He ate with tax collectors, played with children, and seemed unafraid of anyone. And while he did not speak of overthrowing the Romans, he did talk of a kingdom.

So, they celebrated! They praised God and called Jesus their new King. Their joy could not be restrained.

But this parade would not take them where they wanted to go. This was the path to sacrifice, not freedom. By Friday they had tired of their new messiah. Their hopes had fizzled and their disappointment turned ugly.

Right now, even on a donkey, they were willing to take Jesus as king. But once reality set in, the parade would end and, for them, he would be king no more.

Of course, there will be another parade, a heavenly one. The King is coming, and his name is **Jesus**.

> And when he drew near and saw the city, he wept over it, saying, "Would that you, even you, had known on this day the things that make for peace! But now they are hidden from your eyes."
>
> Luke 19:39-44

SEPTEMBER 16

Jesus approached Jerusalem with much emotion. Many were shouting the right things, but he knew they did not really understand what was happening.

At some moment in his journey Jesus came to a spot that permitted him to cast his eyes over this magnificent place. Whatever happened here seemed to reverberate across the world. What was about to happen would, indeed, resound across the whole creation!

As his eyes surveyed this ancient city his heart filled with grief. Before long, tears rolled down his cheeks as he lamented both what the people were about to do and the consequences that would follow.

A search of the Scriptures will reveal that there are only three occasions in which the tears of Jesus are noted by Bible writers. The first was in Bethany when "Jesus wept" with those who were weeping over the death of Lazarus. This quiet, silent shedding of tears was a genuine, heartfelt compassion for the grief experienced by others. He truly shared their pain. He shares yours, too.

A second instance is in Hebrews (5:7). The writer says that during his life on earth, Jesus "offered up prayers and supplications with loud cries and tears." We recall Jesus being "sorrowful and troubled" prior to his arrest (Matthew 26:37). In fact, Jesus told Peter, James and John, "My soul is deeply grieved, to the point of death" (Matthew 26:38). Jesus' tears came as he wrestled with which way to go.

But the tears that now fall to the ground are are tears of grief, grief for a people determined to ignore the evidence. Jesus wept over the city because they rejected him as their King. Even more, his heart ached for their suffering which would come as a consequence of their decision.

It is said that you can tell a lot about a person if you know what makes the person laugh and what makes the person cry. Jesus wept for hurting people. No one's tears ever meant so much to us as the tears of **Jesus**.

> And when he entered Jerusalem, the whole city was stirred up, saying, "Who is this?"
> And the crowds said, "This is the prophet Jesus, from Nazareth of Galilee."
>
> Matthew 21:10-11, 14-17 (Mark 11:11)

SEPTEMBER 17

Jesus was filled with emotion as he made his way toward the holy city, and he was not alone. There was great excitement in Jerusalem. The Passover brought thousands of Jews from many distant places. The roads to Jerusalem were clogged with pilgrims and the streets of the city were already stirring with great expectations for this festive week.

But while the carnival atmosphere prevailed over the city, Jesus' thoughts were far more somber. This was the last week, *his* last week. By Friday the people who spread their cloaks before him and shouted praises to the King would be singing a very different song. They might be celebrating his presence just now but by week's end they would be shouting for his removal.

Jesus' arrival at the temple drew a crowd, especially those seeking healing. Interestingly, among those attracted to this temple spectacle were some children. We don't know their ages or how many there were, but there were enough to form a small chorus!

Maybe they were the children of those who came for healing. Perhaps, they were there when Jesus rode into the city on a donkey and they listened to the way their parents shouted praises to him. Whoever they were and whatever the reason for their presence in the temple, they sang a wonderful song!

Unfortunately, everyone wasn't excited about the song selection. "Hosanna" was a term reserved for the Savior of God's people, not some peasant riding in on a donkey. The religious leaders were angry that the children sang such words, but they were infuriated that Jesus would allow it!

"Don't you hear what they are saying?" The question wasn't really about Jesus' hearing but about his failure to rebuke the children for their words. The leaders were offended, so why shouldn't Jesus be?

These guys were the professionals. They knew the Scriptures backwards and forwards. Yet, it took children to sing the truth and provide a glimpse of the future when all the children of God will sing "Hosanna" in praise of **Jesus**.

> And he entered the temple and began to drive out those who sold and those who bought in the temple, and he overturned the tables of the money-changers and the seats of those who sold pigeons.
> Mark 11:12-18 (Matthew 21:18-19a, 12-13; Luke 19:45-48)

SEPTEMBER 18

Jesus started for Jerusalem. He was hungry and spotted a fig tree. Now, since Jesus did nothing on a whim but acted with purpose, we can only conclude that what follows was for the benefit of his disciples.

This tree had the signs of life but was missing the fruit. It promised much but delivered nothing. Israel was like this tree, possessing the signs of life but empty. All the sacrifices, rites and rituals were a mere show. While fruit was to be expected, there was none.

Then, the setting changes to the temple. How are we to understand Jesus' actions? Why did he feel compelled to drive everyone out? Was he angry over the high exchange rates of the money- changers? Was he upset over the exorbitant rates being charged the poor pilgrims who needed to buy animals for sacrifice? Was he angry over the greed and extortion he saw in the temple concessions?

But suppose that the exchange rate was fair and the price of the animals was good. Would Jesus have approved? No! Jesus was not primarily concerned for those things but for the absence of any sense of God's presence! There was no reverence for God, no sense of His holiness!

The business of the temple courts simply reflected the lives of people who did not respect God. They lived as they desired and then came into the temple thinking that everything was just fine, that here they were religiously safe.

The cursing of the fruitless fig tree and the cleansing of the temple spoke to the failures of a nation that, even with every opportunity and benefit, had failed to be faithful to God. There was a consequence. The fig tree withered and the temple would be destroyed. Sin never permits a life to stay the same.

Disrespect for God will not be tolerated by **Jesus**.

"Whoever loves his life loses it, and whoever hates his life in this world will keep it for eternal life."

John 12:20-26

SEPTEMBER 19

Jesus' triumphal entry into Jerusalem probably set the disciples to thinking about Jesus being crowned king. After all, the whole world seemed to be in his corner. Even some Greeks, probably God-fearers, came desiring to see him. Were they genuine seekers or just curious to see a celebrity?

Jesus' agricultural imagery would have been easily grasped by his listeners. After all, their food supply depended on one seed producing many seeds. His point was clear: the means of his glorification was death. As the seed dies in the ground, yet brings forth new life, just so the death of Jesus would result in new life.

But there was more! Those who followed him must be willing to die, too! Surely, we must have heard wrong!

Die to live. It is not what we want to hear. But Jesus says that is the path to real life and receiving the blessing of God. If you live only to please yourself, you will lose everything...even the very self you are trying to please.

Sometimes, our own notions distort Jesus' call to discipleship. For example, we argue, "We must be true to ourselves." Wrong! Where did we get the idea that the secret to life, the solution to being happy is to be true to one's self? Satan! Satan told us that starting with Eve. The reason we are in the trouble we are is because we relied on ourselves rather than trusting God. We were true to ourselves and it took us in the wrong direction.

Or, we might say, "I know what is best for me." Wrong. Not only do we not know what is best for us, we don't even do what is best when we think we know it! But the Lord does know what is best and deciding to follow him is our expression of trust in him. Following him is "what is best for me."

This is the unique call of Christianity: in order to live you have to die. The glory of God is accomplished not only through the death of Jesus but through the death of disciples, too. We die to live, just like **Jesus**.

"Now is my soul troubled. And what shall I say? 'Father, save me from this hour'? But for this purpose I have come to this hour. Father, glorify your name."

John 12:27-36a

SEPTEMBER 20

Jesus knew exactly what lay ahead. Until this week the 'hour' had always been in the future. Before this, he often said, "my hour is not yet come." Now, his 'hour' was here. And he knew what that 'hour' held for him.

Jesus didn't come just to live among us, or to teach great and inspirational lessons, or to perform amazing miracles. Jesus came into the world to die. He was the "lamb slain from the foundation of the world."

Scores of books have been written trying to explain God's thoughts and His ways. Innumerable sermons have been preached attempting to explain why God does what He does. Perhaps, God knew that we would be unable to grasp all this and, rather than explaining it, He just wanted us to trust Him.

But Jesus' words do provide a window to his heart. The conflict is real! Jesus **is** one of us! And because he is one of us, he grapples with what he desires as a man as it conflicts with what God wants. But the issue is decided because his greatest passion is to do the will of the Father, and because he loves us so much. He identifies with the Father and with us.

"Father, glorify your name!" There is no higher, greater purpose in the whole of human existence! It is the sole reason why we exist! The heart beats, the lungs breathe, the body lives so that every moment of our time may be for the praise of His glory!

The cross was a horrible way for a person to die. It was cruel and barbaric. Even so, the cross of Jesus becomes glorious because it is the ultimate statement of praise to the Father. The cross is the greatest declaration ever of what life is all about: absolute surrender to the will of God! Thus, we are without excuse. In his death Jesus has shown us that we may, indeed, put the Father's will above our own.

The cross has made our purpose clear, conquered our enemy and shown us an unimaginable love. No wonder it serves to draw all people to Jesus. We are not forced to come to him. We are free to choose our path. We have the right to refuse. But why would we? Everything we have ever wanted is found in **Jesus**.

Though he had done so many signs before them, they still did not believe in him...
                                                    John 12:36b-41

SEPTEMBER 21

Jesus came displaying his goodness and power in ways that seemed beyond dispute. He turned water to wine, walked on the waters of the lake, and he calmed the stormy seas. He healed the blind and the lame, and he cleansed the lepers. He even raised the dead. Absolutely amazing!

But the response to him was equally amazing. Instead of having hearts flooded with appreciation, worshiping him and trusting his every word, the majority chose not to believe or accept him at all.

Perhaps, we learn something important in all this unbelief. We are inclined to think that, if people today could just see some wonderful miracle, then folks would want to give their lives to the Lord. But the truth is a bit disappointing: miracles alone do not guarantee faith.

So much power, so many miracles. Why so few believers? John wrote of eyes that could not see and hearts that could not feel. They had become insensitive to God and to His ways.

How could this happen to them? Could they not see? Could they not hear? How could this happen to us?

Isn't it amazing that Isaiah would write about Jesus long before his arrival in Palestine and be so specific about his reception? How could that be? Certainly, Isaiah was guided by the Spirit of God. But could it also be that Isaiah just knew human nature. After all, he had first-hand experience with hardheaded people! His own experiences would have taught him that the very people who should know better can sometimes be the most disappointing.

There is a very important law of life found here. We dare not miss it. Here it is: What you choose—what you pursue—is not only what you get but is also what you become. If we are determined to dismiss the wonderful words and works of Jesus, then our choice means we lose our sensitivity to the truth we so badly need to know. And worst of all, we miss out on the very thing we so desperately seek: the healing that comes only from **Jesus**.

And Jesus cried out and said, "Whoever believes in me, believes not in
  me but in him who sent me.
And whoever sees me sees him who sent me."
John 12:42-50 (Mark 11:19)

SEPTEMBER 22

Jesus' followers were not many, but they would have been more if not for their fear. Afraid of losing their place among their peers, certain believing leaders chose to stay quiet. They were unwilling to experience any kind of personal sacrifice for Jesus. Even so, he would still die for them...and for us.

But the rejection of Jesus is even more serious than it first appears. Simply put: the Father and the Son go together. To accept one is to accept the other; to reject one is to reject the other. In fact, Jesus says, "What I say is what the Father has told me to say. What I do is what the Father wants me to do."

In this age of tolerance his words rub us. We would prefer options and choices. His words sound narrow and exclusive. "When a man believes in me, in fact, when he just looks at me, he is seeing God!"

Anytime, anywhere, anyone tells you that he or she can live their life pleasing God without following Jesus, take them to John 12. Jesus says in unmistakable language: What you do with me is what you do with God.

We live in a world of words, millions of them every day. From the moment we get up in the morning until our eyes close at night, we are bombarded with words. These words convey ideas, and these ideas form the basis of our thoughts and actions.

Jesus said, "Listen to me. My Father told me what to say." Shouldn't that settle the question of listening?

Everyone listens to someone. How we live each day is determined by whom we listen to. Jesus says, "When all is said, my words are the only words that will matter."

Wow! Think for a moment about that! When you have drawn your last breath, the words of your peers won't matter anymore and the words of family and friends won't matter anymore. The only words that will still matter will be those of **Jesus**.

> "Truly, I say to you, whoever says to this mountain, 'Be taken up and thrown into the sea,' and does not doubt in his heart, but believes that what he says will come to pass, it will be done for him."
> Mark 11:20-25 (Matthew 21:19-22; Luke 21:37-38)

SEPTEMBER 23

Jesus is not giving a formula or recipe for throwing mountains into the sea, but he is telling us how important it is for us to have faith in God when we face difficulties in our lives that are too large for us. Of course, trusting an unseen God who works in mysterious ways to accomplish purposes that we do not understand is very challenging.

To pray with faith does not mean believing that God will always give us everything that we ask for, as long as we ask for it without any doubt. We have all prayed for things that were not granted to us.

But the purpose of prayer is not to give us a means or way of getting God to give us what we want. In fact, God does not always do what we would like or want Him to do. But He always does what is right! To pray with faith is to trust that God's will really is what is best, even when His will does not match our desires or even make sense to us.

Trust can be difficult. Equally challenging is forgiving people who have hurt us. Our humanness tends to seek revenge, to want justice, not forgiveness.

Our lives are filled with wounds and insults, heartbreak and pain. Jesus knew that this would be very, very difficult for us. How could we possibly forgive? We can. Jesus said so.

Jesus is not saying that our willingness to forgive other people earns us the right to receive forgiveness from God. Not at all! But overwhelmed by His love, we cannot keep it to ourselves; overwhelmed by His grace, we must show it to others. We do not forgive because they deserve it, but because God has forgiven us.

It is difficult to imagine two commands any more challenging for us than these: trust God and forgive people. There is certainly nothing about our world that champions such ideas. No surprise there. The only person who talks like this is **Jesus**.

"By what authority are you doing these things, and who gave you this authority?"

Matthew 21:23-27 (Mark 11:27-33; Luke 20:1-8)

SEPTEMBER 24

Jesus may have looked like any other Jewish guy but he was not. His words and actions were definitely not typical. This was all very unsettling to the religious leaders. They just did not know what to make of Jesus. To make matters worse, the people followed him and listened to his teachings. They even proclaimed him king.

So, they asked him about his authority. "By what authority are you doing these things and who gave you this authority?"

What "things" were they talking about? First, there was his entry into Jerusalem. The people had responded to him as a king, and had shouted "Hosanna to the Son of David!" Jesus accepted their praise.

A second "thing" was his dramatic behavior in the temple. Jesus had exercised authority in the temple by driving out the people who violated the temple's purpose. In doing so, he said, "It is written, 'My house shall be called a house of prayer', but you are making it a robbers' den." "My house," he said.

Then, Jesus healed the blind and the lame that came to Him in the temple! (21:14) Although these religious leaders carried a lot of authority, none of them had power to give sight to the blind or strength to the lame.

No wonder these fellows were nervous! This man Jesus received the praise of the people as the Lord, spoke of the temple as his house, and demonstrated his power by healing people. Still, they refused to acknowledge him or his authority. They refused to admit the truth before their eyes!

Since creation we have struggled against divine authority. We do not want even God telling us what to do. We so much want to believe that we have charge over our soul, and that we have the final word on all that really matters.

Jesus did not answer their question. They would not have accepted his answer if he had. His authority was the result of his identity as God in the flesh, but they were resisting that idea. But neither their stubbornness nor ours changes anything. The ultimate authority in all lives is **Jesus**.

Jesus said to them, "Truly, I say to you, the tax collectors and the prostitutes go into the kingdom of God before you."
Matthew 21:28-32

SEPTEMBER 25

Jesus told a story about a father and his two sons. Unfortunately, one son was disrespectful to his father and the other son was disobedient to his father.

The father gave similar instructions to each son: "Go and work today in the vineyard." The first son refused to go. However, he later thought better of his foolishness and went to the vineyard to work. The second son told his father he would go and work, but he never followed through on his words.

Jesus made his own application of the story. He compared the tax collectors and prostitutes to the son who at first said "no," but then repented and obeyed his father. He compared the chief priests and elders to the son who at first said "yes," but then did not follow through.

Everyone knows the answer to Jesus' question. Both sons were wrong. But the difference is that one changed and obeyed his father. That change, or repentance, is what marks the difference in the two sons, and what signified the difference between the religious leaders and tax collectors and prostitutes.

Remember, too, that the son who said he would go to the vineyard did not put himself under obligation to obey simply because he said he would go. That obligation already existed, whether he recognized it or not.

Like the religious leaders of Jesus' day, it is easy to talk about God and His authority. But it is entirely something different to live in such a way that reveals we really do respect what God says. At the end of the day, it does not matter so much what we say about God's authority—it only matters what we do.

Thankfully, we do not have to be perfect. But our willingness to repent in the face of our wrongdoing is essential. Remember: The measure of a person is not that he or she made a mistake (we all make mistakes). Rather, the true measure of a person is what they do after they have made that mistake.

The doors of the kingdom are closed to those who won't repent. But those doors are open to those who will humble themselves before **Jesus**.

> Jesus said to them, "Have you never read in the Scriptures: "The stone that the builders rejected has become the cornerstone; this was the Lord's doing, and it is marvelous in our eyes'?"
>
> Matthew 21:33-46 (Mark 12:1-12; Luke 20:9-19)

SEPTEMBER 26

Jesus' story of a vineyard was the story of a nation and, in particular, her leaders. But God's people, symbolized by the vineyard, did not act like God's people. Thus, God did not receive the harvest that was due.

This was not the first time Israel had heard such a story. Her history was full of messengers calling the people back to God. At first, they might have thought Jesus was just another prophet like the others. They were to discover that he was far more than a prophet.

As people richly blessed, surely it was not too much to ask that they return to God what was His. What did God want in return? Their love and worship; their obedience and praise. He wanted them to be a light among the nations so that everyone might know of the living God. Instead, they gave Him little or nothing.

So, God sent servants, or prophets, to remind the people, or tenants, of their agreement and to collect the owner's portion that was due. But these servants were mistreated. In His wonderful patience, God sent prophet after prophet, presenting opportunity after opportunity, so that His people might change their ways and honor Him. But they remained rebellious and ungrateful.

Finally, God sent one final messenger: His Son. This final messenger was of a different quality and character from those who preceded him. He was more than a prophet. He was the Son of God.

There is in every life a time when accounts must be settled, when the issue of who owns the vineyard must be settled. If you are in a tussle with God over who owns what, who do you think is going to win? Here is what you need to say—"Lord, all I've ever had, all I have now and all I will ever have are yours. I am all yours. You are the owner."

There is nothing the Lord will withhold from you if you live for Him. He desires only your love and praise. We know that because of **Jesus**.

> "Go therefore to the main roads and invite to the wedding feast as many as you find.'"
>
> Matthew 22:1-14

SEPTEMBER 27

Jesus said that a certain king prepared a "wedding banquet" for his son. No doubt, he did this with great joy because he loved his son and with much anticipation for a wonderful occasion that could be shared with chosen guests.

The king sent out his servants to tell everyone to come join the party, but those who had been invited refused to come. But the king was incredibly patient with these people and sent out messengers once more inviting folks to come to the celebration. But those invited just could not be bothered and indicated they had other things to do.

Now, for the king to extend a third invitation to these ungrateful people was certainly a demonstration of great longsuffering on his part. Unfortunately, it made no difference. The people simply did not want to come. In fact, some made light of it while others mistreated the messengers.

Understandably, the king was furious. Now, he sent an army rather than another invitation. He punished these ungrateful people and then extended an invitation to everyone who would come. Just imagine: one day you are peddling bread or fishing on the sea and the next you are getting ready for a royal banquet!

Jesus used this picture to confront the religious leaders with the truth of what they, and the nation, were doing: rejecting the kingdom rule of God's Son. Ultimately, the invitation would go out to the Gentiles.

Here's the point. Take the happiest, most joyful experiences on earth you can think of. Imagine the best party or banquet you have ever attended, or the finest food you have ever eaten. Put it all together in one place. God has something even better planned. And **you** are invited! The greatest, most important invitation in the world has gone out — and you got one!

But don't presume on God's grace. You can't crash this party. You dare not ignore the terms of entrance. It is not enough to have an invitation; you must accept it and come. And remember: the party goes on whether you come or not. You have the invitation in hand. No one wants to see you there more than **Jesus.**

"Therefore, render to Caesar the things that are Caesar's, and to God the things that are God's."
Matthew 22:15-22 (Mark 12:13-17; Luke 20:20-26)

SEPTEMBER 28

Jesus was no stranger to tough questions or efforts to trap him in his words. But it must have saddened him to witness how they spent so much time and energy opposing God.

The Herodians were a political group of Jews who supported Herod Antipas and supported Roman taxation. The Pharisees were religiously focused and objected strongly to paying anything to Rome, claiming it was heresy to do so. But these strange bedfellows were united by a common enemy: Jesus. So, they devised a question—"Is it right to pay taxes to Caesar or not?" – to trap him.

Jesus answered their question by pointing to the image on the denarius. The coin was Caesar's so give it to Caesar. And in that same way, submit to God that which bears His image. That's us!

Jesus recognized the authority of Rome, whether it was fair and good or not. He was not a personal lawbreaker. His enemies wanted to arrest him but could find no charge to make.

And Jesus did not teach others to break the law. In spite of the persecution he knew his disciples would receive, he never counseled them to fight back.

Jesus did not lead in demonstrations to protest the unjust laws of Rome, and there were many unjust laws. He led neither violent nor non-violent demonstrations.

Even though he saw daily the injustice of the social system, Jesus did not advocate a radical and immediate overthrow of that system.

If we take the writings of Paul and Peter as a reflection of Jesus' will on what actions should be taken with respect to government, then we are going to be people who pray for our leaders (1 Timothy 2:1-2) and live good lives to win the respect of others (1 Peter 2:12-14). The Christian should be the best citizen.

Our society will never be made morally better by the laws we pass or the increase in the size of the police force. We cannot fight a spiritual battle with earthly means. The very best thing we can do for our country is to be like **Jesus**.

> But Jesus answered them, "You are wrong, because you know neither the Scriptures nor the power of God.
> For in the resurrection they neither marry nor are given in marriage, but are like angels in heaven."
> Matthew 22:23-33 (Mark 12:18-27; Luke 20:27-40)

SEPTEMBER 29

Jesus consistently emphasized the words and actions of God. In fact, he was the very Word of God and, when people saw him, they were seeing God in action! Unfortunately, then as now, many failed to get the message.

Unlike the religiously conservative Pharisees, the Sadducees tended toward the liberal side and were very political. Wealthy and influential, they controlled the temple and priesthood. Perhaps, it wasn't until Jesus drove the concessionaires from the temple that they saw him as a real threat to their privileged position. Now, regardless of their differences with the Pharisees, they were united in a single objective: getting rid of Jesus.

Seeking to ruin Jesus credibility with the crowds, the Sadducees cited what Moses said in the law (Deuteronomy 25:5-6) about a special marriage provision called Levirate marriage. Although strange to us, the law apparently served an important purpose in maintaining families and inheritance. If a man died childless, his widow would be given to his brother who would maintain his brother's name in the community by naming the firstborn in the place of his brother. So, the Sadducees presented this story based on the Levirate marriage law to embarrass Jesus and make light of the doctrine of the resurrection.

As to the matter of the resurrection, Jesus affirmed the Scriptures. "'I am the God of Abraham, the God of Isaac, and the God of Jacob'? He is not the God of the dead, but of the living." These men are alive! This is music to our ears! We are right to believe that there is life beyond the grave!

Today is a gift from God. You may use it as you choose. The difficult part will be deciding what is true and who to trust. Jesus' words point you in the right direction. Think of it this way: If you had only hours to live, nothing would be more important to you than knowing what God says (the Scriptures) and trusting what God can do (His power). The secret of living well today is listening to **Jesus**.

"Teacher, which is the great commandment in the Law?"
And he said to him, "You shall love the Lord your God with all your heart and with all your soul and with all your mind."
Matthew 22:34-38 (Mark 12:28-30)

SEPTEMBER 30

Jesus knew that eventually we would want to know which commandment was the **most** important. It is the way we are. Who is the greatest ballplayer? What is the most popular song? What is the largest animal? Where can one get the best hamburger? No matter the categories, we want to know who or what comes first.

While the most recent exchanges with religious leaders were attempts to stump Jesus or to lead him into saying something that would be self-incriminating, this questioner may have had an honorable motive.

Jewish rabbis identified 613 commandments contained in the Torah or the five books of Moses. The commands were divided into two groups: negative and positive. The negative commandments numbered 365 while there were 248 positive commandments in the Law. So, when this questioner asked Jesus about the greatest commandment, Jesus took him immediately to the Scriptures, Deuteronomy 6:5 and Leviticus 19:18.

"You shall love the Lord your God with all your heart and with all your soul and with all your mind." Every corner and crevice, every segment and part of our lives should reflect our devotion and affection for the one true God. We are to love God with our whole being.

While some may debate whether our nature ever permits perfection, there is no debating that Jesus holds out for us the ultimate commandment. The greatest commandment is not about church structure, mission trips or benevolent endeavors. The command is not about baptism, the Lord's Supper, or end times. The greatest commandment is about a relationship established on love and devotion.

God did not command us to love Him because of self-interest. Rather, He knew that loving Him was best for us! No matter what this world may offer us, we are never richer than when we love God with our whole being!

What is the first and greatest thing you can do with your life today? Love God. Life does not get any better than this. We know this because we've seen **Jesus**.

And the second is like it: 'Love your neighbor as yourself.'
All the Law and the Prophets hang on these two commandments."
                                    Matthew 22:39-40 (Mark 12:31-34)

OCTOBER 1

Jesus' second commandment was like the first: centered in love and focused outside of one's self. The combination is always challenging.

Of course, it would have been easier if Jesus had put some qualifiers on the identity of the neighbor. For example, loving those who love me would have been okay. Or, loving those that share similar interests and beliefs would have been manageable, too. But he did not provide conditions.

Love is pretty easy to talk about. Everyone has an opinion about what it is, what it looks like, and how it behaves. But for Jesus, love just loves. There are no "if" statements that accompany this love. There are no conditions to discuss. Loving people doesn't require any kind of test to see if they deserve it or involve any type of measurement to see if they are worthy. Loving people isn't about what they have done or failed to do in the past, or what they intend to do in the future. Loving people isn't about what they can do for you today or ever. Loving people isn't about time or distance or calendar. Love just loves.

Jesus taught us that real love only happens when we are willing to make ourselves vulnerable. Fear often keeps us from loving others. After all, we may expose our hearts to them only to suffer rejection. It is much easier, and safer, to hold our love in check until we're sure of how things are going to go.

But if Jesus had loved us that way, we would have had no hope at all! Instead, he came to us and exposed his heart and his love without regard for our response. He loved us in spite of our treatment of him! And he asked us to love others in the same way!

For all the movement of armies and all the decrees of kings, for all the laws passed by governments and all the money that moves the world, love remains the single most powerful force for transforming a life. Love always makes some kind of difference. We are proof of that. Thank you, **Jesus**.

> He said to them, "How is it then that David, in the Spirit, calls him Lord, saying, "'The Lord said to my Lord, Sit at my right hand, until I put your enemies under your feet'"?
> Matthew 22:41-46 (Mark 12:35-37; Luke 20:41-44)

OCTOBER 2

Jesus' claims were well-known to the religious leadership of Israel. That he was a man they had no doubt; perhaps, even some kind of holy man or prophet. But God? No way!

So, Jesus questioned them. "What do you think about the Christ? Whose son is he?" They knew he was the son of David.

Jesus then quoted from Psalm 110. These Jewish leaders recognized this psalm as referring to the Messiah. They understood that David was speaking of his promised offspring, someone to follow that would be the Messiah. But how was it that David referred to his Promised Son as his "Lord"? How could the Messiah be the Son of David and David's Lord at the same time? The only way that David could speak to his own human offspring and call him "Lord" would be if his offspring was more than a mere man!

This is the heart and center of Christianity: that Jesus Christ is both God and man. The whole foundation of the Christian faith rests upon this truth.

However, there are many people who have drifted toward the acceptance of a lowered view of Jesus as a good and influential man, an inspiring example rather than an almighty Savior. Thus, Jesus is honored for being so much better than most humans but he is still only human.

Does it matter? It does if he is the Son of God. As long as Jesus is only a man, even a very good man, as long as he is only a man, then there is no real responsibility on your part to listen or to obey him. But in that moment in which you admit that he is really the Son of God, then you have acknowledged that he has the right to your life. If he really is the Son of God, following him is the single greatest decision of your life.

So, celebrate! You and your day belong to **Jesus**.

"Woe to you, scribes and Pharisees, hypocrites!"
Matthew 23:1-15 (Mark 12:38-40; Luke 20:45-47)

OCTOBER 3

Jesus was angry. In fact, Jesus was very angry.

This is one of the most unpleasant chapters in all the Gospels. It begins with accusations and closes with condemnations. Our tendency is to dismiss his words as being for the Pharisees of long ago and far away. But the Pharisees were not pagans but the most religious, the most conservative, the most obey-the-commands, go-by-the-book kind of people in all of Israel. So, why was Jesus so upset with these guys?

The Pharisees' approach to righteousness made religion a burden. Loaded down with laws to know and rules to keep, the average person was discouraged rather than encouraged by the Pharisaical method.

If our idea of kingdom living is keeping rules, then we have the wrong idea. There is nothing inspiring about rule-keeping. If our religion is reduced to nothing more than this, then we lose the joy and every good work becomes another task. We are busy keeping up with the numbers on the ledger, not caring for people.

Also, we do not read of a humble Pharisee. Now, it wasn't that Pharisees couldn't be humble; rather, their system of righteousness simply made no provision for humility. Any thought of humility would have been drowned out by the shouting: "Look at me! Look what I've done!"

The Pharisees are gone, but their ways are still with us. It is a system about people, for people, by people, to glorify people. It produces individuals who believe that good deeds increase their worth and that they do God a favor by joining His team. They have all the answers. They deserve to be honored and served. They deserve the better seats. They deserve heaven.

It is no wonder that Jesus clashed with the Pharisees. His call to follow made no provision for pride. Sinful people are saved by God's grace. What is there to boast about? Whatever good we do is to His glory, not ours. Whatever in us may be called good is only the Spirit at work in us.

Human righteousness, however well-crafted by well-intentioned people, always fails. Also, it draws the anger of **Jesus**.

"Woe to you, scribes and Pharisees, hypocrites! For you tithe mint and dill and cumin, and have neglected the weightier matters of the law: justice and mercy and faithfulness."
Matthew 23:16-24

OCTOBER 4

Jesus did not tolerate attempts to lower the standard. Yet, the Pharisees' approach to righteousness did exactly that. Their goal was to be better men who were praised by other men. For that to happen, they needed rules they could keep.

Human righteousness lowers the standard and makes righteousness easy and cheap. Jesus commands that we just be honest, honoring what we say. But we feel the need to come up with some nifty rules that give us exceptions to honesty. Jesus calls for us to love our neighbors. We feel the need to first define who the neighbors are. Jesus told us to forgive. We set up rules which determine who can be forgiven and who cannot.

The righteousness of God is clearly boundless. It turns the other cheek, gives away the cloak, and goes the extra mile. It lends to the borrower, loves the enemy, and offers prayers for persecutors. It places no limits on sharing, loving or forgiving. In the end, it will joyfully sacrifice all to be true to the Father. If only people could see the boundless nature of discipleship! They can...if we are like God.

Also, like the Pharisees, we often miss what is truly important because we are so easily distracted by the less important, even the trivial. We can make a crusade out of something that means little in the greater scheme of life.

Sadly, this is why many find disappointment with the church. Church is often irrelevant. People that are jobless, or going through a divorce, or facing serious surgery, or living with broken hearts over their children don't care who the Amalakites were and they don't care about the genealogy of Jesus and they don't care what Paul said about the Lord's Supper and they don't care about the mode of baptism. They are looking for hope, and for mercy. They are longing for friendship and someone who really cares. They want to hear about forgiveness, love and another chance. And the wonderful thing is that all of that can happen for them—through you—when they come to know **Jesus**.

> "So you also outwardly appear righteous to others, but within you are full of hypocrisy and lawlessness."
>
> Matthew 23:25-39

OCTOBER 5

Jesus' scathing denunciation of the ways of the Pharisees probably had everyone afraid to move, much less speak. After all, these guys were the best! No one did religion better.

But that was their problem: they did religion. They were the best givers, prayers, and fasters around. They did it better and more often than anyone. But Jesus could see through the facade. No wonder they hated him!

Righteousness of our own making always leaves us desperate. The Pharisees were desperate men. They lived each day desperate to satisfy the demands of law. Not until they had accomplished each day's list, dotting every i and crossing every t, could they go home with a sense of satisfaction. Hours later the task of keeping their own rules would start all over again.

But that is the way of human righteousness. Once we craft our own way to righteousness, we follow our little list of rules and accomplish each task because it is our duty. We feel superior as if righteousness belonged only to us. Whether meeting the requirements of church or taking care of the rules of work and family, we take pride in what we are doing and seek nothing beyond what is explicitly required by our list. We do our duty and are satisfied with that. But worst of all, we have settled for so much less than was possible.

Of course, love is much different. Love has no limits, no satisfaction line. When we are in love with God, we cannot get enough of Him. No matter how much we give, we want to give more. No matter how often we pray, we cannot get enough. No matter how much time we spend in the Word, we find ourselves hungry for more. Every taste of goodness, every experience of God only stirs a greater hunger. It is the way of love.

Be on guard! The hardest thing is to know when we've crossed that line from love to duty. Most of us begin with the best of intentions. But somewhere along the journey we start listening to the praise. We like it! We deserve it! We want it! And that's often where we lose touch with **Jesus**.

"Truly, I say to you, this poor widow has put in more than all those who are contributing to the offering box.
For they all contributed out of their abundance, but she out of her poverty has put in everything she had, all she had to live on."

Mark 12:41-44 (Luke 21:1-4)

OCTOBER 6

Jesus missed nothing. And he saw what others could not see: the heart. Mark says she was "a poor widow," but he didn't really have to tell us that. Most widows in Israelite society endured lives of poverty and were completely dependent on the kindness and generosity of others.

Her offering was very small: two small copper coins. It was hardly a gift worth noticing at all. So, while the sound of many coins falling into the bronze containers would have signaled a large donation, hers may have hardly made a sound. Even so, Jesus was watching.

No matter where you are in your journey, money is an issue. Not many interests in life can be totally separated from the consideration of money. Knowing this, God has filled the Bible with stories and proverbs, sermons and letters providing direction on being good stewards. Even so, it does not seem to be a very popular sermon topic. Perhaps, that's because we tend to feel guilty whenever the subject comes up. No matter how we are handling our money and things, we feel like we could do better.

Also, we know that what we do with what we have says a lot about us. One glance at our checkbook or online register reveals much about our interests and priorities. The money tends to go in the direction of our heart.

We give to those causes or ideals, those groups or organizations that we believe in. We give to what has touched us in a personal way. We give to something we believe makes a difference to lives. We give to what has changed us. We give to what we are grateful for. We give to whatever offers us hope. We give to what we love.

Your giving speaks volumes about you and your perspective on life and God. What you do with your money reflects the love of your heart. And isn't that really what drew the attention of **Jesus**?

"And because lawlessness will be increased, the love of many will grow cold.
But the one who endures to the end will be saved."
Matthew 24:1-14 (Mark 13:1-13; Luke 21:5-19)

OCTOBER 7

Jesus spoke of things that were to come. So, it was only natural that his disciples would ask about such things. Their curiosity was particularly aroused when he spoke of things that seemed improbable!

Herod's temple was described by Josephus as being an incredible building. Evidently, the disciples agreed! It was then that Jesus foretold of a not so glorious future for the temple. Naturally, the disciples wanted to know more.

Four disciples, Peter, Andrew, James and John, asked two primary questions and each question had two parts. First, regarding the temple, they wanted to know when the temple would be destroyed and what signs would precede this destruction. Their second question regarded the second coming. What signs will precede the coming of Jesus? And, what signs will precede the end of the world? Since the coming of Jesus will be the end of the world, Jesus answered both questions by his response.

Jesus first took up the question of the temple and Jerusalem. He warned them to be watching out for deceivers claiming to be the Christ. He said that many would make such a claim and that many would be deceived by these frauds.

Also, he told them of the violence which lay ahead. There would be wars and rumors of wars but they were to remain calm. These conflicts were necessary before the end. Also, famine and earthquakes would affect many people.

Hated because of their faithfulness to him, they would be arrested for their faith and then executed. We can only imagine what thoughts filled their minds as they considered his words. Sadly, even family members would betray them and this betrayal would mean their death. But faithfulness to the end would be rewarded!

The only positive sign in this prelude to destruction was that the gospel would be preached to the whole world. Then, said Jesus, the end will come.

The end. Two words that always signal a change. Two words by which we mark time. Two words that always mean God is doing something.

And it all happened just as it was foretold by **Jesus**.

> "So, when you see the abomination of desolation spoken of by the prophet Daniel, standing in the holy place (let the reader understand), then let those who are in Judea flee to the mountains."
> Matthew 24:15-28 (Mark 13:14-23; Luke 21:20-24)

OCTOBER 8

Jesus answered his disciples' questions, not only telling them what signs to watch for, but also giving them instructions about what to do when all of this destruction began. "The abomination of desolation" or the Roman army around Jerusalem was the final sign. After that, the end was in sight.

As soon as they realized the danger, they were to flee to the mountains. The rough terrain would discourage the Romans from chasing after scattered peasants. While such an existence might be rough, at least they would be alive!

Timing was everything! Go immediately! Don't return to the house to pack or arrange or organize or take care of last-minute items. Flee! There is nothing left behind that is worth the risk. Also, the days will be difficult enough but especially so for those pregnant women and nursing mothers.

Naturally, prayer would be in order. In the face of what is coming, pray that the season is conducive to travel and that it won't be the Sabbath.

Jesus knew that his own disciples would be vulnerable to claims that the Messiah had returned, tempted to confuse the Jerusalem events with his coming. So, he warned them to believe no one on this matter. He was not out in the desert and he was not in some building. But when he did return, like lightning is seen across the sky, they would most definitely know it was he!

Why did Jesus provide so much detail? Why the signs? Why the instructions? Jesus loved them and he wanted to spare them.

But isn't that what his story is—signs and instructions? Isn't his very presence in our world a sign of something? Are not his words the instructions we need to read for that final day of judgment?

Jesus came to us as the unmistakable sign of the Father's love. God came to us! And every time he opened his mouth, he gave us words to guide us from danger to the safety of the Father's arms.

God's greatest sign to you is **Jesus**.

> "Then will appear in heaven the sign of the Son of Man, and then all the tribes of the earth will mourn, and they will see the Son of Man coming on the clouds of heaven with power and great glory."
> Matthew 24:29-35 (Mark 13:24-31; Luke 21:25-33)

OCTOBER 9

Jesus answered his disciples about the future of the temple. But while they were pondering his words, he told them of his own return.

What would be the signs of the coming of Jesus and the end of the world? Who wouldn't want to know?

Jesus said that "the sun will be darkened, and the moon will not give its light; the stars will fall from the sky, and the heavenly bodies will be shaken." What were the disciples to make of that! What are we to make of that?

The language is apocalyptic, the kind we see most often in Bible books like Ezekiel, Daniel, and Revelation. Apocalyptic language is composed of symbols that strike the imagination and grab our attention. This language is used to denote that something of incredible proportions and importance is going to happen.

Jesus told them a loud trumpet call would bring angels to gather the followers, wherever they were; thus, the end of life on planet earth.

At this point, Jesus returns to the first theme: the temple. "You will see these things," he says. "Like the fig tree tells you about the seasons, the signs I have given you will tell you when this is about to happen." Then, he adds, "Your generation will live to see this. You have my word on it!"

But in the very next verse (36) Jesus says, "No one knows about that day or hour..." Jesus told his disciples that they would be able to know in advance and actually see "these things," this first great event. However, he gave no such personal assurance concerning "that day," the second incredible event.

To this moment in time, the greatest event in the history of the world was the life of the divine among the human. But we so badly missed his first coming that we rejected him. The greatest news is that he is returning, and he is returning for us! Today might just be the day that brings **Jesus**.

> "But concerning that day or that hour, no one knows, not even the angels in heaven, nor the Son, but only the Father.
> Be on guard, keep awake. For you do not know when the time will come."
> Mark 13:32-33 (Matthew 24:36-41)

OCTOBER 10

Jesus said, "No one knows." But his words have not kept us from trying. The time of his return is such a carefully guarded secret that neither the angels nor Jesus himself know the day or the hour. Evidently, it is God's intention to keep the time of the second coming a secret. It is, you might say, the best-kept secret in the universe.

But what about the conditions in our world at the time of his coming? Well, what did Jesus tell us? "As it was in the days of Noah..." So, how was it? Evidently, people were going about their normal routines. Folks were eating and drinking, and getting married and doing all the things folks do with their days. In fact, right up to the moment that Noah entered the ark everything was just as normal as always. No one had any reason to believe that something incredible was about to happen.

But, in a moment, all of that changed in dramatic fashion! It will be the same when Jesus comes the second time. Men and women will be working at their jobs and taking care of their kids. Just regular stuff...right up to the very last second!

We read the words but we are not easily convinced. After centuries of waiting, it is difficult to believe that today is the day. In fact, unless we are intentional about it, we probably won't even think about it.

But could this be the day that Jesus comes? Maybe. Maybe not. But what if we lived today as though we expected him. What would the day look like? What would we look like? What would we do differently? What would we do that we have always intended to do but kept putting off? If today was the day, how would you use it? Well, isn't that the way life is supposed to be lived?

What if this is the day you see **Jesus**?

"But watch yourselves lest your hearts be weighed down with dissipation and drunkenness and cares of this life, and that day come upon you suddenly like a trap.
For it will come upon all who dwell on the face of the whole earth."
Luke 21:34-36 (Matthew 24:42-44; Mark 13:34-37)

OCTOBER 11

Jesus is intense! His language is passionate! His words are forceful! His meaning is unmistakable!

"Watch! Be alert!"

Jesus was concerned that believers would lose their zeal and become indifferent. Their failure to be always diligent would leave them unprepared for his return.

To illustrate, Jesus presented an all-too-common scenario: a thief breaking into a home. Obviously, if the owner knew the thief was coming and the time of his arrival, then the owner would prepare for the thief and catch him in his mischief. But, as everyone knows, that's not the way thievery works.

Jesus' point: the believer must be always ready and do all he can to be prepared for the sudden coming of the Son of Man. Like the thief, the Son of Man will come at an hour when you do not expect him.

But why are Christians sometimes slow to give up their own bad habits and deceitful ways? The answer: they do not feel the sense of urgency.

Urgency is all about time, isn't it? In fact, urgency takes over when time is short. If your term paper is due tomorrow, urgency takes over. If the house catches on fire, urgency takes over. If war is declared, urgency takes over. Some kind of danger plus limited time equals urgency!

When people began making excuses for their failure to be obedient to Jesus, they simply show that they do not feel the sense of urgency. "I know that I need to make a change in my life. But I'm waiting on my mate." No urgency! Or, "I plan to do something someday." No urgency!

No one goes to heaven without a sense of urgency! No one becomes a genuine follower of Jesus without the attitude and understanding that this is what must be done and done now! Time is short! Life is uncertain! And the most important decision we ever make is what we are going to do with **Jesus**!

"Who then is the faithful and wise servant, whom his master has set over his household, to give them their food at the proper time? Blessed is that servant whom his master will find so doing when he comes."

Matthew 24:45-51

OCTOBER 12

Jesus would not stop talking about it. In one story after another, he wanted his listeners to understand that being ready for the Master's return was extremely important.

Of course, it is just like us to start thinking and acting like we have all the time in the world. It is just like us to think that we can live as we like now and worry about making changes later. But what if we run out of days before we decide to make those changes? What if he returns before we commit to following him?

Maybe we are thinking that following Jesus will be easier when certain things fall in place. After all, life is pretty full and busy right now.

If you are waiting for a convenient time to do the right thing, you are waiting for what will never come. Jesus wants you to respond to him because of who he is, not because it fits what is convenient for you. The convenient day is the day that will never come.

Did you travel through the pages of the morning paper and count the number of people whose deaths are reported? How many of them do you think made plans for today just like you did? How many of them had made plans for next week?

How many people across America got up yesterday morning...talked with their family members about the day's events....kissed their loved ones goodbye....and walked out the door on their way to what they thought was an ordinary day? We are talking about people who thought they had plenty of time to do all the things they had planned and to make all the changes they needed to make. Sadly, they were wrong.

"Be prepared! Get ready! Don't wait to get your life in order! Be faithful!"

The saying is: "There's no time like the present." That is especially true if we are talking about being ready for **Jesus**.

> "Then the kingdom of heaven will be like ten virgins who took their lamps and went to meet the bridegroom. Five of them were foolish, and five were wise."
>
> Matthew 25:1-13

OCTOBER 13

Jesus was a master story-teller. His stories came out of the everyday experiences of his listeners and the messages connected with their hearts. Jesus wasn't spinning tales but revealing the Father and the nature of a kingdom unlike anyone had ever seen before. His stories made people think about the most important things. No wonder the crowds grew so large.

Jesus tells a story about ten excited girls who are planning to take part in a marital celebration. They all seem equally delighted to participate and they all appear to be equally prepared for the occasion. They are all wearing their wedding finery and each one has a lamp. While they each know there is going to be a wonderful ceremony, they do not know the exact time of the bridegroom's arrival.

As the bridegroom delays, they became drowsy and fell asleep. Suddenly, they were startled by a shout that the bridegroom was coming. Quickly they trimmed their little lamps, which had burned up all the oil. Five of the girls had made good preparation and had enough foresight to bring some extra oil. As a result, they went out to meet the bridegroom with brightly burning lamps. But the other five now found themselves without oil for their lamps. So, they ran off to buy some. But when these girls hurriedly returned, the door was already closed and the celebration had begun. They were shut out. They were too late.

The bridegroom's delay is the delay of the second coming of Jesus. The sudden appearance of the bridegroom is the coming of the Son of Man at a time when least expected. And the closed door with the foolish virgins standing on the outside is the judgment pronounced on those who fail to prepare themselves for the Savior's return.

Why wouldn't we be ready? Is there really any good reason for failing to prepare for the greatest celebration the world will ever see?! What fools we would be to be on the wrong side of the door when it is shut by **Jesus**.

"His master said to him, 'Well done, good and faithful servant.'"
Matthew 25:14-30

OCTOBER 14

Jesus spent much of his last hours talking about time. Time for him was short. Time for us is short, too.

The three servants only had so much time before the master returned. We understand time pressure. At some point, the term paper is due, the report has to be turned in, the deal has to be closed, the taxes come due, a decision has to be made. We are used to that. We only have so much time with which to work. Failure to plan carefully often spells trouble.

But the story was about more than time; it was about the use of blessings. Each man was given something. A talent was a large amount of money. The master sent none away empty-handed. All had something to work with. Each man was treated as an individual and received what the master decided. Thus, their starting positions were different.

But this was not some kind of competition between the servants. What mattered was not the size of the gift but what the person did with the gift. The men were not judged by the amount they were given but by what was accomplished for their master.

Jesus wants you to write these words across your heart: Whatever you do with the gifts of God, you must answer to Him. We are stewards of His blessings. If God gave you Christian parents, or a healthy body, or a loving spouse, or a child, or a job, or a house, or a car, or a talent, or any other blessing, then you must answer to God for what you have done with His gifts.

But does that mean that we must always show an increase of blessings? One car must become two or a small house must be replaced by a larger one?

No, the story is not about increase but faithfulness. "Well done, good and faithful servant! You have been faithful with a few things…" The invitation to share in the master's happiness was the result of faithful effort in behalf of the master.

Life is not fair and blessings are not evenly distributed. But real success is always measured the same way. Faithfulness to **Jesus**.

> "And he will place the sheep on his right, but the goats on the left."
> Matthew 25:31-40

OCTOBER 15

Jesus spoke the most welcome word of all: "Come." It is the loveliest word with the happiest sound for one who loves Jesus. "Come!"

Amazingly, those who hear the word "come" will enter, not because of power or wealth, office or title, but because they offered themselves in the most simple service to other people. In doing so, they showed their love and gratitude to Jesus the King.

The six examples—feeding the hungry, giving drink to the thirsty, showing hospitality to strangers, clothing the naked, caring for the sick, and visiting the imprisoned—are acts of kindness that do not depend on wealth, talent, or intelligence. They are the kind of things that we can do. They are the things that we ought to do. They are the kind of deeds that make a difference one person at a time. This is the kind of difference Jesus asked us to make!

Interestingly, these sheep could not recall any occasion in which they realized the King was in need or they offered any help to him. In other words, they did not serve others because they expected some reward for their service.

Although this is a wonderful, inspiring picture of judgment, the scene may not generate confidence in us. The reason: the basis of judgment is the treatment of others. But it is not just the treatment of others but the care of others. And it is not just the care of others, as in our family, or our friends, or fellow church members, but the care of people who are in prison and homeless and needy.

Furthermore, this isn't ministry by committee or service by a hireling or assistance by writing a check. This is a judgment that targets personal involvement, individual service.

"Come" was not extended to those who attended a certain church, had a baptismal certificate in hand, or believed a certain set of doctrines. Instead, "come" was the invitation offered to those who treated others as if they were treating **Jesus**.

> "Then he will say to those on his left, 'Depart from me, you cursed, into the eternal fire prepared for the devil and his angels."
> Matthew 25:41-26:5 (Mark 14:1-2; Luke 22:1-2)

OCTOBER 16

Jesus thrilled the hearts of some (the sheep) with a single word: "come." It was the most wondrous, most exhilarating, most joyous moment of their existence! The greatest desire of their hearts had come true! By this word he gave them what was always their greatest desire: to be forever with him.

But "come" was not the only word that came from Jesus' lips. There was another word that possessed all the sadness and tragedy of human existence. This was the word none wanted to hear. "Depart." It is the worst of all words that could come from the mouth of Jesus.

Everyone gets one word. In this very moment, one of those words is your word. One of those words is what you would hear if everything stopped right now. Which word would it be? "Come" or "depart"?

Very few people like to talk about hell. The idea of 'eternal fire' is something we would prefer not to think about at all. It is natural that we would not like the sound of it but it is important to remember that it is Jesus' description. Whatever may be the nature of this place, Jesus did not want anyone to go there. His cross shouted that loud and clear!

One of the most striking parts of the story is the surprise by all that serving others was serving Jesus. The goat people could recall no situations in which they failed to minister to Jesus. But their failure was in not ministering to people around them.

Perhaps, they felt compelled to shout, "If only we had known! If only we had known that serving others was serving Christ." But how could they not know? How could **we** not know?

Could we read the Gospels and miss seeing Jesus loving and serving people? Could we not tell from his words that people were precious to him and the Father? Did he not tell us that his very reason for being here was to love and to serve people, and that we should be like him? How could we not know?

So, now we know what makes a lasting difference to us and to **Jesus**.

And while he was at Bethany in the house of Simon the leper, as he was reclining at table, a woman came with an alabaster flask of ointment of pure nard, very costly, and she broke the flask and poured it over his head.

Mark 14:3-9 (Matthew 26:6-13; John 12:2-8)

OCTOBER 17

Jesus was the guest of honor in the home of Simon the Leper. Jesus had healed him of leprosy and he wanted to honor Jesus with a meal in his home.

Also, Lazarus was there, along with his sisters, Mary and Martha. They also had good reason to honor Jesus. Jesus raised Lazarus to life!

And the disciples were present, too. They were probably entranced by the table conversation between a former leper, a former dead man and the man who brought life to each.

Martha served. What else would we expect from Martha? Her service was from the heart and it was her way of showing her love for Jesus.

But on this day, it was Mary who joined Jesus at center stage. She broke an alabaster jar and put expensive perfume on his feet. At some point, she began wiping his feet with her hair. As the fragrance filled the room, the group reclined in stunned silence. It was, to be sure, an extravagant expression of her love.

Judas had a ready eye for something valuable and he quickly calculated the perfume's value and realized that this could have been money in his pockets as he was the treasurer for the group. So, he pretended concern for the poor. Mary's actions might be considered extravagant but that is how love behaves. She may have acted spontaneously, but she wanted to express her love and devotion to Jesus and that could not be done according to convenience or minimal investment.

Her actions were courageous. She stepped away from the socially accepted customs of the day and stepped into a man's world to express herself. She had to know that she would draw frowns and criticisms.

But in the end, the only voice that mattered was that of Jesus, and he said, "She has done a beautiful thing to me." What sweet words those must have been to Mary. Extravagant love is pleasing to **Jesus**.

Then Judas Iscariot, who was one of the twelve, went to the chief priests in order to betray him to them.
Mark 14:10-11 (Matthew 26:14-16; Luke 22:3-6)

OCTOBER 18

Jesus predicted betrayal. Now, a deal was about to be made.

How do we explain the actions of Judas? Like the other disciples, he left things behind to follow Jesus. But he never caught the dream; he never grasped the truth. He was never transformed like the others. Somehow, he followed but he never really gave his heart.

"Satan entered Judas." Can you think of anything worse to say about someone?

Perhaps, Judas assumed, as we often do, that making a bargain with the world was the best way to get ahead. Maybe he was willing to sacrifice loyalty to Jesus for the sake of gaining acceptance by others. But he later learned how little others cared about him. When he tried to return the money, acknowledging Jesus' innocence, all he got was, "What is that to us? That's your responsibility."

Remember: the world does not value you, only what you can give.

Whatever Judas envisioned, whatever he thought his betrayal would accomplish for him, it never happened. His disloyalty was one more example of how painful life becomes whenever we sacrifice integrity for our own desires.

Today, though his name figures prominently in history, he is remembered for none of those qualities that call for admiration – love, sacrifice, devotion, generosity, compassion, faithfulness – but only for the one thing that no one admires: betrayal.

Would you betray Jesus? Don't answer too quickly. All too often we have witnessed the fall of some folks we thought were spiritual giants. All that it takes is giving the devil a foothold in your life. Out of our unhappiness or pain, out of our worry or disappointment, out of our troubles or stress, Satan seeks to gain just a foothold, just enough opening to gain entrance to our lives. We give it to him when we choose to believe that his way is the answer to our needs. But it is always a lie!

Would you really believe Satan and betray **Jesus**?

> "For who is the greater, one who reclines at table or one who serves? Is it not the one who reclines at table? But I am among you as the one who serves."
> Luke 22:7-16, 24-30 (Matthew 26:17-20; Mark 14:12-17)

OCTOBER 19

Jesus sent two men, Peter and John, to make preparations for what would be his final meal with the disciples before the cross. Jesus intended to observe the Passover meal with these men had been his comrades in kingdom labors and stood by him in his trials. Sharing this final evening with them was very important.

Peter and John secured the room, purchased the lamb and the other necessary supplies, and then got everything ready for what would prove to be a most memorable evening. Although the writers provided no specific time, to avoid drawing a crowd Jesus probably arrived under the cover of darkness.

Throughout history artists have given us some incredible portraits of what this gathering might have looked like. Usually, the paintings depict Jesus seated in the middle of a long table with six disciples on each side. However, the text says they "reclined at the table." In keeping with the customs of the time, they did not sit in chairs but rested on one elbow and ate with the other hand. It provides a more meaningful picture when thinking of Jesus washing the disciples' feet.

It is difficult to determine the chronology of events in the upper room. However, at some point after the meal began, a quarrel broke out among the disciples. Who started it? What prompted them to veer into a debate about who was the greatest among them? And why did they feel compelled to resolve this matter at all?

There is a part of our nature that longs for recognition and praise. We want to serve; we just don't want it to go unnoticed. In fact, we prefer to be honored above all the others who serve.

This was not the first time they had argued about greatness. Evidently, they had learned little from earlier rebukes. So, they sat around the table thinking of how wonderful they were and arguing their personal case for greatness. And just think: they did all of this in front of the perfect man. **Jesus.**

> Now before the Feast of the Passover, when Jesus knew that his hour had come to depart out of this world to the Father, having loved his own who were in the world, he loved them to the end.
>
> John 13:1-11

OCTOBER 20

Jesus knew that it was almost time to say goodbye. It was time to say what must be said, to say what was on his heart.

For three years Jesus had shared himself with them. Yet, for it all, there was so much they did not understand...as they did not understand what was soon to happen. And they did not understand what he wanted for them in their own relationship to one another. Within sight of the cross there remained a spirit of competitiveness and of jealousy among them.

In this special time Jesus wanted them to know the full extent of his love. More than that, he wanted them to show this love to one another. Words would not be enough.

As Jesus moved around the room washing feet, we can imagine an awkward silence fell on the group. All seemed unable to speak. Well, everyone but Peter. Peter was having trouble with the idea of Jesus washing feet, especially Peter's feet.

Jesus was saying, "I want you to follow my example. I want you to serve people. I want others to see the full extent of my love through you."

Only later would the disciples appreciate fully the magnitude of what they had experienced. Then, they would realize that the King of Kings had not only washed their feet but he had done so at a most difficult time in his earthly life. And later, they would reflect on the faces in the room and recall that Jesus had washed the feet of Judas, the very one who betrayed him! The full extent of love is serving anyone.

Our tendency is to offer our service, when convenient, for high profile, high-demand tasks. After all, we like being noticed and appreciated. But Jesus calls us to the highest standard: service anytime, anywhere, doing anything, for anyone. And just so we won't be confused about it all, he shows us what this service looks like. This is the love of **Jesus**.

"If I then, your Lord and Teacher, have washed your feet, you also ought to wash one another's feet.
For I have given you an example, that you also should do just as I have done to you."

John 13:12-17

OCTOBER 21

Jesus was the ultimate teacher. His words were carefully chosen for each audience and simple so all could understand. Many of his lessons came in stories that reflected the everyday experiences of his listeners. He spoke with an authority that gave his hearers confidence that he knew what he was talking about. And his words always pointed people toward God and the right way to live.

But Jesus wasn't merely the best teacher because of what he said. Jesus taught by doing, too. While the multitudes could observe him from time-to-time, no group was so close to his life as his chosen disciples. He was their teacher in words and in ways.

Washing their feet created silence in the room. Except for Peter's brief exchange with Jesus, we wonder if anyone else made a sound. Washing feet was a lowly and unpleasant task reserved for those who were truly servants. Even so, Jesus moved from one disciple to another, performing this menial job. But why?

Time was short. This was their last evening together. Whether they understood all that he had to tell them right now, they would later. And while words might grow fuzzy with time, an example would be hard to forget. So, he washed their feet.

"I am your Teacher and your Lord. As I have served you, you serve one another."

Service. From the moment his ministry began, he was all about service. People were most important and he came to serve them. He wanted his disciples to do the same. So, he used a towel and basin of water to show them.

Most of us don't mind a bit of service now and then. We prefer to choose our chores and we like to perform those tasks that won't go unnoticed. And we even have preferences about whom we think should be served.

That's why Jesus was teaching, to help us see what service looked like. The blessing is not in knowing about service but in serving. The blessing to others and to ourselves is in being like **Jesus**.

After saying these things, Jesus was troubled in his spirit, and testified, "Truly, truly, I say to you, one of you will betray me."
John 13:18-30 (Matthew 26:21-25; Mark 14:18-21; Luke 22:21-23)

OCTOBER 22

Jesus knew the heart of Judas. Clearly, Judas did not know the heart of Jesus.

We are not Judas, but we could have been. We've turned our back on Jesus to satisfy our longing for things. We've rejected his words to indulge ourselves in pleasures of the flesh. We've denied we knew him so we could be accepted by others. We've scorned his ways because we believed in our own ideas. We are not Judas, but we have certainly behaved like him!

It was Judas who shared the bread with Jesus and it was Judas who lifted up his heel against him. The sharing of bread was descriptive of their relationship and being bound together in loyalty. Of course, it wasn't true. Lifting up his heel was descriptive of his treachery. That was true enough.

When did Judas begin his slide away from Jesus? What happened to make him think this betrayal was worth doing? And how could he look Jesus in the face knowing what he was going to do to him?

Satan. If evil is happening, Satan is involved.

There was a moment, a place and time, maybe even an event, when Satan first gained a very small spot in the heart of Judas. Once in, he never quit. Up and down the dusty roads of Palestine, through the towns and villages, Judas pondered on this one idea. Satan helped keep it alive. Through the sermons and the miracles, the idea grew and grew. In time, Satan and Judas both wanted the same thing. Satan had found a home. Loyalty to Jesus was no longer on the mind of Judas.

Our failure to be loyal to Jesus is not something we can take back or undo, and it is not easy to forget. But our hope rests in God who demonstrated His amazing grace in the Son He gave for us. So, with our lives, we give thanks for the grace we find in **Jesus**.

> "A new commandment I give to you, that you love one another: just as I have loved you, you also are to love one another.
> By this all people will know that you are my disciples, if you have love for one another."
>
> John 13:31-35

OCTOBER 23

Jesus' followers have frequently sought for ways to mark themselves as his followers. Some have chosen to wear a certain type of clothing (gray and black have been popular colors). Others have lived out a rather odd lifestyle or simply withdrawn from society altogether. Some have chosen to be noticed by the way they cut their hair or a chain about the neck. But in each case, there was a desire to be recognized as devoted to the Lord. We can admire their devotion even if the Scriptures say nothing about those kinds of markings.

However, Jesus has provided a distinguishing mark for the Christian. This mark or badge is called love. "By this all men will know that you are my disciples, if you love one another."

Such love, of course, is very challenging. Our inclination is to lower the standard so that it is more doable. For example, if Jesus had just said to love certain people, then this would have been easier. Loving your family, or your friends, or the church folks, or other Americans would have provided parameters. We could work on that.

Or, if he had only said to love others in special situations or under certain conditions, then we would have a better chance of managing that. By loving people in a certain income bracket or those with certain problems or those having specific health issues we could come closer to actually living up to this standard.

But Jesus didn't identify any special groups or designate any certain situations. He just said, "You love as I have loved you." "As I have loved you"–that is the standard.

This love is not a warm, fuzzy feeling but a decision we make and an action we take. It is a deliberate effort to be like Jesus.

Wouldn't it be fantastic if people watched the way you loved others and concluded: There is another follower of **Jesus**.

Peter said to him, "Even if I must die with you, I will not deny you!" And all the disciples said the same.
Matthew 26:31-35 (Mark 14:27-31; Luke 22:31-38; John 13:36-38)

OCTOBER 24

Jesus' selection of Peter as a disciple probably raised a few eyebrows. Sure, the guy had a lot of energy and was a hard worker, but his impetuousness often got him into trouble and he was a bit of a showoff. He was given to stubbornness and, although well-intentioned, he could be argumentative. In short, Peter was pretty ordinary. Maybe that's why we feel drawn to him. His journey with Jesus seems to parallel our own: good days and bad days, moments of courage and times of fear.

Of course, we are all flawed. It is hard to admit, but true. Like Peter, we often have good intentions and understand exactly what is required. But we are weak and simply don't always choose what is right.

But this is Peter we are talking about! How could this happen to Peter, the rock? This guy saw the miracles and heard the sermons of Jesus! Peter walked on water, at least briefly, and boldly declared that Jesus was the Son of God! How could this happen to Peter?

Jesus told Peter what would happen and Peter told him, "Well, that's just your opinion. You have your opinion, I have mine." In fact, all of the disciples took the same approach. They all disagreed with Jesus.

Peter believed that he knew better than Jesus what was right for Peter. Does that sound familiar? Disagreeing with Jesus is not very smart.

Naturally, we think we are different. Peter did. He wanted Jesus to know that the other disciples might be wimps when the moment of truth came, but not him! They might lack backbone, but not Peter! He would be different!

Although Peter could hardly appreciate it at the time, Jesus was telling Peter that he had a wake-up call coming. The rooster was Peter's wake-up call. It would jar him and shake his life in dramatic fashion. But the change would be wonderful before it was over!

Are you arguing with Jesus about anything in your life right now? Ask yourself: do you really believe that you know what's best for you more than **Jesus**?

> **Now as they were eating, Jesus took bread, and after blessing it broke it and gave it to the disciples, and said, "Take, eat; this is my body."**
> **Matthew 26:26-29**
> **(Mark 14:22-25; Luke 22:17-20; 1 Corinthians 11:23-26)**

OCTOBER 25

Jesus normally returned to Bethany in the evenings of this final week. However, this night he stayed in the city with his disciples, meeting in an upper room to participate in the Passover meal. Earlier, Jesus had sent two of his disciples, Peter and John, to prepare the meal. Now, with his disciples around him, Jesus could focus on them and what they needed to know for the journey ahead.

At some point in their meal, Jesus took the bread and the cup and pointed to their significance. He said, "Do this in remembrance of me."

No other event in Christianity is quite like this. Nothing else so powerfully reminds us that we are in this together...that we stand on level ground...that we continue to possess the very same need in every minute: grace. Christians are never closer than when, at the table, our collective eyes are fixed on the cross of our Savior.

And the most exciting news of the table is that there is more! This simple meal anticipates a feast. These few minutes anticipate eternity. This is the moment when the Lord meets his people at his table...and this meeting is a taste, an introduction, a symbol of meeting him at his table in heaven.

Of course, we often come to this table distracted by the many problems of life. We come with anxieties and questions, with pressures and fears. There are pains of the body and the heart. We have questions we can't answer and problems we can't solve. Amazingly, Jesus always welcomes us to the table with open arms. Then, once more, as we remember what he has done for us, we realize that he is really all we need.

Not surprisingly, the table of the Lord becomes a place of resolve. It is here that we commit ourselves once more to being like Jesus. Even so, we know in our hearts that the next time we come to the table we will be doing it yet again. But, for now, it is enough.

"Remember me." How could we ever forget **Jesus**?

"Let not your hearts be troubled. Believe in God; believe also in me. In my Father's house are many rooms. If it were not so, would I have told you that I go to prepare a place for you? And if I go and prepare a place for you, I will come again and will take you to myself, that where I am you may be also."

John 14:1-3

OCTOBER 26

Jesus knew exactly what the next few hours would bring. His disciples had no idea. So, he tried to prepare them.

Already they were troubled. They were troubled at the thought that a traitor was among them. They were troubled that Jesus continued to speak of his own death. They were troubled that he was so troubled.

These disciples needed hope and they needed encouragement for what lay ahead. And we do, too! So, Jesus told them—and us—the only thing he could: "I want you to trust me."

Now, Lord, surely after all this time, after all that we have experienced, surely you have more than that! "No, that's it. I want you to trust me."

Think about it. Everyone experiences those moments when it seems you are alone and abandoned, when it feels like you face a hopeless situation. What keeps you going when your heart is broken? The certain knowledge that, no matter what, God rules and you are going to be safe with Him.

But why is this trust so hard for us? Two reasons. First, we feel more secure with what we can see and touch. If I could just see God the way I see my grandchildren or touch Him the way I hold them, it would be a lot easier to believe! We tend to trust our senses above everything else.

Second, we like to be in control. Trusting someone else makes us feel like we have relinquished control, and that can be a scary thought.

Jesus says, "Trust me. I am preparing a place for you. I am coming back. And I am going to take you to be with me." We have never received a better offer.

In a world where so many things break our heart, we have but one real choice, and it is the best choice of all. Trust **Jesus**.

Jesus said to him, "I am the way, and the truth, and the life. No one comes to the Father except through me."

John 14:4-7

OCTOBER 27

Jesus said a number of things that tend to rub us the wrong way. But of all the things he said, these may be his most offensive words. Talk about a politically incorrect statement!

Yet, listen again to his words. "I am the way and the truth and the life. No one comes to the Father except through me."

How many ways are there to God? The spirit of our time argues that all roads lead to God. All religions are identical and all people will be saved.

While there may be many similarities and many good things about each one, there are also some serious and irreconcilable differences. Perhaps, the most significant difference centers in the action of God in behalf of humanity. Other religions emphasize the need to do something to connect with God and earn His favor. But Christianity affirms that God reaches down to connect with us and does so because He loves us.

The story of the Bible is that because of our sins we have no way to God. There is no door, no road, no path, no way. We cannot make one. God must make a way. The way is a person. Jesus.

Jesus said, "I am the truth." Although not a popular notion in our day, his words require a definitive answer: yes or no.

Whatever life is, whatever life could be, Jesus says, "That's me. I am the life."

A cursory look will reveal that Jesus wasn't "living it up" as we tend to think of it. In fact, he had none of the trappings with which we associate "really living." So, what was he talking about?

For the first time we were in the presence of someone who was actually living the life God intended for us to live. Everything he said and everything he did was intended to bring glory to the Father. He was what we were supposed to be! Thus, the only life that matters is the life of **Jesus**.

"Whoever has seen me has seen the Father."

John 14:8-14

OCTOBER 28

Jesus seemed amazed that Philip had failed to grasp his true nature. "Show us the Father." How could Philip make such a request? Where had he been for these last three years? Had he seen and heard nothing?

In spite of the overwhelming evidence, in spite of the wonders, the words and the ways of Jesus, the reality is this: most people do not believe in him. Then, as now, many people see Jesus as nothing more than a man. Why?

Perhaps, they are so busy with life that they have no time or interest in pausing to consider what connection Jesus might have to their life. Or, maybe they are content to accept what others tell them about him. No doubt, many are looking for someone with a bit more pizazz, more excitement. Even to those who saw Jesus, he looked like another Galilean peasant.

And like them, some of us are afraid. We are afraid of committing ourselves to something we don't completely understand. We are afraid to trust ourselves to someone we can't actually see.

But how could they not see God? Throughout his ministry Jesus had told them, "The Father sent me" and "I and the Father are one." Who did they think they were seeing when the water turned to wine, the storm became still, the blind man could see, and Lazarus walked out of the tomb? Who did they think they were hearing when he said, "If the Son sets you free, you will be free indeed" or "the Son of Man will come with his angels?" After so many miracles and so many sermons, why were the disciples still filled with questions and doubts? Why did they still not get it?

"Anyone who has seen me has seen the Father." We have always wanted to know what God was like, what He wanted and did not want from us, and what was really important to Him. Now, we know.

We are really important to Him. And the incredible thing is that He came all this way to tell us Himself. And His name is **Jesus**.

> "Whoever has my commandments and keeps them, he it is who loves me."
>
> John 14:15-24

OCTOBER 29

Jesus said that love and obedience go together. However, we have a difficult time with both. To some people, loving the Lord simply means being sincere, well-intentioned. As long as the heart is in the right place, everything else is of minimal importance. To others, obeying the Lord is all that matters. Regardless of how you feel or what you think, the only thing that counts with God is just doing what He says. In each instance, there is a failure to understand the true meaning of love and obedience.

The word "love" gets a lot of press. As the subject of most songs, secular and religious, and the primary word we use to describe how we feel about peanut butter, football, grandmother, and America, love has come to mean little more than warm, fuzzy feelings. Applied to virtually everything, it has come to mean practically nothing.

But love is not some mysterious force that moves in and out of our lives without our say. Love is a decision we make. Our feelings (about anything) are going to rise and fall with varying life experiences but our love is to be constant. And because of that love we want to be obedient.

This does not mean that being obedient is all that matters. Obedience is important but so also is the reason for that obedience. Just because we do right does not mean we are right. Just because we do what he said does not mean we love him.

Real obedience does not come from fear, guilt or duty. None of that would be honoring to the Lord. He seeks our hearts. He seeks followers whose passion is to live for him, no matter what. He wants our actions to rise out of hearts that desire to please Him, no matter what.

We know the rules and commands of God are for our good. Following His instructions is the only way to live a rich and meaningful life. But we obey, not because we love the rules or commandments, but because we love the Person! Our love moves us to obey and our obedience reflects our love. Working together, these two make beautiful lives in **Jesus**!

"Peace I leave with you; my peace I give to you. Not as the world gives do I give to you. Let not your hearts be troubled, neither let them be afraid."

John 14:25-31

OCTOBER 30

Jesus had peace. He wanted his disciples to have that peace.

The disciples did not really understand everything that was about to happen. Perhaps, from Jesus' references to death and the tone in his voice they could sense that something bad was going to occur. Maybe they felt a sense of dread, even fear. So, Jesus told them that he would give them his peace.

Becoming a Christian does not provide immunity against the sorrows and pains of life. But while we may not be free of such troubles, we can be free of fear, anxiety and worry! Jesus said so! That is the kind of peace we want!

The world system tries every day to convince you that it is good at providing peace. "Just make more money, lose weight, get married, get divorced, get a hobby, buy a new car, get a face lift...then you will finally be at peace!" In other words, do something that will make you feel good now. Of course, it won't be long and you will be searching again for that elusive peace. The world cannot provide what it does not have.

The peace that Jesus gives does not come by changing the circumstances or engaging in some activity. Rearranging the load may be a wise move, but doing a little more of this or a little less of that leaves the heart unchanged. And, after all, this is really a heart matter.

We were made for closeness with God. It is only in this fellowship with Him that we experience the peace and joy we so desperately seek. Whenever we are away from Him, peace and joy are missing, too. We may search in all directions and in a thousand places but we will never find it apart from God.

Like the disciples in the upper room, we, too, often face the unknown with apprehension. Unable to control the events and determine the outcome, we feel helpless and hopeless. What we want is the peace that calms our hearts and gives confidence to our souls. We want the peace that comes only from **Jesus**.

"I am the vine; you are the branches. Whoever abides in me and I in him, he it is that bears much fruit, for apart from me you can do nothing."
John 15:1-11

OCTOBER 31

Jesus would soon lead his little group out of the house and toward the Garden of Gethsemane. Mindful of how little time he actually had left, he talked with them about the things on his heart. Their relationship was one of those things. So, he illustrated their relationship by drawing on what was familiar to them: a vineyard. His union with these men was like the relationship of the vine to the branches. The vine is the source of life. If the branch is separated from the vine for any reason, it will die.

Real life is the result of our union with him. We are powerless if we lack connection to him. Everything that we need, all that we value, and all that sustains us comes from being united with Christ.

The vine is the source of fruit, too. If we are to do anything of real, eternal value, then it will be because we remain in Christ. Apart from him, no matter how hard we labor, we can produce nothing of lasting value.

There is no suggestion that one is unable to be happily married, enjoy parenting, or succeed in one's vocation simply because he or she is not connected to Christ. What is affirmed is that, if one is to live a life in keeping with the purpose for which he or she was made, the person must be connected to the one who provides guidance and gives strength for the living of that life.

Jesus' words leave us with several things to think about. First, there is this obvious expectation that disciples will bear fruit. After all, that's why we are here. Second, the key to bearing fruit is remaining in him. There is no fruit apart from Jesus. And third, there are always unpleasant consequences for not bearing fruit. God takes the matter seriously.

We are tempted to measure our lives by what we accumulate and achieve. But Jesus said that the fruit of our lives that matters most is that which brings glory to the Father and which shows that we are disciples of **Jesus**.

> "This is my commandment, that you love one another as I have loved you. Greater love has no one than this, that someone lay down his life for his friends."
>
> John 15:12-17

NOVEMBER 1

Jesus said, "This is my command." Of all the things he could or might command, this is the one: love one another.

To help his disciples, and us, Jesus provided a standard: himself. "Love each other as I have loved you." How we wish Jesus had made the standard something other than himself! He could have made it easier on us by specifying who to love or how to love or when to love. But he identified no certain group or specific action or special situation. Instead, he made himself the rule on the subject of love.

Sadly, we are too often pursuing the lowest standard in matters of the heart. Jesus wanted love to be the badge of his followers, the way by which his disciples were known. Unfortunately, as his followers we are too often recognizable for words and behavior that in no way sets us apart from the world.

"Love as I have loved you." What can we say of his love? His love was freely given. Those who would crucify him probably thought they were taking his life from him. Little did they realize that he was freely giving it.

And his love was sacrificial. He made the ultimate sacrifice, surrendering his life to save us. He kept nothing back. He could not give any more.

Loving as Jesus loved is not easy; in fact, it is very difficult. It calls for tough decisions and strong commitment. Your love will be tested. People will hurt you. You will have to make hard choices in the midst of emotions that tell you to hate and to strike back. And loving as Jesus loved will leave you vulnerable. Jesus knew all about what can happen when you truly love people.

His cross represented the most incredible, most unbelievable love that the world has ever known. He did not die for those who saw themselves as his friends, though such would be an incredible love. He died for those who saw themselves as his enemies. Now, we are to love like **Jesus**.

> "If you were of the world, the world would love you as its own; but because you are not of the world, but I chose you out of the world, therefore the world hates you."
>
> John 15:18-16:4

NOVEMBER 2

Jesus anticipated persecution for his followers. Discipleship was costly. He would not have his followers believe otherwise.

But why must it be this way? Why such hostility against people who are just trying to be and do good like their Teacher?

Jesus said, "Because the world hates me." In fact, he even quoted from the psalms to indicate that this was to be expected. But why did they hate him so much?

Jesus was a man of integrity. His words were always true; his actions always right. He refused to play religious games, do the politically correct thing, or simply echo what others had said before him. He had no regard for religious traditions that were bound on people and he emphasized the spiritual above the material. He had complete respect for God's Word and called upon others to respect it as well. And he focused on grace in dealing with people.

But hating Jesus is only part of it. Hostility to his followers comes because, like him, we do not belong to the world. Jesus said so. We have joined the ranks of Jesus' followers and our identity is with him. We don't really fit here anymore.

We must be careful lest we be lulled into believing that the world is our friend and that our presence is welcome. We are out of step and traveling in a different direction. Our values and goals are different. We don't fit here, and we never will! While Satan will endeavor to convince us that friendship with the world is possible, Jesus' words indicate something quite the opposite.

Humility and patience, kindness and love, service and submission. These words describe Jesus but they don't describe the way the world operates. The tension was inevitable. The world refused to give an inch. In fact, it pushed back and killed the Son of God. Those who wear his name and walk in his steps can expect nothing less than what the Master received. But it is okay. We have been chosen out of the world by **Jesus**.

"Nevertheless, I tell you the truth: it is to your advantage that I go away, for if I do not go away, the Helper will not come to you. But if I go, I will send him to you."

John 16:5-11

NOVEMBER 3

Jesus spent the evening with his disciples, the last evening. He showed them the extent of his love and the meaning of service. He warned them of betrayal in their own company and mistreatment at the hands of others. He told them that he was leaving but he would return. He encouraged them not to be troubled in their hearts or afraid of what would soon occur. And he promised them he would not leave them alone.

One of life's most thought provoking and most troubling questions is found in the little word 'why.' "Why me? Why now? Why this?" We ask "why" because we seek an explanation, a reason for what is happening in our lives. We believe that knowing would help us handle the matter better, that understanding would allow us to make some sense of it all, and that this understanding would enable us to endure. However, the Bible suggests that God sees this differently.

Sometimes, God does reveal to us a reason for what happens. Sometimes, the reason may be obvious. But often there is no explanation at all. Nothing seems to make sense. "Why" goes unanswered. It is in those times that we need to remember this truth: In life's most troubling moments, most painful hours, and darkest days, real hope and genuine peace are not in explanations or reasons but in promises.

Jesus knew his disciples had many questions and few answers. He knew they did not understand what was about to happen. So, he gave them promises to hold onto.

Before everything else, he wanted them to know that he would not abandon them. "I will not leave you alone. I will send the Spirit to you."

Believers are never alone! We may feel alone and we may appear to be alone, but we are never alone. Jesus promised.

Sometimes things make sense, sometimes they don't. We still have to face whatever confronts us. What is important is the knowledge that we are not alone. What makes the difference is holding on to the promises of **Jesus**.

> "I still have many things to say to you, but you cannot bear them now. When the Spirit of truth comes, he will guide you into all the truth..."
>
> John 16:12-15

NOVEMBER 4

Jesus and this little band of twelve were not the only group awake and meeting at this late hour. Jewish religious leaders were huddled in deep and serious discussion plotting his death.

Jesus knew about their plans and warned his disciples so that they would not be taken by surprise when trouble came. It was, of course, more than they could understand. In fact, Jesus had so much that he wanted to tell them but they were simply not able to handle more just now. "But," he said, "the time is coming when you will have all the truth you need."

The Spirit "will guide you into all truth." What did they understand Jesus to be saying? What did they expect would happen? Did they have any idea how this promise would affect their lives?

Debate about the Holy Spirit has raged for centuries. Who or what is he? What exactly does he do and does he do this for everyone or just a special few? We have so many questions and not so many answers about the Spirit.

But right then, for these men, Jesus' words were intended to encourage them. Everything they needed to know would be given to them. The Spirit would provide. While they could not fully appreciate his words just yet, later, on Pentecost, they would experience the Spirit's coming and know that Jesus had, indeed, kept his promise. Their inabilities, their deficiencies would not slow the advance of the Lord's kingdom. The Spirit would make the difference!

Today, we pick up our Bible and read the words the Spirit provided. There are still things that confound us and some tough questions remain, but we have everything we need to navigate through this world on our journey home. We have "everything we need for life and godliness" (2Peter 1:3). Nothing of importance has been left out.

On that night long ago, as religious leaders weighed their options, Jesus was telling his disciples about someone who would change their lives. He changed ours, too, with the truth. God's Spirit came for us just as we were promised by **Jesus**.

"I have said these things to you, that in me you may have peace. In the world you will have tribulation. But take heart; I have overcome the world."

John 16:16-33

NOVEMBER 5

Jesus predicted joy! And not just any joy, but a joy that no one could take away!

This meal was a solemn occasion for Jesus and his disciples. We can easily imagine a rather subdued table conversation. Jesus knew that "the time had come for him to leave this world." He shared that with his disciples. That gave them much to think about. And then there was that statement about one of them betraying him. That created no little bit of wondering and they had that on their minds, too. Peter was still turning over in his mind what Jesus told him about his three denials before the crowing of the rooster.

Also, Jesus had spoken of going to another place and returning to take them with him. What was that all about? And he spoke of another Comforter coming who would replace him in some way. How were they to understand how that worked?

And if that was not enough on their plates, he told them they would be hated and mistreated. If they followed him, they could expect to receive what he received.

So, the mood in the room was one of confusion and sadness, uncertainty and perhaps a bit of fear. They were listening to Jesus but looking to each other to figure out his meaning.

Into all of this Jesus interjected the very best news. Life! But their minds were already crowded with much they didn't grasp and this seemed to be only one more item for the list.

Jesus understood. So, he helped them, and us.

"In a little while, your hearts will hurt for what happens to me and for what you fear will happen to you. But your time of grief will be brief. I will see you again and you will forget your sorrow and you will rejoice like a mother giving birth to her child. It is an indescribable joy and you will have it forever!"

Today, no matter what, trust him. No one brings joy like **Jesus**!

> "And this is eternal life, that they know you the only true God, and Jesus Christ whom you have sent."
>
> John 17:1-5

NOVEMBER 6

Jesus looking toward heaven and praying is no surprise to those who have read his story. Whether selecting disciples or giving thanks for food, prayer was a consistent feature in his life. Now, in these closing hours with his disciples, it is only natural that he would turn to the Father in prayer.

"Father, the time has come." Jesus knew the end was near. He was only hours away from arrest, trials, and crucifixion. But this was what he had come to do. He came into the world to die.

Jesus came into the world with a mission: to be the Savior of the world. Everything he said and everything he did was with that mission in mind. Or, to say it another way: everything he said and everything he did was with you in mind.

But what exactly was he offering? Was this eternal life simply an unending existence? Was it merely some kind of prolonged duration?

Jesus defined eternal life as the quality of life that comes from a relationship with the Father, Son and Spirit. It is in knowing the one true God that we can live in keeping with the purpose for which we were created. Knowing God doesn't mean increased knowledge about God, but it does mean having a relationship with Him, knowing His heart and His ways. But the only way to know the Father is through the Son, Jesus Christ. And the Spirit is the gift to those who believe.

In the course of his ministry, Jesus had occasionally stated that the Father had sent him to finish His work. Now, that work was almost done. It is not without significance that Jesus' last word from the cross was, "it is finished" (John 19:30).

Now he repeats the request and defines the glory for which he prays: the glory that he had with the Father before the world existed. This is an unmistakable claim of his preexistence.

Jesus' prayer was not a selfish request. He was acknowledging that the Father's will was foremost in his mind and that his work was almost finished. In other words, you were still the first priority in the heart of **Jesus**.

"I do not ask that you take them out of the world, but that you keep them from the evil one.
They are not of the world, just as I am not of the world.
Sanctify them in the truth; your word is truth."

John 17:6-19

NOVEMBER 7

Jesus loved these guys. These were his men. He had spent three years with them. They had shared practically everything. No one knew him better.

The Father had sent him into the world with a message of good news. Now, he was sending them into the world with that same message. So, he prayed for them.

"They are not of the world." If they were, Jesus could not have used them. At one time, each of them was very much of the world. Their passions and goals, their interests and concerns were all about this world. But Jesus had come into their lives and they had not been the same since. Their days with him had opened their eyes to wonder and beauty, to wisdom and power, to so many things they had never imagined possible!

By virtue of their walk with Jesus, they had learned to see people in new ways and to value things in different light. They had discovered that even tax collectors could change and that a Samaritan could show kindness to a Jew. By watching Jesus, they had learned that love and kindness could change a room or a village. Their experiences with him had taught them that all things are possible with God. By listening to his words and watching his ways they had come to know God!

They had spent three years with the most "real" man since creation, only to discover that he was "not of the world." Now, they had a better understanding than ever of what it meant to be "not of the world."

Now, Jesus was ready to send them out. Hours from his own death, he was ready to send them out with the only message that really mattered: the good news of God! So, he prayed.

No group of people had ever received a greater commission! No group ever had a greater story to tell. It is your story, too: the story of **Jesus**.

> "The glory that you have given me I have given to them, that they may be one even as we are one…"
>
> John 17:20-26

NOVEMBER 8

Jesus chose disciples to make other disciples. So, he prayed for the unity of all who became believers. And further, he prayed that their unity might be a sign to the world of the Father's love and presence.

Why, of all the things he might have mentioned, did he pray for our unity? Maybe Jesus asked for this because he knew it would be one of the hardest things for us. History has certainly proved him right. We all have our own ideas, our own personal agendas. Jesus knew how difficult it would be for us to be of one heart.

It was, however, a unity based on acceptance of one another, not uniformity of members. Sameness would not ensure oneness. The body of Christ has variety. God is pleased with variety. He made it. Unity's answer to the issue of diversity was not conformity but a spirit of acceptance and loving self-denial, which leads to peace among those who believe.

Our own life experiences tell us that relationships and conflict go hand-in-hand. People don't always see things the same way. We don't expect our relationships to be free of any disagreement, but we do hope that people on both sides are committed to the relationship and will keep working together on the issues. Often, that does not happen and heartache usually follows.

Actually, our times of disagreement serve to demonstrate how really committed we are to the Lord and to one another. What should distinguish the church from the world is not the absence of any disagreement but the way the disagreement is handled. Jesus said that the world would know to whom we belong, not because we never disagree, but because we don't seek to hurt one another when we disagree. Unfortunately, the church has not always been a good example.

Ultimately, Jesus sought only to glorify the Father. Thus, he prayed that the completion of his work, the preaching of his disciples and the unity of his followers would do exactly that.

And to us is the privilege and blessing of being a part of the answer to the prayer of **Jesus**.

And he said to them, "My soul is very sorrowful, even to death. Remain here and watch."

Mark 14:32-34
(Matthew 26:30, 36-38; Mark 14:26; Luke 22:39; John 18:1)

NOVEMBER 9

Jesus returned to a familiar spot. The Synoptic writers, Matthew, Mark, and Luke, identified the area as the Mount of Olives. But only Matthew and Mark actually specified the place as Gethsemane. John was content with simply identifying it as an orchard or grove. It was, in fact, an olive grove.

Also, Matthew and Mark mention that Jesus separated himself from eight of the disciples and took with him Peter, James and John. To the others he gave a simple instruction: "Sit here while I pray."

Did they wonder about the subject of his prayer? Were they still pondering the words and events in the upper room? Could they see that he was distressed about something?

There are two gardens in the Bible that have become famous because of the decisions that were made by those in the gardens. The decision in one took us away from God while the decision in the other drew us back to Him.

While we don't tend to think of Jesus as being visibly shaken or overwhelmed by anything, it is obvious that he was truly feeling as we do when facing something painful, frightening and deadly. Jesus' distress was probably evident to Peter, James and John. But if it was not, he told them. "My soul is overwhelmed with sorrow to the point of death."

A promise to the patriarch Abraham, a word through the prophets of old and a hope in the hearts of people was now coming closer to reality. However, it was not in the way in which people imagined. This garden scene did not have the look of victory. An observer would never see in the distress of Jesus or in his fearful disciples reason to celebrate a coming triumph.

Yet, this was God's plan. The journey of redemption required this time in the garden. There would be no victory, no celebration without the distress.

Jesus told the three, "Stay here and keep watch." Did they understand why? Did they know what to watch for?

"To the point of death." Jesus knew where this was going.

Never doubt it. Your distress is known and understood by **Jesus**.

> "Father, if you are willing, remove this cup from me. Nevertheless, not my will, but yours, be done."
> And there appeared to him an angel from heaven, strengthening him.
>
> Luke 22:41-44 (Matthew 26:39; Mark 14:35-36)

NOVEMBER 10

Jesus was now separated from his disciples and all his focus and energy was on the appointment ahead. As he had done on so many other occasions, he once more went to his Father in prayer.

Matthew says that Jesus "fell with his face to the ground." Luke says that he "knelt down and prayed." Jesus was driven to the ground by the weight of what the several hours would require of him. The demeaning trials, the enormous suffering, the sin of the world – these all combined to make standing impossible!

But there was more! His own struggle with this plan sent him to his knees. "If there was just another way...." Some Plan B. Some alternative. But God's planning is always perfect. There was only one plan and this was it.

The image of Jesus praying alone in the Garden of Gethsemane is one of the Bible's most poignant pictures. The disciples have fallen asleep on the job. Thus, Jesus seems completely alone at a time when good friends can mean so much. And, of course, it is dark and things always seem worse in the night. It would be difficult to find a darker moment in Jesus' life than this one.

So, there he is. Stretched out over the ground of the garden. Praying with all his might. Alone.

Then, something remarkable happened. Luke says that an angel came to comfort Jesus as he prayed.

What a special assignment! What a special angel! How long the angel was there and exactly what he did to help are not things we are told. But clearly, God was providing His Son comfort and strength for what was to come.

But for all that is being felt and being said, all that really matters to Jesus is what the Father wants. His acceptance of the Father's will would forever change what was possible for you. Your future lay in the obedient heart of **Jesus**.

> Then he came to the disciples and said to them, "Sleep and take your rest later on. See, the hour is at hand, and the Son of Man is betrayed into the hands of sinners."
> Matthew 26:40-46 (Mark 14:37-42; Luke 22:45-46)

NOVEMBER 11

Jesus seemed alone. Now, in a dark place and his soul in distress, those who had been his companions for three years were absent. They were asleep.

It had been a long day. There was much to think about. Now, sitting in the darkness they found sleep came easier than contemplation. Luke says that they were exhausted from sorrow. We would fault them but we know we are just like them.

We mean well. We have every intention of doing our best, standing for right, thinking things through, serving others without being asked, giving with genuine motive, and a thousand other noble things. But sometimes we just wear out. And always there is Satan to dissuade us from our good intentions.

Jesus wasn't really alone. Satan was close. We can imagine he offered his usual fare. "Jesus, do you see anyone who really cares about you? Do you know that no one is coming to rescue you? Why bother going through with this? Do you think anyone is going to appreciate it anyway?"

What thought or time, if any, Jesus gave to the devil's temptations is unknown. But if a reply was called for, we have a pretty good idea what it would sound like: "not my will but the Father's will be done in my life."

Eventually, we all find ourselves in a dark place. We may even feel alone. But we can be sure that we are not alone because of Jesus. He has been there himself and he understands exactly how we feel. He knows the sense of distress, the feelings of fear, and the longing to escape. He also knows that Satan will promise us anything if we will abandon righteousness.

But fortunately for us, Jesus also knows where the victory lies. Jesus knows that the best result for us is always the one when God's will is done. No matter what it may seem at the time, what we need most is to be in the will of the Father. We learned that by watching **Jesus**.

And when he came, he went up to him at once and said, "Rabbi!" And he kissed him.

Mark 14:43-46
(Matthew 26:47-50; Luke 22:47-49; John 18:2-9)

NOVEMBER 12

Jesus was born to die. But his death was not the result of some misguided purpose or poor planning. It was God's plan for Jesus to be the sacrifice for our sins. For this reason, he stood in the garden awaiting the soldiers. There may have been parts of him that wanted to run, to flee, but it was his passion for the Father's will that made him stay.

While Jesus was praying, Judas was conducting his own business. Thirty pieces of silver was a paltry sum for such a deed! The Jewish authorities were using Judas to secure that "inside" information about Jesus. They wanted to seize Jesus privately and avoid a riot. Judas could help. He knew the places Jesus went.

But why? Why betray Jesus? Was Judas trying to force the hand of Jesus so that he would prove himself for all to see? Had Judas given up hope and decided that Jesus was a fraud after all? Was it really just about the money?

Judas had arranged in advance that he would identify Jesus with a kiss. In the darkness of the garden and in the midst of so much commotion, a signal was necessary. A kiss would have been a usual way of greeting in that time and especially so between a disciple and his teacher. But in this instance, it wasn't out of respect or love. It was merely a signal of identification in the darkness.

There is an ongoing conflict between good and evil, between the ways of God and those of Satan. If we were to judge the outcome of this contest by the events in the garden, we would be left in complete despair.

But there is a difference between appearance and reality, and that is especially so when considering the ways of God. In fact, God is doing what God came to do: die for you. In a dark garden with a traitor and soldiers, the only person who knew what was really happening was the one you trust: **Jesus**.

"Do you think that I cannot appeal to my Father, and he will at once send me more than twelve legions of angels?"
Matthew 26:51-54 (Mark 14:47; Luke 22:50-51; John 18:10-11)

NOVEMBER 13

Jesus surely appreciated the brave but foolish attempt of Peter to change the outcome of these events. Already known for his impetuous, even foolhardy, actions, Peter meant well but there was no possibility of a last-minute rescue of Jesus. Even Jesus would not agree to that.

Peter had a sword. How he came to have it and how long he had carried it are questions without answers. His decision to go on the offensive was simply Peter acting in his own strength trying to do things his own way. His track record was not exactly one that would engender confidence.

Was Peter trying to save Jesus? Did he really believe that his brief attack would change the outcome? Was he hoping to inspire the other disciples to join his efforts? With Peter we can only imagine.

But even if we cannot be sure of what he was thinking, we can be certain of one thing: Peter didn't mean to just take off an ear. It might distract a fellow but it won't slow him down! No, Peter meant to split his head wide open. But Peter probably wasn't very good with a sword. After all, he was a fisherman, not a soldier.

And as he had done on other occasions of Peter's missteps, Jesus intervened to spare Peter worse problems. Jesus restored the ear of Malchus. The Savior's last miracle was an unrequested act of kindness to an enemy. We are not surprised.

In commanding Peter to put away the sword, Jesus was conveying to this disciple his acceptance of these things. He knew that he did not have to go with them. He had options! Twelve legions of angels was one option. But Jesus made his decision regarding the Father's will and not even the well-intentioned actions of Peter would change that.

Contrary to what it seems, the story of the garden was not one of defeat and despair. We are not watching the end but the beginning! We are not seeing the victory of the dark side but the sovereignty of **Jesus**!

> "When I was with you day after day in the temple, you did not lay hands on me. But this is your hour, and the power of darkness."
> Luke 22:52-53
> (Matthew 26:55-56; Mark 14:48-52; John 18:12a)

NOVEMBER 14

Jesus was not caught by surprise in the garden. He knew what Judas was doing and he knew that his hour was near. The arrival of soldiers in such a serene place, especially at night, would have been startling, even frightening under normal circumstances. But Jesus was expecting them.

Armed soldiers were sent to arrest Jesus but they would have been helpless if he had refused them. But resistance was never an option for him because he was compelled by his desire to place the Father's will above his own, to place your need above his own.

His death was not merely a sacrifice, but self-sacrifice. He was no victim. He was no martyr. He did not die because he could not help himself but because he could not help us if he didn't. So, with his face set toward the cross, the events in the garden were but a step toward the goal.

Although Jesus had moved about in the open and made no attempt to elude the authorities, their fears of the people had kept them from taking action. All that changed with Judas and thirty pieces of silver.

And under the cover of darkness, the disciples who had spent three years with him and knew his ways and words better than anyone had scattered to save themselves. These men, who were more than friends, had heard his prayers and his stories, watched his kindness and his miracles, and felt his hands wash their feet, were now running from the very one God sent to save them.

So, under the cover of darkness, we did our deed. We arrested the one person who could help us the most and we deserted the one person who could save us from certain destruction. And he was not surprised by either action.

We have a Savior who is more willing to save us than we are willing to be saved. That's why we love the name of **Jesus**.

> Then he began to invoke a curse on himself and to swear, "I do not know the man." And immediately the rooster crowed.
>
> Matthew 26:74
> (Matthew 26:58, 69-75; Mark 14:54, 66-71; Luke 22:54b-62; John 18:15-18, 25-27a)

NOVEMBER 15

Jesus knew this would happen. In fact, he even told Peter it would happen. Peter, of course, was equally adamant about his faithfulness and made it plain that he would never turn his back on Jesus. So much for his claims!

Peter was a sincere, dedicated follower of Jesus. He had every intention of being true to Jesus to the end. No one would have expected him to be afraid. Just two hours earlier he was whacking off somebody's ear. Peter was no coward.

So, what happened? Peter was caught by surprise. Caught off guard, he lied. One lie would lead to another.

Most of the disciples had drifted into the darkness. They were both shocked and afraid. But Peter wanted to be close. So, he tagged along behind the crowd hoping no one would notice him.

The night had a chill and standing beside the fire was especially nice. Soldiers were milling around and servants were running errands. A few folks were just waiting to find out what was happening with Jesus. Peter was hopeful that no one would pay any attention to him.

But someone did notice him, and that led to a question. So, Peter lied. Minutes passed and then another question. He lied again. Peter breathed a sigh of relief. Maybe he would get out of this after all.

"Didn't I see you with him in the olive grove?" That did it! He would have to lie and curse his way out of this!

It is helpful to remember that Jesus knew Peter would fail but still had a place for him in kingdom work. In fact, Peter would do much more for Jesus after his failure than he ever did before.

Sometimes we give in to the pressures. Perhaps, we deny the Lord by keeping quiet when we should speak up. Maybe we act embarrassed about being Christians.

Take heart! Do not despair! Peter's story gives us hope. We are known and loved by **Jesus**.

> And the high priest stood up in the midst and asked Jesus, "Have you no answer to make? What is it that these men testify against you?" But he remained silent and made no answer.
>
> Mark 14:55-61a (Matthew 26:57, 59-63; Mark 14:53; Luke 22:54a; John 18:13-14, 19-24)

NOVEMBER 16

Jesus was finally in the hands of the authorities. The mere word of his capture brought a sigh of relief to the Jewish leaders. Perhaps, now they could bring this whole Messiah fiasco to an end and return to some semblance of normalcy. Little did they realize how wrong they were!

Facing the prospect of arrest themselves, the disciples had fled into the night. Jesus predicted it. Maybe some lingered in the darkness to see what would happen. Maybe they all agreed to meet later at some particular place. But just now they were scared!

Jesus' first stop in the trial sequence was at the house of the former high priest, Annas. Annas must have been frustrated with Jesus. Accustomed to people answering his questions and obeying his commands, Jesus' response was hardly what Annas wanted to hear. But if Annas was looking for answers about Jesus' teaching, he could go ask those who knew best: the people who heard him teach. Nothing about his teaching was secretive. It was proclaimed for all to hear.

Disappointed, Annas sent Jesus to Caiaphas. The Sanhedrin had assembled in the hope of settling the "Jesus issue." The Sanhedrin was the supreme court of the Jews and would now examine Jesus. As noted by Mark, this was not a fact-finding mission but an effort to justify a conclusion already reached: Jesus must die. In order to help the cause, witnesses gave false testimony. However, their testimony did not agree. Jesus did not honor their lies with even a comment.

The Sanhedrin met with the goal of silencing this teacher. Now, more than two thousand years later, Jesus' teachings are available to everyone in the Scriptures and may be seen in the lives of those who walk in the way of **Jesus**.

"I have sinned by betraying innocent blood." They said, "What is that to us? See to it yourself."

And throwing down the pieces of silver into the temple, he departed, and he went and hanged himself.

Matthew 27:3-10

NOVEMBER 17

Jesus was condemned, but it was Judas who felt guilty. Thirty pieces of silver lay on the temple floor. The coins were a sign of a life gone wrong.

The verdict should have come as no surprise and we can only wonder what Judas was thinking and what kind of outcome he imagined. While various theories continue to be offered to explain his actions, it is evident that the result was not quite what he had in mind. Ultimately, the reason for the betrayal is unimportant. What does matter is that he did betray Jesus and he is filled with guilt.

Guilt is not always a bad thing. In fact, it can be a very good thing. It is a signal that something is very wrong and needs attention. God has given us a conscience and, when we violate that conscience, we have the unpleasant feelings of guilt. Failure to have those feelings is not a good sign.

Just feeling badly that things turned out as they did is not the same thing as possessing a changed heart. It is not enough to say you are sorry, not enough to feel regret. Also, it does not do any good to engage in some action to make up for the wrong. Judas' act of throwing the money into the temple accomplished nothing. Doing some good deed, giving to some charity as an effort to atone for sin is worthless.

Every time we do wrong, every time we violate God's will, there is an ache, a pain, that won't leave us alone. The joy is gone from life and everything seems out of sync. God is responsible for that. It is God's way of saying, "I want you back." But we have to listen to the signal and respond.

Before Jesus ever went to the cross, Judas was dead at his own hands. He made wrong choices, but the greatest wrong choice was to miss the forgiveness of **Jesus**.

Again the high priest asked him, "Are you the Christ, the Son of the Blessed?"
Mark 14:61b-65 (Matthew 26:63b-68; 27:1; Luke 22:63-65; Mark 15:1a; Luke 22:66-71)

NOVEMBER 18

Jesus was going to die. It was just a matter of when. These fellows were never interested in the truth. His words had kept the people stirred up and his actions had generated considerable debate. The sooner he was gone, the sooner things would return to normal.

One of the more fascinating debates of our time centers in the issue of what Jesus really believed and said about himself. It has become increasingly popular to argue that Jesus never thought of himself as God's Son or the Messiah of the Jews, much less said so. Evidently, the Jewish authorities saw this differently and were not hesitant to accuse him of making such claims.

Although their original plan was to wait until after the Feast of Passover to arrest Jesus, as they were afraid of the people's reaction, the opportunity presented to them by Judas was simply too good to miss. But having initiated the arrest in private the previous night, they now were faced with certain deadlines.

As they examined Jesus in the early morning hours of Friday, they realized that the Sabbath was only hours away. They would prefer to get this matter cleared up before then rather than have to wait past the Sabbath to begin again.

They were also facing the challenge of getting the Romans to respond to their wishes in relatively short time. The Jews did not have the power of the sword and, thus, were dependent on the Romans to do this for them. They would have to develop a convincing case and then get it before Pilate right away if this was all to be done today!

So, here in the early morning hours in Jerusalem, the Sanhedrin reached the only conclusion they sought. They determined that Jesus was deserving of death and they abused him time and again for their own enjoyment. Jesus' humiliation and public suffering had begun.

So, Caiaphas pressed him. "Are you the Christ, the Son of the Blessed One?"

Are you listening for the answer? With so many opinions and views surrounding Jesus, don't you want to know for sure, to hear it from Jesus' mouth?

"I am," said **Jesus**.

> So Pilate went outside to them and said, "What accusation do you bring against this man?"
> They answered him, "If this man were not doing evil, we would not have delivered him over to you."
> John 18:28-32 (Matthew 27:2; Mark 15:1b; Luke 23:1-2)

NOVEMBER 19

Jesus was taken by the Jewish authorities to the house of Pilate, the Governor of Judea. It was early morning, perhaps, at the first sign of light. Concerned for the matter of being clean for the Passover, they refused to enter the residence of Pilate. Although this would have been insulting, Pilate was probably used to this kind of attitude and behavior from the Jews.

As governor, Pilate was in charge of administering all aspects of Roman law. In addition to his role as the head of Rome's judicial system in Judea, he also was responsible for the collection of taxes, appropriate spending in the province, and maintaining order among a conquered people.

Regardless of what can be known of Pilate's life, his actions with the prisoner Jesus are beyond dispute. However, Pilate did not start as a willing participant. In fact, he was happy for the Jews to take Jesus and judge him by their own law.

However, the Jews needed Pilate and they said so. "But we have no right to execute anyone." And that was the real point of this whole matter.

The Jewish leaders were not looking for the truth, nor were they seeking to know the true identity of the prisoner. They were not trying to better understand Jesus' teachings and they were not wanting to engage him in any kind of meaningful discussion. Simply put: they wanted him dead! That required the Romans.

Throughout your day, Jesus will be speaking to your heart. He will be calling you to honesty in your words and purity in your thoughts. He will be calling you to humility in your attitude and service in your actions. In other words, he will be calling you to be like him.

Will you be listening and considering his words? Or, will you feel compelled to find some way to silence him? Each day is another opportunity to decide about **Jesus**.

> Jesus answered, "My kingdom is not of this world."
> John 18:33-36 (Matthew 27:11; Mark 15:2; Luke 23:3)

NOVEMBER 20

Jesus spoke to Pilate about a subject that the two men had in common: kingdoms. Pilate knew all about kingdoms. He was a part of the largest kingdom humanity had ever seen. But from the moment the conversation turned to kingdoms, Pilate could tell this would not be your typical kingdom discussion.

Their goals were entirely different. World kingdoms, like Rome, were primarily interested in controlling the populace. Power and authority were important to Pilate. A kingdom like Rome possessed no expectation that people could be trusted to do right.

The Lord's kingdom, however, is all about hearts. The emphasis is not on making laws to govern people but changing hearts so people will choose what is good. The focus is not on what people are made to do but on what people can become.

Also, the methods of each kingdom were nothing alike. Pilate knew all about diplomacy. But he also knew that, if diplomacy failed, the Roman legions were always ready. If brute force was needed to accomplish the goal, then so be it.

But before him stood a 'king' who championed love as the most powerful agent of change. The struggle of this kingdom was not against flesh and blood, and the weapons used were not the weapons of the world.

It is no wonder Pilate felt frustration. They both knew a lot about kingdoms, but the kingdoms were nothing alike. In fact, Jesus said his kingdom was not of this world!

Not much has changed in two thousand years. We still have a hard time coming to grips with Jesus' idea of kingdom. This 'turn the other cheek' and 'go the extra mile' approach is catchy but seems impractical. 'Loving your enemies' and 'not being anxious' are good ideas, even if we have doubts that such ideas will work in our real world. We like the notion of love as a change agent, but more often than not, we choose force to make our point.

So, there they stood. Pilate and Jesus. Two men whose lives were intertwined with their respective kingdoms. Which man had the better idea? Well, whose kingdom is still here? The kingdom of **Jesus.**

Then Pilate said to him, "So you are a king?" Jesus answered, "You say that I am a king. For this purpose I was born and for this purpose I have come into the world—to bear witness to the truth."
John 18:37-38 (Matthew 27:12-14; Mark 15:3-5; Luke 23:4)

NOVEMBER 21

Jesus is a king, but not just any king. He is THE King. Of course, he is also the Good Shepherd and the Door. He is the Bread of Life and he is the Light of the World. Jesus is the Way, the Truth and the Life. And Jesus is the Resurrection and the Life. The images are several and each one is helpful to our understanding of Jesus. But one of them really rubs us. The King.

Kings rule. Kings govern. Kings tell other people what to do. We like the idea that Jesus is an entry way or nourishment. We like the notion that he guides us. But we are not so keen on the thought that he would rule us.

We heartily embrace the pleasant images of Jesus as Shepherd, Counselor and Friend. Those images are not threatening. But suggesting Jesus is King immediately calls to mind certain concepts, like submission and obedience. We are not so eager to embrace those ideas.

His coming into our world to live among us was to give to us that which we so desperately needed: the truth. And how better to reveal the truth about God and life than to send the Son, the very image and reflection of God, into the world.

Not surprisingly, Jesus' words were met with skepticism by this Roman leader. He had crisscrossed the empire often enough and knew the way the world worked. He had seen 'truth' twisted and distorted enough times that he lacked any confidence that there was really anything that was completely true.

But Jesus speaks of truth that comes from outside our world. The world doesn't make or form this truth. It isn't a truth that is subject to change. And it is not a truth for me and a different truth for you. It is THE TRUTH for all of us and it comes to us from the One who is the image of the true God: King **Jesus**.

> So when the crowd had gathered, Pilate asked them, "Which one do you want me to release to you: Barabbas, or Jesus who is called Christ?"
> Matthew 27:15-21 (Luke 23:5-19; Mark 15:6-11; John 18:39-40)

NOVEMBER 22

Jesus was fast becoming a political liability to Pilate. This entire matter was turning into a no-win situation. Pilate possessed no inclination to give in to the demands of Jews. On the other hand, he had to maintain peace in his region. Convinced that Jesus was no serious threat to him or the Roman Empire, Pilate started probing for ways to be rid of Jesus.

An opportunity presented itself. On hearing that Jesus was a Galilean and under Herod's jurisdiction, he sent him to Herod, who happened to be in the city. Hopefully, Herod could settle this.

Evidently, Herod was hopeful that one day he might meet this man who performed miracles. That day had arrived. But whatever questions Herod put to Jesus, Jesus gave him no answers. Herod must have been both frustrated and disappointed. But, at the end of the time, much to Pilate's dismay, Herod sent Jesus back to Pilate.

Since the 'Jesus issue" came to his door, Pilate had tried to avoid that final decision as much as he could. Besides his hope that Herod would resolve the problem for him, he had made several attempts to find some solution that would pacify the Jews. The release of a prisoner now seemed a good option. This was a goodwill gesture. Pilate saw this as a way of releasing Jesus and, thus, ridding himself of a difficult political problem.

The man's conscience is telling him the right thing to do. His conscience is telling him that there is something very unusual about Jesus and that Jesus is innocent of the charges. But there is a problem. Pilate has a lot to lose. He has power and advantage. He is respected. He has money and a future. If he listens to his conscience, he may lose all that he has accumulated in his life.

If only the Jews could be pacified...if only Herod had settled this matter...if only the people had called for Jesus. No, like you, Pilate would have to decide for himself what to do with **Jesus**.

And the soldiers twisted together a crown of thorns and put it on his head and arrayed him in a purple robe.

John 19:1-5

NOVEMBER 23

Jesus was now the ball in the pinball machine. No one really wanted to have to deal with him and he was shuffled around before Pilate decided to do something. He chose to give Jesus a flogging.

No doubt, Pilate was hopeful that this might help nudge things forward to a solution. He was much busy with the affairs of state and not a little irritated at having to become enmeshed in some Jewish religious problem.

The crown of thorns and the purple robe only heightened the enjoyment of the soldiers. Making fun of a Jew was always fun, but to have one who claimed to be a king just added to the merriment!

We are not Roman soldiers at the foot of the cross, but we still have our ways of making fun of Jesus. From the stage comedians to the office jokes to the classroom sarcasm, Jesus is the object of 'playful humor' that is often dismissed as being harmless.

Our lack of respect for Jesus is evident when we throw his name around with our irritations and frustrations. We use it the same way we do those four-letter words when we are angry.

"Here is the man!" What deep, unfathomable theology is captured in those four words! What incredible love and what a carefully crafted plan are reflected in those four words!

"Here is the man!" And what a man! Pilate had no idea that he was presenting to this crowd the only perfect man that any of them had ever seen!

Jesus was the man that we were created to be. He was living the life we were created to live. We were made to live in union with our God. Jesus was doing that!

As we know, things are not always what they seem. By all appearances, the day belonged to the amused soldiers, the disinterested governor, and the howling mob. But the day really belonged to the bloody and beaten man wearing the crown of thorns and the purple robe. The day belonged to God; this was His plan. For your sake, the day belonged to **Jesus**.

Pilate said to them, "Then what shall I do with Jesus who is called Christ?" They all said, "Let him be crucified!"
Matthew 27:22-23 (Mark 15:12-14; Luke 23:20-22; John 19:6-11)

NOVEMBER 24

Jesus speaks and lives in front of us and then departs, but not without leaving us facing the most important question. It happens to everyone who meets him. It happened to Pilate.

"What shall I do, then, with Jesus who is called Christ?"

What are you going to do with Jesus? Do something with him you must. Only two choices are possible; neutrality is not one of them.

Why is it so important that you decide for Jesus? There are two very good reasons. First, because what you decide about Jesus will determine the character of every day for as long as you live. And second, because what you decide about Jesus will determine the character of every moment of your life after your time on this earth is over.

Pilate, however, was doing his best to avoid having to make any decision. But if Pilate was bothered that an innocent man was being charged, there was something else that bothered Pilate even more. The Jews said that Jesus had to die "because he claimed to be the Son of God." This charge drove Pilate back inside the palace to question Jesus. It was one thing to claim to be king of the Jews but quite another to claim to be the Son of God! Suddenly, Pilate felt compelled to get some answers. However, Jesus was through talking.

But Pilate still had to decide. The question would not go away.

Jesus was never powerless. He was never at the mercy of others because he lacked the strength to do anything for himself. He was never pushed around by others because he was unable to push back. He was never held against his will. And that is what makes this story so incredible!

Jesus possessed the power that is God's! Yet, he accepted this mistreatment because his purpose was greater than anything ever known: the redemption of the human race. Only by yielding and submitting to our cruel and unjust treatment could he save us. We thought the power was with us. Thankfully, we were wrong. Indeed, all the real power was (is) with **Jesus**.

So when Pilate saw that he was gaining nothing, but rather that a riot was beginning, he took water and washed his hands before the crowd, saying, "I am innocent of this man's blood; see to it yourselves."

Matthew 27:24-26 (Mark 15:15; Luke 23:23-25; John 19:12-16)

NOVEMBER 25

Jesus was a thorny problem that required a solution from Pilate. On his shoulders rested the final decision. His perplexing dilemma is adequately expressed in his own question: "Then what shall I do with Jesus who is called Christ?" His answer: he washed his hands in the basin called neutrality.

Of all the illusions nursed by modern men and women none is more pathetic or dangerous than the illusion of neutrality. It is the mistaken notion that one can detach himself from the conflict and merely be a spectator. It is the misguided belief that straddling the fence is some sort of virtue.

But there are a couple of things you should know about neutrality. First, in matters of God, there is no such thing as neutrality. It is an illusion. The refusal to choose constitutes a choice. You may refuse to make up your mind but you cannot refuse to make up your life. That gets made up one way or another.

Also, you need to know that God does not recognize neutrals. Consider the language of Scripture—right and wrong, good and evil, righteous and unrighteous, light and darkness, narrow road and broad road, wise and foolish, kingdom of God and kingdom of Satan, fruitful and unfruitful, of the Spirit and of the flesh, salvation and damnation. What you won't find is some safe, neutral zone. You can walk around shouting, "I'm neutral! I'm neutral!" God does not know what you mean.

So, why do we do it? Because in our minds we are not really choosing neutrality. We are choosing peace over chaos. We foolishly believe that neutrality allows everyone to win.

All of life is a crucial conflict between the kingdom of Christ and the kingdom of Satan. Neutrality is an illusion. No one can be neutral about **Jesus.**

> And kneeling before him, they mocked him, saying, "Hail, King of the Jews!"
>
> Matthew 27:27-30 (Mark 15:16-19)

NOVEMBER 26

Jesus was simply an amusement to the Roman soldiers. It wasn't often they got to 'play' with a man who claimed to be royalty. So, it was that Jesus would be treated as the king he claimed to be. It took only minutes to find a robe, bend into shape a crown of thorns, and come up with a staff. Now he was a king. Let the mocking begin.

The soldiers took turns falling down in front of him and feigning praise. It was to be expected that, when they grew weary of this mocking, they would resort to the next level of ridicule and abuse: spitting and hitting. Such disrespect and contempt came natural to these soldiers stationed in a faraway land, especially since Jesus was a Jew. Jesus was nothing more than a bit of fun, a temporary distraction in this hostile country!

The spectacle was shameful. We cringe as we think of how cruel humans can be to one another. To hear of abuse, especially the abuse of someone who has done no wrong, stirs us with anger. We see ourselves as too educated, too civilized to ever behave in such disgusting fashion.

We may, indeed, possess no desire to inflict physical harm on anyone, but are we any better than the soldiers when we scoff at Jesus' teachings or make light of his ways? Are we really so different from the soldiers when we make Jesus the object of our jokes or when we ridicule his ideas on holy living? Are we actually separated from these soldiers when we scorn the call to discipleship and treat with contempt his suffering for our sake?

Stripped, mocked, spat on, beaten. Yet, Jesus made no effort to defend himself or escape his situation. He did not revile or threaten his persecutors. He made no appeal to a higher court and he did not ask anyone to come to his aid. This was not about him standing up for himself. This was about God standing up for us. Today is your day to stand up for **Jesus**.

> And when they had mocked him, they stripped him of the purple cloak and put his own clothes on him. And they led him out to crucify him.
>
> Mark 15:20-21 (Matthew 27:31-32; Luke 23:26; John 19:16b-17a)

NOVEMBER 27

Jesus began the journey to Golgotha carrying his own cross. The journey through the streets of Jerusalem to the place of the skull was not unplanned. Peter would later remind the Jews that "the cross of this carpenter is no accident–the death of this man is no unplanned tragedy. It has been in the mind of God since the creation and Jesus has known all this time that one day we would nail him to a cross" (Acts 2:22-23).

God's plan for us always called for a cross. Throughout his ministry, Jesus told the disciples what lay ahead. Jesus used those last hours with his disciples to instruct, comfort and encourage...but the cross never left his thoughts.

Jesus knew treachery was coming. He told them at the table. The bread and wine lay before him on the table–reminders of the cross. In Gethsemane the cross was nearer, and he admitted that his soul was overwhelmed with sorrow.

Now the cross was looming larger than life. It was once so far away... once it was only in the mind of God...once it was only something on the lips of a prophet...once it was centuries away. But now...now it was only minutes away.

Everything happened so quickly! Betrayed — arrested — tried — condemned — scourged! And suddenly there it was — large, rough wooden timbers. As it was laid on his back, he could feel the rough wood against his lacerated skin. He could feel the weight of the timbers pressing into his bruised shoulders.

This was it! He had lived all these years for this day–for this cross! The plan for a cross was now reality.

You see, the cross was always in God's plan because you were always in God's plan. He planned for the cross because He planned for you. The cross was always in his heart because you were always in his heart.

He gave up everything to come to us and, in return, we gave him a cross to carry. Now, what will you give up for **Jesus**?

And there followed him a great multitude of the people and of women who were mourning and lamenting for him.
But turning to them Jesus said, "Daughters of Jerusalem, do not weep for me, but weep for yourselves and for your children."

Luke 23:27-32

NOVEMBER 28

Jesus wasn't the only man headed to his death that day. To add to his humiliation, Jesus was to be executed with two others, both criminals.

Jesus had no need for self-pity because he was fulfilling the Father's plan. Every step was toward the completion of what the Father sent him to do. Throughout his ministry he had emphasized that he came to do the will of the Father. Even though he was already hurting in the garden as he contemplated the great pain that lay ahead, he still placed the Father's will above his own. No, Jesus did not feel sorry for himself. His sorrow was for those who failed to see and understand what was happening.

But neither did Jesus want the pity of the crowd. Instead, he wanted them to believe.

It is not difficult to imagine the scene. People pressing close to the prisoners as they stumbled along between Roman soldiers. Some were there for the spectacle, others were friends and followers. Some were jeering. Some were crying and weeping. Some were praying. Some were exultant.

At some point in the journey Jesus stopped and turned to the crowd. In particular, he turned to the women and said, "Daughters of Jerusalem, do not weep for me; weep for yourselves and your children." His words must have caught them off guard. He seemed to be saying that their situation was more serious and tragic than his own.

Just think! If this happens when the tree is green, can you imagine what will happen when it is dry? How terrible for those who would reject the gospel!

Isn't this just like Jesus? In the midst of his own painful ordeal, his thoughts are on what will happen to these people. Their pain, not his own, is what he's thinking about.

But then, isn't that what the cross is all about? God's incredible concern for your pain is what brought the cross of **Jesus**.

> And when they came to the place that is called The Skull, there they crucified him, and the criminals, one on his right and one on his left.
> Luke 23:33 (Matthew 27:33-35a; Mark 15:22-24a; John 19:18)

NOVEMBER 29

Jesus was executed at a place called "the skull." Located outside the city, Golgotha was the site of public executions. It was a shameful place where society's worst were permanently removed in cruel fashion.

Crucifixion was a method of execution that subjected a person to the utmost indignity and extreme pain. Although our art is sympathetic to the dignity of Jesus, it is likely that Jesus was crucified naked. Designed to torture a person without immediately injuring any vital organs, crucifixions might last several hours or several days. There would be excruciating pain from the nails in hands and feet and a continual need to push up on those feet to catch a breath. The whole experience was torture until death gave the person relief.

Crosses would have been a common sight in Palestine. In his travels over the land Jesus surely saw men hanging on crosses. Did he ever stop for a moment to look at what lay ahead for him? Did his gaze ever fasten on the wounded hands and feet?

Today, we wear a cross on a bracelet or necklace. We have a plastic one as a bookmark. We attach one to the bumper or hang one from the rearview mirror. We put crosses on books, roofs, furniture, letterheads, and signs. We have taken a first-century symbol of shame and made it acceptable. We have turned a torture tool into an ornament. Perhaps, in doing so, we have emptied the cross of its power.

Why did he endure such horrible agony? Because sin – *our* sin – created a chasm between God and us. Unable to help ourselves draw near to God, He drew us to Him by the sacrifice of His Son.

The mystery of the cross is not just that a man died a horrible death or even that the man crucified was innocent of the charges. The mystery of the cross is that the "him" we crucified was the Son of God and he chose to be there!

"Mercy there was great and grace was free." Think about that today as you make decisions for **Jesus**.

And Jesus said, "Father, forgive them, for they know not what they do."
Luke 23:34a

NOVEMBER 30

Jesus now prayed.

To anyone standing close enough to hear him, Jesus' words must have sounded insane. "Father, forgive them, for they do not know what they are doing." No crucified person ever asked forgiveness for the executioners!

And Jesus prayed for us, too. We were not there in person, but we were there. Our sins were there. Our sins put Jesus there. So, Jesus prayed for us, too. In the midst of incredible pain and agony, he prayed for us. Even when we were at our very worst as human beings, he was at his very best...asking the Father to forgive us.

Our temptation is to defend ourselves, to argue that we are not like those people. "Why, we would never do anything like that!" But we would. We do.

If we had been there, we would have shouted as loud as anyone. If we had been there, we would have mocked him like the others. If we had been there, we would have held the nails for the soldiers. We are neither different nor better.

It is our nature to want to believe that we are capable of rising above the worst in us. We want to believe that whatever ground with God was lost in Adam can be reclaimed by our own efforts at goodness. We will try harder! We will do better! We promise! But it is a promise and an effort that we cannot keep. We inevitably fail and discover over and over that God always knew best. That's why he sent His Son.

What we did to Jesus is unforgivable. What deed could be worse than to murder the sinless Son of God? What could possibly be worse than the cruel rejection of God's incredible expression of love?

Yet, even in his suffering, he was thinking of our salvation. Unforgivable is replaced by unbelievable.

Even now, so far removed from the time and place, it is hard to grasp the magnitude of our sin. We still don't want to believe it was us. But it was. But thank God that the story does not end there. On the absolute worst day of your life and mine, we received forgiveness because of **Jesus**.

> When the soldiers had crucified Jesus, they took his garments and divided them into four parts, one part for each soldier; also his tunic.
> John 19:23-24 (Luke 23:34b; Mark 15:24b-25; Matthew 27:36)

DECEMBER 1

Jesus was nailed to the wood at nine o'clock on a Friday morning. The whole process would not have taken very long. These guys were professionals. They knew the drill. They had crucified lots of men. Once their task was finished, the soldiers concerned themselves with a bit of gambling for a seamless garment.

In those few hours, the most incredible thing was happening. But those at Golgotha had no idea.

That was certainly true of the Romans. They had no idea of the role they were playing in this world-changing event. They could not conceive of God becoming a man or behaving unselfishly. They had no notion of a Messiah or any awareness that they needed a Savior. What they did, they did in ignorance. So, Jesus prayed for them.

The Jews were just as confused, even if they should not have been. They could not imagine that God would become a man or that the Messiah could be a suffering servant. And, even if they expected a Messiah, he wouldn't look like this Jesus. What they did, they did in ignorance. So, Jesus prayed for them.

Amazing! Jesus prayed for the forgiveness of his executioners while they concerned themselves with a bit of business. No reason to let a man's death get in the way of a bargain. He prayed. They gambled while the world was saved.

That is so much like us! Created to see what is truly valuable, we often live with our eyes fixed on what is worthless. Made to possess the eternal blessings of God, we often pursue the temporal things of earth. Created by God to be like Him, we often get down in the dirt to make deals for what does not matter.

You know this day will be full. Your life is busy and your heart is easily distracted. The noisy things are not always the most important ones. Some days, it's hard to catch your breath, much less keep priorities straight.

So, to stay connected to what truly matters, remember this: nothing of this life has value apart from **Jesus**.

> **Pilate also wrote an inscription and put it on the cross. It read, "Jesus of Nazareth, the King of the Jews."**
> **John 19:19-22 (Matthew 27:37-38; Mark 15:25-27; Luke 23:38)**

DECEMBER 2

Jesus' claim of being a king was the single most serious and controversial accusation made against him. And it was true.

Seeing the Jews' irritation with Jesus and possessing no sympathy for them, Pilate seemed to enjoy irritating them even more by referring to Jesus as their king. "Behold your king!" he said. "What shall I do with your king?" he asked them. Then, there was the sign on the cross. Naturally, they wanted him to change the wording, but he refused. It was, in its own way, a kind of joke on the Jews. Pilate enjoyed that.

It was not uncommon for the condemned man to have a placard hung about his neck providing the details of his crime. The sign could also be nailed to the cross. This particular title for Jesus was in three languages: Aramaic, Greek and Latin.

Jesus was not your usual king. There is nothing new or unusual about the subjects pledging their loyalty and lives to the king. Thousands have died for king and country. But in this kingdom, it is the king who dies for the subjects.

But amazingly, Jesus did not have to die! He could have called twelve legions of angels at any time. What king wouldn't do that to save himself and his kingdom? But not this king.

Jesus is a king who rules in the hearts of his subjects. The Pharisees asked Jesus about this kingdom. Jesus told them it wasn't a kingdom to which people point and say, "There it is," but a kingdom within people (Luke 17:20-21).

Jesus is a king with no kingdom in the usual sense. No castle or palace. No congress or parliament. No army, no navy, no special forces. There are no immigration issues, budget problems, or territorial arguments. There is no currency or coinage that carries the king's picture.

We see the results of his rule, but we don't actually see his rule. The reason is because he rules in our hearts. At least, he does if we invite him.

Pilate was right. "Behold your king!" His name is **Jesus**.

> So also the chief priests with the scribes mocked him to one another, saying, "He saved others; he cannot save himself. Let the Christ, the King of Israel, come down now from the cross that we may see and believe."
>
> Mark 15:29-32a (Matthew 27:39-43; Luke 23:35-37)

DECEMBER 3

Jesus was often challenged to prove his claims. Now, as life flowed out of him, the mocking would be among the last things he heard.

There were two groups of mockers. The first group questioned his integrity. Throwing his words back in his face, they challenged him to prove that he was telling the truth. If he wasn't, then that was proof that he was a fraud and they did not need him.

Jesus repeatedly told his disciples that he must go to Jerusalem and be killed. If he did not die, but saved himself, how would we ever know that he could accomplish the other things he promised. If he could change his plans about dying for humanity, how do we know he wouldn't change his plans about coming back for us?

He proved the integrity of his words by staying on the cross! If Jesus came down from the cross, you couldn't trust him! But because he stayed on the cross, you can know that he means what he says and he will do what he promises!

Group two questioned his identity claims. "Where is the power that would prove you are who you claim?"

The irony is that they would ask Jesus to abandon the cross in order to demonstrate his power. What they failed to see was that staying there **was** the proof! The very demonstration of power they were seeking was happening in front of them! God was staying on the cross!

The problem wasn't that Jesus could not prove that he was God's Son. The problem was we didn't recognize God! "Prove you are who you claim to be!" He is doing that! This is the way God is! It was not because he could not, but because he would not.

Now, if that is how much being with you means to him, how much should being with him mean to you? Every day, you get to tell **Jesus**.

And he said to him, "Truly, I say to you, today you will be with me in Paradise."

Luke 23:39-43 (Matthew 27:44; Mark 15:32b)

DECEMBER 4

Jesus' cross stood between two men. There was a sinner on each side. While they shared many things in common, these two thieves were not at all alike in that singular way that matters most: their response to Jesus.

On the one side was a man who possessed no spirit of brokenness or guilt, no remorse or humility. Even at this moment in his life he seemed unconcerned about truth or right, only how to save his earthly skin. His appeal to Jesus was based, not on any faith in Jesus, but on his own desire to be delivered from his suffering.

For all that he had done wrong in his life, the man on the other side did fear God. God was real to him; at least, to the extent that he knew he must answer for his life. He freely admitted that he was guilty.

What is especially striking is that this robber recognized something in Jesus that few others did. "This man has done nothing wrong." Did he know Jesus before? Had he heard Jesus teach? Had he once been a disciple? Or, did something happen during those hours on the cross?

Jesus' words to this man must have given hope to his heart like nothing he had ever experienced. "Today you will be with me in paradise." Whatever and wherever paradise might be, he didn't care! He was now facing death with hope!

The salvation of this thief has been the subject of much debate through the centuries. But if Jesus is God in flesh and the Savior of humanity, then he can save whomever he wants wherever and whenever he wants.

At Golgotha, there were two thieves separated by a cross. One had a change of heart. The other did not. One repented. The other was defiant to the last. One was arrogant. The other asked for mercy. One went with Jesus. The other did not.

There are only two kinds of people: those who follow Jesus and those who don't. There are no others. And the two groups are forever separated by their response to the cross of **Jesus**.

When Jesus saw his mother and the disciple whom he loved standing nearby, he said to his mother, "Woman, behold, your son!" Then he said to the disciple, "Behold, your mother!" And from that hour the disciple took her to his own home.

John 19:25-27

DECEMBER 5

Jesus owned no property or house that would occupy his concern at the end of his life. He had no worldly investments or business holdings that would require his attention. All those material items that usually require some care as we face death were not the things that concerned him.

But Jesus did have a mother. The one action he does take regarding his departure is to see that his mother would receive care. As the eldest son, Jesus would not leave her to the mercy of the society.

The relationship between Mary and Jesus will always contain an element of the unknown. Our questions far outnumber our answers. But this particular moment speaks volumes about their care and love for each other. She is there in his most difficult moment. His words show that she is on his mind even as he faces his final hours.

Although the Gospel writers do not focus attention on all those watching the event at Golgotha, this brief reference by John tells us that not everyone was hostile to Jesus. Mary was accompanied by three women. Evidently, they were near enough to the cross for Jesus to be heard.

"The disciple whom he loved" was John. It is likely that John was the disciple "known to the high priest," (John 18:15-16) and this had permitted him access to some of the events in the last hours of Jesus' life, including nearness to the cross.

It is natural that, if Jesus were to entrust his mother's care into the hands of another, it would be to this man. For reasons not given, they formed a special friendship and Jesus now called upon that friendship for this one earthly matter that was important to him.

Although bearing in his mind an unimaginable weight for all humanity and suffering in his body the agony for all our sins, Jesus remained sensitive to those most basic needs of human life.

This was just one more reminder that whatever we need is important to **Jesus**.

> And about the ninth hour Jesus cried out with a loud voice, saying, "My God, my God, why have you forsaken me?"
>
> Matthew 27:45-49 (Mark 15:33-36; Luke 23:44-45; John 19:28-29)

DECEMBER 6

Jesus was dying. No one was coming to rescue him; not his eleven disciples, not his followers, not even God.

There was an unnatural darkness, a strange and weird darkness that settled over the earth, a darkness only God could cause. Perhaps, the darkness was there to cover our most heinous act. Maybe the darkness covered the land to emphasize just how great was our rejection of God, to underscore how far we would go to have our own way. Truly, these were humanity's darkest hours.

And what shall we make of Jesus' anguished cry: "My God, My God, why have you forsaken me?" Was he quoting from this Messianic psalm in order to declare that the psalmist's words found fulfillment in him? Was the question intended to attach some sort of blame to God for allowing this to go this far? Or, as some suggest, was Jesus simply coming to terms with reality and expressing his disillusionment over his life's work?

It is not to be expected that we could ever grasp the full meaning of Jesus' cry. But of this we can be sure: God did not abandon His Son. The darkness and the torn temple curtain were signs that God had not distanced himself from what was happening. Jesus cried to the only one who could save him from what had been decided before the creation of the world. The Father chose not to intervene but that choice was anything but abandonment. This was the plan. Together they would see this through to its completion.

Periodically, moviegoers have been presented with graphic and moving portrayals of the Golgotha event; yet, there is always the knowledge that we are only watching actors. We read and re-read the words of the Golgotha story. Images form in our minds. Yet, for all the effort, we find it impossible to capture the magnitude of his suffering or to adequately explain how what he endured brought our reconciliation to God or to fathom such wondrous love.

Ultimately, it is our life that must be our testimony to the indescribable sacrifice of **Jesus**.

Then Jesus, calling out with a loud voice, said, "Father, into your hands I commit my spirit!" And having said this he breathed his last.
Luke 23:46 (Matthew 27:50; Mark 15:37; John 19:30)

DECEMBER 7

Jesus is dead. Why? Why did he have to die? And what did executing an innocent man really accomplish?

"For Christ also suffered once for sins, the righteous for the unrighteous, that he might bring us to God..." (1 Peter 3:18) There it is: "To bring **us** to God." Everything that God was doing for centuries was to bring you to Him. From the promise to Abraham to the leadership of Moses, from the throne of David to the prophecies of Isaiah, everything was so that you might come to God.

Jesus said, "It is finished." But what was finished? Certainly, more than just a man's life; more than just a ministry to needy people; and certainly more than just a good idea about how human life should be lived.

Jesus finished the business of redemption. As the perfect sacrifice for our sins, he rendered futile any other effort on our part to gain access to God's presence. He accomplished in living and dying what we could never accomplish.

Admittedly, this makes little sense to us. From our perspective, we cannot fathom how one man can die in place of another, bearing his penalty, and this result in a right standing before God. But remember: the issue is not whether it makes sense to us, but is it true and do we believe it.

If the cross of Jesus is anything, it is a solemn statement on the ugliness of humanity and how far we will go to keep God from interfering in our lives. But it is also a glorious statement on the beauty and magnitude of God's love and holiness and how far He will go so that we may be restored to fellowship with Him. In spite of our every effort to push God away, He pursues us. The cross is the final effort of that pursuit. If we would ever love and serve Him, this is the place it will happen. The cross is where the pursuit ends and life with God begins.

"To bring you to God." That is the work that was finished by **Jesus**.

And being found in human form, he humbled himself by becoming obedient to the point of death, even death on a cross.

Philippians 2:5-11

DECEMBER 8

Jesus was/is God! He was not pretending to be God or simply claiming to be God. He did not have to grasp the divine nature or seize it for it was already his.

But he emptied himself. He made himself nothing. He went from the highest position imaginable to the lowest precisely because such selfless love was an expression of his deity. Jesus humbled himself by becoming one of us.

Jesus did not abandon his divine nature. He did not cease to be God. If he did, then he was only a man. Nor did he merely appear to be man. He was not playing a part. He was really one of us.

He ate our food, drank our water, breathed our air, walked on our streets and wore our clothes. He sang, danced, laughed and sighed along with us. He cried over our tears and loved us in our pain. And like us, he bled from his head, hands, feet, back and side. And like us, his heart stopped and he died.

Was it not humiliating enough for God to become a man? And not just a man but a servant?

Was not this humility by obedience enough? He stooped even more becoming obedient to death. Death for us is a necessity. For him it was obedience.

But it was not just any death. It was death on a cross! It was a terrible, violent, painful, agonizing, and humiliating death!

How could we do what we did to God?

We could do what we did to him because of sin, and sin is the very reason he permitted it to be done. The cross is all about our pride and his humility, our selfishness and his selflessness, our hate and his love, our filth and his purity. The cross is all about the beauty of God in a man and the ugliness of man without God.

Even today, this is the story of all stories: God becoming man. This is the best news of all good news: you are the reason He came. And that's why, to us, the most beautiful name of all names must be **Jesus**.

And behold, the curtain of the temple was torn in two, from top to bottom. And the earth shook, and the rocks were split.
The tombs also were opened. And many bodies of the saints who had fallen asleep were raised...
Matthew 27:51-53 (Mark 15:38; Luke 23:45b)

DECEMBER 9

Jesus took his last breath. That is when it happened. Everything was changed.

Jesus cried out from the cross, "It is finished!" and, in that moment, that thick curtain in the temple was torn from the top to the bottom. Matthew emphasized that the curtain was completely severed. We are to understand that this is God's action.

First in the tabernacle and then in the temple, there was veil or curtain that separated the Holy Place and the Most Holy Place. No one could pass through the curtain into the Most Holy Place except the high priest, and then only on one day, the Day of Atonement. Having made atonement for himself, he would enter to make atonement for the people. The curtain was a continual reminder of the barrier between God and people. That curtain was gone!

But there was more! "The earth shook and the rocks split." Then, tombs burst open and folks, once dead, emerged into the day. It was heaven's response to our inglorious deed, as well as the announcement of a new day dawning. Things were changing and it was all good news!

No more animals to sacrifice. No more special priests. No more laws to keep on leprosy, property, feasts or offerings. No more curtains to separate believers. No more pilgrimages to Jerusalem. No more Sabbath observances. No more tassels on the garments and no more dietary regulations. No more Jubilee Years or Days of Atonement.

Today, we belong to Jesus. Our words and our ways reveal how we trust him. We are not perfect, but we are forgiven. Our strength for today and our hope for tomorrow are tied to the inconceivable and astonishing display of love and sacrifice at Golgotha. And because God reached down and tore the veil, we now have full and free access to our Father through His Son, Jesus Christ.

Everything that matters about our lives changed forever with that last breath of **Jesus**.

When the centurion and those who were with him, keeping watch over Jesus, saw the earthquake and what took place, they were filled with awe and said, "Truly this was the Son of God!"
Matthew 27:54-56 (Mark 15:39-41; Luke 23:47-49)

DECEMBER 10

Jesus' suffering and death brought a response from heaven. A surprising darkness in the day, an earthquake that shook the city, a temple curtain torn in two, and opened tombs with the dead coming to life were startling events. Even if the general populace missed the significance of this, it all had a profound effect on one man: the centurion.

But why did this centurion become convinced that Jesus was a man worth praising? Why did he conclude that Jesus was a good man? What caused him to praise God and shout out as he did, "Truly this was the Son of God!"?

Suppose that you could interview the centurion regarding his statement and you asked him for an explanation. Would he provide some academic answer? Would he give you some philosophical theory that helped him? Not at all.

Perhaps, the centurion would say that his nearness to the cross allowed him to see and hear everything that occurred. He might add that, due to the nature of his job, he had seen hundreds of executions, but he had never seen one quite like this. The obvious goodness of Jesus was easy to see, he would say. Also, it was difficult to miss the hatred that so many had for Jesus, yet equally hard to miss his words of forgiveness for the haters.

The centurion might speak of the remarkable conversations he heard: Jesus thoughtful words to John about the care of his mother and his encouragement to the thief who asked to be remembered.

And if you asked the centurion for his overall impression of Jesus, he would tell you that Jesus had a remarkable and lovely spirit in a terrible situation and that the ways and words of this condemned man touched his heart and the disturbing signs of the day confirmed his thoughts. He would tell you that Jesus was not like other men. The centurion would tell you that Jesus knew how to live and he knew how to die. And you would agree that no one can help you with those things but **Jesus**.

But when they came to Jesus and saw that he was already dead, they did not break his legs.
But one of the soldiers pierced his side with a spear, and at once there came out blood and water.

John 19:31-37

DECEMBER 11

Jesus remained the focus of Jewish attention even as he was breathing his last. While he was dying, two requests came to Pilate. The first request was made by those who despised Jesus. They wanted his legs broken so that death might come sooner rather than later. The second request would come from those who sought to honor him by giving him a respectable burial.

Old Testament law mandated that a body was not to be left on a tree overnight (Deuteronomy 21:22-23). However, it would be expected that the Romans would care little for such Jewish scruples. But the Jewish leaders were pressing the matter because the next day was the special Sabbath, or high Sabbath, that fell on Passover week.

So, the Romans made sure that all the men on the crosses would die quickly. The action of breaking the legs would make it exceedingly difficult to catch a breath by pushing up with the feet and legs. They would suffocate sooner with broken legs. It turned out that Jesus was already dead, so they didn't need to break His legs. Just to make sure He was dead, one of the soldiers drove a spear into Jesus' side.

The deed was done. The rejection of Jesus seemed complete. All that remained was to do something with the body.

A popular custom in today's scholarly circles is to express doubt as to whether Jesus really died on the cross. Apart from openly accusing the writers of lying, some modern scholars seem to doubt the ability of the Roman soldiers to tell when a person was truly dead. In any other story this would not be all that significant. However, when someone promises to rise from the grave, being dead first is rather important!

Jesus was dead. No one present doubted it. Three years of ministry had come to this horrific end. The voice that had called people to a loving Father was now quiet. The hands that had brought healing to so many were now still. But we know that only three days separated the world and the truth of **Jesus**.

Now in the place where he was crucified there was a garden, and in the garden a new tomb in which no one had yet been laid.
So because of the Jewish day of Preparation, since the tomb was close at hand, they laid Jesus there.

John 19:39-42 (Matthew 27:57-60; Mark 15:42-46a; Luke 23:50b-56)

DECEMBER 12

Jesus was destined for a pauper's grave on "boot hill." The disciples were keeping their distance and family members lacked the influence to secure the body of Jesus. The matter was even more difficult because time was running out. It was late in the day and the bodies needed to be buried before dark.

But into this situation stepped two unlikely characters. It is unclear when Joseph and Nicodemus agreed to work together, or when they commenced their efforts to prepare for the burial of Jesus.

Joseph of Arimathea was a prominent member of the Sanhedrin. He was a rich man, but more important, he was a good and upright man, a man looking for the kingdom, and a man of the Sanhedrin who had not joined in the condemnation of Jesus.

It is only from John's Gospel that we even know of Nicodemus. He is the same man who "came to Jesus by night" (John 3). It is also John who tells us that Nicodemus openly defended Jesus' right to a fair hearing (John 7).

Nicodemus brought a mixture of myrrh and aloes weighing about seventy-five pounds and, along with Jospeh, wrapped Jesus' body with spices in strips of linen, in accordance with Jewish burial customs. The tomb where Joseph buried Jesus was his own new tomb, hewn out of solid stone. It appears the reason for using this tomb was not because it belonged to Joseph, but because it was close, and it seemed expedient since time was short. They placed Jesus' body in Joseph's tomb and then rolled the stone against the entrance.

What do we make of these "secret disciples?" And what was their motivation for this special care of Jesus' body? The answers may lie beyond us for now but we can say that these two stepped out and identified themselves with Jesus in a way that no others did. In this worst of all possible scenes, where secrecy was safe and discipleship was dangerous, two men said, "We are not ashamed of **Jesus.**"

Pilate said to them, "You have a guard of soldiers. Go, make it as secure as you can."

Matthew 27:62-66

DECEMBER 13

Jesus lived a life like no one else. Yet, there were those who could not wait until he was dead. They rejected his words, discounted his deeds and accused him of being a fraud. They could not stand against his words, nor could they explain away his deeds, nor could they prove any charge they made against him. But for them, it did not matter. They were not pursuing truth but the end of a person. Finally, they got what they were seeking.

Now, they had a smug look of satisfaction on their faces as they talked of his death among themselves. "Did you see how he died? Just like any other man. Nothing very special about him."

Jesus wouldn't be bothering anyone anymore. Although he had seemed threatening at times, the religious leaders of the Jews had managed to weather the storm. Although the peace of the status quo had been momentarily shaken, things had been restored to their rightful place. It just took the death of Jesus to do it.

So, if everything was back to normal and there was nothing to be concerned about, why all the security around the tomb? Well, there were those rumors about Jesus being raised. Nobody believed it, of course, but they had to be careful.

Jesus was dead. They no longer had reason to be afraid of what he might do. But his disciples were capable of anything. So, seal the tomb, guard the tomb, and put an end to any talk by his followers about him coming to life.

Now, nothing will ever get in and nothing will ever get out. We are all safe; the world is safe. Jesus will not trouble anyone ever again. End of story.

Isn't it fascinating (and sad) that we would think we could write a better conclusion to our story than God? Just imagine! Our ending was to write Jesus right out of our story! He leaves and we keep what we've got.

But in God's story, Jesus lives and we receive far more than we could have imagined! All because there is no "end of story" when we speak of **Jesus**.

> And he said to them, "Do not be alarmed. You seek Jesus of Nazareth, who was crucified. He has risen; he is not here."
> Mark 16:1-8 (Matthew 28:1-8; Luke 24:1-8; John 20:1)

DECEMBER 14

"Jesus has risen!"

Whether we realize it or not, with those words, our lives were forever changed. From the way we speak of the years on a calendar to the way our landscape is dotted with crosses to the songs we sing in our saddest or happiest moments, our world changed with those three words. From the way we view Sundays to our private devotional practices to our perspective on death, "Jesus has risen" changed everything.

In some ways, the resurrection of Jesus was as quiet as the arrival of Jesus. At his birth, only a few shepherds and wise men were privileged to know of the event. At his resurrection, only a few women first received the news. Also, like the announcement of his birth, the resurrection was announced by angels. And in both instances, the religious establishment found the news troubling.

Perhaps, the news was too big a shock, too overwhelming to grasp. Maybe these women could only imagine a terrible violation of body and tomb had occurred. Or, maybe they just could not believe what they were hearing.

In time, answers would come to fill in some of the blanks. For now, they were left to consider what they had seen and heard.

But isn't that the way God often works? In our haste, we want answers. We are very impatient. Yet, we often experience events that bring questions. Sometimes we feel overwhelmed by it all. We may pray to God and discuss it with others, but answers don't seem immediate. Perhaps, the time is to allow us the opportunity to grasp something that was too big to be handled all at once. Then, as windows open to clearer vision and to better understanding, we can see both God's hand at work and we can understand how the time helped us get ready for what God had in mind. And what God has in mind for you is always tied to **Jesus**.

Then Simon Peter came, following him, and went into the tomb. He saw the linen cloths lying there, and the face cloth, which had been on Jesus' head, not lying with the linen cloths but folded up in a place by itself.

John 20:2-10 (Luke 24:9-12)

DECEMBER 15

Jesus wasn't where he was supposed to be. For people accustomed to an ordered and explainable world, this was difficult to handle. How could they make sense of this?

First, Peter and John had to see for themselves. But seeing the empty tomb only seemed to create more questions than answers and they were already running low on answers.

So, what now? Still failing to grasp the full truth of all that was happening as revealed by God in the Scriptures, they simply went to their homes. After all, what could they do about a missing body?

But does it really matter? Couldn't they still go forth telling people of the marvelous person, Jesus? Couldn't they still show people the way of Jesus without having to explain what happened to his body? Does it matter whether Jesus rose from the dead?

In an age in which so many people determine what is true by what is acceptable and helpful to them, a surprising number seem all too willing to accept Christianity, with or without a body. All that really matters is whether Christianity works for them, whether it helps them.

But does Christianity without a body really work for us? Does it really help us?

Do you have any hope of seeing your deceased loved ones again?

Do you have any confidence in the reality of a place called heaven?

In fact, do you have any hope for any life beyond the grave?

Everything that truly matters is tied to that empty tomb! Knowing what happened to the body of Jesus means everything to us! Without the knowledge that Jesus was raised, Christianity is nothing more than another philosophy of life, and not a very credible one at that.

The resurrection of Jesus Christ is God's global warning that repentance is necessary and judgment is coming. And it is His wonderful good news to us that real life is in the Son He raised. **Jesus.**

> Mary Magdalene went and announced to the disciples, "I have seen the Lord"—and that he had said these things to her.
> John 20:11-18 (Mark 16:9-11)

DECEMBER 16

Jesus loved Mary of Magdala. But his relationship with her was not like many suggest. He was not her lover; she never became his wife. They never had three children and moved to Rome or France or anywhere else. Creating such stories may sell more books or create more speaking engagements but it doesn't reflect the plain words of the Bible.

Mary Magdalene was consumed with sadness. Her uncontrollable sobbing is a reflection of the intense sorrow and pain she felt over the loss of someone who changed her life. Her thoughts were now focused on a single idea: Someone has taken the body of Jesus!

She was one of a group of women who were followers of Jesus and who were supporting his ministry out of their own means (Luke 8:1-3). Some of the women in the group had been demon possessed and Mary was one of them. In fact, she had seven demons that had come out of her. How she came to be in that awful state is not revealed. But her gratitude and devotion to Jesus was understandable.

So, on that morning she came to the tomb with a desire to do honor to the body of Jesus only to be disappointed once again. What happens next is a dramatic turn of emotions.

At first, two angels spoke to her. Then, it was Jesus who spoke to her. Maybe her tears clouded her vision. Perhaps, the light made it difficult to see clearly. Whatever the reason, she did not recognize him.

But that changed when Jesus called her name. "Mary." In that moment everything that was wrong with the world and life suddenly was forgotten. Jesus is alive!

Joy swept away all the sadness! Relief replaced all the anxiety! This was the very best day of her life! Jesus said, "Go and tell my brothers." Can you imagine how quickly she ran to tell the disciples?

Today, the news is all good. "I have seen **Jesus**!"

> Then Jesus said to them, "Do not be afraid; go and tell my brothers to go to Galilee, and there they will see me."
>
> Matthew 28:9-15

DECEMBER 17

Jesus was not expected to rise...by anyone! Two fellows stepped forward to bury the body. Some women were making preparations to anoint the body. The disciples were in hiding trying to figure out what happened to the plan for a kingdom. No one was waiting to see him! No one was watching for him!

Why not? Why, after three years of watching and listening, did no one expect him to be anywhere but in the tomb?

The easiest and most reasonable explanation for the missing body was the explanation chosen first: the disciples stole the body. This rumor was helped along by paying the soldiers to say it.

This explanation assumes that these disciples, too frightened to even stand with Jesus when he was alive, would now choose to act courageously for Jesus when he was dead. But the greater question is why. Why would these disciples steal the body, go preach a lie about Jesus, and then suffer so severely the rest of their lives for something they knew was never true? What is the sense in that?

Some critics of the biblical account argue that Jesus' body was never found because it was eaten by wild dogs. This was a fate common to crucified criminals.

Others have claimed that Jesus' body never left the tomb and the disciples only imagined they saw Jesus because they wanted to so much.

In spite of the story of his treatment, there are some who argue that Jesus never really died. He was alive after the crucifixion because he did not die on the cross and revived in the tomb. Of course, this assumes that he could, in his condition, roll away the stone and elude the guards. If so, the guards could have reported it.

History is replete with skeptics and critics of the empty tomb.But what do you believe? Your answer makes all the difference to the way you live. If you believe in his resurrection, then you won't be surprised if today is the day you see **Jesus**.

Then one of them, named Cleopas, answered him, "Are you the only visitor to Jerusalem who does not know the things that have happened there in these days?"

Luke 24:13-24 (Mark 16:12-13)

DECEMBER 18

Jesus was in the news. They had heard the reports. An empty tomb. Angels said he was alive. But it was too difficult to believe. In fact, they were now more confused than ever.

These two, Cleopas and his friend, began their seven-mile walk to Emmaus even as the rumors of resurrection circulated. It was a walk of sadness and gloom, frustration and doubt. As they walked, they shared their thoughts and emotions as they searched for answers and meaning to all that had happened.

Because of their slow, trudging walk, Jesus overtook them and joined their company. They didn't know him. At some point, he asked, "What are you talking about?" They stood still with downcast faces.

"Where have you been?" Cleopas was surprised that this stranger was unaware of recent happenings in Jerusalem. "What things are these?" Jesus asked, prompting these two to explain.

"We had hoped that he was the one who was going to redeem Israel." They were looking for a Messiah who would restore Israel as a nation to its place of prominence in the world. Notice the past tense in their voice- "He **was** a prophet, powerful in word and deed" and "we **had** hoped that he was the one." It is as though they had pieces of the puzzle but couldn't quite figure how they fit.

These fellows were going home disappointed and discouraged, disillusioned about the whole Jesus project. Jesus did not do what they expected him to do. And when he died on the cross, their hopes and dreams died, too.

We expect to be disappointed by people. But when it seems that God has let us down, it is so much worse.

But remember: If all you know and the only conclusion you can reach is based only on what you can see with your eyes, then you don't know the whole story and you don't know God!

Today, you are blessed. And the blessings of your day are far greater than anything you could hope because of what God did for you in His Son, **Jesus**.

And they found the eleven and those who were with them gathered together, saying, "The Lord has risen indeed, and has appeared to Simon!"

Luke 24:25-35

DECEMBER 19

Jesus said these two were "slow of heart." They were not slow of mind but they were slow in their willingness to believe all the prophets had spoken. They were quick to believe in the promises of a coming kingdom, but they were slow to believe the prophecies of a suffering Savior.

Then he studied with them. What a Bible study that must have been! Perhaps, he started with Genesis 3:15, the bruised heel passage. Or maybe he explained to them about Moses lifting up the serpent in the wilderness. Or, perhaps, he focused on the suffering Servant of Isaiah 53.

Now, don't miss this. Jesus believed the answers they needed could be found in the Scriptures! Isn't that still true?

As they drew close to Emmaus, Jesus seemed to be going on without them. They strongly urged him to stay with them. So, he did. Later, at the table, they recognized him.

Eyes opened. Hearts burning. What an incredible experience with Jesus!

It was seven miles back to Jerusalem, but this time there was a skip in their step. They had a story to tell, a most unbelievable story.

There is so much pain in our world, so much heartache, so much death. Anguished by what we see and experience, we cry, "Why hasn't God done something?" "Why hasn't He done something about our pain? Why hasn't He done something about our broken hearts? Why hasn't He done something about our fears? Why hasn't He done something about death?"

And the answer from Scripture rings in clarion tones: HE HAS! This is what Christianity is all about! What God HAS done!

God gave His Son! God raised His Son! And God promised life in His Son!

That last moment comes for all of us. The book is closed. The body is at rest. No breath. No motion. No life. But it is in that silent and still moment that we will discover what God has done.

Are your eyes open to see Him, to see His love for you? Does your heart burn with an excitement and energy to live for **Jesus**?

So the other disciples told him, "We have seen the Lord." But he said to them, "Unless I see in his hands the mark of the nails, and place my finger into the mark of the nails, and place my hand into his side, I will never believe."
John 20:19-25 (Mark 16:14; Luke 24:36-42)

DECEMBER 20

Jesus was with his disciples. Well, he was with most of his disciples. One was absent. Thomas.

Why wasn't Thomas with the disciples when Jesus appeared to them? We don't know. Maybe he was disappointed. Maybe he was afraid. Maybe he was brooding over the failure of the whole thing. Maybe he just needed some time to think about what to do next.

Oh, Thomas wanted to believe them. He wanted to accept their word. He wanted to feel a part of the group. But, right now, he couldn't.

He was there. He saw the whole thing. When the day was done, Jesus was dead. He had seen the body. His hopes had been dashed once. He didn't want to set himself up for more disappointment.

Thomas is the world's most famous doubter. His reputation has crossed the centuries and everyone knows him as 'doubting Thomas.' Of course, the Bible never described Thomas that way. It tells of this one, solitary incident when he doubted, but most people remember nothing else about him

Thomas was struggling. But can you blame him? What these men were saying was beyond anything in his experience. Dead folks don't come back to life! Had he forgotten about Lazarus?

Thomas was not going to pretend. He was honest about his doubts. He did not claim to understand what he really didn't or believe in what he did not. He was not going to rattle off some words to save face or to be a part of a group.

So, he would trust his own senses. He would accept nothing as true unless he could see it and touch it himself. He wouldn't believe it just because someone said it. One way or the other, his faith would be his own!

That is a wonderful way to seek **Jesus**.

Thomas answered him, "My Lord and my God!"

John 20:26-29

DECEMBER 21

Jesus appeared to his disciples again. This time, Thomas was there. Jesus invited Thomas to touch him and encouraged him, "Stop doubting and believe." Thomas' response indicates that he did!

Of course, Jesus could have said, "Too little, too late," and booted him out. But he didn't. Jesus won't kick you out because you don't have an answer to every question or send you on your way because you don't yet understand everything. He won't disown you because your faith struggles over certain things. He does want you to be honest with him. Don't pretend.

Some people seem to think that once you become a Christian you should never have doubts. But that is not so.

Asking questions is not bad. Admitting that we don't understand everything is not bad. Asking God to make something clearer is not wrong. The Bible is full of people who did exactly that! Thomas is just one in a long line of honest folks who raised their voices to ask difficult questions.

And to their credit, the disciples were also receptive to Thomas, even with his doubts. They could have chosen to exclude him since he refused to accept their word and believe exactly as they did.

In a world of enormous uncertainty and confusion, the Christian community should be the one place where people feel free to come with their struggles and questions. The church is for people who don't have it all together, for people who don't have all the answers, for people who are struggling with life's frustrations and irritations.

The church is the place where people should be able to say, "I don't understand this...I don't yet see it that way....I'm not where you are....I need to think about that some more....." And when people say that, we need to throw our arms around them and say, "Welcome, you are at the right place. We are all learners and seekers."

There is a bit of Thomas in all of us. We seek certainty. We have been disappointed often enough. But remember: we walk by faith, not by sight!

Any uncertainties? Any fears? Any doubts? Any questions? It's okay. No one of us has all the answers but we know whom we can trust. **Jesus.**

> Now Jesus did many other signs in the presence of the disciples, which are not written in this book; but these are written so that you may believe that Jesus is the Christ, the Son of God, and that by believing you may have life in his name.
>
> John 20:30-31

DECEMBER 22

Jesus was the reason John wrote. It was never about explaining history or storytelling. It was never about ethics or apologetics. It was always about one thing, one person: Jesus.

John was there when Jesus fed five thousand, and when Lazarus walked out of the tomb. He knew Nicodemus came to Jesus at night and that Jesus washed the disciples' feet. He saw Jesus walking on water and he watched him heal a blind man who had been blind since birth. John was writing what he knew to be true!

John told many stories of Jesus. But these were not just stories to entertain or amuse, or cause us to think more deeply. These stories were told to open our eyes and hearts to reality. He wanted us to see through the stories how God reached down to us. The stories were the connection between the God who walked among us and the people He came to save.

What we have is a fragment. It is incomplete. John said so. "Jesus did many other miraculous signs..." So, why just these few? His favorites, perhaps. Maybe the ones he could remember best. John knew he could never write it all down. So, he had to be selective. Of all that Jesus did, these he selected so that we might know the truth and come to faith.

John wrote for a reason; he wrote with a goal in mind. John wrote so we would come to know Jesus Christ and believe in him. Why? Because John knew that God loved us and that real life was found only in Jesus.

Yes, **real** life. Living the life that you were created to live. Jesus showed us what that life looks like.

The words are not the goal. The stories are not the answer. But the words and the stories do point us to the goal and to the answer. Thus, we don't love the book that tells us about Jesus. We love **Jesus**.

> When Simon Peter heard that it was the Lord, he put on his outer garment, for he was stripped for work, and threw himself into the sea.
> John 21:1-14

DECEMBER 23

Jesus "is going ahead of you into Galilee, the angel said" (Matthew 28:7). So here they were but there was no sign of Jesus.

Perhaps, it was restlessness that got to them. Some have suggested that Peter went fishing to get his mind off his failure. Perhaps. Or maybe he just needed to be busy doing something that counted.

And what might we say of the other disciples? They have many questions. What is going to happen next? Is the kingdom to begin now? What will be their job? How long should they wait? Evidently, in the absence of answers, they decided they might as well go fishing.

They fished through the night and didn't have anything to show for their effort. Not even one lousy fish!

In the morning, Jesus called to them from the shore. He told them to toss their nets on the right side of the boat and they would find some fish. Sure enough, the fish came in! 153 large fish. Jesus is the perfect fish finder!

At some point, John recognized Jesus and said so. In his typical impetuous way, Peter jumped in and started swimming to shore. The rest simply traveled by boat, towing the heavy net full of fish behind them.

Once they all arrived at shore, Jesus invited them to bring some of their fish and they could all share breakfast together. Maybe Jesus shared the meal to impress upon them once more that he was truly alive. Maybe this déjà vu experience was intended to remind them of their calling to be fishers of men. Perhaps, Jesus wanted to remind them one more time that he was with them and all that they needed would be provided. Whatever his reasons for appearing to them just now, all that mattered to them was being with him.

Perhaps, their failure to catch any fish was intended as a message: this is a picture of your life without Jesus. How many signs like that do we experience? How often do we have a déjà vu experience that reminds us of the blessings that come from being a follower of **Jesus**?

Again Jesus said, "Simon son of John, do you truly love me?"
He answered, "Yes, Lord, you know that I love you."
Jesus said, "Take care of my sheep."

John 21:15-17

DECEMBER 24

Jesus waited until the meal was eaten before turning his attention to Peter. While all of the disciples had questions about the future, perhaps no one wondered about their role more than Peter. Did Jesus still have a place for him in this kingdom?

"Simon son of John, do you truly love me?"

It seemed like a simple question. But Peter's response revealed that it was more complicated for him than a simple yes or no.

Scholars have long debated the implications of what came next: Peter changing the term for love. Jesus asked Peter about his love and used the Greek verb 'agapao.' The noun form, agape, is more recognizable to most people. But Peter responded by using a different verb, 'phileo.' The same thing would happen in the second round of question-answer. In the third question Jesus changed to phileo.

Agapao is the strongest expression of love. This is unconditional love, tenacious love. It is love that endures difficult circumstances and painful disagreements. It is love that persists through misunderstanding and mistreatment. This is the very love that God showed us even though we were still sinners (Romans 5:8). "Peter, do you deeply love me, even above all the others?"

While Peter did declare his love for Jesus, two things are absent in his words. First, he did not make any comparisons between his love and that of the other disciples. Failure has now removed any sense of superiority. Second, he exhibits none of that brash self-confidence that filled him before Jesus was arrested.

Jesus said to him, "Simon, take care of my sheep."

So, what is this all about? What is actually happening here? It is this: Simon Peter is being given the gift of another day. He is being given another chance. He is being given another opportunity to become that 'rock' for the kingdom. Jesus still believed in Peter and he had a place and a task for him.

How often we have received the gift of another day! It is always grace. It is one more day, one more opportunity to show that we really do love **Jesus**.

> "...but when you are old, you will stretch out your hands, and another will dress you and carry you where you do not want to go."
>
> John 21:18-25

DECEMBER 25

Jesus and Peter appear to have left the campfire meal and gone for a walk. Peter probably welcomed the privacy. Perhaps, he was a bit unsure of what Jesus would say to him. He had failed miserably and everyone there knew it. Like us, he preferred to be dealt with privately.

Jesus told Peter that, unlike the present, the day would come when others would be in charge of him. In fact, they will "lead you where you don't want to go." Sober words for a man who was trying to get back on the right track with his life.

According to John, Jesus said these words to Peter so that he would know something about his death. What thoughts were racing in Peter's mind now?

Then, Jesus said to Peter, "Follow me!" It had been about three years since Peter first heard Jesus say that. How incredible his life since that first day!!

As Peter contemplated what Jesus said, he became aware of someone following. He turned to see that it was John. Whether he spoke out of curiosity or it was simply his impetuous nature prompting him to speak without thinking, Peter asked Jesus, "What about him?"

Jesus' reply was quick and to the point: "That is not your concern! Your concern is to follow me."

Wow! Don't we all need to hear that?

We are so tempted to be interested in what is happening in the lives of others and how we compare to them. In fact, we may even decide the faithfulness of our own walk with God by comparing ourselves to others. And we find it particularly difficult to resist trying to determine how God may be blessing them in comparison to us.

The Lord deals with each of us as he determines. He does not measure us against one another. We are not loved or accepted more or less than another. Whether blessing or discipline, we live today knowing that we will receive only what is right and best from **Jesus**.

"Go therefore and make disciples of all nations, baptizing them in the name of the Father and of the Son and of the Holy Spirit, teaching them to observe all that I have commanded you."
Matthew 28:16-20 (Mark 16:15-18)

DECEMBER 26

Jesus' words are a call to action! Time is short. Final instructions must be given.

Jesus said, "All authority...everywhere...is mine." Authority is the power or the right to control, command, or determine. Jesus says there is no place on the planet where my word is not the authority. Everyone and everything are subject to his voice! Jesus alone has the authority to forgive sins.

"Therefore, go and make disciples of all nations..." Jesus said. The scope of this work is the world, wherever there are people.

And this mission is **our** mission! It was given to no one else! Evangelism is the responsibility of the Christian community to bear witness to the saving work of God in Christ. We do not convert the world. We do not convict the world. We do not save the world. Our total contribution to the salvation task is to make possible an encounter between Jesus and lost people. But do we feel the urgency?

The temptation here is to believe that our failure to feel the urgency is because we don't really love the lost. There is certainly some truth to that. But perhaps the deeper reason is that we don't really prize or treasure our own salvation. We may have come to take it for granted. We have no deep sense of our own sinfulness, no real appreciation for the price paid for our redemption, no genuine understanding of salvation by grace. We don't mean to feel that way, but sensitivity is often lost over time. Lacking such sensitivity in our own lives, we could not possibly feel urgent for those who are not Christians. If we are not deeply aware of what God's grace means in our lives, we are not likely to give much thought to what God's grace can mean in the life of another.

Jesus sent them (and us) into the world with the only story of salvation. This is Good News about what God has done. But time is precious. People need to know **Jesus**.

> "Thus it is written, that the Christ should suffer and on the third day rise from the dead, and that repentance and forgiveness of sins should be proclaimed in his name to all nations, beginning from Jerusalem. You are witnesses of these things."
>
> Luke 24:44-49

DECEMBER 27

Jesus said, "You are witnesses." Indeed, the disciples were witnesses. For almost three years they had seen and heard the most incredible things! No man ever spoke as Jesus did, and no person had ever done the things that Jesus did. The time had come to tell others what they knew to be true: God had kept His promise. The Messiah had come. The kingdom had arrived.

Like lepers who have been cleansed or blind that can now see, like the lame that can walk again or the diseased who are healed, we find it impossible to keep such good news to ourselves. And why would we? Gratitude and generosity motivate us.

We want people to know that a person does not have to greet each day with loneliness and guilt, with hopelessness and regret. We want people to know that God is real and true, that He is close and He cares. We want people to know that God's fullest expression of Himself and His love for us is found in His Son, Jesus.

But they will never know those things by looking at the stars or considering the skeletal system. These are not truths found under a microscope or discovered by searching in the ocean's depths. Rather, God reveals Himself to people, and people share that revelation with one another.

As witnesses for Jesus, the disciples' task (and ours) was far more than simply sharing their own experiences or feelings. It would be impossible for them to share the good news without including the stories of how their own lives were changed by the man from Nazareth. However, the focus of their message was not on themselves but on Jesus. He was (is) the good news!

Now, the task is yours. Actually, it is much more than a task; it is a privilege. After all, someone shared the story with you. They did it because they loved you. Now, you can share with those you love the wonderful story of **Jesus**.

> "Men of Galilee, why do you stand looking into heaven? This Jesus, who was taken up from you into heaven, will come in the same way as you saw him go into heaven."
>
> Acts 1:9-12 (Mark 16:19-20; Luke 24:50-53)

DECEMBER 28

Jesus always planned to leave. He told his disciples this day was coming. "I am going to the Father" (John 14:12, 28; John 16:28).

It all happened so quickly. One moment he was with them, talking about the kingdom. Then, he was rising and disappearing in the clouds. The disciples stood there, probably with their mouths wide open, watching something that was completely outside their experience.

So many questions must have flooded the minds of these eleven men as they watched Jesus disappear in the clouds. Where did he go? What do they do now? Would it not have been better if Jesus had stayed? How could his leaving be a good thing?

They may have felt overwhelmed by the mission they were given. "You will be my witnesses to the remotest parts of the earth?" What a task! In all likelihood, these fellows had never traveled beyond the borders of Palestine.

Also, they had spent three years with Jesus. He was their master and teacher. They had looked to him for guidance and strength. How could they possibly take on a world-wide assignment without his presence?

But they were not alone! Two men in white stood beside them with fantastic news: Jesus would return! The questions might linger until the Spirit came but they knew that Jesus had not left them alone and he would come back! With that knowledge their hearts rejoiced as they returned to Jerusalem.

When Jesus ascended and sat down at the right hand of the Father, he demonstrated that his sacrificial work for humanity was completed. Even more, it was the singular action that declared his supremacy over everything, including death. The ascension was the coronation of the King of Kings!

You awakened this morning knowing that love is more powerful than hate, that giving is more fun than getting, that death is not to be feared, and that Satan is not going to win. All of this you know because the one on the throne is **Jesus**.

> "...this Jesus, delivered up according to the definite plan and foreknowledge of God, you crucified and killed by the hands of lawless men.
> Acts 2:22-23

DECEMBER 29

Jesus was the plan of God — "God's set purpose and foreknowledge." Peter's words could be heard above the troubled whisperings of the crowd. "The cross of this carpenter is no accident–the death of this man is no unplanned tragedy. It has been in the mind of God since the creation."

We wonder why he waited all those centuries to come. The wonder is that he came at all. Since the beginning of time he has known that the cross was waiting for him. But he came anyway...to help us. The cross tells us that there was no other alternative, no other option, no other choice. Once we understand that, we then can see why those who would go home to the Father must pass through Jesus and the cross.

The cross is the turning point of history. It is in this precise moment of chaos that this world suddenly makes sense...it is in this exact moment of supreme hate and cruelty that love finds its fullest expression....it is in this very moment of man at his worst that God is at His best....it is in this Calvary moment, in this Golgotha moment, in this place of the skull moment, that peace, joy and hope become real....

For all those centuries Jesus could think of nothing else but that cross and you. For all those centuries his every action was focused on that cross and you.

In God's mind you and the cross go together. He cannot speak of you or bless your life or envision your presence without the cross coming to mind. The reason: the cross was required so that He could say, "My child, come home to your Father."

In our minds God and the cross go together. We cannot speak of Him or praise His name or envision His presence without the cross coming to mind. The reason: the cross was required so that we could say, "Father, we want to come home." And the plan for home was always centered in **Jesus**.

> Since therefore the children share in flesh and blood, he himself likewise partook of the same things, that through death he might destroy the one who has the power of death, that is, the devil, and deliver all those who through fear of death were subject to lifelong slavery.
>
> Hebrews 2:14-18

DECEMBER 30

Jesus' death forever changed the way we look at our own.

Since the beginning of our days we have struggled with the grim fact that all of our labors and dreams must one day be swallowed by the grave. Every death is a reminder of our frailty. Every cemetery is a reminder that our days are numbered and we will return to dust.

Death is a dreaded word. We fear the process of dying and we have fears of the unknown. We fear the separation from those we love and we are afraid of judgment.

The days of our lives are being subtracted and we are drawing ever closer to the last ones. There is no escape, no way to bypass this exit. No amount of pleading or tears, no amount of denial or pretension can change what must be.

The time is coming when our life will be measured in days, then hours, then minutes, then seconds...four, three, two, one. Gone! No word on the lips. No breath in the nostrils. No sound in the chest. No life. Just still.

And in that moment, in that silent moment, in that utterly unique moment, is the trumpet blast of angels proclaiming victory! And in that moment, you will be more alive than you have ever been.

Sometimes, in anguish over the death of someone we love or even the reality of our own death, we cry, "Why hasn't God done something?" He has! God became one of us so that we might never have to be afraid again.

Nothing so profoundly determines the way you feel about life as the way you feel about death. For you, death is but a doorway from earth to heaven, a passageway to the throne of God. One person changed everything about your life by changing everything about your death. That one person is **Jesus**.

"Behold, I am coming soon…"
Revelation 22:12-13 (Revelation 19:11-16)

DECEMBER 31

Jesus promised you he would rise, and he did. Jesus promised you he would be the pathway to the Father, and he is. Jesus promised you he would return for you, and he will.

He came the first time as a helpless baby. From the moment his star appeared, his enemies began lining up. Though "God with us," he arrived without any earthly title that would set him apart from other men. Though he made the world, he owned no house or land, no waterfront property or mountain retreat. Though he lived as God is and he spoke as God speaks, his words and his ways were an irritation we could no longer ignore. Even though he loved us, we hated him. And though he was God and possessed authority and power over all, he allowed us to do to him whatever we wanted. So, after we had beaten him and mocked him, we killed him.

As he promised, Jesus will return to us. This time, however, he will not come as a helpless baby but as the King and Commander that he is. Like a conquering General leading his army to war, he will ride a white horse. This time everyone will know the title he wears is a reflection of his person. He is the One who is always trustworthy.

We walk in light and know the truth, but only because of Jesus. We know the love of God and experience His grace, but only because of Jesus. We are saved and blessed, but only because of Jesus.

Jesus is the reason for every day. Jesus is the meaning behind every word and every action. Jesus is the hope we hold in our hearts. Jesus is the courage to rise when we have fallen, to confess when we have strayed. Jesus is the faith when we are afraid. Jesus is the answer to all our questions and the solution to all our problems. Jesus is the story that gives us a story. Jesus is the life that fills us when our eyes open in the morning and close at night. Jesus is the love that makes us the Father's child. Now, we wait for him from morning to evening.

"Come, Lord **Jesus**."

CPSIA information can be obtained
at www.ICGtesting.com
Printed in the USA
LVHW050320191119
637662LV00010BB/284/P